Iris and Periocular Recognition using Deep Learning

Iris and Periocular Recognition using Deep Learning

Ajay Kumar
The Hong Kong Polytechnic University,
Hong Kong

ACADEMIC PRESS

An imprint of Elsevier

Academic Press is an imprint of Elsevier
125 London Wall, London EC2Y 5AS, United Kingdom
525 B Street, Suite 1650, San Diego, CA 92101, United States
50 Hampshire Street, 5th Floor, Cambridge, MA 02139, United States

Notices
Knowledge and best practice in this field are constantly changing. As new research and experience broaden our understanding, changes in research methods, professional practices, or medical treatment may become necessary.

Practitioners and researchers must always rely on their own experience and knowledge in evaluating and using any information, methods, compounds, or experiments described herein. In using such information or methods they should be mindful of their own safety and the safety of others, including parties for whom they have a professional responsibility.

To the fullest extent of the law, neither the Publisher nor the authors, contributors, or editors, assume any liability for any injury and/or damage to persons or property as a matter of products liability, negligence or otherwise, or from any use or operation of any methods, products, instructions, or ideas contained in the material herein.

ISBN: 978-0-443-27318-6

For Information on all Academic Press publications
visit our website at https://www.elsevier.com/books-and-journals

Publisher: Mara Conner
Editorial Project Manager: Sara Greco
Production Project Manager: Omer Mukthar
Cover Designer: Christian Bilbow

Typeset by MPS Limited, Chennai, India

Contents

Preface

Recent advances in deep neural networks have opened exciting possibilities for pushing the boundaries of biometric identification and diagnosis. These cutting-edge capabilities hold immense promise for real-world applications and immersive applications in the metaverse. Deep learning is a powerful branch of machine learning that harnesses the capabilities of artificial neural networks to recover discriminative features and representations. The term *deep learning* is often used interchangeably with *deep neural networks*, with the adjective *deep* referring to the utilization of multiple layers in progressively recovering the high-level features from raw images or signals. However, it is essential to recognize that any direct application of widely available deep neural network architectures can only yield limited performance. Specialized network architectures and training mechanisms must be devised to fully exploit the unparalleled uniqueness of iris and periocular features, especially considering the scarcity of biometric (training) data. This book systematically presents notable advancements in developing these specialized deep network models while offering profound insights into their underlying algorithms.

The availability of a book that is exclusively devoted to deep learning–based iris and periocular recognition techniques is expected to greatly benefit not only the graduate students but also further research, development, and deployment efforts for these technologies. Some of the contents in this book have appeared in some of our research publications or reports. However, many of the important details, explanations, and results that have been previously overlooked in the publications are included in this book.

This book is organized into 11 different chapters. The first chapter introduces current trends in acquiring and identifying iris images using conventional methods. This introductory chapter focuses on the non-deep learning–based methods for iris segmentation and matching and presents standards for sensing, template storage, and performance evaluation. An explanation of the most successful iris and periocular recognition methods is included and serves as the key baseline for deep learning–based methods. It also explains the algorithmic specializations introduced for accurately matching iris images acquired from mobile biometric devices and smartphones. This chapter bridges the journey from conventional iris and periocular recognition methods to the deep neural network–based methods that begin from the second chapter onwards.

In the second chapter, we will delve into the significance of using a specific network architecture tailored for iris recognition using deep learning. The main objective of this chapter is to provide a comprehensive explanation of the theory and design behind deep neural networks that can effectively extract powerful feature templates from normalized iris images. The focus is on developing a simplified deep neural network architecture to achieve superior match *accuracy* and *speed*, making it suitable for a wide range of real-world applications.

Chapter 3 presents a unified framework that harnesses the power of deep neural networks to detect, segment, and match iris images. This approach addresses the limitations of the method presented in Chapter 2. This unified system elevates the reliability and uniformity of iris segmentation and feature optimization, offering deeper insights into creating an end-to-end network that can be designed to fully avail the potential of deep neural networks.

Chapter 4 presents the design and results from a systematic investigation aimed at enhancing match accuracy through a newly adopted framework that extracts more representative features across different scales. The framework leverages residual network learning with dilated convolutional kernels, optimizing the training process and aggregating contextual information from iris images without needing down-sampling and up-sampling layers. The results demonstrate promising outcomes, validating the potential of multiple kernels to significantly enhance iris match accuracy.

Chapter 5 focuses on improving the accuracy of matching iris images acquired from different spectrums and sensors. The chapter introduces a specialized deep learning framework that enhances the recognition of these iris images. It provides a detailed design for creating a pipeline that is aimed at amplifying the accuracy of matching iris images acquired under disparate spectrums.

Chapter 6 introduces the deep learning techniques to match periocular images obtained from less-restricted environments. Periocular recognition is useful when accurate iris recognition is not feasible due to factors like visible illumination, an unconstrained environment, or when the entire face is unavailable. This chapter details the remarkable ability of deep neural networks to recover intricate contextual details from previously unseen periocular images. Leveraging such uncovered details, this framework can further enhance match accuracy, even with limited availability or the number of training samples.

Chapter 7 introduces a multiglance mechanism where specific components of the network focus on important semantical regions, namely, the eyebrow and eye regions within the periocular images. The remarkable performance of this approach underlines the significance of the eyebrow and eye regions in periocular recognition, emphasizing the need for special attention during the deep feature learning process.

Chapter 8 presents a deep learning–based dynamic iris recognition framework to accurately match iris images acquired from increased standoff images under cross-distance and nonideal imaging scenarios. The framework presented in this chapter is designed to account for the differences in the effective area of available iris regions, thereby dynamically reinforcing the periocular information to achieve significant enhancement in the matching accuracy.

Convolutional neural networks share the same parameters across an entire image; the distinctive features of iris images are often spatially localized, which can render parameter sharing futile. Thus, to surmount this challenge, Chapter 9 introduces a specialized solution, a positional convolutional network (*PosNet*) that incorporates positional-specific convolutional kernels trained for each pixel. This chapter systematically introduces this specialized network architecture to extract highly discriminant features, yielding superior accuracy with considerably low complexity.

For the metaverse to thrive, it is crucial to adopt a security model with strict identity checks while real-world users are seamlessly connected to the virtual world using popular augmented reality, virtual reality, or mixed reality devices. Ocular images are inherently acquired during the immersion experiences from such devices and offer tremendous potential for high security. Chapter 10 presents a specialized pipeline for detecting, segmenting, and normalizing iris details from *off-angle* images and a generalized framework that dynamically matches such iris images to achieve high security in various metaverse applications.

Finally, Chapter 11 reviews the limitations of some of the deep learning—based iris recognition algorithms introduced in related literature and analyzes the factors influencing the achievable performance and application scenarios for different iris recognition algorithms. High-level feature representation for iris images is essential to realize the full potential of iris images. A range of new ideas and frameworks, including iris recognition using adversarial learning and graph neural networks, are also introduced to advance iris recognition capabilities for challenging and large-scale applications.

I would like to express my gratitude to the numerous students and staff at *The Hong Kong Polytechnic University* who have directly or indirectly supported the completion of this book. *Zijing Zhao* and *Kuo Wang* deserve special thanks here as they have been instrumental in advancing many of the research outcomes reported in this book. I would also like to acknowledge *Yulin Feng* as he played a significant role in developing *PosNet* architecture, although regrettably, circumstances compelled him to relinquish his research midway.

Ajay Kumar
Hong Kong

1

An insight into trends on advances in iris and periocular recognition

Advanced capabilities to automatically establish the unique identity of humans are highly sought in a range of e-governance, e-business, and law-enforcement applications. Although research and development on automated methods for iris recognition began during the late 80 and early 90s [1−3], the development idea of iris biometrics is believed to be over 100 years old [4]. Although iris recognition systems have been increasingly deployed, several studies have shown that it has limitations, such as a false nonmatch rate of approximately 1.5% at a false positive rate of 0.1% when searching against a population of 1.6 million iris images [5]. Another study on iris recognition in India's Aadhaar program [6] revealed a false rejection rate of 0.64% at a false acceptance rate of 0.001% for millions of enrolled subjects. Therefore iris recognition has attracted continued research and development efforts to achieve faster, more accurate human identification, especially for a range of real-world applications where the iris images are acquired from greater standoff distances or under less constrained environments. This chapter begins by discussing the anatomy of ocular patterns and their distinctiveness as biometrics. Section 1.2 provides a summary of iris segmentation, while iris recognition algorithms in the literature are summarized in Section 1.3. Section 1.4 overviews specializations for accurately matching iris images acquired from smartphones or mobile biometric devices. Section 1.5 summarizes leading periocular image-matching methods using conventional, or nondeep learning, algorithms. Finally, Section 1.6 briefly overviews advances in iris recognition using multispectral imaging.

1.1 Ocular patterns and biometrics

Ocular region among humans can be clearly identified from a distance and includes eyebrows, pupil, and iris as well as other geometric shape details like the tear duct. Fig. 1−1 illustrates a sample image acquired by an iris sensor. The textured patterned region between the sclera and pupil represents the iris. The uniqueness of iris patterns is attributed to the randomness of complex patterns, such as furrows, ridges, freckles, or crypts. These patterns are randomly formed during the 3rd−8th month of fetal development and are quite protected by a transparent covering known as the cornea. It's impossible to surgically alter iris patterns without unacceptable risks, which makes it a preferred biometric trait for highly secured person identification.

The term periocular has been applied to the region surrounding the eye. In addition to the iris, such regions include eyelids, tear ducts, eyelashes, and eyebrows Several studies

Iris and Periocular Recognition using Deep Learning. DOI: https://doi.org/10.1016/B978-0-443-27318-6.00007-3

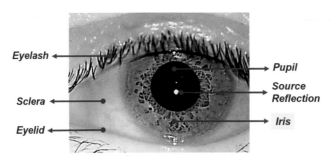

FIGURE 1–1 Sample iris image from a commercial iris sensor.

have suggested that the periocular region is as distinctive as the face itself. Considering iris recognition, it is noteworthy that the periocular region is inherently captured by conventional sensors that are widely used for acquiring iris images. Thus periocular recognition can be employed to augment the accuracy of iris recognition.

Commercially available iris sensors are widely required to conform to ISO 19794-6:2011 standard [7]. Such sensors support the auto capture that can generate rectangular segmented images, with respective iris masks, and generate images in JPEG 2000 format (2−10 kb size). Iris sensors deployed for law enforcement and large-scale national ID programs should also meet several functional device characteristics. Table 1−1 lists some of the reference specifications for the iris sensors deployed in large-scale Aadhaar program [6,8,9].

1.1.1 Biometrics systems and performance evaluation

A typical biometric identification can be considered as a pattern-matching system that has sensors for signal or image acquisition, preprocessing steps that often include segmentation, and template generation using such segmented or region-of-interest images. These templates are matched using some matching criterion or a matching distance that generates respective match scores with the templates that are stored in a database from the registered identities or subjects.

Iris recognition systems, or any general biometric systems, can be operated in a verification or identification mode.

1.1.1.1 Iris segmentation performance

Iris images acquired from the conventional sensors using the stop-and-stare mode of imaging often provide high-quality images that can enable accurate segmentation of pixels in the iris region, that is, enabling proper extraction of segmentation masks that are widely used to mask noniris areas of the acquired images. Extraction of such iris segmentation masks can be more difficult for the iris images obtained under relaxed imaging constraints or from the subjects on the move. The accuracy of iris segmentation algorithms can therefore be quantified using the segmentation error and is often used to judge the effectiveness of different iris segmentation algorithms, especially for *nonideal* iris images [10]. Such quantification uses

Table 1–1 Functional characteristics for a typical iris sensor.

S. no.	Iris sensor characteristics	Specifications
1.	Pixel resolution	>10 pixels/mm
2.	Spatial resolution	>50% at 1 LP/mm
3.	Spectral wavelength	700–900 nm
4.	Pixel depth	At least 8 bits per pixel
5.	Sensor signal-to-noise ratio	>30 dB
6.	Capture time	<5 seconds
7.	Image margins	Left and right $\geq 0.6 \times$ iris radius
		Top and bottom $\geq 0.2 \times$ iris radius

manually annotated ground truth masks that serve as a baseline to ascertain iris segmentation masks that are automatically generated from any given iris segmentation algorithm. Iris segmentation or classification error E can serve as a quantitative metric for the performance evaluation and can be written as follows:

$$E = \frac{1}{c \times r} \sum_{c'} \sum_{r'} G(c', r') \otimes M(c', r') \qquad (1-1)$$

where G represents manually annotated ground truth masks, M represents the automatically generated iris segmentation masks from a given algorithm, while c and r, respectively represent the width and height of the iris image. The "$\otimes$" represents an XOR operator which evaluates the disagreeing pixels between the ground truth G and the segmented iris mask M (Fig. 1−2).

The segmentation error E effectively counts the number of disagreed pixels between ground truth mask G and the results M generated by the employed segmentation algorithm. Any improved iris segmentation algorithm can lead to improved iris recognition performance but *not always* [11] because, in many cases, noniris pixels appearing due to the poor iris segmentation can be consistent and aid in the improved matching/recognition of such iris images.

1.1.1.2 Iris recognition performance
Performance for the iris recognition algorithms can be quantified under the verification or identification modes. The verification mode is also referred to as *one-to-one* matching, and the identification mode is referred to as *one-to-many* matching. The quantitative metric to ascertain performance under these two modes is detailed in the following.

1.1.1.2.1 One-to-one matching
Biometrics authentication or verification systems use *one-to-one* matching and therefore iris template matching algorithms are often evaluated under this mode. Secure access control at border crossings, large-scale national ID programs for e-governance, unauthorized access control in secured buildings and personal gadgets like smartphones, or construction of

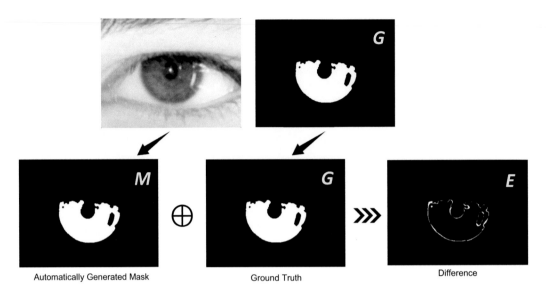

FIGURE 1–2 Illustration for quantitatively computing iris segmentation error (*E*).

biometric cryptosystems for data security, are some examples of iris recognition algorithms with the one-to-one matching mode of operation.

Iris authentication or one-to-one matching problem can be formulated as follows: let the feature representation, that is, template from the unknown or query iris image be represented by U while the R represents that registered or enrolled template for the identity class that is claimed as C. One-to-one matching task is to determine whether this pair (C, U) belongs to the *Genuine* class G that can be authenticated, or it belongs to *Impostor* class I that must be rejected by the iris recognition system. The match score $s\,(U, R)$ between two templates, that is, unknown query U and the registered template R, is used to decide the class G or I using one-to-one matching as follows:

$$(C,U) \in G \quad if \quad s(U,R) \le t \tag{1-2}$$

$$(C,U) \in I \quad if \quad s(U,R) > t \tag{1-3}$$

This match score s is generally Hamming distance score for the *IrisCode*-based algorithms or Euclidean distance score for the templates that are matched using deeply learned neural networks. The variable t represents the decision threshold whose value is determined using the learning or calibration stage and its choice can also depend on the nature of security expected from the deployment [12].

Performance of iris matching algorithms can be conveniently visualized using the receiver operating characteristics (ROC) which is the plot of false acceptance rate (FAR) and false reject rate (FRR) at any possible value of decision threshold t which represents the operating point of respective biometric system. The FAR represents the fraction of genuine class template comparisons during the one-to-one matching for which the respective match scores are smaller than or equal to the decision threshold. The term false nonmatch rate and FAR are used interchangeably[1] in the literature and can be computed as follows:

$$FAR(t) = \frac{1}{K}\sum_{i=1}^{K}[s_i \leq t] \quad \text{where} \quad s_i \in G \qquad (1-4)$$

where K is the total number of class comparisons perforned and [...] represents 1 if the boolean expression inside the brackets is true and 0 otherwise. The FRR represents the fraction of impostor class template comparisons during the one-to-one matching for which the respective match scores are greater than the decision threshold. The term false match rate and FRR have been interchangeably used in the literature. FRR at any operating or decision threshold t can be computed as follows:

$$FRR(t) = \frac{1}{L}\sum_{i=1}^{L}[s_i > t] \quad \text{where} \quad s_i \in I \qquad (1-5)$$

where L is the total number of impostor class comparisons performed during the performance evaluation. Typical performance evaluation in the literature uses all possible match scores s_i as the decision thresholds to record respective values for FAR and FRR.

The plot of $FRR(t)$ against $FAR(t)$ is referred to as the ROC and serves as the key performance indicator for the iris recognition system deployed for the one-to-one matching or authentication applications. Such plot provides a vital *tradeoff* between the false acceptance of fraudulent users and incorrect rejection of legitimate users trying to access the system. This is the reason that such plots are also referred to as detection error tradeoff (DET) plots in the literature. The ROC plots should be presented in a semilog scale, that is, with logarithmic x-axes which can ensure that the operating points of wider interest, that is, low FAR values where iris recognition systems are deployed for high-security requirements, can be visualized with ease. Instead of presenting FAR versus FRR plots, many references in iris recognition literature present one-to-one matching performance using genuine acceptance rate (GAR = 1 − FRR) against FAR in a semilog scale. Such alternate visualization of ROC has been found to be more convenient, especially while viewing closely performing competitive performance ROC curves at operating points offering higher security, and is widely employed for the comparative performance evaluation [13].

1.1.1.2.2 One-to-many matching

In contrast to the one-to-one matching of iris images for the verification problem, the identification problem requires one-to-many matching of iris templates and is used to determine the identity of unknown iris template U. Let this identity of the unknown user providing

---

[1] ISO/IEC SC 37 Working Group [8] uses FMR and FNMR for the comparisons resulting from *single* samples, while FAR and FRR are used to define the matching performance observed from the complete transactions that may include multiple user attempts or multiple iris acquisitions.

the template U be represented by U_c which need to be identified among any one of the N registered identities, that is, $U_c \in \{C_1, C_2, \ldots, C_N, C_{N+1}\}$ where C_{N+1} represents the identity corresponding to the users that are not enrolled in the system. Let R_i represent the corresponding templates for the N registered identities in the iris recognition system.

$$(U_c, U) \in C_i \; if \min^i s(U, R_i) \leq \tau \quad i = 1, 2, \ldots, N \tag{1-6}$$

$$(U_c, U) \in C_{N+1} \quad if \quad \min^i s(U, R_i) > \tau \tag{1-7}$$

One-to-many matching performance employed for such open set identification problem receives an unknown or presented iris template which is searched against the database of registered templates from known users. A candidate is returned from Eq. (1−6) when the match score is below a predetermined threshold τ. A false positive is returned from Eq. (1−7) when such search returns a candidate C_{N+1} which is *not registered* in the database. Therefore false positive identification rate (FPIR) quantifies the proportion of such rejected search results with at least one nonmatched candidates. When such search fails to return correct candidate from Eq. (1−6) for a legitimate user that is registered in the database, a false negative return is identified. Therefore false negative identification rate (FNIR) quantifies the proportion of such matched search results from Eq. (1−6) that are incorrectly identified. These two performance indicators for the open set identification [14] can be defined as follows:

$$\text{FPIR}(\tau) = \frac{1}{K} \sum_{i=1}^{K} h(\tau - s_{i1}) \tag{1-8}$$

$$\text{FNIR}(\tau) = 1 - \frac{1}{M} \sum_{i=1}^{M} h(\tau - s_{ic}) \tag{1-9}$$

where K represents the number of searches for the unregistered images, M is the number of searches for the registered images, s_{i1} is the match score from the first rank in ith search, s_{ic} is the match score of the true class from ith search while h represents the unit step function. It can be observed that higher values of decision threshold τ is expected to reduce FPIR but increase the FNIR. Therefore such tradeoff for these two error rates are visualized from the DET plots between FPIR and FNIR.

Iris recognition performance is quantified using average recognition rate when evaluated for the closed-set identification problem that involves one-to-many matching. For a range of civilian and forensic applications, average recognition accuracy for higher ranks can also be of interest. Therefore cumulative match characteristics plots representing the variation of average recognition accuracy with the cumulative ranks, corresponding to the registered identities, have also been used to ascertain one-to-many matching performance in the literature.

1.1.1.3 Template size and computational complexity
In addition to the match accuracy, template size and complexity of algorithm are essential aspects to ascertain the comparative performance from iris recognition algorithms. Smaller template size and faster template generation time can reduce storage and enhance speed

and are important factors for large-scale programs, such as e-governance. Smaller template is also expected to result in faster matching speed among the templates. Computational complexity has two important aspects, that is, template generation time and match or search speed. It is quite possible that larger templates, or slower matching algorithms, may offer superior matching accuracy. Therefore it is important to judiciously consider these related factors while evaluating comparative performance from various iris recognition systems. This is also the reason that in addition to the FTE and average FNIR accuracy on a very large dataset, ongoing IRIX 10 [13] comparatively reports the performance using search time, template creation time, and template size, for submitted algorithms.

1.2 Iris segmentation

Iris recognition requires eye images that are acquired from a specialized iris image sensor. Such eye images (Fig. 1−1) also contain unwanted portions, such as eyelid or pupil. Therefore acquired images require are subjected to a set of preprocessing operations to extract region of interest (ROI), or iris images. This preprocessing includes extraction of ROI and the masking of the unwanted or noisy portions from such recovered ROI images. Such iris segmentation process should also ensure that the extracted ROI images are translation and scale invariant for the reliable iris recognition. Fig. 1−3 illustrates typic preprocessing steps involved for the automated segmentation of iris images and are briefly discussed in the following.

The pupil in the acquired eye images from the iris sensors usually contains reflection(s) from the illumination source. Such source reflections form some bright spots in the pupil and can be suppressed to aid in further processing for the localization of pupil center. One

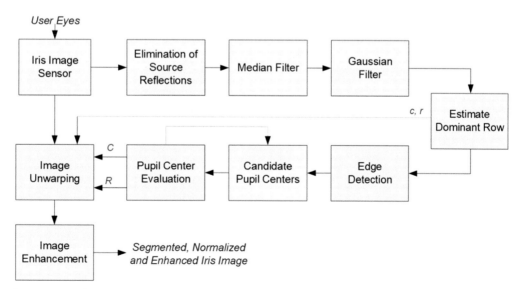

FIGURE 1–3 Sample preprocessing steps for the segmentation of iris using the eye images acquired from closer distances.

of the simplest approaches is to replace every pixel value by some neighborhood pixel if the pixel value inside the pupil is over a particular threshold (200 for image in Fig. 1−4). This operation almost fills the circles but still it is not good enough to apply a global threshold for the pupil circle estimation. Therefore the resulting image is subjected to denoising using a median filter (7 × 7 for sample in Fig. 1−4). The contrast from the image filtered from the median filter is generally higher and therefore it can be subjected to the Gaussian filtering to suppress noise (Fig. 1−4C) and from the iris texture.

The pupil is usually very distinct black circle especially in the processed images as shown in Fig. 1−4C. Therefore the pupil center can be estimated by scanning the image row-wise as shown in the blue and red lines illustrated in Fig. 1−4C. The number of consecutive pixels whose value is less than a certain threshold (say 65 for Fig. 1−4C) can be computed for every row of image pixel. The row containing the *highest* number of such consecutive pixels is expected to represent the diameter of pupil. Therefore the half of such maximum value corresponds to the radius r of the

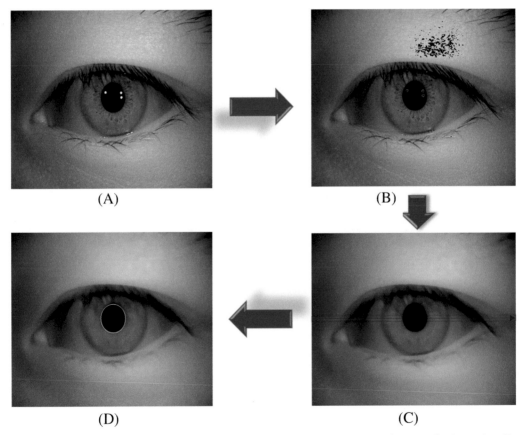

FIGURE 1–4 (A) Sample image acquired from iris sensor, (B) image after the suppression of source reflection and median filtering, and (C) Gaussian filtering of image in (B). Image (C) also illustrates overlaid red and blue lines representing the directions for scanning to estimate largest number of connected (black) pixels to localize iris. Image in (D) illustrates white circle depicting pupil circle drawn from the estimated pupil center and radius from operations in image (C).

pupil, the *y* coordinate of the center *c* of pupil is the row of the diameter and the *x* coordinate is calculated by adding radius of pupil to the column from where the consecutive pixels started. Such localization of pupil can be seen from the image in Fig. 1−4D. The location of pupil (*r*, *c*) is further used for iris segmentation as can be observed from the block diagram in Fig. 1−3.

The processed image in Fig. 1−4D is further used for the edge detection and such canny edge detector results are shown in Fig. 1−5. After the edge detection, a fixed size (20 × 20 in Fig. 1−5) window is chosen in the edge detected image around the estimated center of the pupil. Then, every pixel in *this* window is assumed as the center (candidate centers) and the numbers of white pixels, that are encountered at the perimeter of circle, with radius varying from 80 to 120 pixels, are computed. The winner, that is, the radius (among 80−120 pixels) and the center (among all 20 × 20 pixels) for which the maximum white pixels are encountered, is located. That radius *R* corresponds to the radius of the iris and pixel which was chosen as the center *P*.

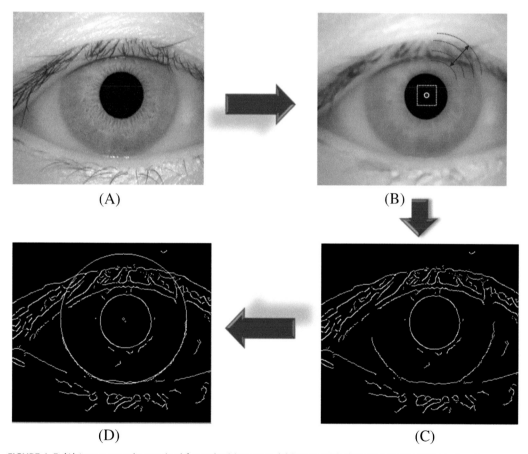

(A)

(B)

(D)

(C)

FIGURE 1–5 (A) Image sample acquired from the iris sensor, (B) image with detected pupil center and radius as shown in Fig. 1−4 and possible iris canter's (square box at pupil center) and radiuses (red arcs) for the evaluation, (C) processed image with edge detection operator that also reveals large portion of likely iris circle, and (D) image in (C) with overlaid iris circle as selected from the possible candidates in (B).

Once the pupil circle (Fig. 1–4) and iris circle (Fig. 1–5) are detected, the region between two circles defines the iris pixels of interest for the recovery and matching

1.2.1 Image normalization

The responsive nature of iris and the variations in the imaging environments or distances influence the size of the acquired iris image. The image unwrapping model shown in Fig. 1–6 can compensate for the stretching of the iris texture due to changes in pupil's size. This model can effectively remove the nonconcentricity of the iris and the pupil, and unwrap the iris image into a rectangular iris images, for example, rectangular region of 64×512 pixels as shown in Fig. 1–7.

In above Fig. 1–6, R represents the iris radius and r represents the pupil radius with "i" and "p" as their respective centers, while "d" represents the distance between the two centers.

$$R = |iB|, \quad r = |pA|, \quad d = |ip| \tag{1-10}$$

It can be observed that the angle ϕ is the angle between ip and pC, while angle α is the angle between ip and pA. The angle α for any angle θ can be obtained as:

$$\alpha = \phi - \theta; \tag{1-11}$$

The angle Ψ (Fig. 1–6) and distance pB and AB are computed using the following relations.

$$\frac{\sin(\psi)}{ip} = \frac{\sin(\alpha)}{iB}, \quad \frac{\sin(\alpha + \psi)}{pB} = \frac{\sin(\alpha)}{iB}, \quad AB = pB - pA \tag{1-12}$$

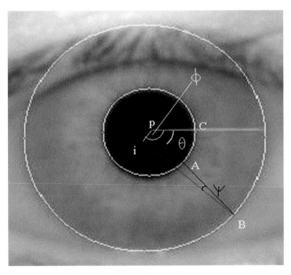

FIGURE 1–6 Image normalization model to normalize iris images.

FIGURE 1–7 Unwrapping iris pixels into rectangular images.

Using this distance *AB* and for θ varying from 0 to 360 degrees, the region of acquired image with iris pixels is unwrapped into a rectangular strip as shown in Fig. 1−7. The size of 64 × 512 is used for the unwrapped images shown in Fig. 1−8.

1.2.2 Image enhancement

The normalized iris image generally presents low contrast and may have nonuniform brightness caused by the position of illumination sources. Therefore the normalized or rectangular iris images are subjected to the enhancement operation by removing the average background illumination as can also be observed from the steps illustrated in Fig. 1−8. The first step here is to obtain the illumination profile (Fig. 1−8B) of the normalized iris image which can be obtained by computing average of each of the (say) 8 × 8 pixels from image in Fig. 1−8A and then interpolating the resulting reduced size image to the original size image using bicubic interpolation. This illumination profile image can be subtracted from the original image in Fig. 1−8A to obtain to normalize the illumination. The resulting image is further enhanced using the histogram equalization to obtain the image shown in Fig. 1−8D. Such preprocessing improves the contrast of the image, removes the nonuniform illumination, and enables the finer texture properties of the iris more distinct.

1.2.3 Eyelash and eyelid removal

Eyelashes and eyelids often occlude the iris region pixels which can degrade the match accuracy, therefore such occluded pixels in the iris region should be identified during the iris segmentation stage and excluded during the matching stage. Therefore respective binary mask that represents such occluded or noisy pixels, in the rectangular unwrapped images, is also generated during the iris segmentation process. One such simplified process for the generation of such iris mask is discussed here. Once the parameters for iris and pupillary circle are known from the normalization process discussed in Section 2.1, the edge detected image can be scanned from bottom to top starting from the topmost point of pupillary circle to topmost point of iris circle (leaving some margins). If any white pixel is encountered then a window of 80 × 8 pixels (red colored region in Fig. 1−9A) is scanned for white pixels. If the count of the white pixels in this region is more than the length of that window, then it can be considered as noise from the eyelash or eyelid (while line in Fig. 1−9B). At the *lowest* row of such a window, the iris image is separated as noisy and noiseless part of the image. The same

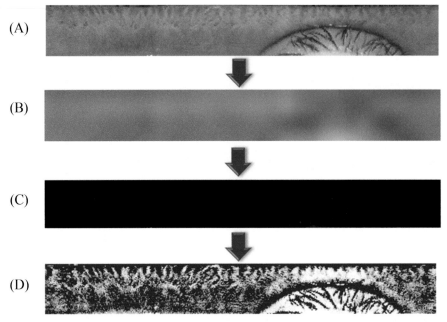

FIGURE 1–8 (A) Normalized or unwrapped iris image, (B) mean image, that is, estimate of the background illumination, (C) resulting image from the subtraction of image (A) with (B), and (D) enhanced iris image after histogram equalization of image in (C).

process is incorporated for lower eyelids but with a different threshold (say 70 for the example case in Fig. 1−9). Fig. 1−10 illustrates sample iris images from different sensors and overlaid regions from different steps during the iris segmentation.

1.2.4 Less constrained iris segmentation

Conventional iris segmentation algorithms [4] have shown to work quite well on the images that are acquired using iris sensors (Table 1−1) under stop-and-stare mode of acquisition. Such algorithms are therefore widely employed in the deployed iris recognition systems for access control and enrollment of citizens in the national ID programs. Degradation in iris image quality, due to lack of adequate user cooperation, variations in the ambient illuminations, acquisition distances, etc., can challenge performance from such iris segmentation algorithms. Therefore a range of more complex but accurate iris segmentation algorithms have been introduced for such less-constrained iris segmentation. These algorithms [15,16] have been primarily evaluated for their improved efficacy on iris images that are acquired from a distance, for example, [17,18] or those from visible illumination [19]. Notable advancements in such efforts are reflected from [11] that also provides source codes for benchmarking iris segmentation algorithms. More advanced iris segmentation

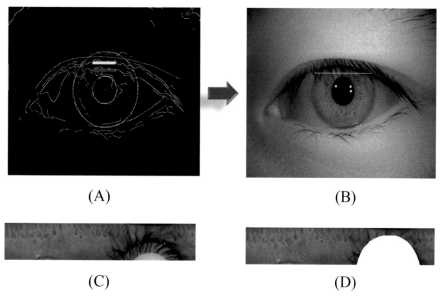

(A)   (B)

(C)   (D)

FIGURE 1–9 (A) Edge detected image with overlaid colored window illustrations, (B) image with white line marker to illustrate the detection of noisy pixels from the eyelash or eyelid, (C) respective normalized image, and (D) image in (C) with overlaid iris mask that identifies occluded iris pixels.

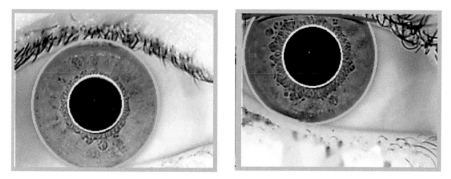

FIGURE 1–10 Sample iris images with overlaid pupillary circle (yellow color), iris circle (green color), and iris mask (red curve) that are automatically detected during the iris segmentation process.

approaches typically use fully convolutional neural networks and such method appears in [20] using *MaskNet*, which can generate more accurately segmented iris images [21] for the conventional and less-constrained iris recognition. In this context, there are several other references [22] that also present impressive results and use deep neural networks. However, some of these are less reliable as fair comparisons cannot be guaranteed when some images are excluded [23] during such performance evaluation.

1.3 Iris recognition

Conventional iris recognition using analysis of the random iris texture has attracted lot of attention and researchers have presented a variety of approaches in the literature. This section briefly summarizes such methods that have shown to offer competing accuracy on various databases and platforms.

1.3.1 2D Gabor filters

The most significant and widely deployed method of iris recognition uses *IrisCode* and has been introduced by Daugman [4,24]. This highly accurate method to match normalized iris images uses 2D Gabor filter(s) to generate binary iris codes, like a typical bar code, that are generally of 2048 bits and its generation is briefly discussed in the following.

   Each of the unwrapped and enhanced iris images are subjected to 2D Gabor filtering operation and respective responses, that is, band pass filtered images, are obtained. The analytical form of a 2D Gabor filter G in spatial domain can be expressed as in the following:

$$G(x, y, \theta, u, \sigma) = \frac{1}{2\pi\sigma^2} \exp\left(-\frac{x^2 + y^2}{2\sigma^2}\right) \times \exp\{2\pi i(ux\cos\theta + uy\sin\theta)\} \qquad (1-13)$$

where x and y represent the horizontal and vertical spatial index for the filter elements. The first part in the above equation is a 2D Gaussian function with standard deviation of σ while the second part represents a sine and cosine function that modulates the Gaussian function with the modulation frequency of u. Typical distribution of Gabor filter elements in the real and imaginary part of a Gabor filter is shown in Fig. 1–11. The filter elements from Eq. (1–4) can be separated into the real $Re(G)$ and imaginary $Im(G)$ part of the 2D Gabor filter. Therefore

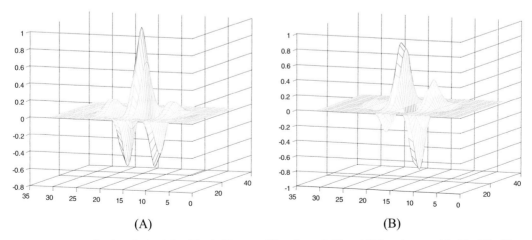

FIGURE 1–11 Visualization of a 2D Gabor filter in 3D space: (A) real part $Re(G)$ and (B) imaginary part $Im(G)$ of the filter.

conventional 2D convolution operation, that is, "*" on the normalized iris images I_n using the real part and imaginary part of Gabor filter, will respectively generate two filtered images.

These filtered images are used to recover discriminant features from each of the iris pixel locations. Instead of utilizing the magnitude of such Gabor filtered image, phase information is used for the generation of feature templates as the phase information has shown [4] to encode most discriminant features from the two Gabor-filtered responses. However instead of directly using the phase information, that is, $\tan^{-1}\left(\frac{Im(G*I_n)}{Re(G*I_n)}\right)$, the phase information from *each* of the pixels is quantized to a fixed, or four possible, levels for *IrisCode* representation. Such quantization of phase information can significantly enhance the robustness of the features to the noise. Such phase quantization is achieved as follows.

$$b_r = 1 \quad \text{if } Re\{G*I_n\} \geq 0$$
$$b_r = 0 \quad \text{if } Re\{G*I_n\} < 0$$

$$b_i = 1 \quad \text{if } Im\{G*I_n\} \geq 0$$
$$b_i = 0 \quad \text{if } Im\{G*I_n\} < 0$$

$$(1-14)$$

The pair (b_r, b_i) of binary bits corresponding to each of the pixels in iris image I_n encodes the gray level information in one of the four phase quadrants and requires two bits. Such quantization of phase angle responses from the Gabor filter, into one of the possible quadrants in the complex plane representing real and imaginary parts of filtered responses, is shown in Fig. 1−12. The total number of bits in resulting iris template will be twice of the angular resolution (512 pixels in Fig. 1−7) times the radial resolution (64 pixels in Fig. 1−7). We should note that this size of iris template, or *IrisCode*, is obtained when only one Gabor

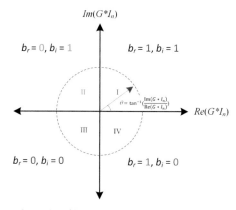

FIGURE 1–12 Quantization of complex Gabor filter response using its phase angle, into one of the four-phase quadrants, to generate two-bit binary code for every pixel in the normalized iris image I_n.

filter is employed and the use of multiple Gabor filters, for example, representing different scale and/or orientation parameters, will accordingly increase the size of *IrisCodes*.

The match score between two binarized feature templates, say *A* and *B*, is computed using the Hamming distance which represents the normalized sum of disagreeing (exclusive OR, XOR operator) number of corresponding bits between these two templated.

This match score is only computed from the valid bits in two templates, that is, those bits that are not representing the noise or occlusions and this information is adequately represented from respective masks say M_A and M_B. Therefore the normalized match score between two *IrisCode* templates can be represented as follows: -

$$s_{A,B} = \frac{\sum_{i=1}^{M} \sum_{j=1}^{N} \begin{Bmatrix} A_R(i,j)\ XOR\ B_R(i,j)\ AND\ M_A'(i,j)\ AND\ M_B'(i,j) \end{Bmatrix} + \sum_{i=1}^{M} \sum_{j=1}^{N} \begin{Bmatrix} A_I(i,j)\ XOR\ B_I(i,j)\ AND\ M_A'(i,j)\ AND\ M_B'(i,j) \end{Bmatrix}}{2\begin{Bmatrix} (M \times N) - \sum_{i=1}^{M} \sum_{j=1}^{N} M_A(i,j)\ OR\ \ M_B(i,j) \end{Bmatrix}} \qquad (1-15)$$

Above score s_{AB} will only consider those bits that are zero, or not marked as noisy pixel, in both the iris masks M_A and M_B. The complemented bits in respective iris masks M_A and M_B are represented as M_A' and M_B' to ensure such computation. To account for the rotational changes in the acquired iris images, one of the templates is circularly shifted to the left and right, say $\pm k$ bits, and match score s_{AB} is computed from *each* of the such successively shifted templates. The best or the *minimum* of such match scores s_{AB} among all $\pm k$ shifts is used as the final match score for the identification.

1.3.2 Localized Radon transform

Another efficient and effective extraction of iris features can be enabled uses localized Radon transforms (LRT) and can help to significantly reduce complexity of pixel-wise convolutional operations required using Gabor filters for the *IrisCode* approach. The feature extraction process exploits the orientation information from the local iris texture features using finite Radon transform [25]. The dominant orientation from these Radon transform features is used to generate a binarized and compact feature representations.

The LRT of a discrete image $g[m, n]$ on a finite grid R_q^2 can be defined as:

$$s[L_\theta] = M_g(\theta) = \sum_{(x,y) \in L_\theta} g[x,y] \qquad (1-16)$$

where $R_q = \{0, 1, \ldots, q-1\}$, q is a positive integer, and R_q^2 is centered at (x_0, y_0). The L_θ represents a set of points on R_q^2 such that

$$L_\theta = \begin{cases} \{(x,y)|y = \tan(\theta) \times (x - x_0) + y_0, x \in R_q\}, & \theta \neq \dfrac{\pi}{2} \\[2ex] \{(x,y)|x = x_0, y \in R_q\}, & \theta = \dfrac{\pi}{2} \end{cases} \qquad (1-17)$$

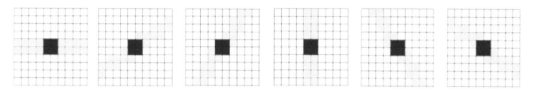

FIGURE 1–13 Illustration for computing LRT in a 10 × 10 iris pixel regions, in the directions of 0 degrees, π/6, π/3, π/2, 2π/3, 5π/6, while the L_θ is 2 pixels wide.

where $\theta \in [0, \pi)$ and denotes the angle between line L_θ and the positive x-axis, and L_θ is the line passing through the center (x_0, y_0) of R_q^2.

The orientation of the line-like patterns like blobs and furrows is estimated from the values of LRT. Since we are interested in the dark line-like features in the iris image, the orientation (Fig. 1–13) that corresponds to the *minimum* value is selected as the *dominant* direction. This can be mathematically represented as follows:

$$O_p(x_0, y_0) = arg\left(\min_p(s[L_\theta])\right), p = 1, 2, \ldots, D \qquad (1-18)$$

where the $O_p(x_0, y_0)$ represents the estimated direction of pixel $g[x_0, y_0]$, and D represents the number of directions (i.e., in Fig. 1–13, $D = 6$ since six directions can be selected). This operation is repeated as the center of lattice R_q^2 moves over all the iris pixels in the normalized iris image. At each position, the dominant orientation O_p is computed, and encoded using binary numbers (three-bit binary code representation for LRT steps shown in Fig. 1–13), to form the feature vector for the normalized iris image.

The match score S between two feature vectors (templates) R and T, with the corresponding masks M_A and M_B, is computed as follows:

$$S(R, T, M_A, M_B) = \min_{\forall i \in [0,2w], \forall j \in [0,2h]} \left(\frac{\sum_{x=1}^{m} \sum_{y=1}^{n} \psi\left(\hat{R}(x+i, y+j), T(x,y), M_A(x+i, y+j), M_B(x,y)\right)}{\sum_{x=1}^{m} \sum_{y=1}^{n} M_A(x,y) \cap M_B(x,y)} \right)$$
$$(1-19)$$

where $\hat{R}$ is the registered feature template with width and height expanded to $2w + m$ and $2h + n$.[2] We can define w, hm and $\hat{R}$ as follows:

$$w = \text{floor}\left(\frac{m}{8}\right), h = \text{floor}\left(\frac{n}{3}\right) \qquad (1-20)$$

$$\hat{R}(x, y) = \begin{cases} R(x - w, y - h) & x \in [w+1, w+m], \quad y \in [h+1, h+n] \\ -1 & \text{otherwise} \end{cases} \qquad (1-21)$$

---

[2] Relatively large amount of shifting in both directions can be employed to account for the segmentation errors, translational and rotational variations in the normalized images.

while the operator ψ can be defined as follows:

$$\psi(J,K,M,N) = \begin{cases} 0 \text{ if } M = N = 1 \text{ and } J = K \neq -1 \text{ or } & J = -1 \\ 1 & \text{otherwise} \end{cases} \tag{1-22}$$

Detailed analysis for this approach in [25] indicates that the *LRT*-based feature extraction approach requires about $2Kw$ times (K and w stands for the filter size and chosen line width, 10 and 2, respectively for example in Fig. 1–13) *fewer* operations as compared to those from the conventional Gabor filter-based approach for the *IrisCode*. In addition, the size of template (feature vector) is reduced by a factor of w^2 as compared to those for the *IrisCode* approach. Therefore this approach can be computationally attractive alternative for a range of online applications.

1.3.3 Log-Gabor, Gaussian derivative, and Cauchy filters

Gabor filters have been utilized to generate *IrisCode*, mainly due to their orientation selectivity, and maximum possible joint resolution in spatial and spatial-frequency domain. However, these filters may under emphasize low frequency contents or over emphasize on the high frequency contents in iris images. Log-Gabor filters can address such bandwidth-related constraints in traditional Gabor filters. The frequency response of log-Gabor filters has elongated tail in the high frequency part which can help to efficiently capture fine details from the high-frequency areas of the iris texture.

The 2D log-Gabor filter can be defined in frequency domain (u,v) as follows [26]:

$$H_B(u,v) = \exp\left(-\frac{\ln^2\left(\sqrt{u^2 + v^2}/f_0\right)}{2\ln^2(\sigma/f_0)} \right) \tag{1-23}$$

where f_0 is the center frequency and σ/f_0 is the parameter that controls bandwidth b for the bandpass filter H_B. The bandwidth of 2D log-Gabor filter can be computed as follows:

$$b = -2\sqrt{2\ln 2}\log_2(\sigma/f_0). \tag{1-24}$$

There are also other examples of 2D bandpass filters that can be effective to encode iris texture. The 2D Cauchy filter can be defined as follows [27]:

$$H_B(u,v) = \left(u^2 + v^2\right)^{a/2} \exp\left(-\sigma\sqrt{u^2 + v^2} \right) \tag{1-25}$$

where a/σ is the center frequency and a is a parameter for the bandwidth. The bandwidth b of this filter can be computed as follows [28]:

$$b = \log_2\frac{L_{-1}(c)}{L_0(c)}, c = -\frac{2^{-1/a}}{e}. \tag{1-26}$$

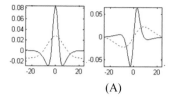 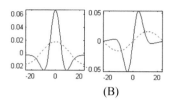 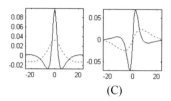

(A)   (B)   (C)

FIGURE 1–14 Spatial representation of real and imaginary parts of a typical 1D (A) Cauchy, (B) Gaussian derivative, and (C) log-Gabor filter. The dotted line in red color illustrates respective plot for different scale with thrice the center wavelength.

where L_{-1} and L_0 denote two branches of the Lambert L function which is the multivalued inverse function of xe^x [29]. Normalized iris images can be subjected to any of the above band pass filters Eqs. (1.23)–(1.25) and its phase information can be quantized, using similar steps as illustrated in Eq. (1−14), to generate *IrisCode* like *binary* templates that can be matched using Eq. (1−15). Use of respective 1D filters, instead of 2D as in Eq. (1−4), can offer computationally simpler alternative to generate *IrisCode* templates. Fig. 1−14 illustrates such spatial representation of a Cauchy, Gaussian derivative and log-Gabor filters. Several references use *IrisCodes* generated using 1D log-Gabor filters as the baseline method, and this mainly due to availability of such implementation in public domain [30] which has enabled easy and reproducible performance comparisons.

1.3.4 Quaternionic quadrature filters

The bandpass filters introduced in the previous section can also be used to generate quaternionic quadrature filters (QQF) for the iris recognition. Such decomposition can be achieved as follows [27]:-

$$\text{QQF} = (1 + \text{sgn}(u))(1 + \text{sgn}(v))F_1(u, v)H_B \tag{1−27}$$

where

$$\text{sgn}(u) = \begin{cases} 1, & u > 0 \\ 0, & u = 0 \\ -1, & u < 0. \end{cases} \tag{1−28}$$

Fig. 1−15 illustrates spatial domain representation of quaternionic quadrature filters. The phase information from each of the pixels in the normalized iris images can be encoded in four bits, instead of two bits for the *IrisCode*. Such representation using the quaternionic filters is referred as *QuaternionicCode* and can be computed as follows:

$$A_{\{1,2,3,4\}}(x, y) = \text{sgn}^+_{\{1,i,j,k\}}((qqf * I_n)(x, y)), \tag{1−29}$$

where $\text{sgn}^+_{\{1,i,j,k\}}$ extracts the nonnegative signs of respective $1, i, j, k$ parts (Fig. 1−15) of a quaternion, *qqf* is the spatial domain representation of *QQF* defined in Eq. (1−18), while

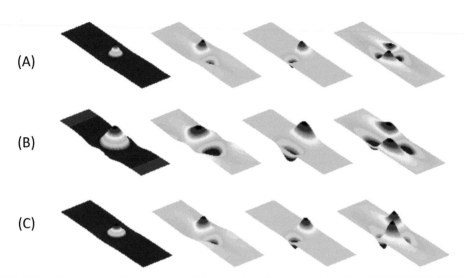

FIGURE 1–15 Spatial representation of a sample (A) quaternionic log-Gabor, (B) quaternionic Gaussian derivative, and (C) quaternionic Cauchy filter. The first column illustrates real part of respective filter while rest illustrates *i,j,k* (complex) part of filters, respectively.

$I_n(x, y)$ is normalized iris image. The match score between two *QuaternionicCodes* is computed using their normalized Hamming distance, that is, simple extension of Eq. $(1-15)$ from two-bit to four-bit templates.

The monogenic quadrature filters [26] can also be used for the phase encoding of iris texture and generate three bits per pixel binary representation which is referred to as *MonogenicCode* [31,32]. Despite notable increase in the template size of *MonogenicCode* and *QuaternionicCodes*, over the *IrisCode* representation, it may be attractive for the higher match accuracy in other biometric modalities.

1.3.5 Haar wavelet

Another successful approach to recover discriminating from the iris texture is to use multi-scale wavelet decomposition to analyze texture features from different resolutions. The Haar wavelets [33] can efficiently encode sharp discontinuities in the spatial gray-level iris texture transitions, by repeated application of following low-pass (g) and high-pass (h) filters:

$$g = \frac{1}{\sqrt{2}}\begin{bmatrix} 1 & 1 \end{bmatrix}, h = \frac{1}{\sqrt{2}}\begin{bmatrix} 1 & -1 \end{bmatrix} \qquad (1-30)$$

The above filters are separately applied to the rows and columns of the unwrapped iris images, resulting in four channels or outputs, that is, LL, LH, HL, and HH decomposition corresponding to filters $g^t * g$, $g^t * h$, $h^t * g$ and $h^t * h$, respectively, where "*" and t, respectively, represent conventional convolution and transpose operation. The recursive application of this decomposition is used to construct higher-level decomposition. We can consider feature extraction using the four-level Haar wavelet decomposition [34,35] as an *example* case. When the diagonal coefficients from the fourth level are employed, we can obtain 4×32 real values for the normalized iris image shown in Fig. $1-7$, 64×512. In addition to these 128 values, the average of diagonal coefficients from the first-, second-, and third-level decomposition can also be employed. Each of those 131 $(3 + 128)$ values can be quantized to binary values by simply converting the positive values to 1 and negative values to 0. Therefore the feature vector from such sample decomposition will result in iris template of 131 bits. The Hamming distance, similar to as in Eq. $(1-15)$, is used to efficiently match two feature vectors and generate a match score for the identification.

1.3.6 Ordinal filters

Another effective approach to encode normalized iris images uses (multiple) pairs of Gaussian kernels and encodes their *relative* output, from the local convolutional operations [32]. This relative output can be considered to the quantization operation in Eq. $(1-15)$, from the different portions of varying sinusoidal lobes, that also generates binary code that represent relative measurements among the distribution of local gray level texture features. Such relative or ordinal measurements are computed from a set of Gaussian kernels which can be represented as follows [36]:

$$\text{OM} = C_1 \sum_{i=1}^{K_1} \frac{1}{\sqrt{2\pi\sigma_i}} \exp\left[\frac{-\left(X-\mu_i\right)^2}{2\sigma_i^2}\right] - C_2 \sum_{j=1}^{K_2} \frac{1}{\sqrt{2\pi\sigma_j}} \exp\left[\frac{-\left(X-\mu_j\right)^2}{2\sigma_j^2}\right] \qquad (1-31)$$

where μ and σ, respectively, represent the spatial position and standard deviation of respective Gaussian filter while K_1 and K_2 respective define the number of positive and negative lobes. The coefficients C_1 and C_2 are incorporated to ensure that the average of OM kernel remains zero, that is, $C_1 \ K_1 = C_2 \ K_2$. The ordinal filters in Eq. $(1-22)$ are similar to difference-of-offset-Gaussian [37] and effective in encoding relative distribution of local iris texture elements. The Gabor filters used in *IrisCode*, Haar wavelets in [38], or Derivative of Gaussian filters in [37] can also be considered as the ordinal operators in encoding iris texture features along the $X-Y$ plane while carefully designed filters in [39] can also enable ordinal measurements along the Z direction using such 2D images. The sign of the local convolutional operation, with the normalized iris images, from the OM is used to generate a binary code or the template. These templates are matched using Hamming distance, similar to in Eq. $(1-15)$, to generate normalized match score.

1.3.7 Discrete cosine transform

Another effective approach to encode iris texture features is to use phase information from the zero crossings of the one-dimensional DCT for each row of pixels in the normalized iris images. The DCT coefficients $C(u)$ from the signal $f(x)$ of length L are obtained as follows:

$$C(u) = \varepsilon(u) \sum_{x=o}^{L-1} f(x) \cos\left[\frac{\pi.u}{2.L}(2x+1)\right], \ \forall \ u = 0, 1, \ldots, L-1 \qquad (1-32)$$

where $\varepsilon(u) = \frac{2}{L}$ for $u \neq 0$ and $\varepsilon(u) = \frac{2\sqrt{2}}{L}$ for $u = 0$. More specific details on the implementation and results from the iterative tuning to achieve best performance appear in [40,41]. The skewing of successive rows by one pixel to the right can be used to extract the blocks that are orientated at 45 degrees. To suppress the degradations from the noise, a weighted average from a Hanning window of 1/4th the length is computed on each of such blocks. The resulting vector is then windowed again, using a similar Hanning window, in the vertical direction before computing its DCT. Next, the difference of adjacent DCT output vectors is computed and the *feature* vector is obtained from their zero crossings. The match score s between two such iris templates is computed from a *modified* version of Hamming distance, in which the product of sum of respective bits corresponding to each block:

$$S = \left(\prod_{i=1}^{M} \frac{\sum_{j=1}^{N} \text{Block1}_{ij} \oplus \text{Block2}_{ij}}{N} \right)^{1/M} \tag{1-33}$$

where M is the number of bits per block in the vertical direction and N is the total number of blocks. This method of consolidating the Hamming distance has shown to offer better separation of genuine and impostor matches.

1.3.8 Fast Fourier transform

The phase information from the local frequency variations in the normalized iris images can also be used for the iris recognition [42]. Such approach first divides the normalized images into the pixel blocks that are aligned at 45 degrees. As detailed in [40], the average of these blocks in the horizontal direction is multiplied by a Hanning window to generate a 1D signal corresponding to each block. This signal $f(x)$ is then employed to compute the one-dimensional FFT coefficients, say $F(k)$, as follows:

$$F(k) = \sum_{x=1}^{L} f(x) \exp \left\{ \frac{-2\pi j(k-1)}{L} \right\}, \ \forall\, k = 1, 2 \ldots, L \tag{1-34}$$

The difference in the magnitude of adjacent blocks is computed and a binary feature vector is formed from the zero crossings of each difference. Each of the normalized iris image (sample in Fig. 1–7) can generate feature vector of 8160 bits, when the block size of 8×12 with an overlapping of 4 pixels in the vertical direction and 6 pixels in the horizontal direction is chosen. The match scores between such feature vectors is generated using their normalized Hamming distance.

1.4 Iris recognition using mobile phones

Iris recognition using popular mobile phones has increasingly been popular to support a range of applications, that is, from safeguarding a vast amount of personal data that generally resides on such smartphones to support a range of other online applications, such as the mobile banking. There is a difference between the design of algorithms deployed for the conventional iris recognition and those for the iris recognition on mobile phones. These differences can be in two categories, that is, (1) those relating to the design of sensors and detection/segmentation algorithms and (2) those relating to the design of algorithms for the matching the feature templates. These can be briefly summarized as in the following.

The design of algorithms to detect and segment iris images is closely related to the design of sensors and factors, such as the number of illuminators, placement of sensors, resolution of camera, depth of focus, and field of view from the camera lenses. There are several studies on the design of such algorithms for acceptable quality of iris images with at least 100 pixels diameter of iris (to meet ISO/IEC standard [1]). Reference [43] explains the selection of a good quality iris image from a consistent sequence of eye images. This method uses the position and quality of corneal specular reflections relative to the pupil. to the pupil. More insightful study on the iris detection using mobile phone is presented in [44] and it introduces algorithm to detect high-quality iris images in when users wore glasses which generates multiple corneal specular reflections. Reference [45] details a more efficient algorithm to detect iris images from mobile phone using a simplified combination of four classifies that detect relating brightness of iris with neighboring regions. This study positioned two 850-nm LED illuminators at a distance of 1.1 cm iris camera position on mobile phone. for the size of a 7 cm $\times$ 13.7 cm phone. Modern smartphones can acquire very high-resolution images without any additional zoom and focus. These smartphones have used conventional, that is, nondeep learning-based methods [45] to detect and segment iris images. Recent studies have shown that a deep neural network based methods can more accurately detect and segment iris images acquired from the smartphones.

The second difference is related to the design of algorithms to accurately match images acquired from mobile phones. Once the image detection, segmentation, and normalization are achieved, most of the classical methods (Section 3.1−3.8) can be used to generate feature templates. In the context of limited computational power, more simplified versions for the feature generations are preferred this can include just one pair or one component of 2D Gabor filters to generate *IrisCode* or use of Radon transforms (method detailed in Section 3.2) to avoid computationally demanding convolutional operations. Several research studies [46,47] have shown that not all components of iris feature templates are not equally important in generating reliable match scores. Such *fragility* of different iris bits in *IrisCodes*, or different components in feature templates, is more serious in the iris images acquired under less constrained environments or from mobile phones. The key reason for the fragility, or the reliability, of different features, from different locations, in the same iris images can be related to (1) sensing (illumination, distance, sensor noise, etc.) and (2) process of generating iris texture randomness (pupil dilation and contraction).

1.4.1 Identification of fragile bits in less constrained iris images

The existence of the fragile bits has been observed and effectively used in [46] to improve the matching accuracy. Reference [48] further extended this work based on the knowledge of fragile bits by weighting each bit to achieve improved recognition performance. Several studies have shown that such occurrence of fragile bits is more pronounced in the iris images acquired under less constrained environments, such as using mobile phones. We can use the following example to estimate the probability or extent of fragility of any particular bit, in the iris template. This example in table below shows five *corresponding* bits (in a column) from the instances in templates (*IrisCodes*), for five different iris images, of the same subject or eye. Therefore these bits are expected to remain stable but occasional changes in these bits (brown color) indicate the inconsistency. The numbers in the last row represent the estimated probability of such fragility associated with the respective bit.

	1	0	0	1	1
	0	0	0	1	1
	0	0	1	0	0
	0	0	0	1	1
	1	0	0	1	1
$\frac{\theta_n}{K} =$	0.6	0	0.2	0.2	0.2

The fragile bits which are estimated from the training images can be considered as an outcome from the noise perturbation. Therefore a nonlinear weighting strategy can be more effective in quantifying the consistency of each iris bit in the remapped normalized iris image [49]. The iris bit (in *IrisCode*) which is more consistent will be assigned with higher weight (close to one) to emphasize its importance while the iris bit which is less consistent is assigned a lower weight (close to zero). Given K preprocessed training normalized iris images $\left\{ \hat{I}_i^j \right\}_{i=1}^K$ of the jth class, we can firstly obtain the corresponding iris code representations $\boldsymbol{C}^j = \left\{ C_i^j \right\}_{(i=1)}^K$. Then, the consistency of nth bit can be estimated from the $\boldsymbol{C}^j$ by measuring the number of times that the nth is fragile. Note that $\boldsymbol{C}^j$ here is aligned with respect to the minimum Hamming distance obtained from the circular bit shifting before the consistency of iris bits is estimated. Let θ_n denote the number of times that nth bit is fragile. Then, the consistency of nth bit can be estimated from a probability value which can be defined as follows:

$$p_n^j = 1 - \frac{\theta_n}{K} \in [0, 1] \tag{1-35}$$

Hence, a probability map $P^j = \left\{ p_1^j, p_2^j, \ldots, p_N^j \right\}$ can be obtained based on the knowledge of the fragile bits estimated from some iris codes $\boldsymbol{C}^j$. The P^j has the identical dimension as the iris code of N bits, with each p_n^j corresponding to the consistency of the nth iris bit. Fig. 1−16 illustrates two examples of the probability maps obtained from the five *IrisCodes*.

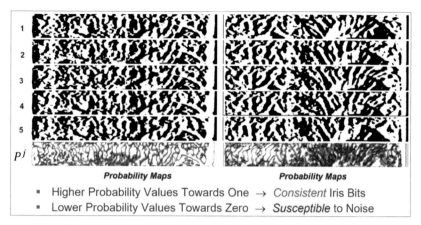

Probability Maps   **Probability Maps**

- Higher Probability Values Towards One → *Consistent* Iris Bits
- Lower Probability Values Towards Zero → *Susceptible* to Noise

FIGURE 1–16 Examples of the probability map (last row) estimated from five *IrisCodes* (first five rows marked from 1–5). Brighter pixels in this map indicates the respective bits are more stable while darker pixel indicates otherwise.

It can be observed that the iris bits where are estimated to be more consistent have higher probability values (higher intensity values), while the iris bits which are less consistent are indicated by lower probability values (lower intensity values).

$$w_n^j = \left(p_n^j\right)^{\alpha^j} \quad \text{where} \quad \alpha^j = \begin{cases} \dfrac{|P_{max}|}{\mu^j} = \dfrac{1}{\mu^j} & \text{if } \mu^j > 0 \\ 1 & \text{if } \mu^j = 0, \end{cases} \tag{1-36}$$

To more effectively emphasize (penalize) those bits which are highly consistent (inconsistent), a nonlinear weighting strategy is introduced as follows:where $\mu^j = 1/N \sum_{n=1}^{N} p_n^j$ and P_{max} represents the maximum probability value of P. The α^j exhibits the same function as the crest factor (peak-to-average signal ratio) which is employed here to ascertain overall quality of the P^j. The weighting function formulated in Eq. (1−36) exhibits several interesting properties which can be summarized in the following:

- The weighting function *preserves* the local consistency value for the highly consistent (inconsistent) bits, that is, when $\boldsymbol{p_n^j} = \{\boldsymbol{0,1}\}$, regardless of the crest factor α^j. As such, the weights for those highly consistent (inconsistent) bits will not be affected by α^j. This phenomenon can also be observed in the earlier illustration in this section which estimated the fragility (θ_n/K) of five different bits and its respective p_n values are illustrated in the following.

probability map of class j				
$p_n^j =$ 0.4	1	0.8	0.8	0.8
$w_n^j =$ 0.3	1	0.75	0.75	0.75

where $\mu^j = 1/N \sum_{n=1}^{N} p_n^j = 0.76$

- For $\mu^j = \{0,1\}$, which are the two special cases when the crest factor at its extremum, the weight remains the same, that is, $w_n^j = p_n^j$.
- For $K = 1$, the computed weight map $W^j = \left\{ w_1^j, w_2^j, \ldots, w_N^j \right\}$ is identical to the generated iris code C^j, such that the $w_n^j = \{0,1\}$. Therefore Eq. $(1-36)$ can be considered as the generalized representation for the conventional *IrisCode* representation.

The similarity between a query *IrisCode* C_{query} and reference gallery *IrisCode* $C_{gallery}^j$ of class j can be computed using modified Hamming distance [48] as in the following:

$$\text{HD}^j = \frac{\left\| \left(C_{query} \oplus C_{gallery}^j \right) \times W^j \right\|}{\left\| W^j \right\|} \qquad (1-37)$$

A range of experimental results presented in [39] using less constrained iris images indicates that this strategy can offer significant performance improvement over [46,48].

There are some computationally simpler alternatives to identify fragile bits, and these do not need multiple image frames, or samples, to ignore or suppress such inconsistent bits. The key idea is that bits corresponding to complex Gabor filter responses near the axes of the real or imaginary part which are smaller than a threshold (say t_f) should be excluded while computing the match distances between any two *IrisCodes*. Reference [50] introduces a simplified approach that adaptively determines t_f, from the statistics of respective filter responses, for each of the iris image frames. Such approaches have shown to be quite efficient and effective for the iris images acquired from mobile phones.

The thresholds for the real and imaginary parts of generated *IrisCodes* are different (Fig. $1-17$A) and are adaptively determined from the range of feature values, generated from the convolution with the Gabor filters. Results presented in [47] indicate another approach to determine and mask fragile bits from the iris image frames in *video* frames can be more effective. Instead of determining the fragile bits from the values that are closer to either the real axis or the imaginary axis, the fragility in this approach is determined using the relative magnitude of distance (feature value after convolution with Gabor filters) from the origin, that is, it masks those bits in *IrisCodes* that are *too close* to the origin or *too far* from the origin (Fig. $1-17$B). Motivation for masking larger values, that is, far away from the origin, is supported by the observation that most of the outliers due to the surface reflections or eyelashes generate larger values and should be ignored to generate more reliable match scores. It is worth noting the estimation of fragile bit is not limited to the iris templates represented by *IrisCodes* which was only used as an example. It has been shown to be effective for other classical methods of feature encoding and especially for images from mobile devices.

1.5 Periocular recognition and fusion with iris

The region around the eye is referred to as the periocular region, and there is no strict definition or standard, from professional or research bodies like NIST, on the anatomical extent of this region. Periocular recognition can be useful when accurate iris recognition cannot be

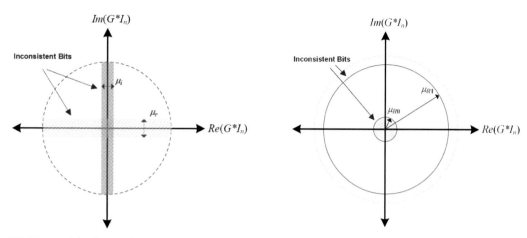

FIGURE 1–17 (A) Adaptive determination of fragile bits using different thresholds for the real and imaginary part of *IrisCodes* and (B) fragile bit localization using absolute distance from the origin, which masks too near and too far (small and large) feature values.

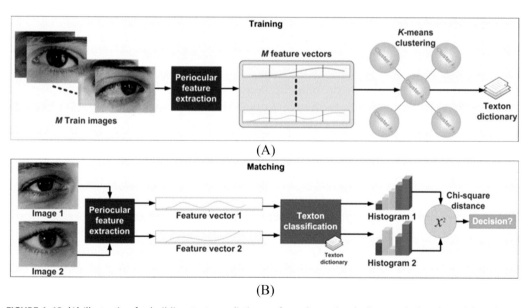

FIGURE 1–18 (A) Illustration for building *texton* a dictionary from the periocular images during the training phase and (B) the process of matching two periocular images.

ensured, due to imaging challenges due to lack of sufficient imaging resolution, or iris quality, especially for images using mobile phones and under an unconstrained environment. It is also helpful for a range of real-world applications, like surveillance which can generally present low-resolution or nonideal images, or when the entire face region is not available as commonly observed due to popular face masks. It has also been shown that the periocular region is more resistant to expression variations and aging as compared to other regions in the face. In addition to serving as an independent biometric modality, periocular information can also be simultaneously combined with the iris [16,51] and/or face [52] to improve overall recognition performance. However, matching periocular images, particularly under less constrained environments, is a challenging problem as this region itself contains less information than the entire face and is often accompanied by high intra-class variations along with occlusions like from glasses or hair.

Iris images acquired from conventional iris sensors inherently reveal periocular features. Therefore its natural for the researchers and developers to jointly use such available periocular features to enhance iris recognition capabilities. Reference [53] provides a good reference to understand human interpretable and discriminant features that can be reinforced to advance conventional iris recognition capabilities. It has been shown [16] that the dictionary represented from the global periocular features, instead of the local features that are extracted from localized eye regions, can offer more cues and achieve better matching accuracy. Therefore either the source iris images from the conventional iris sensors or the complete eye images as detected by a robust eye detector from the face images (e.g., partial or full face images using mobile phones) should be used to utilize the full potential of such periocular recognition.

A range of classical periocular recognition methods have been introduced in the literature [54]. It may not be helpful to discuss such periocular recognition methods, but prudent to discuss a few state-of-the-art conventional methods (i.e., nondeep learning based) that have convincingly demonstrated their merit from the performance evaluation using challenging but reproducible protocols. Two such methods are briefly discussed in the following two sections.

1.5.1 Periocular recognition using texton dictionary

The term *texton* was first introduced in [55] and later empirically (re)defined in [56] as an elementary unit of image analysis. This approach can allow us to construct a universal *texton* dictionary from the feature set that can be derived from a large number of periocular images in the training set. Several classical feature extractors, for example, such as SIFT [57], GIST [58], LBP [59], HoG [60], and LMF (Leung Malik Filters) [61], can be considered as the feature extractors to build such a *texton* dictionary. Comparative experimental results on several public periocular image databases indicate that dense SIFT [62] and LMF can better characterize periocular features at such (relatively low) resolutions.

The global periocular region, that is, entire ocular image made available during the iris imaging, is particularly useful if the iris segmentation fails or when the quality of the segmented iris image does not meet the minimum requirements. Unlike the local periocular region (i.e., normalized regions often used for periocular image matching), the size and the location of the global periocular region are less consistent as the such region is highly dependent on the detected eye region. This challenge can be addressed by a choice of superior feature descriptor, such as LMF and DSIFT adopted in this approach.

The training and the matching processes for the periocular image matching using such *texton* dictionary are summarized in Fig. 1−18. During the training phase, a *k-texton* dictionary can be constructed as follows. The (DSIFT or LMF) features are firstly computed from the periocular images in the training set. Then the *texton* dictionary is constructed by clustering the computed feature vectors using the *k*-means clustering approach. To select the best or, say *k* representative *textons*, a discrete set of *k*-values is computed for the candidate feature extraction methods, that is, the best or optimal *k* is computed during the training phase using a simple search. During the matching process, the features from the query periocular images are computed in a similar manner as during the training process. These periocular features are then classified using the trained *texton* dictionary, and the number of occurrences of each classified *texton* is computed to form a *k*-bin histogram (Fig. 1−18B). The match score between two such templates is computed using the Chi-square distance.

1.5.2 Periocular recognition using patch-based similarity prediction

Many real-world periocular images, especially those from surveillance or general face imagery, can depict significant, off-axis, defocus, illumination, and scale changes. Therefore consolidation of match scores generated from different patchers can be used to generate more reliable match scores. The key to the success of this approach lies in the alignment among the patches, that is, capability of generate match scores despite defocus, off-axis or scale changes. Such matching can be more accurately achieved in frequency domain by computing cross-correlation. Such cross-correlation requires discrete Fourier transform and inverse discrete Fourier transform which can be computationally demanding, especially for a large number of patches. This approach can however offer superior match performance and is detailed in reference [63] (Fig. 1−19).

Each of the query periocular images is first partitioned into a fixed number of nonoverlapping patches. The cross-correlation (amplitude of the observed peak) between two arbitrary patches in the training data can represent extent of correlation even under deformed or degraded patches. The training data in gallery can however lack deformation, pose, or occlusion cues. Such limitation is addressed by building a likelihood and prior distribution which can help to account for such variability in different periocular regions. The region represented by the pixels in patches can provide limited information and therefore multiple feature sets are recovered to build a more robust template. This step requires a bank of Gabor filters whose responses are subjected to a rectified linear unit to extract such feature sets. The experimental results illustrated in [63], on a range of public databases, are quite impressive.

1.6 Advancing iris recognition with periocular and multispectral images

Conventional iris sensors inherently acquire periocular details, to a varying degree, and therefore simultaneous use of such discriminant features to enhance iris recognition

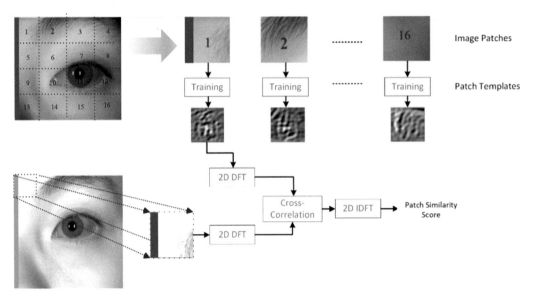

FIGURE 1–19 Generating periocular patch similarity score from the peak of the cross-correlation, using a set of augmented patch templates generated during the training phase.

capability has been widely investigated with some successful deployments. It is not just in references like [16] or [51], and many commercial iris recognition systems [64] are also believed to incorporate periocular and image quality features to enhance the iris recognition performance. Therefore *true* iris recognition performance evaluation from the acquired iris image datasets can be revealed by intentionally masking the noniris regions, similar to the use of automatically recovered iris masks in conventional iris recognition. This is also the reason that some comparative evaluation for iris recognition performance will (manually) mask noniris pixels before subjecting those images to estimate iris recognition performance.

The combination of such iris and periocular can be achieved using match score fusion. Weighted match score combination of multiple pieces of evidence is computationally simpler and more efficient. Therefore such fusion is widely preferred in many practical biometrics systems. Other methods of combinations, like feature-level fusion, can offer rich and more discriminant feature representation. However, such fusion is more challenging using classical feature representations, which can be attributed to the difficulty in combining wider variations in their conventional feature representations, for example, binarized *IrisCodes* for iris and real numbers as vectors for the periocular features.

Multispectral iris images can be acquired in single-shot imaging and provide rich pieces of discriminant information, as the same iris can reveal different features when observed under different spectrums [65]. However, enhanced complexity and cost associated with such multispectral imaging have prohibited the realization of multispectral iris recognition systems. Recent advances in sensing techniques and the availability of low-cost bi-spectral sensors, that is, single-shot visible and near-infrared images of the iris, have enabled the realization of such a system. Reference [66] details the development of such a bi-spectral iris recognition system which can simultaneously recover iris images from two spectra and generate two templates, for example, two *IrisCodes* for each of the iris images, that is, one from the visible and another from the near-infrared spectrum. Segmentation of the iris from the images acquired under the visible spectrum [15], especially for a large proportion of the population which has darker pigmentation, is quite challenging and complex as compared to those acquired under near-infrared illumination. Therefore the key to the success of such a bi-spectral system is the *pixel-to-pixel correspondences* in the iris images between the near-infrared and visible spectrum iris images that are instantly generated from the presented eye for the imaging. This can allow direct segmentation of iris pixels from the visible images from those locations that are identified for the iris segmentation in respective near-infrared images which is highly accurate. The mechanism for such precise pixel-to-pixel correspondences is also illustrated in Fig. 1−20, which utilizes a dichroic prism that can accurately segregate incoming images for the visible sensor and the other one for the near-infrared sensor/camera.

It is important to note the role of iris pigmentation on the multispectral iris recognition. Iris with light pigmentation reveal rich iris texture than those with darker pigmentation, which is prevalent in vast populations, especially in Asia. At visible wavelengths, conventional iris matchers are known to perform better for iris with lighter pigmentation than for those with darker pigmentation, while the reverse is true for irises acquired with darker pigmentation at near-infrared wavelengths. A recent NIST study [67] also underlines such observation and observed a noticeable improvement in performance for the light pigmentation when the match score fusion was employed for the scores acquired at 900 nm and 700 nm.

Many large-scale deployments of iris recognition technologies use dual eye identification as many commercial iris sensors can acquire both, that is, left and right, iris images in a single imaging shot. This has enabled many large-scale national ID programs, like Aadhaar [68].

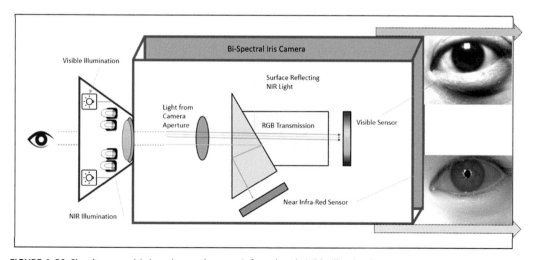

FIGURE 1–20 Simultaneous iris imaging under near-infrared and visible illumination.

and high-security applications, like prison management or de-duplication, to widely deploy such two-eye iris identification systems. Many large-scale performance evaluations for such dual eye identification [13] indicate that the performance improvement, for example, FNIR at FPIR of 0.01, over the use of just single eye identification, is much more than double.

1.6.1 Advances for the next-generation iris recognition technologies

Almost all large-scale deployments of iris recognition systems widely use classical methods that run on conventional CPU-based machines. This is also the reason that the ongoing NIST evaluation [13] only uses conventional[3] CPU machine for the comparative performance evaluation from the commercial algorithms submitted by different vendors. Deep neural network-based methods can offer power feature representation and capabilities to more accurately match iris images. However, the development and evaluation of such specialized deep learning-based algorithms are quite recent, and their commercialization will require upgrades on existing hardware infrastructure, and large-scale performance evaluation and consideration for such transition can only be gradual, requiring time.

---

[3] Ongoing IRIX X [14] evaluation in 2024 utilizes Dell PowerEdge M910 blades with Dual Intel Xeon X7560 2.3 GHz CPUs (with eight cores per processor) for comparative performance evaluation.

2

Unlocking the full potential of Iris recognition with deep learning

In recent years deep learning has gained tremendous success, especially in the area of computer vision, and accomplished state-of-the-art performance for a number of tasks, such as general image classification and recognition. However, unlike face recognition, iris recognition using deep learning has received relatively low attention, and there is a need to systematically understand expectations from the iris-specific network architecture to utilize the potential of the deep learning techniques fully. The focus of this chapter is to systematically explain the development of a powerful iris feature representation, from the normalized iris images, using a simplified deep neural network architecture.

2.1 Limitations with classical iris recognition techniques and challenges

Despite the popularity of iris recognition in biometrics, the conventional or classical iris feature descriptors do have several limitations. The summaries of earlier work [6,69] reveal that existing methods can achieve satisfactory performance, which is also revealed from their deployments. However, there is a need to enhance such performance to meet the expectations for a broader range of deployments. Conventional iris features, from classical methods, such as *IrisCode*, are mostly based on empirical models which incorporate hand-crafted filters or feature generators.

As a result, these models rely heavily on parameter selection when applied to different databases or imaging environments, that is, sensor and imaging types. Although there are some standards on iris image format [1], the selection of parameters for feature extraction remains empirical or based on training methods, such as boosting [70]. This situation can be observed from many quality references, for example, [36] uses eight different combinations of parameters for ordinal filters delivered varying performance on three databases, or from [40], which employed two sets of parameters for the log-Gabor filter on two databases by extensive tuning. Another limitation is that due to the simplicity of conventional iris descriptors, they are less promising in fully exploiting the underlying distribution from various types of iris data available today. Advanced capabilities of deep learning can enable accurate learning from large amounts of samples to significantly enhance the matching accuracy.

Deep learning capabilities offer tremendous potential to address the above-noted limitations (Fig. 2−1) since the parameters in deep neural networks are learned from data *instead* of being empirically set, and deep architectures are known to have good generalization capability. However, new challenges emerge while incorporating typical deep learning architectures, for example,

Iris and Periocular Recognition using Deep Learning. DOI: https://doi.org/10.1016/B978-0-443-27318-6.00003-6

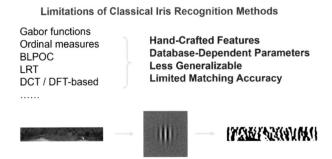

FIGURE 2–1 Key motivation for developing deep learning-based solution for iris recognition.

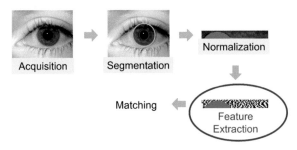

FIGURE 2–2 Conventional iris recognition pipeline and the key focus (red text) of the network design considered in this chapter.

convolutional neural network (CNN), for iris recognition, which can be primarily attributed to the nature of iris patterns. Different from the face, the iris patterns are observed to reveal little structural information or meaningful hierarchies. Iris's texture is believed to be random [71]. Earlier work in iris recognition [36,41,42,72] mainly employed small-size filters or block-based operations to obtain iris features. Therefore we can infer that the most discriminative information in the iris pattern comes from the *local* intensity distribution of an iris image rather than the *global* features, if any. CNN is known as effective for extracting features from low level to high level, and from local to global, due to the combination of convolutional layers and fully connected layers [73]. However, as discussed above, high-level and global features may not be optimal for iris representation.

2.1.1 Spatial correspondences in templates and chapter focus

The focus of this chapter is to design a specialized network that can generate the most discriminative iris feature templates by preserving spatial correspondences, in feature templates with respect to the normalized or input iris images. Fig. 2−2 can underline this objective, and we will extensively discuss postnormalization operations to develop a more accurate and robust deep learning-based iris feature representation framework to uncover the tremendous potential of deep learning for iris recognition. The focus of this chapter is *not* to discuss or introduce iris detection or normalization using deep neural networks, and this problem is discussed in the *next* chapter three. There are several references in the literature, for example [22], that are basically a direct application of typical CNN without many optimizations on iris representation, and also fail to provide any *fair* performance comparisons with the optimized iris representation, which will be discussed in this chapter.

2.2 Network architecture to generate optimized iris templates

The task of generating highly discriminant iris feature templates is achieved using a specialized deep neural network. This highly optimized and unified deep neural network architecture, referred to as *UniNet*, is used for iris feature extraction and masking noniris pixels. It is based on a fully convolutional network (FCN) [74], which is motivated to generate spatially corresponding iris features, as illustrated in Fig. 2−3. It uses a new customized loss function, named Extended Triplet Loss (*ETL*), and is developed to accommodate the nature of iris texture for supervised learning. The motivations and technical details of this network architecture are explained in the following sections.

2.2.1 Iris image preprocessing

As stated in Section 1.1, the focus of this chapter is on the design of specialized deep-learning architecture to extract discriminant iris features. Therefore the most matured conventional iris segmentation method was incorporated for the detection and normalization of the iris regions. This method [11], also provides publicly available codes [75] for easy reproducibility. The resolution of iris images after the normalization is uniformly set to 64×512 pixels for all the experimentation reported in Section 2.6. A simplified image contrast enhancement process is incorporated to adjust the image intensity so that 5% of pixels are saturated at low and high intensities. Fig. 2−4 illustrates the key steps of image preprocessing employed on the raw iris images provided in various databases. The normalized and enhanced images are used as the input to train the deep neural network, and also for the performance evaluation during the test phase.

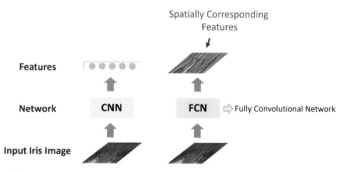

FIGURE 2–3 Inter-pixel feature relationships can be preserved in the encoded iris features by ensuring spatial correspondences in the iris templates.

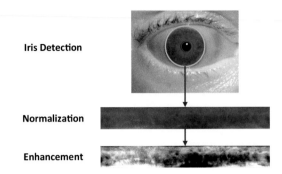

FIGURE 2–4 Illustration for key iris preprocessing steps.

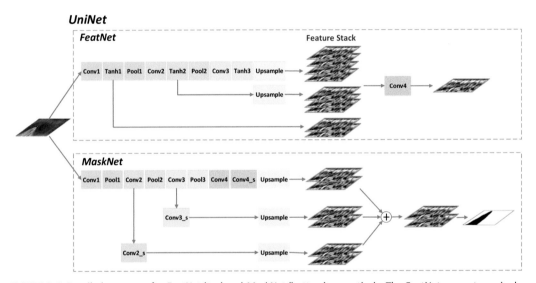

FIGURE 2–5 Detailed structures for *FeatNet* (top) and *MaskNet* (bottom) respectively. The *FeatNet* generates a single-channel feature map for each sample for matching. The *MaskNet* outputs a two-channel map, on which the values for each pixel along two channels represent the probabilities of belonging to iris and noniris regions, respectively.

2.2.2 Fully convolutional and unified neural network

Such a unified network referred to as *UniNet* is composed of two subnetworks, *FeatNet* and *MaskNet*. The detailed architecture of these subnetworks is presented in Fig. 2–5 and Table 2–1. Both of these two subnetworks are based on FCN architecture, which was originally developed for semantic image segmentation [74]. Different from the common CNN, the FCN does not have a fully connected layer. The major components of FCN are convolutional layers, pooling layers, activation layers, *etc.* Since all these layers operate on local regions around pixels from their bottom map, the output map can preserve the spatial correspondence with the *original* input iris image. By incorporating up-sampling layers, FCN is able to perform pixel-to-pixel prediction. The two components of *UniNet* are detailed in the following two subsections.

Table 2–1 Configuration for different layers in *FeatNet* and *MaskNet*.

FeatNet				
Layer	**Type**	**Kernel size**	**Stride**	**# Output channels**
Conv1	Convolution	3×7	1	16
Conv2	Convolution	3×5	1	24
Conv3	Convolution	3×3	1	32
Conv4	Convolution	3×3	1	1
Tanh1, 2, 3	TanH activation	/	/	/
Pool1, 2, 3	Average pooling	2×2	2	/

MaskNet				
Layer	**Type**	**Kernel size**	**Stride**	**# Output channels**
Conv1	Convolution	3×3	1	16
Conv2	Convolution	3×3	1	32
Conv2_s	Convolution	1×1	1	2
Conv3	Convolution	3×3	1	64
Conv3_s	Convolution	1×1	1	2
Conv4	Convolution	3×3	1	128
Conv4_s	Convolution	1×1	1	2
Pool1, 2	Max pooling	2×2	2	/
Pool3	Max pooling	4×4	4	/

2.2.2.1 FeatNet

The *FeatNet* is an abbreviation for the feature network as it is designed to extract discriminative iris features, which can be used for more accurate matching. As shown in Fig. 2−5, the input iris image is forwarded by several convolutional layers, activation layers, and pooling layers. The network activations at different scales, that is, Tanh1, Tanh2, and Tanh3 are then up-sampled, if necessary, to the size of the original input. These features form a multichannel feature stack that contains rich information from different scales and are finally convolved again to generate an integrated single-channel feature map.

The reason for selecting FCN, instead of CNN, for iris feature extraction primarily lies in the previous analysis of iris patterns presented earlier in Section 2.1, that is, the most discriminative information of an iris probably comes from small and local patterns. FCN is able to maintain local pixel-to-pixel correspondence between input and output, and therefore is a better candidate for the iris feature extraction.

2.2.2.2 MaskNet

MaskNet is set to perform noniris region masking for normalized iris images, which can be regarded as a specific problem for semantic segmentation. It is basically a simplified version of the FCNs introduced in [74]. The *MaskNet* is supervised by a pixel-wise softmax loss, where each pixel is classified into one of two classes, that is, iris or noniris. In our practice, *MaskNet* is trained with 500 randomly selected samples from the training set of the ND-IRIS-0405 [76] database, and we manually generated the ground truth masks during the offline training process. It is important to note that the focus of the network architecture (*FeatNet*) is on learning an effective and most discriminent iris feature representation. *MaskNet* is developed to provide adequate and intermediate information for masking noniris image regions, which is necessary for our newly designed loss function (will be detailed in Section 2.3) and also for the matching process. The placement of *MaskNet* in the unified network also preserves the possibility that iris masks may be jointly optimized/fine-tuned with the feature representations, which is one of our future research goals. At this stage, however, *MaskNet* is pretrained and fixed during the learning phase for the iris features. A sample evaluation for its performance evaluation for the *MaskNet* appears later in Section 2.6.6 of this chapter.

2.2.3 Network training under triplet architecture

A triplet network [77] was implemented for learning the convolutional kernels in *FeatNet*. The overall structure for the triplet network in the training stage is illustrated in Fig. 2−6. As shown in the Figure, three identical *UniNets*, whose weights are kept identical during training, are placed in parallel to forward and back-propagate the data and gradients for anchor (*A*), positive (*P*), and negative (*N*) samples, respectively. The anchor-positive pair should come from the same person, while the anchor-negative pair should come from different persons. The triplet loss function in such architecture attempts to reduce the anchor-positive distance and, meanwhile, increase the anchor-negative distance. However, in order to ensure more appropriate and effective supervision in the generation of iris features by the FCN, we improve the original triplet loss by incorporating a bit-shifting operation. The improved loss function is referred to as *ETL*, whose motivation and mechanism are detailed in Section 2.3.

2.3 Extended triplet loss function

This Section details the development of a specialized loss function designed to enhance the efficacy of iris feature learning. The newly developed loss function comprises two distinct versions - one optimized for real-valued features and the other tailored to binary feature codes. The motivation for

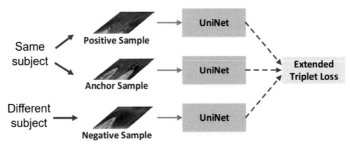

FIGURE 2–6 Network training using triplet-based architecture.

creating the binary version is grounded in extensive research on iris recognition, which has consistently suggested that binary features are better suited for iris pattern representation and can exhibit greater robustness to noise [24,25,36,41]. Therefore developing an end-to-end deep learning framework capable of directly learning (*IrisCode* like) binary iris features would be worthwhile. In the subsequent section, we present *both* versions of the newly developed loss function.

2.3.1 Triplet loss function incorporating bit-shifting and iris masks

The original loss function for a triplet network is defined as follows:

$$L = \frac{1}{N}\sum_{i=1}^{N}\left[\left\|\boldsymbol{f}^{A}_{i}-\boldsymbol{f}^{P}_{i}\right\|^{2}-\left\|\boldsymbol{f}^{A}_{i}-\boldsymbol{f}^{N}_{i}\right\|^{2}+\alpha\right]_{+} \qquad (2-1)$$

where N is the number of triplet samples in a mini-batch, $\boldsymbol{f}^{A}_{i}, \boldsymbol{f}^{P}_{i}$, and $\boldsymbol{f}^{N}_{i}$ are the feature maps of anchor, positive, and negative images in the ith triplet respectively. The symbol $[\bullet]_{+}$ is the same as used in [77] and is equivalent to $\max(\bullet, 0)$. α is a preset parameter to control the desired margin between anchor-positive distance and anchor-negative distance. Optimizing the above loss will lead to the anchor-positive distance being reduced and the anchor-negative distance being enlarged until their margin is larger than a certain value.

In our case, however, using Euclidean distance as the dissimilarity metric is far from sufficient. As discussed earlier, we propose using spatial features with the same resolution as the input, the matching process has to deal with noniris region masking and horizontal shifting, which are frequently observed in iris samples, as illustrated in Fig. 2−7. Therefore in the following, we extend the original triplet loss function, which we refer to as the *ETL*:

$$ETL = \frac{1}{N}\sum_{i=1}^{N}\left[D(\boldsymbol{f}^{A}_{i},\boldsymbol{f}^{P}_{i})-D(\boldsymbol{f}^{A}_{i},\boldsymbol{f}^{N}_{i})+\alpha\right]_{+} \qquad (2-2)$$

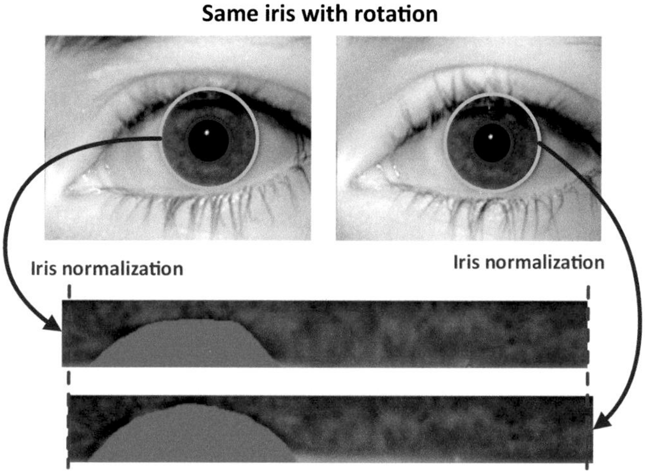

FIGURE 2–7 Illustration of occlusions (blue colored mask) and horizontal translation which usually exist between two normalized iris images even from a same iris.

where $D(f^1, f^2)$ represents the Minimum Shifted and Masked Distance (MMSD) function and the symbol $[\bullet]_+$ is equivalent to $\max(\bullet, 0)$ which means that in the case when $(f^A_i, f^P_i) - D(f^A_i, f^N_i) + \alpha < 0$, the anchor-positive distance (AP) and anchor-negative (AN) distance are already well separated, there is no need to learn from such (easy) training samples, and therefore the loss is set to zero. The distance function $D(f^1, f^2)$ can be defined as follows:

$$D(f^1, f^2) = \min_{-B \leq b \leq B} \{FD(f_b^1, f^2)\} \qquad (2-3)$$

where f_b represents a shifted version of f obtained by horizontally shifting it by b pixels and FD is the fractional distance. The spatial correspondence between the original feature map and the shifted feature map is as follows:

$$f_b[x_b, y] = f[x, y] \qquad (2-4)$$

$$x_b = (x - b + w) \mod w$$

where w represents the width of the 2-D feature map, x, y are the spatial coordinates and x_b is obtained by shifting the pixel to the left by a step of b. Note that when x is less than b, the pixel position will be directed to the right end of the map, as the iris map is normalized by unwrapping the original iris circularly and the left end is therefore physically connected with the right end. When b is negative, the bit-shifting operation would shift the map to the right by $-b$ pixels. The relative difference between two feature maps within the nonmasked regions is quantified by the FD as incorporated in Eq. (2-3). This value is then normalized by the number of pixels (M) involved in the calculation:

$$FD(f^1, f^2) = \frac{1}{|M|} \sum_{(x,y) \in M} d(f^1_{x,y}, f^2_{x,y}) \qquad (2-5)$$

where M is the set common nonmasked pixel positions for the two feature maps and can be computed as follows:

$$M = \{(x, y) | m^1_{x,y} \neq 0 \text{ and } m^2_{x,y} \neq 0\} \qquad (2-6)$$

where m^1 and m^2 are the binary masks for two feature maps, that is, blue colored regions for two normalized irises being matched in Fig. 2-7, where zero represents the current position of noniris pixels in respective masks.

The selection of the element-wise difference function $d(\bullet)$ in Eq. (2-5) is contingent upon the specific version of ETL employed, namely the real-valued or binary version as previously mentioned. For the real-valued version, the difference function is defined as the square of the difference.

$$d_{real}(f_1, f_2) = (f_1 - f_2)^2 \qquad (2-7)$$

whereas in the binary version, to measure the fractional Hamming distance, the exclusive-or (XOR) operator can be used to compute this distance as follows:

$$d_{binary}(f_1, f_2) = f_1' \oplus f_2' \qquad (2-8)$$

$$f' = \Psi(f) = \begin{cases} 1, & \text{if} \quad f \geq 0 \\ 0, & \text{otherwise} \end{cases} \qquad (2-9)$$

where Ψ (•) represents a step function. Eqs. (2−3) and (2−5) highlight that the newly introduced iris-specific loss function solely assesses feature differences within nonmasked iris regions, and also incorporates a shifting operation to account for horizontal translation (Fig. 2−8). This ensures that the matching of spatially corresponding iris features is both accurate and relevant. In the subsequent section, we will outline the gradient computations for the ETL, enabling the implementation of back-propagation (BP) for the learning process. Notably, the cases for the real-valued and binary versions of ETL are markedly distinct and will therefore be addressed separately.

2.3.2 Back-propagation using real-valued extended triples loss

As all components of the real-valued ETL are differentiable, the computation of gradients is a relatively straightforward process. First, in order to maintain simplicity of the notations for the following derivation, we denote the offsets that fulfill the MMSD of AP-pair and AN-pair as follows:

$$b_{AP} = \underset{-B \leq b \leq B}{\operatorname{argmin}} \left\{ FD(f^A{}_b, f^P) \right\} \qquad (2-10)$$

$$b_{AN} = \underset{-B \leq b \leq B}{\operatorname{argmin}} \left\{ FD(f^A{}_b, f^N) \right\}$$

During the back-propagation operation in the network training process, the gradients (or partial derivatives) of the new loss on the anchor, positive, and negative feature maps need

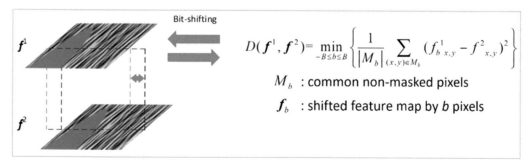

FIGURE 2–8 Computing minimum of the shifted and masked distance during the network training.

to be computed. For simplicity, let us firstly derive the partial derivative w.r.t. the positive feature map f^P. From Eq. $(2-2)$ it can be derived that for one sample in the batch:

$$\frac{\partial ETL}{\partial f^P} = \begin{cases} 0, & \text{if } ETL = 0 \\ \frac{1}{N}\frac{\partial ETL}{\partial D(f^A,f^P)}\frac{\partial D(f^A,f^P)}{\partial f^P}, & \text{otherwise} \end{cases} \qquad (2-11)$$

Again from Eq. $(2-2)$, we can observe that $ETL = 0$ is equivalent to $D(f^A,f^P) - D(f^A,f^N) + \alpha \le 0$. We only need to show the derivation when ETL is not 0. Let us define the set of common valid iris pixel positions for AP pair as:

$$M_{AP} = \{(x,y)|\boldsymbol{m}^A[x,y] \ne 0 \text{ and } \mathbf{m}^P[x_{b_{AP}},y] \ne 0\} \qquad (2-12)$$

From Eqs. $(2-3)$ and $(2-11)$, we can compute the following pixel-wise derivatives:

$$\frac{\partial D(f^A,f^P)}{\partial f^P[x,y]} = \frac{\partial FD(f^A_{b_{AP}},f^P)}{\partial f^P[x,y]} = \begin{cases} 0, & \text{if } (x,y) \notin M_{AP} \text{ or } ETL = 0 \\ \frac{-2}{|M_{AP}|}(f^A[x_{b_{AP}},y] - f^P[x,y]), & \text{otherwise} \end{cases} \qquad (2-13)$$

And apparently $\frac{\partial ETL}{\partial D(f^A,f^P)} = 1$, therefore using Eqs. $(2-11)$ and $(2-13)$.

$$\frac{\partial ETL}{\partial f^P[x,y]} = \begin{cases} 0, & \text{if } (x,y) \notin M_{AP} \text{ or } ETL = 0 \\ \frac{-2(f^A[x_{b_{AP}},y] - f^P[x,y])}{N|M_{AP}|}, & \text{otherwise} \end{cases} \qquad (2-14)$$

Similarly, for the partial derivatives on the negative feature map, we have:

$$\frac{\partial ETL}{\partial f^N[x,y]} = \begin{cases} 0, & \text{if } (x,y) \notin M_{AN} \text{ or } ETL = 0 \\ \frac{2(f^A[x_{b_{AN}},y] - f^N[x,y])}{N|M_{AN}|}, & \text{otherwise} \end{cases} \qquad (2-15)$$

The final step is to compute the derivatives of loss function with respect to the anchor feature map. It can be observed from Eqs. $(2-3)$ to $(2-5)$ that the shifting (horizontal translation) of first map to the left by b pixels is equivalent to shifting the second map to the right by b pixels. Making use of this property, we can write $FD(f^A_{b_{AP}},f^P) = FD(f^A,f^P_{-b_{AP}})$ and $FD(f^A_{b_{AN}},f^N) = FD(f^A,f^N_{-b_{AN}})$. It is therefore quite straightforward to further simplify Eq. $(2-15)$, using $(2-2)$ to $(2-4)$, as follows:

$$\frac{\partial ETL}{\partial f^A[x,y]} = -\frac{\partial ETL}{\partial f^P[x_{-b_{AP}},y]} + \frac{\partial ETL}{\partial f^N[x_{-b_{AN}},y]} \qquad (2-16)$$

After calculating the derivative maps with respect to f^A, f^P, and f^N respectively, the rest of the BP process is the same as for common CNNs. Above derivation shows that gradients will be computed only for pixels that are not masked. In this way, features are learned only within valid iris regions, while noniris regions will be ignored since they are not of our interest. After the last convolutional layer, a single-channel feature map is generated which can be used to measure similarities between the iris samples.

2.3.3 Back-propagation using binary valued extended triples loss

When it comes to the binary version of ETL, the sole discrepancy from the real-valued counterpart is the different computation of distance function (2.8). Specifically, the step function $\Psi(\bullet)$ generates either undefined gradients or zero, rendering it unfeasible to directly apply BP with gradient descent. This can be connected to an open research problem in the literature, namely, learning binary features or Hash codes using deep neural networks [78]. Prior approaches, such as in [79] and [80], have typically leveraged *smooth* versions of the step function to mimic the binarization process, thereby achieving compatibility with gradient descent. However, we here consider a completely different strategy to address this issue. Rather than emulating the step function using "soft" versions, we interpret the binarization process as a binary classification problem. Our objective is to accurately classify each pixel or element in the feature maps f^A_i, f^P_i, and f^N_i, such that the forward loss *ETL* computed from Eq. (2−8) is minimized.

   To begin with, we calculate the forward loss using Eqs. (2−2) to (2−5) and (2−8), and we focus on triplet samples that produce nonzero *ETL*, subject to the threshold α. Since the forward loss cannot be back-propagated, we can consider feature binarization as binary classification problem. To this end, we create a dependent backward loss L_{cls} using widely used logistic (or cross-entropy) loss function for each pixel.

$$L_{cls}(f) = -y\log(p) - (1-y)\log(1-p) \qquad (2-17)$$

where $y \in \{0,1\}$ is the latent target label for the current pixel, and p is the probability of the respective pixel being in class $y = 1$. This probability p is estimated with sigmoid function as follows:

$$p = \sigma(f) = \frac{1}{1 + e^{-f}} \qquad (2-18)$$

   The key issue is that the correct class label y for each pixel is unknown in our case. However, we can leverage the logical relationship among the anchor, positive, and negative samples in the triplet architecture to deduce the desired labels and reduce the forward loss. Assuming that the feature maps are aligned with Eq. (2−3) and that a particular pixel position is not masked, the ideal scenario for that aligned pixel position is when A, P, and N have distinct labels, that is, $y^A = y^P \neq y^N$. This arrangement causes the anchor-positive distance to shrink while the anchor-negative distance increases. We therefore assign the following *pseudo-labels* to each pixel in the anchor feature map.

$$\hat{y}^A = \begin{cases} \Psi(f^P), & \mathit{iff}^P, f^A > 0 \\ 1 - \Psi(f^N), & \text{Otherwise} \end{cases} \qquad (2-19)$$

The objective of above assignment described above is straightforward - to reinforce the pattern where the anchor has the same binary code as the positive sample, and the opposite binary code to the negative sample. It is important to note that the feature values from the other branches ($\boldsymbol{f}^{P}_{i}$ and $\boldsymbol{f}^{N}_{i}$) are treated as constants with respect to the anchor feature $\boldsymbol{f}^{A}_{i}$. Using the pseudo-labels, we can derive the derivative of the logistic loss function, which is a well-known result.

$$\frac{\partial L_{cls}}{\partial \boldsymbol{f}^{A}} = p^{A} - \hat{y}^{A} = \frac{1}{1 + e^{-f^{A}}} - \hat{y}^{A} \qquad (2-20)$$

By using the pseudo-labels and the resulting derivative, we can perform BP. Currently in this implementation, the gradients are only computed for the anchor branch, but the weight updates are combined for all three branches at each iteration.

The above optimization strategy does not simulate the step function like other approaches but incorporates the real binarization step into forward and backward processes by modeling it as a binary classification problem. To optimize the features, we construct a backward classification loss that closely aligns with the forward target loss *ETL*. This approach can be more effective than numerical simulation, which often requires additional consideration of quantization loss and data distribution priors.

2.4 Fine tuning and feature fusion

The feature level fusion can be better learned to reduce the matching complexity and fine-tune the model for the better representation of iris features. Such feature fusion can be accomplished by a resizing layer and a convolutional layer, as also illustrated from simplified illustration in Fig. 2−9. The first part of this model can be obtained in the pretrain stage and is *frozen* during the fine-tuning stage. The output of the pretrained model contains feature maps at three different scales. The features at smaller scales can then be passed through resize layers, which resize them to the same resolution as the largest scale. The resized feature maps can then be concatenated (stacked) as a new multichannel feature map, followed by a convolutional layer that only generates a single-channel output. In such implementation (Fig. 2−9), we can uniformly set the size of the convolutional

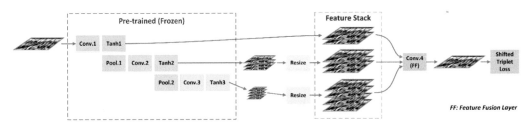

FIGURE 2–9 Simplified network architecture with feature fusion learning. It should be noted that there are three identical networks in parallel as required by the triplet loss, but only one is shown for saving space.

kernels of this layer to 3×3. This newly added convolutional layer can serve as a feature selector and the fuser, which is expected to select and consolidate the most discriminant features from input maps. The feature fusion learning process can *again* be supervised by the *Shifted Triplet Loss* function, as what is employed in the pretraining stage. The fused features, however, do not need to be activated or normalized by the nonlinear (TanH) function. Since the input feature maps are already well scoped between the fixed ranges, the output values are expected to be relatively aggregated and can be directly used as the features in computing their similarity.

The fine-tuning stage can be trained with the same set of training data as used in the pre-train stage, provided that this model (Fig. 2−5) has sufficient generation power; or it can be trained using a different set from any target database to fully exploit the cross-database variations. Fig. 2−10 presents a typical visualization for part of the learned convolutional kernels, intermediate feature maps and the final fused iris feature map.

2.5 Feature encoding and matching

For the real-valued features output from *UniNet*, we perform a simple encoding process for the feature map output. The feature maps originally contain real values, and it is straightforward to measure the fractional Euclidean distance between the masked maps for matching, as the network is trained in this manner. However, binary features are more popular in most of the research works on iris recognition (e.g., [36,40,42,45,46,81]), since it is widely accepted by the community that binary features are more resistant to illumination change, blurring, and other underlying noise. Besides, binary features require smaller storage and can enable faster matching. Therefore we also investigated the feasibility of binarizing our features with a reasonable scheme as described in the following:

For each of the output feature map, the mean value of the elements within the non-masked iris regions is firstly computed as m. This mean value is then used as the threshold to binarize the original feature map. In order to avoid marginal errors, elements with feature values v close to m (i.e., $|v - m| < t$) are regarded as less reliable and will be masked together with the original mask output by *MaskNet*. Such a further masking step is conceptually similar to "Fragile Bits" discussed in Section 1.4.1 of Chapter 1, which underlines that some bits in *IrisCode*, with filtered responses near the axes of the complex space, are less consistent or unreliable. The range threshold t for masking least reliable bits is uniformly set to 0.6 for all the experiments. Such feature encoding process can also be visualized in Fig. 2−11. For matching, we use the fractional Hamming distance HD (c^1, c^2), which is the same as discussed in Chapter 1 (Eq. (2−6)), from the binarized feature maps and extended masks. Such match score can be computer as follows:

$$HD(c^1, c^2) = \min_{-B \leq b \leq B} \left\{ \frac{1}{|M'_b|} \sum_{(x,y) \in M'_b} c^1_{b\,x,y} \oplus c^2_{x,y} \right\} \qquad (2-21)$$

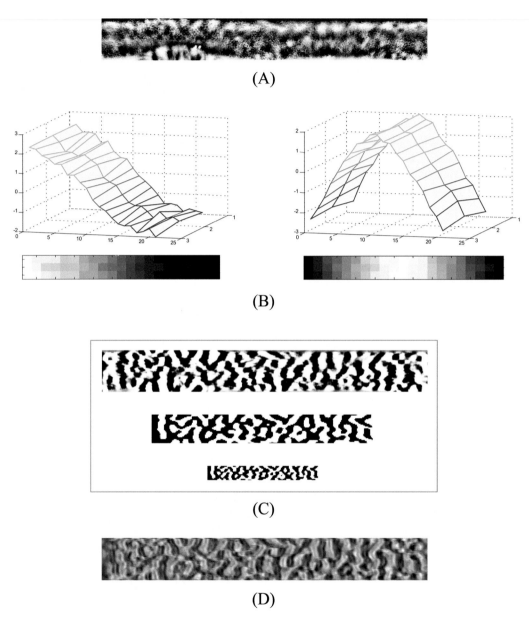

FIGURE 2–10 Sample visualization of (A) a normalized iris input image, (B) part of the learned convolutional filters, (C) part of the learned intermediate feature maps from three activation layers, and (D) the fused feature map of the input image.

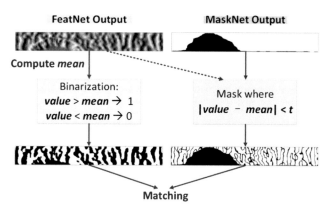

FIGURE 2–11 Illustration of feature binarization process.

where c^1, c^2 represents the binary codes or feature maps to be matched, c_b^1 represents shifted version of c^1, M_b' represents the common nonmasked areas between the two codes, and $\oplus$ represents Boolean exclusive OR (XOR) operation. It has been empirically observed that using the binary features does not degrade the performance compared with using the real-valued features, and even yield slight improvements in some cross-dataset scenarios, presumably due to the factors discussed earlier in this section.

2.6 Experiments and results

This section will present rigorous experimental results to evaluate the performance of the proposed approach from various aspects. The following sections firstly details on the experimental settings for these reproducible [82] results presented in this section.

2.6.1 Databases and protocols

We employed the following four publicly available databases in our experiments:

- ND-IRIS-0405 iris image dataset (ICE 2006)
     This database [76] contains 64,980 iris samples from 356 subjects and is one of the most popular iris databases in the literature. The training set for this database is composed of the first 25 left eye images from all the subjects, and the test set consists of first 10 right-eye images from all the subjects. The test set, after *removing* some falsely segmented samples, contains 14,791 genuine pairs and 5,743,130 imposter pairs.

- CASIA iris image database V4—distance

    This database (subset) [17] includes 2,446 samples from 142 subjects. Each sample captures the upper part of face and therefore contain both left and right irises. The images were acquired from 3 m away. An OpenCV-implemented eye detector [83] was applied to crop the eye regions from the original images. The training set consists of all the right eye images from all the subjects, and the test set comprises all the left eye images. The test set generates 20,702 genuine pairs and 2,969,533 imposter pairs.
- IITD iris database

    The IITD database [84] contains 2,240 image samples from 224 subjects. All of the right eye iris images were used as training set while the first five left eye images were used as test set. The test set contains 2,240 genuine pairs and 624,400 imposter pairs.
- WVU Nonideal iris database—Release 1

    The WVU Nonideal database [85] (Rel1 subset) comprises 3,043 iris samples from 231 subjects which were acquired under different extends of off-angle, illumination change, occlusions, etc. The training set consists of all of the right eye images, and the test set was formed by the first five left eye images from all the subjects. The test set has 2,251 genuine pairs and 643,565 imposter pairs.

From the above introduction we can observe that the imaging conditions for these databases are quite different. Sample images from the four employed datasets are provided in Fig. 2–12, where noticeable variation in image quality can be observed. It is therefore judicious to assume that these databases can represent diverse real-world deployment environments.

The details on the division of the training set and the test set on the four employed databases are provided in Table 2–2. Both the training set and the test set are formed with the first X ($X = 25$, 10, or 5, shown in Table 2–2) or all of the left/right eye images from each of the subjects. If a subject has less than X images in the respective database, then all images from this subject will be included.

| ND-IRIS-0405 | CASIAv4-distance | IITD | WVU Non-ideal |

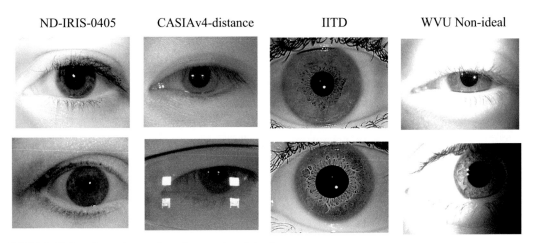

FIGURE 2–12 Sample raw images from four employed databases.

Table 2-2 Summary of the division for training set and test set on the employed databases.

Database	Training set				Test set			
	# subjects	# images/subject	Side	# images	# subjects	# images/subject	Side	# images
ND-IRIS-0405	All 356	First 25	left	9,301	All 356	First 10	Right	3,394
CASIA.v4-distance	All 411	First 25	Left	6,840	All 411	First 10	Right	3,939
IITD	All 224	All	Right	1,052	All 224	First 5	Left	1,120
WVU Nonideal	All 231	All	Right	1,511	All 231	First 5	Left	1,137

During the training phase, the triplet-based architecture detailed in Section 2.2 requires the input data to be triplet sets (anchor−positive−negative entries) instead of single images. Therefore the training images in each of the databases need to be presented as triplet entries which are generated from the combinations of images. However, enumerating all the possible triplet combinations in the training set will lead to high storage and computational complexity, we therefore selectively generate part of the possible triplet entries for training, as described in the following: For each training set, we firstly enumerate all the possible anchor-positive (genuine) pairs, since the numbers of available genuine pairs are relatively small; for each anchor-positive pair, we randomly select five negative samples that are from different subjects than the anchor subject, and form the anchor-positive-negative triplet. In other words, each genuine pair in the training set will generate five triplet entries for training.

2.6.2 Test configurations

We incorporated the following two configurations during the test phase for extensive evaluation of the proposed model.

- Cross-Database Performance Evaluation (*CrossDB*)

    In the *CrossDB* configuration, we use the ND-IRIS-0405 as the training set. During testing, the trained model was directly applied on CASIA.v4-distance and IITD *without any further tuning*. The purpose of the *CrossDB* setting is to examine the generalization capability of the proposed framework under challenging scenario that few training samples are available.

- Within-Database Performance Evaluation (*WithinDB*)

    In this configuration we use the network trained on ND-IRIS-0405 as the initial model, then fine-tune it using the independent training set from the target database. The fine-tuned network is then evaluated on the respective test set. Being capable of learning from data is the key advantage of deep learning, therefore it is judicious to examine the best possible performance from the proposed model by fine-tuning it with some samples from the target database. The fine-tuned models from the *WithinDB* configuration are expected to perform better than the one with *CrossDB*, due to higher consistency of image quality between the training set and test set.

It should be noted that in both of the above configurations, training set and test set are totally separated, that is, none of the iris images are overlapping between the training set and test set. All the experimental results were generated under all-to-all matching protocol, that is, the scores of every image pair in the test set have been counted.

2.6.3 Comparations with state-of-the-art baseline methods

We present comparative experimental results using several highly competitive benchmarks. Gabor filter based *IrisCode* [24] has been the most widely deployed iris feature descriptor, largely due to the fact that few alternative iris features in the literature are universally accepted as better than *IrisCodes*. Instead, the majority of related work on real-world iris biometric have been focussed on enhancing the segmentation and/or normalization models [11,86] applying multiscore fusion [40] or feature bits selection [46]. In other words, in the context of iris feature representations, *IrisCode* is still the most popular and highly competitive approach, and therefore is definitely a fair benchmark for the performance evaluation. *IrisCode* has a number of enhanced versions or implementations. From the publicly available ones, we selected OSIRIS [87], which is an open source tool for iris recognition. It implements a band of multiple tunable 2D Gabor filters that can encode iris patterns at different scales, therefore is a highly credible competitor. Another classic implementation of *IrisCode* is based on 1D log-Gabor filter(s) [30,81], which is claimed to encode iris patterns more efficiently, and is also widely chosen as benchmark in a variety of related work, for example [11] or [81]. Therefore this approach is also investigated. Apart from the Gabor filter bank, ordinal filters proposed in [36] can serve as a different type of iris feature extractors to complement the comparisons. The aforementioned benchmarks have been extensively tuned on target databases during testing to ensure as good performance as possible. In the following subsection, the parameter tuning for the three baseline methods is systematically explained.

2.6.3.1 Selection of best parameters for baseline methods

We have extensively tuned the benchmarking methods (i.e., OSIRIS [87], 1D log-Gabor [30], and ordinal [36]) to ensure that their best possible performances are used for the fair comparisons. We iteratively adopted possible combinations of the parameters for these approaches on each of the training sets within the empirically selected ranges, similar[1] to as in many references (e.g., [30,36,40]). The best-performing parameters on the training sets were then employed on the respective test sets for the performance evaluation.

- Parameters for *IrisCode* (OSIRIS 2D Gabor filters):

    A Gabor filter band containing six filters is provided in the original OSIRIS implementation [87]. In addition to the default one, we generate five Gabor filter bands for tuning this tool to obtain the best performance. Based on this implementation, the parameters for the 2D Gabor filter $g(x, y)$ for generating *IrisCode* can be formulated as:

$$g(x,y) = e^{-\left(\frac{x^2}{\alpha^2} + \frac{y^2}{\beta^2}\right)} e^{-i\omega x} \qquad (2-22)$$

Each set of parameters (α, β, ω) can be used to generate two filters which are the real and imaginary parts of the complex filter kernel in Eq. (2−22). We incorporate three sets of parameters to form a band of six filters. The five additional Gabor filter bands are then generated using the following set of parameters:

1. $(\alpha, \beta, \omega) \in \{(3, 1.5, 0.4\pi), (5, 1.5, 0.2\pi), (7, 1.5, 0.1\pi)\}$
2. $(\alpha, \beta, \omega) \in \{(3, 1.5, 0.4\pi), (5, 1.5, 0.3\pi), (7, 1.5, 0.2\pi)\}$

---

[1] It is essentially a grid search for the best set of parameters and it also appears in *Appendix A* of [88].

3. $(\alpha, \beta, \omega) \in \{(5, 2, 0.3\pi), (7, 2, 0.2\pi), (9, 2, 0.1\pi)\}$
4. $(\alpha, \beta, \omega) \in \{(3, 2, 0.3\pi), (6, 2, 0.2\pi), (9, 2, 0.1\pi)\}$
5. $(\alpha, \beta, \omega) \in \{(5, 1.5, 0.3\pi), (7, 1.5, 0.2\pi), (9, 1.5, 0.1\pi)\}$
- Parameters for *IrisCode* (1D log-Gabor filter):

     Based on the model employed in [30], two parameters for the baseline comparisons are selected as follows: σ/f (bandwidth over frequency): ranges from 0.3 to 0.6, with a step of 0.05. λ (wavelength): ranges from 15 to 40, with a step of 1. Therefore a total of 182 combinations of parameters are employed.
- Parameters for ordinal filter-based method:

     Based on the model presented in [36], four parameters are tuned using the following set of combinations:

     n (number of lobes): ranges between $\{2, 3\}$.
     s (size of each lobe): ranges among $\{5, 7, 9\}$.
     d (distance between lobes): ranges among $\{5, 9, 13, 17\}$.
     σ (standard deviation of each lobe): ranges among $\{1.5, 1.7, 1.9\}$.

Therefore a total of 72 combinations of different parameters are employed for the selection of best set of parameters.

The best parameters are automatically selected using the above detailed steps are summarized in Table 2–4. It can be observed that such optimal parameters vary for one dataset to another, which underlines the *need* for selecting parameters for baseline or conventional methods according to the imaging environments and the quality of images for different databases. In contrast, our *CrossDB* model is able to deliver stable and satisfactory performance on the four public databases without any tuning, as can be observed from the results in Fig. 2–13 and Table 2–3.

Table 2–3 Summary of false reject rates (FRR) at 0.1% false accept rate (FAR) and equal error rates (EER) for the performance comparisons.

	ND-IRIS-0405		CASIA.v4-distance		IITD		WVU Nonideal	
	FRR	EER	FRR	EER	FRR	EER	FRR	EER
IrisCode (OSIRIS)	3.73%	1.70%	19.93%	6.39%	1.61%	1.11%	13.70%	4.43%
IrisCode (log-Gabor)	3.31%	1.88%	20.72%	7.71%	1.81%	1.38%	11.63%	6.82%
Ordinal	3.22%	1.74%	16.93%	7.89%	1.70%	1.25%	9.89%	5.19%
Ours-CrossDB (Real-Bin)[a]	-	-	13.27%	4.54%	0.82%	0.64%	5.46%	2.83%
Ours-WithinDB (Real-Bin)[a]	1.78%	0.99%	11.15%	3.85%	1.19%	0.73%	5.00%	2.28%
Ours-CrossDB (Bin)[b]	-	-	14.35%	5.06%	**0.76%**	**0.61%**	5.02%	2.69%
Ours-WithinDB (Bin)[b]	**1.62%**	**0.93%**	**10.27%**	**3.34%**	1.01%	0.73%	**4.35%**	**2.23%**

Bold values show the 'minimum' value of the error
[a]Back-propagation using the real-valued ETL (Section 2.3.2).
[b]Back-propagation using the binary-valued ETL (Section 2.3.3).

Table 2–4 Best performing parameters for *IrisCode* [30,87] and Ordinal filters [36] on four iris images databases.

Method	Parameter	ND-IRIS-0405	CASIA.v4-distance	IITD	WVU Nonideal
IrisCode (2D Gabor—OSIRIS)	Config.	Default	(iii)	(ii)	(i)
IrisCode (1D log-Gabor)	σ/f	18	24	18	15
	λ	0.45	0.35	0.4	0.55
Ordinal filter	n	3	3	2	3
	s	5	9	7	9
	d	9	13	5	5
	σ	1.9	1.7	1.9	1.9

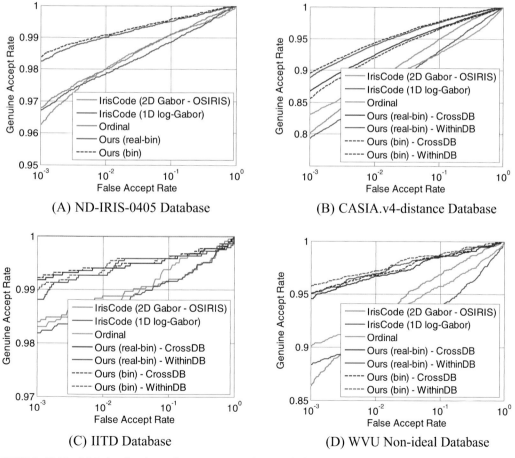

(A) ND-IRIS-0405 Database

(B) CASIA.v4-distance Database

(C) IITD Database

(D) WVU Non-ideal Database

FIGURE 2–13 The ROC plots for the performance comparisons with the conventional (non-deep learning based) state-of-the-art methods on the four publicly accessible iris image databases. (A) ND-IRIS-0405 database. (B) CASIA. v4-distance database. (C) IITD database. (D) WVU Nonideal database.

It is worth mentioning that we do *not* use the original or built-in iris segmentation/normalization procedures from OSIRIS and Masek's 1D log-Gabor-based implementation. Iris segmentation has been shown to have significant impact on the recognition accuracy. Therefore to ensure the fairness in the evaluation of proposed deep learning based iris feature representation, we uniformly adopt [11] for iris detection and normalization (as [11] has shown superior results on multiple public databases and also provides implementation codes), and use the output of *MaskNet* as the iris masks for our method and other investigated methods in this chapter.

The comparative performance results are presented in Fig. 2−13 and summarized in Table 2−3 Consistent improvements from our method over others can be observed on all of the four databases, under both *WithinDB* and *CrossDB* configurations. Such results suggest that the proposed iris feature representation not only achieves superior accuracy but also exhibits outstanding generalization capability. Even without additional parameter tuning, the well-trained model from our framework is promising to be directly used in deployment environments with varying image qualities. The relaxation of parameter tuning is apparently a highly desirable property for many real-life applications. An interesting finding is that on IITD database, the *CrossDB* model performs better even than the fine-tuned one. This is possibly because most of the images in IITD are of higher quality and therefore less challenging, and its training set size is not large enough, which can cause slight over-fitting problem.

Our comparative results also indicate that in almost all cases the binary iris features learned through end-to-end training (Section 3.3) can offer noticeable performance gains when compared to their ad hoc binarized real-valued counterparts used during test phase. These results provide evidence of the efficacy of the proposed end-to-end binary feature learning approach, which holds promise for addressing the challenge of deep neural network-based learning to hash.

2.6.4 Comparisons with commercial iris recognition system

Although the baseline methods considered in Section 6.3 are widely cited and have shown to offer competitive performance in the literature, it will be useful to provide comparison with some commercial off the shelf (COTS) solutions for the iris recognition, as they are considered to be more suitable and optimized for the real-life deployment. Therefore such a comparison is presented with a COTS, that is, VeriEye SDK 9.0 [89], which is a commercial product for iris recognition and has gained considerable popularity due to its effectiveness. However, since it is not open source, there may be some underlying factors affecting the final results, for example, additional use of periocular features instead of just iris as in all the baseline methods and *UniNet*. Despite such concern, the comparison may still be interesting. We therefore performed comparative evaluation using a VeriEye iris recognition SDK from Neurotechnology [89], version 9.0, which was available with us. The VeriEye SDK accepts original eye images (without normalization) as input and has its built-in iris segmentation components. Since this software is not open-source for its core functions, we are not able to interfere its iris segmentation process. Therefore the comparison results presented in this section may not fully represent the effectiveness of iris feature representation, which is the key focus of this chapter. Instead, it can be a sample reference for overall performance evaluation. The results of the comparison are shown in Fig. 2–14.

As shown in the figure, on ND-IRIS-0405 and WVU Nonideal databases, VeriEye has better genuine accept rates (GAR) at lower false accept rates (FAR), while our approach consistently outperforms VeriEye on CASIA.v4-distance and IITD iris image datasets. As discussed earlier, the difference in the segmentation process may have a certain impact on the presented recognition results. Besides, VeryEye has a built-in quality assessment function that it does not match images with low quality, which may improve its overall performance to a certain extent, while our approach does not evaluate image quality at the current stage. Considering the above factors, it is judicious to believe that the prototype model introduced in Section 2.2 offers highly competitive performance compared with the well-optimized commercial system.

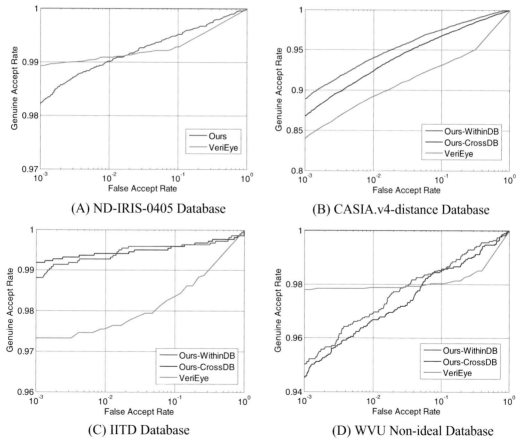

(A) ND-IRIS-0405 Database

(B) CASIA.v4-distance Database

(C) IITD Database

(D) WVU Non-ideal Database

FIGURE 2–14 Receiver operating characteristic (ROC) curves from *UniNet* and a COTS using four iris image databases. (A) ND-IRIS-0405 database. (B) CASIA.v4-distance database. (C) IITD Database. (D) WVU Nonideal database.

2.6.5 Comparison with other deep learning configurations

To ascertain the effectiveness of the proposed network architecture for spatial feature extraction and the *ETL*, we also compared our method against typical deep learning architectures that are widely employed in various recognition tasks. The tested configurations are introduced in the following:

1. CNN + Softmax/Triplet loss

    CNN + softmax is the most widely employed deep learning configurations in the community, such as in [73] and [90]. Besides, CNN + triplet loss loss has been widely employed after it was proposed in [77], and therefore may also be interesting and worth evaluating. For the CNN model, we have chosen the popular VGG-16 which has achieved superior performance in face recognition.

2. FCN + Triplet loss

    Comparative evaluation has also been performed on using the proposed FCN (*FeatNet* only) and the original triplet loss function without incorporating bit-shifting and masking. Such comparison may assert the necessity of extending the original triplet loss.

3. DeepIrisNet [22]

    We also compared our method against the recent deep learning-based iris recognition framework, DeepIrisNet, which reports promising results. This architecture actually belongs to the CNN + softmax category, but we separately inspected it as it is directly proposed for iris recognition. Since the original model in their paper is not publicly available, we carefully implemented and trained the CNN according to all the details in [22].

The comparison with aforementioned configurations was performed on ND-IRIS-0405 dataset, which has the largest number of training images among employed ones. The test set is kept consistent during the comparison. Hyper-parameters of the training processes for above architectures have been carefully investigated to achieve best possible performance. The results of the same test set are presented in Fig. 2–15.

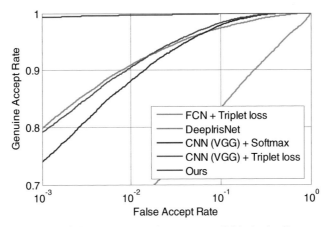

FIGURE 2–15 ROC curves for typical deep learning architectures available in the literature and our method on ND-IRIS-0405.

It can be observed from the comparative plots in Fig. 2−15 that our (*UniNet*) architecture significantly outperforms other deep learning configurations. CNN-based configurations have failed to deliver satisfactory results especially at lower FAR. Such results support our previous analysis that global and high-level features extracted by CNN may not be suitable for iris recognition. The poor performance from (FCN + triplet loss) strongly suggests that it is necessary to account for the inherent bit-shifting and noniris region masking when learning spatially corresponding features through FCN. We also evaluated the computational complexity of the *UniNet*. Such results indicate that the execution time of *UniNet* can meet general real-time requirements, and these results are presented in Section 2.6.8.

2.6.6 Performance evaluation for *MaskNet*

The key focus of this chapter is on design of a deep neural network-based architecture to enable learning of more effective iris feature representation. However, the *MaskNet* is an essential component of *UniNet* for providing immediate and appropriate noniris masking information to the proposed *ETL* function. In order to assert the adequateness of the masking information during the feature learning process, we have performed a sample evaluation of *MaskNet*. For the evaluation benchmark, we use a more advanced iris segmentation approach [11] as this method has already provided comparison with other classical methods in the literature. Similar to as discussed in Section 1.1.1.1 of Chapter 1, the average segmentation error for such evaluation can be defined as follows:

$$\bar{e} = \frac{1}{N \times w \times h} \sum_{i=1}^{N} \sum_{x=1}^{w} \sum_{y=1}^{h} M_i[x,y] \oplus G_i[x,y] \qquad (2-22)$$

where N is the number of test images, w and h are the weight and height of each image respectively, M_i is the ith computed mask and G_i is the corresponding ground truth mask that should be manually generated. $\oplus$ is the exclusive-OR (XOR) operation for two binary values. This error rate measures the level of disagreement between the computed mask and the ground truth. The difference with the performance evaluation in [11] is that we here measure the segmentation error *after* the iris image normalization. The baseline iris segmentation method was especially chosen for the comparative evaluation as its implementation is publicly available and to the best of our knowledge, no other iris segmentation method has presented fair comparison with this method for the iris segmentation performance evaluation.

The *MaskNet* employed in such experiments was trained with 500 randomly selected left eye images from ND-IRIS-0405 database, with manually labeled iris masks as the ground truth. The test sets for its evaluation are also generated from the same database, excluding the training samples. We used the following two sets for the testing: (a) 100 randomly selected samples and their ground truth masks manually created by us and (b) 792 samples and their ground truth masks which are available from a public iris segmentation ground truth database, IRISSEG-EP [92]. The average segmentation errors of *MaskNet* and using the iris segmentation framework presented in [11] are shown in Table 2−5.

Table 2–5   Comparison of average segmentation errors from *MaskNet* and using [11].

Approach	Average segmentation error	
	Set (a)	Set (b)
MaskNet	5.89%	9.00%
Framework in [11]	6.73%	11.83%

Table 2–6   Simplified FCN configurations for the ablation study.

Layer	Type	Kernel size	No. of output channels
Conv.1	Convolutional	3×21	16
Conv.2	Convolutional	3×15	24
Conv.3	Convolutional	3×11	32
Smd.1, 2, 3	Sigmoid activation	/	/
Pool.1, 2, 3	Average pooling	2×2	/

The results shown in Table 2–5 suggest that for both test sets, the developed *MaskNet* can achieve superior segmentation accuracy compared with state-of-the-art iris segmentation approach. It is therefore reasonable to conclude that *MaskNet* is able to provide appropriate information for identifying valid iris region during the feature learning process via *ETL*.

2.6.7 Ablation study

In the architecture of the *FeatNet*, there are multiple channels in each of the feature maps and computing the distance directly can require relatively more time. Among such different channels in one or different scales, it is common to have redundant information which can be suppressed. Since the network outputs are normalized by the same activation function, features in different channels are expected to be in similar numeric scales and will equally contribute to the distance computations. However, in fact, these features from different channels can have unequal importance in terms of discriminant features for distinguishing different subjects/irises. It is for these reasons that we incorporate feature-level fusion in order to obtain the most effective feature representation as well as to reduce computational complexity.

We performed additional experiments during the development of *UniNet* architecture to ascertain the effectiveness of feature fusion layer. We used simplified version of *FeatNet* and these experiments do not include *MaskNet* (and binarization as detailed in Section 2.5). Table 2–6 details the architecture of such network for the ablation study. The comparative performances from using the fused features and the intermediate features (i.e., the feature output from Smd.1, Smd.2, and Smd.3) are presented in this figure. In addition to using intermediate features at each scale independently, we can also independently examine popular score level fusion schemes for combining the match scores obtained at each scale, that is, average, minimum (best score), and linear weighted average of scores. In the linear weighted average scheme, we iteratively tuned three nonnegative weights that sum up to one on the training set and adopted the best-performing combination on the test set. Fig. 2−16A shows the comparative performance using the receiver operating characteristic plots among these schemes. It can be observed that the use of the feature fusion mechanism introduced in our network architecture (*UniNet*) achieves superior performance than using intermediate features without fusion as well as the other simplified score fusion schemes. Another apparent benefit, obviously, is that fusing the multichannel intermediate feature maps into single-channel features can significantly reduce the template size which is one of the performance metric [14] for the large-scale deployments.

During this ablation study, and with the same network architecture (Table 2−6), we also performed comparative performance evaluation to ascertain the performance benefits when the original triplet loss function [77] without bit-shifting has been utilized. Fig. 2−16B illustrates the ROCs from using such network architecture which are trained with STL and original triplet loss respectively. During such test phase for two resulting models, we perform bit-shifting and use the minimum distance l_1 or l_2 as the final match score. These results show that the usage of conventional or original triplet loss function leads to significant degradation in the performance. These results also validate the importance of the bit-shifting operations in learning discriminant and spatially corresponding features.

2.6.8 Complexity analysis

The computational complexity of *UniNet* model has been evaluated to address the potential concerns on the feasibility for the deployment. Since our FCN does not employ fully connected layers, the number of parameters is significantly reduced and therefore it is much spatially simpler than conventional CNN-based architectures. Table 2−7 summarizes the computational time for feature extraction and the storage required by our model, as

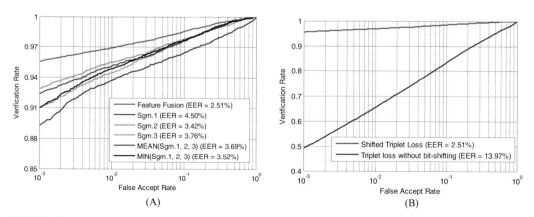

FIGURE 2−16 Performance plots for (A) using fused features, intermediate features without fusion, and intermediate features with simple score fusion schemes and (B) using the ETL and original triplet loss on ICE 2006 database.

Table 2–7 Summary of number of parameters, model storage size, and feature extraction time per image, run with Matlab wrapper and C++ implementation, on Intel i7−4770 CPU, 16 G RAM, and Nvidia GTX670 GPU.

			Feature extraction time	
Approach	# parameters	Model size (B)	GPU	CPU
Ours	~110.7 K	1.5 M	7.6 ms	236 ms
DeepIrisNet [22]	~55,420 K	289.0 M	12.7 ms	335 ms

compared with the CNN-based approach in [22]. It can be noted that the space and time complexities for the approach detailed in Section 2.2 is quite small.

2.7 Chapter summary

This chapter discussed the development of a deeply learned powerful feature descriptor for the normalized iris images. Such descriptor can preserve the spatial feature relationship and accommodate intra-class variations in the normalized iris images. This was enabled by introducing a specialized loss function, *ETL* in Eq. (2−2), to enable the network to focus on learning the discriminant features. This design also required to develop a train *MaskNet* to mask noniris pixels and incorporate the suppression of unstable iris features, that is, fragile bits. In view of limited training data, unlike for other biometric modalities like face, network architecture was designed and training using triplet architecture. Complexity analysis presented in Section 2.6.8 of this chapter indicates that such FCN-based *UniNet* framework is suitable for the online and large-scale iris recognition. Despite consistently outperforming results illustrated in Section 2.6.3 of this chapter, the *UniNet* architecture is not a full-fledged deep learning-based alternative to the conventional iris recognition framework as it uses conventional method [11] to localize iris images. Such limitations will be discussed and addressed in the next chapter.

3

A unified framework for accurate detection, segmentation, and recognition of irises

Traditional iris identification methods typically rely on predefined operators to locate and segment the iris region in images captured by sensors. These operators require calibration to achieve accurate segmentation of the iris. An example of such a pipeline involving these operators has been discussed in Section 1.2 of the first chapter. In the last chapter, a deep learning-based framework was proposed that leverages normalized iris images obtained using traditional methods. In this chapter, we introduce a new deep learning-based approach to detect, segment, and match iris images that overcomes the limitations of the previous method. This unified framework significantly improves the robustness and consistency of the iris segmentation and feature optimization processes.

3.1 Introduction to the framework

Despite the popularity of iris recognition in biometrics, the conventional or classical iris feature descriptors do have several limitations. The framework discussed in Chapter 2 focused on learning discriminant iris feature representation, and the success of such an approach relied on the external and conventional method [11] for the detection of iris circle, which is parameter sensitive and less generalizable to different datasets. This chapter will extend the earlier framework *UniNet* by integrating iris detection and segmentation from the raw eye images, that is, the images acquired from the iris sensors, into a unified framework. Such a resulting framework is completely based on deep learning and referred to as *UniNet.v2* and is shown in Fig. 3−1. Such an approach essentially improves the detection and segmentation accuracy as well as the robustness and finally benefits the iris recognition performance, as will be shown from the extensive experimental results in this chapter. More importantly, by incorporating deep neural networks for the iris detection process, our framework can easily adapt to varying image qualities without additional parameter tuning. The high level of integration of such architecture also enables more consistent and smooth learning for the iris feature representation with respect to the deep learning-based detection and segmentation results. It is worth noting that the term *unified framework* in this chapter refers to the fact that this framework utilizes deep learning techniques to cover all the major tasks, in a typical or conventional iris recognition system. rather than implying an end-to-end optimization process for the framework.

Iris and Periocular Recognition using Deep Learning. DOI: https://doi.org/10.1016/B978-0-443-27318-6.00010-3

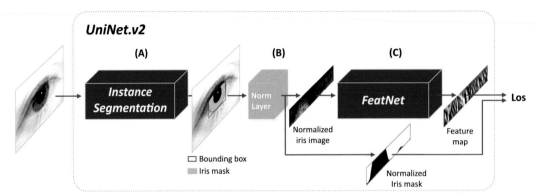

FIGURE 3–1 Overall framework of the *UniNet.v2*. Raw acquired eye image is the input and parsed by an iris-specific (A) This box refers to an iris-specific detector to detect the presence of iris in the images acquired from the iris sensor. (B) This green-colored box refers to the normalization layer, and (C) a feature extraction network referred to as *FeatNet*.

3.2 Network architecture

The overall framework to automatically detect, segment, and match iris images is shown in Fig. 3–1. This unified architecture consists of three key components that are shown as different 3D boxes in above figure. In order to differentiate with the *UniNet* framework introduced in Chapter 1, the framework in Fig. 3–1 is referred to as *UniNet.v2*. The technical specifications and optimization methods for the three subnetworks are detailed in the following sections.

3.2.1 Network architecture for iris detection and segmentation

Accurate iris detection and segmentation are critical for achieving higher performance for iris-based personal identification. Inadequate segmentation can lead to severe degradation of the performance of automated Iris recognition systems. A range of efficient and effective mechanisms have been developed for the *instance segmentation* [93,98,99] and can be employed for module (A) to detect the region of interest pixels (iris) in the presented images. Instance segmentation techniques are popularly used to detect, segment, and classify individual objects or instances in the input image. We can effectively use such methods to classify every pixel in the input images into two classes, i.e., iris pixels and non-iris pixels, to significantly enhance the reliability and accuracy of iris detection and segmentation. Our specific implementation discussed in this chapter uses Mask R-CNN [93] as the iris instance segmentation module as it has also been one of the effective architectures for general *instance segmentation*. Therefore this unified framework is enhanced by incorporating the instance segmentation model, which improves the stability and consistency between the iris masks and corresponding features.

The iris segmentation in any conventional or modern iris recognition approaches generally involves two parts: (1) pixel-level identification of iris and noniris regions (e.g., excluding eyelash, sclera, and reflection) and (2) fitting circles/ellipses or other geometric representations on iris structures to assist part (1) and to serve for normalization. In. earlier works [24,69], part (2) has been the main focus, while more recent and advanced methods [11,16,36] have also heavily addressed part (1). In this chapter, our framework employs Mask R-CNN for part (1) of the iris segmentation process, that is, identifying iris and noniris pixel regions from the input eye images.

3.2.1.1 Brief introduction to Mask R-CNN
The overall structure of Mask R-CNN employed for the framework in Fig. 3−1 is illustrated in Fig. 3−2. Mask R-CNN is built on top of its predecessor, that is, Faster R-CNN [94]. In this framework, the input eye image from the iris sensor is firstly subjected to a backbone convolutional neural network (CNN), which serves as a region proposal network, to obtain initial guesses of regions that may contain a desired object. The proposed regions are then sent to a branch classification network for identifying object classes within each region. However, for our approach, there is only one foreground class (i.e., iris) to be detected. Therefore the classification branch is reduced. In addition, we assume each input eye image contains just a single iris, hence only the proposal with the highest confidence will be processed subsequently.

Such simplification of Mask R-CNN can better regularize the training process to avoid overfitting when it is adopted to learn iris regions and masks. Mask R-CNN includes one more branch, which is a fully convolutional network (FCN) [74], to the Faster R-CNN to segment instance masks simultaneously inside the proposed regions. According to [93], the RoIAlign operation is introduced to recover pixel-level segmentation accuracy on downsampled feature maps, and state-of-the-art performance was reported for the COCO

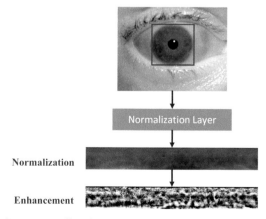

FIGURE 3–2 Illustration of enhancement effect for normalized iris image after the iris detection.

segmentation challenge [95]. Due to its impressive performance and built-in detection segmentation design, Mask R-CNN is highly promising for addressing the reliability and generalizability of iris segmentation as well as constructing a unified framework for iris
recognition.

3.2.1.2 Training of Mask R-CNN for detecting and segmenting irises

To train Mask R-CNN for the specific task of iris detection and segmentation from the input
eye images, a sufficient number of training samples with their corresponding ground truth
bounding box labels and instance masks are required. We can adopt a semimanual procedure to label images from multiple, publicly available databases, to enrich data variation in
the less available time. Initially, a conventional iris segmentation approach with optimized
parameters, as detailed in [11], which also has publicly accessible codes [75], can be incorporated for the training sets from each database. The resulting segmentation (initial segmentation step) is manually inspected to select the best ones. We then incorporate some manual
operations, such as filling holes and removing isolated pixels, to refine the initial segmentation results. Such filtered iris masks are regarded as ground truths and form a training set of
1,700 images and a validation set of about 300 images. These samples were then utilized to
fine-tune a Mask R-CNN model, which had been pretrained on the COCO dataset with some
modifications, as discussed in the previous section.

3.2.1.3 Iris normalization layer

A normalization layer is appended after Mask R-CNN, as shown in Fig. 3−1, (b), to perform
iris and mask normalization (unwrapping) before learning iris features. Input to this layer
is the cropped image and mask from the full-size image, where the crop region centers at
the detected bounding box but is 1.2 times larger in order to accommodate marginal
errors. Within this layer, a simple circular Hough transform, which is similar to the one
used in [11], is employed for detecting iris and pupil circles. However, unlike in [11] where
the circle detection is performed on the entire image as no prior information is known, in
this framework, the search region for the circle center is made near the center of the
bounding box (especially the x-position), and the fitting range for the radius is also set to
be around half of the width of the RoI. With such spatial constraints, the circle detection is
least likely to generate erroneous output as compared with the approach in [11]. It is
important to note that unlike the common iris segmentation approaches, there are no
dataset-specific parameters required for the above circle detection step. Variables like the
possible range of radius (Fig. 1−5B) are automatically inferred from the dynamically
detected RoI from Mask R-CNN to achieve good generalizability. As will be shown from the
experiments, the circle detection accuracy from this framework is much higher than those
from the conventional methods. After the iris and pupil circles are detected, the iris region
and mask are normalized using the classical rubber-sheet model, discussed in
Section 1.2.1, into a resolution of 512×64 pixels. The next step is to learn effective spatially

corresponding features using the *FeatNet* component and extended triplet loss (ETL) function, which is discussed in the following sections.

3.2.2 FeatNet: learning spatially corresponding iris features

3.2.2.1 Image preprocessing
After the iris region is detected and normalized, we incorporate a simple contrast enhancement process, which adjusts the image intensity so that 5% of pixels are saturated at low and high intensities, respectively. The enhanced images are fed into the subsequent network, referred to as *FeatNet*, for extracting comprehensive features. These key steps of image preprocessing are also illustrated in Fig. 3−2.

3.2.2.2 Learning spatially corresponding features
The purpose of *FeatNet* is to extract distinctive iris features, and it utilizes an FCN architecture that was initially designed for semantic segmentation [74]. Unlike the typical CNN, FCN does not include a fully connected layer. Its primary components include convolutional layers, pooling layers, and activation layers, which all operate on localized regions surrounding pixels from their lower-level maps. As a result, the output map can maintain spatial correspondence with the original input image. With the inclusion of up-sampling layers, FCN can accurately perform pixel-to-pixel prediction. The architecture of *FeatNet* is the same as illustrated in Fig. 2−5 and Table 2−1. Although it is also shown in Fig. 3−3 for easy reference, its detailed motivation has been discussed in Section 2.2.2.

The reason for selecting FCN instead of CNN for iris feature extraction primarily lies in the analysis of iris patterns presented in the previous chapters, that is, the most discriminative information about an iris is expected to be embedded in small and localized random patterns. The FCN is able to maintain local pixel-to-pixel correspondence between input and output, enhancing the discriminant capability among the different iris templates and therefore is a better candidate for the extraction of iris features.

Regarding the extent of the recovered iris features and depth of network, there are trade-offs among the level of feature locality, complexity, and compatibility with the conventional iris

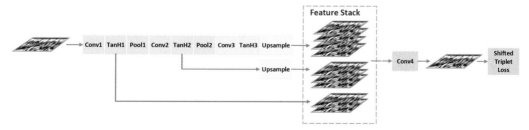

FIGURE 3–3 The *FeatNet* has been designed to consolidate convolutional feature maps from different scales and resizes them to the same resolution to form a feature stack. These features are then fused by a convolutional layer to generate a single-channel feature map that retains spatial correspondences with the normalized input iris image.

recognition systems. When the network goes deeper, the receptive field, which describes how large the input area affects each output element, becomes larger and fine details can be more easily lost, resulting in higher level and more global feature descriptors [96]. As pointed out earlier, global features may not be suitable for iris recognition. On the other hand, networks with shallow layers can hardly capture adequate or comprehensive information from the input images. After extensive exploration, four convolutional layers for *FeatNet*, as shown in Fig. 3−3, were employed to achieve the balance between maintaining feature locality as well as enabling comprehensive feature extraction. Another factor is the number of channels of the output iris feature map. In theory, multichannel or multiscale features can enrich the information in the descriptor and lead to higher recognition accuracy with more complex matching mechanisms [36,97]. However, the primary goal here is to investigate the effectiveness of our feature representation, and therefore we focus on single-channel iris feature maps or templates. It should also be noted that for a *fair* comparison with the other existing or baseline methods, it is important that a single-channel iris template be utilized in such experiments.

3.2.3 Network training and loss function

This network is also trained using triplet-based network architecture, as discussed in Section 2.2.3 (Fig. 2−6). It uses a specially designed loss function, that is, ETL function, which has been systematically explained in Section 2.3, and therefore these details are not repeated here. Please refer to that explanation on the loss function *ETL* which is also used to train the network (Fig. 3−3).

3.2.4 Feature encoding and template matching

For the real-valued features output from *UniNet.v2*, we perform a simple encoding scheme. The feature maps originally contain real values, and it is straightforward to measure the *fractional Euclidean distance* between the masked maps for matching, as the network is also trained in this manner. As discussed earlier, however, binary features are more popular in most of the research works on iris recognition (as summarized in Chapter 1) and are widely used in almost all iris recognition deployments today. It is widely accepted that the binary features generated using classical feature descriptors, such as the *IrisCode*, are more resistant to illumination changes, blurring, and other underlying noise that is often observed in real-world iris images. Besides, binary features consume smaller storage and enable faster matching. Therefore we also investigated the feasibility of binarizing our features with a reasonable scheme, as discussed in the following.

To begin with, the mean value (m) of elements within the nonmasked iris regions is calculated for each output feature map. This mean value is then utilized as a threshold to convert the original real-valued feature map into a binary format. In order to mitigate the effects of marginal errors, elements with feature values (f) that are close to m are considered less reliable and are subsequently masked, along with the original mask generated by *MaskNet*. This additional masking step is inspired by fragile bits discussed in Section 1.4.1, which identified certain bits in *IrisCode*, having filtered responses close to the axes of the complex space

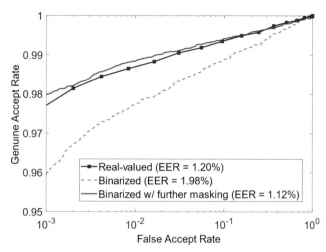

FIGURE 3–4 Comparison of ROCs from diverse deep learning architectures and configurations for the iris recognition problem.

(Fig. 1−18), as less consistent or unreliable. For all experimental results reported in this chapter, a uniform range threshold (t) of 0.6 is set to mask such unreliable bits. This feature encoding process is essentially the same as illustrated in Fig. 2−11 in the previous Chapter. To facilitate matching, we utilize the *fractional Hamming distance* (Eq. (2−21)) from the binarized feature maps and the *extended* masks that incorporate suppression of fragile bits.

The performance comparison between the original real-valued features and the binarized version of the iris templates, as well as illustrating the effect of the additional masking operation, is presented in Fig. 3−4 using ND-IRIS-0405 database [76]. The real-valued features are matched using Euclidean distance within the common valid iris regions, while binary features are matched with Hamming distance, both averaged by the number of valid pixels. As shown in the comparative ROC plots, directly binarizing the real-valued features leads to performance degradation. After masking ambiguous feature points whose original values are close to the mean value, the performance from the binarized feature is improved and becomes even slightly better than the real-valued version. Such improvement can be possibly attributed to the removal of less reliable features and relatively higher tolerance to noise in the binary feature representation. The threshold for selecting the fragile features, 0.6 as mentioned earlier, is empirically determined from the feature value distribution during the training phase.

3.3 Experiments and results

Thorough experiments were conducted to evaluate the performance of the *UniNet.v2* framework from various aspects. The following sections detail the experimental settings along with the reproducible [82] results.

3.3.1 Databases and protocols

Four publicly available databases were employed for our experiments. The details on these databases and the test protocols are precisely the same as those detailed in Sections 2.6.1 and 2.6.2. Therefore please refer to the respective sections for these details. Such consistency is adopted to ensure fair comparisons with *UniNet.v2*.

3.3.2 Iris detection and segmentation accuracy

As the unified framework incorporating iris detection and segmentation is the key extension for the framework introduced in Chapter 2, we first evaluate the performance for this part. The iris detection and segmentation accuracy is of vital importance for the task of reliable iris recognition. Representative results of the iris bounding box detection and mask segmentation are provided in Fig. 3−5, from which it can be observed that the proposed framework can generalize well for varying image qualities. In this section, the key performance comparisons are focused on its earlier version, that is, *UniNet*, which has been discussed in detail in Chapter 2, and conventional method in reference [11] has also been used as the detection and segmentation performance baseline, as it emerged as the most accurate and reproducible [75] method to evaluate iris segmentation performance (Fig. 3−5).

3.3.2.1 Quantifying iris detection accuracy

The term iris detection accuracy here refers to the accuracy in automatically detecting the iris and pupil circle *position*s compared with manually labeled ground truths. To generate ground truth circle positions, 500 sample images from test sets of the four employed databases are randomly selected. These sample images do not have overlapping subjects that were present in the training sets. The positions of both pupil and iris circles are then manually labeled as the ground truths. Let us represent a circle as $C = (x, y, r)$ where x and y are spatial coordinates of the center and r is the radius, and assume we have an automatically

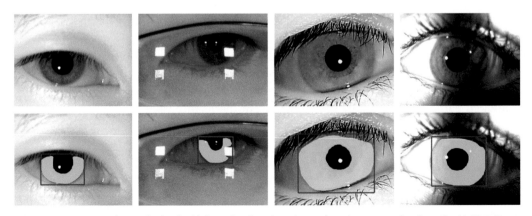

FIGURE 3–5 Representative results for the iris bounding box detection and mask segmentation from the *UniNet.v2*.

detected circle C_d and the ground truth circle C_g. The detection is considered as accurate if the conditions outlined in the following two equations are met.

$$\frac{\sqrt{\left(x_d - x_g\right)^2 + \left(y_d - y_g\right)^2}}{r_g} < 5\% \qquad (3-1)$$

$$\frac{\left|r_d - r_g\right|}{r_g} < 10\% \qquad (3-2)$$

Above two conditions consider the distance between two centers Eq. (3−1) and the difference between the radii Eq. (3−2). An iris is then considered correctly detected if both iris and pupil circles are accurately found. Table 3−1 compares iris detection accuracy from UniNet.v2 and the highly accurate conventional method (introduced in [11]), which was also used as a baseline method in Chapter 2.

The comparative results shown in Table 3−1 indicate consistent improvements in the iris detection accuracy can be achieved by exploiting the instance segmentation module, Mask R-CNN here, in place of a parameter-dependent hand-crafted approach introduced in [11]. Note that the results of our approach are obtained from one model *without* fine-tuning, whereas the parameters of [11] have been extensively tuned for each of the employed databases separately. Therefore we can infer that our model introduced in Fig. 3−1 offers superior generalization capability, which has been the key motivation for the developed framework.

3.3.2.2 Iris segmentation accuracy

Apart from detection accuracy, which evaluates the correctness of the location of the detected iris, we should also examine the segmentation accuracy that measures pixel-level precision for the iris mask. Manually labeled ground truth masks are necessary for such evaluation. The IRISSEG-EP [92] has provided manually labeled iris masks for part of images from ND-IRIS-0405 and IITD databases, and another reference [16] has released ground truth masks for the CASIA.v4-distance dataset. We can utilize these masks as the ground truths for such evaluation. After removing duplicate samples in the training set for training our model, we obtain 819, 1890, and 437 ground truth masks for the images from ND-IRIS-0405, IITD, and CASIA.v4-distance databases, respectively. The segmentation accuracy is evaluated using the average segmentation error, which is widely adopted in the iris recognition literature. The average segmentation error is the same as defined in Eq. (2−22) or as

Table 3−1   Comparison of correct rates of iris detection obtained from this approach and a competitive baseline.

	ND IRIS 0405	Casia.v4	IITD	WVU nonideal
UniNet.v2	94.4%	96%	96.8%	89.6%
RTV-L^1 [11]	92.8%	92%	96%	85.6%

Table 3–2   Comparison of segmentation error rates from different approaches.

	ND IRIS 0405	CASIA.v4	IITD
UniNet.v2	1.68%	0.67%	5.34%
UniNet	1.74%	0.83%	6.63%
RTV-L^1 [11]	1.93%	0.70%	5.89%

Eq. 1−1 and measures the number of inconsistent pixels between the predicted and ground truth masks, which are normalized by the resolution of the image to compute average segmentation error rate. This metric is used to compare the performance from reference [11] and the *MaskNet*, which was introduced with *UniNet* and evaluated in Chapter 2. These comparative results are summarized in Table 3−2.

As shown from the above segmentation results, iris masks generated from the framework (*UniNet.v2*) using Mask R-CNN achieve consistently higher accuracy than those from hand-crafted (RTV-L^1) or post normalization segmentation approaches (*UniNet*). Such observation underlines the usefulness of the instance segmentation scheme (Mask R-CNN here) in addressing the problem of iris segmentation with superior generalization capability. It is again important to note that unlike for the RTV-L^1, there is no dataset-specific parameter tuning employed for this iris segmentation approach.

3.3.2.3 Ablation study for iris recognition

It is prudent to compare the recognition accuracy of *UniNet.v2* with the results from the UniNet, which was introduced in Chapter 2, to investigate possible performance improvements by incorporating the Mask R-CNN for unified iris detection and segmentation. However, it is important to underline a key step to ensure a fair comparison. During the experimental evaluations in Chapter 2, our key focus was on *learning* effective iris features only for the matching, we therefore manually *removed* some samples with badly detected iris circles, or corrected some of the detection results from both the training set and test set to avoid learning meaningless information. This setup has been stated in Section 2.6.1 and adequately reflected in the number of stated match scores. Such manual filtering for test images was identically performed for *each baseline* algorithm to ensure fairness in the comparisons presented in Chapter 2. In the experiment presented in this section, however, as automated iris detection using instance segmentation is also *part* of our new framework, we *skip* such human intervention on the iris detection results to eliminate bias on the earlier version (Chapter 2 experiments using *UniNet*). Comparative ROC plots The framework presented in this chapter (Fig. 3−1) has introduced a fully automated iris segmentation with *no* human intervention, and results have ensured fairness in the comparison. Such results indicate that adding an iris detection and segmentation module using Mask R-CNN, or any other instance segmentation module [98,99] can offer promising enhancement in the recognition performance (Fig. 3−6).

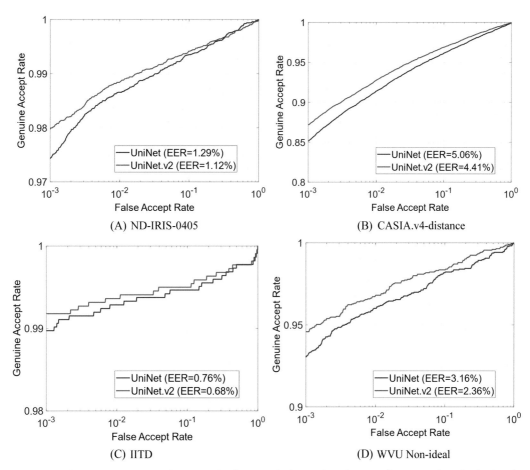

FIGURE 3–6 The comparative ROC plots using the framework discussed in Chapter 2 (*UniNet* with real-valued ETL) on four (A)–(D) different iris databases.

3.3.3 Comparison with baseline methods

In this section, comparative experimental results using several highly competitive baseline methods are presented.

3.3.3.1 Test protocols

During the extensive performance evaluation in the test phase, the following two experimental configurations were considered.

3.3.3.1.1 Cross-database performance evaluation (*CrossDB*)

In the *CrossDB* configuration, ND-IRIS-0405 database images are used as the training set. During testing, the trained model was directly used to evaluate performance from the CASIA.

v4-distance and IITD iris database images without any further tuning. The purpose of the *CrossDB* setting is to examine the generalization capability of the proposed framework under the challenging scenario when only a few training samples are available.

3.3.3.1.2 Within-database performance evaluation (*WithinDB*)

In this configuration, the network trained on ND-IRIS-0405 dataset is used as the initial model, then fine-tuned using the independent training set from the target database. The fine-tuned network is then evaluated on the respective test set. Being capable of learning from domain data is the key advantage of deep neural networks, therefore it is judicious to examine the best possible performance from the proposed model by fine-tuning it with some samples from the target database. The fine-tuned models from the *WithinDB* configuration are expected to perform better than the one with *CrossDB*, due to higher consistency of image quality between the training set and test set. It should be noted that in both of the above configurations, the training set and test set are totally separated, that is, none of the iris images are overlapping between the training set and test set. All the experimental results were generated under an all-to-all matching protocol, that is, the match scores of every image pair in the test set have been considered in the performance plots.

3.3.3.2 Comparative experimental results

Several highly competitive baselines are employed for the comparisons. Gabor filter-based *IrisCode* [24] has been the most widely deployed iris feature descriptor, largely due to the fact that few alternative iris features in the literature are universally deployed or accepted as superior to *IrisCodes*. Rather than focusing on novel approaches to iris biometrics, much of the current research has been aimed at enhancing segmentation and normalization models [11,86], employing multiscore fusion [40], or selecting feature bits [46]. Regarding iris feature representations, *IrisCode* remains the most commonly used and highly competitive method, making it a reliable benchmark for performance evaluation. There are several advanced versions of *IrisCode* available, with OSIRIS [87] being a particularly credible open-source tool for iris recognition. Its implementation employs a bank of multiple 2D Gabor filters, which can encode iris patterns at various scales. Another classic implementation of *IrisCode* uses 1D log-Gabor filter(s) [30], which is a more efficient alternative for encoding iris patterns and is often utilized as a benchmark in various research works (e.g., [81] or [11]). Consequently, this approach is also being investigated. In addition to the Gabor series filters, ordinal filters proposed in [36] can serve as an alternative type of iris feature extractors for comparative analysis. The aforementioned benchmarks have been extensively tuned on target databases during testing to ensure as good performance as possible.

The comparison results are shown in Fig. 3−7 and Table 3−3. Significant and consistent improvements from our deep learning-based methods over other baselines have been shown on all four databases, under both *WithinDB* and *CrossDB* configurations. These results suggest that the feature representation using *UniNet.v2* achieves not only superior match accuracy but also exhibits outstanding generalization capability. Even without additional parameter tuning, the well-trained model from *UniNet.v2* offers promising performance to

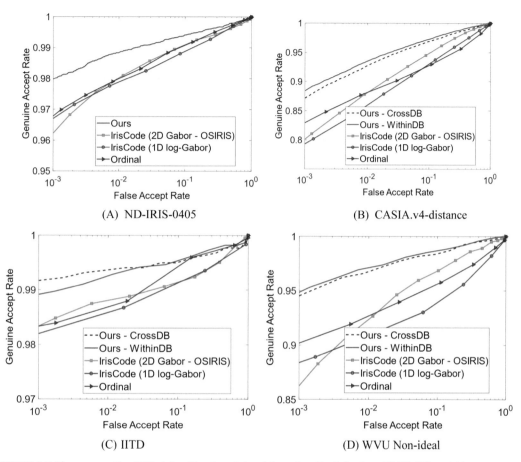

FIGURE 3–7 The comparative ROC plots with other state-of-the-art methods for four (A)-(D) different iris databases.

Table 3–3 Summary of comparative FRR at 0.1% FAR, and EER, values from *UniNet.v2*.

	ND-IRIS-0405		CASIA.v4-distance		IITD		WVU Nonideal	
	FRR	**EER**	**FRR**	**EER**	**FRR**	**EER**	**FRR**	**EER**
IrisCode (OSIRIS)	3.73%	1.70%	19.93%	6.39%	1.61%	1.11%	13.70%	4.43%
IrisCode (log-Gabor)	3.31%	1.88%	20.72%	7.71%	1.81%	1.38%	11.63%	6.82%
Ordinal	3.22%	1.74%	16.93%	7.89%	1.70%	1.25%	9.89%	5.19%
Ours-*CrossDB*	/	/	12.83%	4.41%	**0.82%**	**0.68%**	5.42%	2.36%
Ours-*WithinDB*	**2.02%**	**1.12%**	**11.61%**	**4.07%**	1.12%	0.76%	**5.06%**	**2.20%**

Table 3–4   Execution time for each eye image using the *UniNet.v2* and other methods.

	Detection/segmentation time		Feature extraction time	
	GPU	**CPU**	**GPU**	**CPU**
UniNet.v2	271 ms	4.3 s	5.9 ms	193 ms
RTV-L^1 [11]	/	763 ms	/	/
OSIRIS [87]	/	93 ms	/	17 ms

The resolutions for the original image and normalized template are 640 × 480 and 512 × 64 pixels, respectively.

be directly used in deployment environments with varying iris image qualities. The relaxation of parameter tuning is apparently a highly desirable property for many real-life iris recognition applications. An interesting finding is that on the IITD iris database, the *CrossDB* model performs better even than the fine-tuned one. This is possibly because most of the images in IITD iris database are of high image qualities and less challenging, and its training set is not large enough, which can cause slight overfitting problems.

The experimental results to ascertain the effectiveness of the ETL and the FCN architecture, using comparisons against other popular deep learning architectures, been presented in Section 2.6.5 in the previous Chapter.

3.3.4 Computational speed

The computational efficiency of the *UniNet.v2* framework is also evaluated by measuring the execution time. The programs were executed on a desktop computer with Intel Core 3.4 GHz i7−4770 CPU, 16GB RAM, and NVIDIA GTX 1080 GPU. These results are summarized in Table 3−4. It can be observed from this summary that the overall execution time of the proposed framework is within a reasonable range. It should be noted that: (1) in practical systems, the iris detection, segmentation, and feature extraction are one-time efforts for the online probe sample and template generation for the gallery subjects can be made online during the registration process and (2) the generated iris templates from the *UniNet.v2* are in the same format as those from conventional methods, for example, *IrisCodes*. Consequently, there is no additional computational cost for matching/searching iris templates for the probe to gallery samples compared with existing approaches. It should also be noted that there have been tremendous advances in the speed of GPUs, that is, GTX 1080 is set to obsolete while RTX 4090 is more recent alternative, and such GPUs are also available on the mobile platform.

3.4 Conclusions and further enhancements

This chapter has detailed the development of a novel deep learning-based framework, referred to as *UniNet.v2*, for effective iris detection, segmentation, and recognition. This framework has been shown to offer matching superior performance and generalization capability for the focused iris recognition problem. Higher iris detection and segmentation accuracy have been achieved by introducing the instance segmentation model as compared with the earlier version of *UniNet* introduced in the previous chapter. As for the feature learning, the specially designed ETL function can provide effective supervision for learning comprehensive and spatially corresponding iris features through the FCN.

Fitting irises with more precise representations rather than circles, as used in this work, can lead to better-aligned normalization and also benefit the recognition performance. During the development phase of this work, our primary goal is to explore a more effective iris feature representation (Chapter 2) using deep learning, and therefore the circular Hough transform was adopted for simplicity. During the extension of *UniNet* (Chapter 2) framework to the iris detection and segmentation processes (in *UniNet.v2*), the key effort was devoted to improving the quality of the iris mask with deep learning, while the circle fitting step was not focussed. This can be perceived as a limitation in this framework, which can be enhanced by incorporating more precise contours, for example, [87] can also offer superior iris contour representation in the future version of this work.

The framework presented in this chapter can be further by incorporating more effective algorithms for the simultaneous optimization of the iris segmentation and feature learning processes through the deep networks, including more advanced and backpropagation complaint iris contour fitting and normalization, which is expected to exploit further the spatially corresponding features. The instance segmentation model used in *UniNet.v2* is quite outdated, but it has served its key purpose of validating the deep learning-based alternative for the precise detection and segmentation of iris RoI from the acquired eye images. Therefore further enhancement in this framework, in terms of accuracy and speed, is expected by incorporating more specialized instance segmentation models, such as SOLO [99], YOLO [98], Mark2Former [100], UViM [101], SAM [221], or SEEM [102]. Chapter 8 uses such an instance segmentation model for the detection of pupil and limbic boundaries. A range of generalized but complex segmentation models, such as [103] or [104], have been shown to offer better generalization capability with in-context training and can also be adapted for more accurate iris detection and segmentation tasks.

4

Enhancing iris recognition accuracy through dilated residual features

Specialized deep neural network architecture designed to recover rich feature templates from the normalized iris regions were discussed in the earlier chapter. This chapter presents the design and results from a systematic investigation aimed at further enhancing match accuracy through a newly adopted framework that extracts more representative features across different scales. The framework leverages residual network learning with dilated convolutional kernels, optimizing the training process and aggregating contextual information from iris images without the need for down-sampling and up-sampling layers. Experimental results demonstrate promising outcomes, validating the potential of multiple kernels to significantly improve iris match accuracy.

4.1 Introduction

Although deep network-based iris recognition has not received much attention, several interesting attempts have been made to utilize popular deep network-based architectures for iris recognition. DeepIrisNet in [22] is a notable example, which directly applies typical CNN and inception CNN to identify iris texture patterns and was also used as a baseline method in Chapter 2 for our comparative performance evaluation. In [106], the ResNet18 was employed to extract deep convolutional features, and a two-class support vector machine classifier was used for iris recognition. Another attempt in [105] uses a deep belief network with optimal Gabor filter selection for iris recognition. Effective use of a lightweight CNN to extract feature maps from iris images appears in [254], which also incorporates ordinal measurements [36] and iris mask details for iris matching. Reference [201] investigates the effectiveness of several pretrained CNN models, including AlexNet, VGGNet, InceptionNet, ResNet, and DenseNet, for extracting off-the-shelf CNN features for iris recognition. Pretrained VGGNet and ResNet models are used for iris recognition in [200]. It is worth noting that most of these attempts lack iris-specific design and fair performance comparisons with the method introduced in the last chapter.

4.1.1 Motivation

This chappter is motivated to further enhance the normalized iris image matching capabilities using deep neural networks. The method focussed in this Chapter can create a robust representation of iris features by incorporating a superior feature extraction network that utilizes dilated convolution kernels to handle common deformations between matched iris

Iris and Periocular Recognition using Deep Learning. DOI: https://doi.org/10.1016/B978-0-443-27318-6.00005-X

patterns. The simplicity of this network stems from its use of dilated kernels, and it benefits from residual learning.

The approach offers two significant advantages. Firstly, the dilated convolution kernels in the network allow for nonlinearly expanding receptive fields without decreasing resolution or coverage. Additionally, the use of residual learning blocks is expected to improve matching accuracy by increasing model depth and enriching learning capability through residual information. Another benefit is the network's robustness and simplicity. The *UniNet* introduced in Chapter 2 requires parameters from up-sampling layers which are not trainable in CNN. This increases the complexity of the model and the potential for introducing more errors from the trained network. Although the new architecture discussed in this Chapter uses more layers, as compared with the one in Chapter 2, the parameters trained are not increased. This is because the element-wise combination and instance normalization (IN) layers from the residual network do not include any trained parameters.

4.2 Residual feature learning and dilated kernels for iris recognition

In this study, we explore a framework for precise iris recognition as depicted in Fig. 4−1. This approach is based on the *UniNet*, which serves as an essential baseline for comparisons and is detailed in Chapter 2. The entire framework comprises of *MaskNet* and *FeatNet*, and we begin by training the parameters in *MaskNet*. Subsequently, we freeze the *MaskNet* parameters and fine-tune the weights in our feature extraction architecture called Dilated Residual Feature Net (DRFNet) using the extended triplet loss (ETL) discussed in Chapter 2. During the testing phase, the network receives segmented iris images and automatically produces iris templates and their corresponding masks. With the binarized iris templates and corresponding masks, we can compute the Hamming distance and use it as the match score to distinguish the genuine or the imposter match.

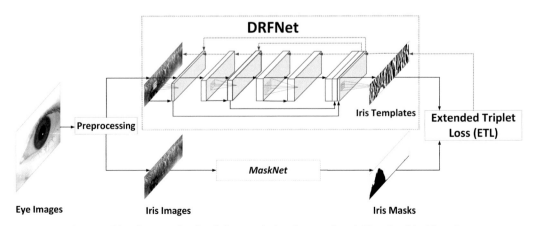

FIGURE 4–1 Iris recognition framework using fully convolutional network and dilated residual learning.

Our primary focus is on the enhancement with the DRFNet architecture to generate more precise binary feature maps than *FeatNet*. To this end, the new architecture employs dilated convolutional neural networks [107] and residual learning kernels [108], with detailed specifications listed in Table 4−1. Additionally, we optimize the training process by employing offline triplet selection [21]. Further details on these techniques are presented in subsequent sections.

4.2.1 Dilated convolutional neural network

Dilated convolutional neural network was introduced in [107] to address the semantic segmentation problem. In a traditional CNN, the output from the previous layer, say j, is always used as the input for the next layer $(j + 1)$. Let us represent $I_j(x, y)$ as the 2-D input for our network and $f_j(x, y)$ as a discrete convolutional kernel. The output feature map from $(j + 1)$th layer using conventional convolution operations can be described as:

$$I_{j+1}(x, y) = (I_j * f_j)(x, y) = \sum_m \sum_n I_j(m, n) f_j(x - m, y - n) \qquad (4-1)$$

where $*$ is the convolution operator. If the filter f is a dilated kernel and let k be a dilation factor, the dilated convolutional operator $*_k$ can be defined as:

$$I_{j+1}(x, y) = (I_j *_k f_j)(x, y) = \sum_m \sum_n I_j(m, n) f_j(x - km, y - kn) \qquad (4-2)$$

Table 4–1   Details of the dilated residual feature network (DRFNet) in Fig. 4−1.

Layer name	Layer type	Kernel size	Output channel	Dilated factor
Conv1	Convolutional	3×3	16	1
Tanh1	*tanh*	–	16	–
Pre_Conv1	Convolutional	1×1	32	1
Imnorm1	Instance normalization	–	32	–
Conv2	Convolutional	3×3	32	2
Tanh2	*tanh*	–	32	–
Res2	Elementwise sum	–	32	–
Tanh3	*tanh*	–	32	–
Pre_Conv2	Convolutional	1×1	64	1
Imnorm2	Instance normalization	–	64	–
Conv3	Convolutional	3×3	64	4
Tanh4	*tanh*	–	64	–
Res3	Elementwise sum	–	64	–
Tanh5	*tanh*	–	64	–
Res	Concatenate	–	112	–
Conv4	Convolutional	3×3	1	1
Tanh6	*tanh*	–	1	–

We can observe that the dilation factor k is the key to control the receptive field of the convolutional kernel. Without losing the resolution and convergence, this controlling factor can be exponentially increased. In this model, the dilated convolutional kernel is incorporated as:

$$I_{j+1}(x, y) = (I_j *_{2^j} f_j)(x, y) \text{ for } j = 0, 1, \ldots n \tag{4-3}$$

This network model uses three scales of dilated convolutional kernels whose receptive fields are illustrated in Fig. 4–2. It is straightforward to observe that the usage of such kernels can process the feature maps from different scales, without increasing the number of training parameters. The up-sampling and down-sampling layers are discarded, which simplifies the network structure. Nonetheless, we can aggregate more information to train the network and introduce less error without the down-sampling layers and up-sampling layers. Incorporating such network is expected to enhance the match accuracy as more robust feature maps are generated from the trained network.

As shown in Fig. 4–1, the feature stack generates dense feature predictions by consolidating the features from three distinct scales using a concatenation layer.

4.2.2 Residual learning blocks

In the previous section, we explained the process of generating feature maps using dilated convolution kernels with Eq. (4–2). However, in our iris recognition framework, the dilated kernel is not employed to learn the feature maps for the next layer but to acquire residual information. The deep residual network introduced in [108] was designed to learn residual information from the input and ease the network training as conventional CNN structures face difficulties approximating the identity mapping due to nonlinear layers. Given a vector input x for the network layer and its corresponding desired output vector $O(x)$, residual learning [108] aims to learn the residue $R(x)$ required for generating the desired output. Assuming the input is x and the desired output is $O(x)$. The ResNet [108] is an architecture aiming to learn the residual $R(x)$ to obtain the desired output.

$$O(x) = R(x) + x \tag{4-4}$$

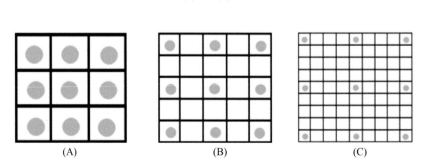

(A)   (B)   (C)

FIGURE 4–2 The dilated convolutional kernels with (A) a dilation factor of one and receptive field of 3×3, (B) dilation factor of two and receptive field of 5×5, and (C) dilation factor of four and receptive field of 9×9.

From Eq. (4−2), we can observe that the input is processed in two different branches. One is for identity mapping, whereas the other one is for the residual information learning. If the identity mapping is an optimal solution, the network could simply train the residual $R(x)$ towards 0. If the residual features are minimizing the loss, we will get a new feature map $O(x)$ from the combination. Compared with the plain network, it does not need more parameters or produce more computational complexity. In our model, we use the dilated convolutional kernel to learn the residual information as introduced in the previous section, so the output from the dilated residual learning kernels can be represented as follows:

$$I_{j+1}(x, y) = \left(I_j *_{2^j} f_j\right)(x, y) + I_j(x, y) \text{ for } j = 0, 1, \ldots n \tag{4−5}$$

The channel number of outputs may be different from x because we need more feature maps with the increase of network depth. We use a preconvolutional layer with a kernel size of one to control this parameter which is similar to the bottleneck design described in [108]. We also use IN instead of batch normalization (BN) which performs better in the dense prediction. The dilated residual feature learning blocks used in this network is shown in Fig. 4−3.

4.2.3 Selection of triplets

The selection of triplets aims to enhance the training process of the network using the triplet architecture as depicted in Fig. 4−4. Triplet pairs are generated by combining an anchor sample with a positive sample and a negative sample. These pairs are respectively fed into

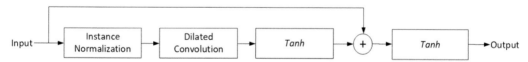

FIGURE 4–3 The dilated residual feature learning block.

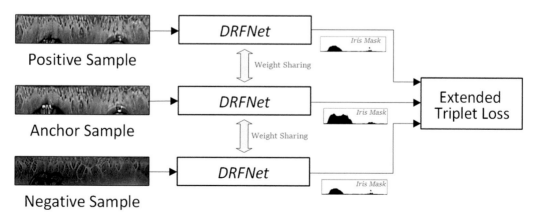

FIGURE 4–4 Training *DRFNet* using triplet architecture.

three network branches, each with identical parameters. Each network branch produces corresponding feature maps F_A, F_P, and F_N, which are utilized during the network training to compute the ETL as follows:

$$\Delta = \frac{1}{M}\sum_{i=1}^{M}\max\left(\left\|F_P-F_A\right\|^2 - \left\|F_N-F_A\right\|^2 + \gamma, 0\right) \qquad (4-6)$$

where M is the batch size and γ is a hyperparameter controlling the margin between the anchor-positive distance and anchor-negative distance. It is crucial to select triplet samples/pairs that can generate nonzero training loss to ensure the effective and efficient training of the network. This means that given F_A we prefer to select corresponding F_P (hard positive) with $argmax_{F_p}\|F_P-F_A\|^2$ and its similarly F_N (hard negative) such that $argmin_{F_N}\|F_N-F_A\|^2$.

However, it is not feasible to compute the *argmin* and *argmax* across the large training set. In addition, this can also result in poor training, as any mislabeled and/or noisy iris samples (outliers) would dominate the selection of such hard pairs. There are two choices to alleviate such limitations. First is to generate the triplets offline after a few thousands of iterations, using the most recent network model to determine the hard pairs in every training subsets. Second choice is to generate triplets online by selecting the hard positive and negative exemplars from within a mini-batch, which can result in significant amount of computing overhead.

In this implementation, we employ the offline generation by dividing the whole training sets into several parts and compute *argmin* and *argmax* within each training subset. It should be ensured that all the identities in each batch are considered to have a meaningful representation of the anchor positive distances. During the experiments, it was also observed that all anchor positive approach instead of only hard positive is more stable and results in faster convergence of the loss during the training process.

Selection of hardest negatives for network training can often lead to poor local minimum during the training process. To mitigate such limitations, preference should be given to select iris image triplets with the following constraints:

$$\left\|F_N-F_A\right\|^2 + \alpha > \left\|F_p-F_A\right\|^2 > \left\|F_N-F_A\right\|^2 \qquad (4-7)$$

Such negative exemplars can be referred to as *semihard*, as they are not expected to be outliers because those negatives lie inside the margin α, but still represent challenging samples because their squared distance is less than the anchor positive distance. As the number of impostor training samples or negative matching pairs greatly exceeds the number of genuine or positive pairs, we generate triplets consisting of all genuine pairs and their respective negative samples that meet the optimization constraints during the training process.

4.3 Experiments and results

We perform a series of experiments on multiple publicly available iris datasets to evaluate the effectiveness of DRFNet-based iris recognition framework. There are four publicly available iris image datasets that are used in Section 2.3 and also used during this evaluation. The experimental protocols are the same as explained in Section 2.6.1, or Table 2−2. The comparative results from the framework introduced in this chapter and other baseline methods are discussed in the following section.

4.3.1 Within-database performance evaluation

Under these sets of experiments, the network is trained using the ND-Iris-0405 dataset, similar to what we did during the performance evaluation in Section 2.3. The trained model is further *fine-tuned* with the *training images from the target dataset* to generate other models. The model of ND-IRIS-0405 dataset is trained from scratch. Our initial learning rate is set to be 0.01. The total number of iterations is set to 384 60,000 while our learning strategy chose multiple steps with the step size 15,000. The parameter update scheme is stochastic gradient descent (SGD) with momentum while the momentum is 0.9. The ratio of positive sample pairs and negative sample pairs in triplets generation is 1:5. During the fine-tuning for the other two datasets, the initial learning rate is changed to 0.001.

The performance evaluation for all the models is performed using the test set images for the respective datasets. Comparative performance is evaluated using the baseline methods that were used in earlier chapters: Conventional *IrisCode* which is a popular benchmark for the iris recognition and Ordinal filters. The UniNet model introduced in the chapter also served as another baseline method. The comparative experimental results with the respective benchmark methods are presented in Fig. 4−5. The equal error rates (EERs) from the respective methods are summarized in Table 4−2.

The ROC plots in Fig. 4−5 indicate that DRFNet-based approach can offer consistently outperforming results on four different public databases. The extent of the performance improvement however varies for the different databases and the observed improvement is also supported by EER in Table 4−2. Some references have also illustrated the area under the curve (AUC) to ascertain the comparative performance. Therefore these numbers for the three (larger) respective datasets are presented in Table 4−3, which can underline the observed performance enhancement.

In addition to the consistent improvement in the match accuracy, this model can also offer a simplified network architecture as it discards the pooling layer and the up-sampling layer. Such simplification can also be observed from Table 4−4 which provides average feature extraction time for the iris image samples, the number of parameters, and total number of float point operations (FLOPs) in the trained model. The employed machine configuration for these comparisons is Intel i9-7900x with 32 GB memory, and all the experiments use one NVIDIA GTX 1080Ti card with 11GB memory.

4.3.2 Cross-database performance evaluation

One of the key benefits expected from the deep learning-based iris recognition lies in the generalization, that is, capability to offer high match accuracy using the model which is trained using completely different or independent iris database. We have evaluated such

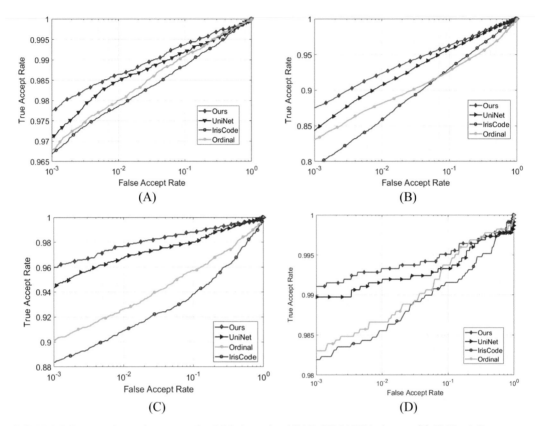

FIGURE 4–5 Comparative performance using ROC plots using (A) ND-IRIS-0405 iris dataset, (B) CASIA.v4-distance dataset, (C) WVU nonideal, and (D) IITD iris images dataset.

Table 4–2   Summary of comparative EER from the within dataset performance evaluation.

	ND-IRIS-0405	CASIA.v4-distance	WVU nonideal	IITD iris database
IrisCode	1.88%	7.71%	6.82%	1.38%
Ordinal	1.74%	7.89%	5.19%	1.25%
UniNet	1.40%	5.50%	2.63%	0.85%
DRFNet	1.30%	4.91%	1.91%	0.72%

cross-database iris recognition performance in earlier chapters and similar cross-database performance evaluation is also performed for DRFnet-based framework. During this evaluation, we employed the model that is directly trained using the ND-IRIS-0405 iris image database [76] and use it to ascertain the match accuracy on the CASIA.v4-distance database [17] and WVU nonideal iris image dataset [85] images directly *without* any fine-tuning.

Table 4–3   Summary of AUC from the within dataset performance evaluation.

	ND-IRIS-0405	CASIA.v4-distance	WVU nonideal
UniNet	0.9963	0.9819	0.9921
DRFNet	0.9970	0.9843	0.9941

Table 4–4   Comparative evaluation of the network complexity.

	Feature extraction time per sample (ms)	Number of parameters	FLOPs
UniNet	8.93	129,872	883.88 M
DRFNet	8.12	125,264	828.67 M

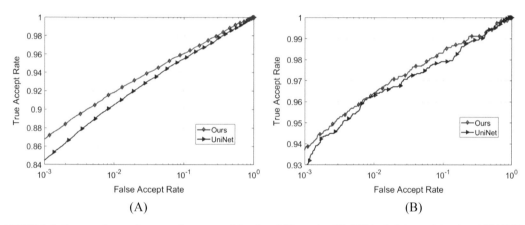

(A)   (B)

FIGURE 4–6 Comparative performance from cross-dataset matching using (A) CASIA.v4-distance dataset and (B) WVU nonideal iris dataset.

The number of test images are same as described for respective databases in the previous section. This evaluation aims to validate generalization capability of the framework when there are limited or no training samples accessible from the target iris database. The comparative performance from the respective databases is shown in Fig. 4–6. Table 4–5 summarizes the respective EER values from such cross-database performance evaluation.

These results for the cross-database matching also indicate improvement using DRFNet-based framework and reveal its generalization capability. We also computed the AUC between the *UniNet* and this framework to ascertain the significant of performance improvement and is summarized in Table 4–6.

4.3.3 Ablation study

This section presents results from two ablation experiments, including the dilated net and residual net, to further investigate the extent of performance enhancement. This ablation study

Table 4–5   Summary of EER values from the cross-database performance evaluation.

	CASIA.v4-distance	WVU nonideal
UniNet	5.61%	3.67%
DRFNet	5.13%	2.31%

Table 4–6   Summary of AUC values from the cross-database performance evaluation.

	CASIA.v4-distance	WVU nonideal
UniNet	0.9804	0.9915
DRFNet	0.9837	0.9927

Table 4–7   Summary of EER values from the ablation study experiments.

	ND-IRIS-0405	CASIA.v4-distance	WVU nonideal
ResNet	1.37%	5.54%	2.71%
Dilated Net	1.32%	5.58%	2.33%
UniNet	1.40%	5.50%	2.63%
DRFNet	1.30%	4.91%	1.91%

helps us to ascertain the effectiveness of our approach or network, over other popular networks (like ResNet [108] or DilatedNet [107]), for the iris recognition problem (Table 4–7).

The EER results are summarized in Table 4–6, and the corresponding ROCs are illustrated in Fig. 4–7. From the results shown above, we can observe the usage of both the residual blocks and dilated kernel contribute to the increase in iris matching accuracy. The residual block learns the residual information and ensemble across layers and makes the learning pattern more representative. The dilated kernels can also learn more accurate features by discarding the down-sampling (maximum pooling) layer and the up-sampling (bilinear) layer whose parameters may not be tunable in *UniNet*. The dilated convolutional kernel can maintain the resolution of input data and help to preserve the contributions from thin and small texture features that are important in correctly matching the iris images.

4.3.4 Comparison with aggregated residual network

A variant of ResNet, codenamed as ResNeXt, has been introduced in [109] which includes several parallel ResNet branches with the same topology, and introduces a hyper-parameter called *cardinality*—the number of independent paths, to provide a new way of adjusting the model capacity. In this set of experiments, we attempted to expand our model with cardinality eight to ascertain possible improvement of wide architecture. Such comparative experimental results using ND-0405-Iris image dataset are illustrated in Fig. 4–8. These results also suggest outperforming results from our approach.

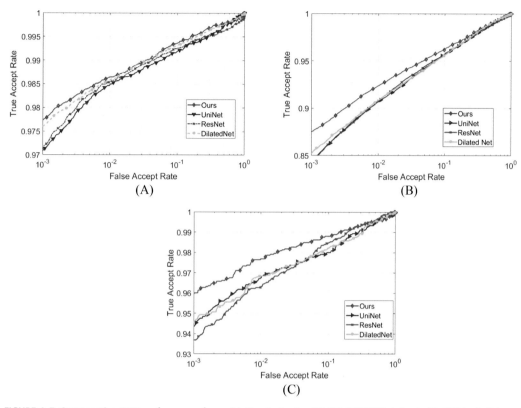

FIGURE 4–7 Comparative ROC performance from ablation test using (A) ND-IRIS-0405 dataset, (B) CASIA.v4-distance iris dataset, (C) WVU Nonideal iris images dataset.

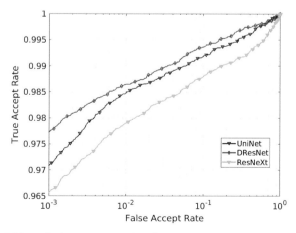

FIGURE 4–8 Comparative ROC results from ResNeXt using the ND-Iris-0405 dataset.

4.3.5 Comparisons with commercial matcher

Comparative performance evaluation with a popular Commercial-off-the-shelf (COTS) system can help to generate some confidence with the effectiveness of DRFNet-based approach. Therefore a popular COTS system [89] was chosen for such a baseline. Fig. 4−9 and Table 4−8 present such comparative results using such COTS on three different public iris databases To ensure a *fair* comparison, the size of test samples for these comparative experiments is exactly same as employed for the experiments in Section 4.3.1, that is, 14,791 genuine and 5,743,130 impostor match scores for the tests using ND-IRIS-0405 iris database, 20,702 genuine and 2,969,533 impostor match scores for the CASIA.v4-distance iris database,

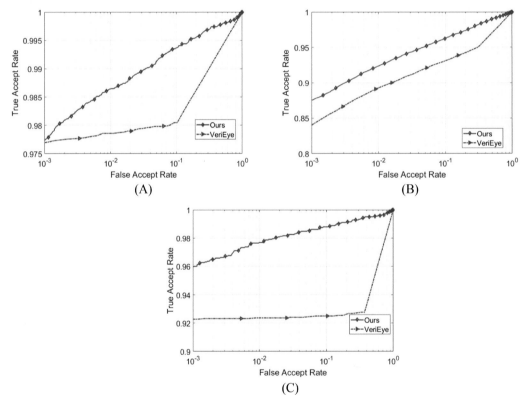

FIGURE 4–9 Comparative ROC results from DRFNet-based framework and a COTS using (A) ND-IRIS-0405 dataset, (B) CASIA.v4-distance dataset, and (C) WVU Nonideal iris dataset.

Table 4–8   Summary of comparative EER values using a COTS.

	ND-IRIS-0405	CASIA.v4-distance	WVU nonideal
VeriEye	1.33%	7.05%	7.20%
DRFNet	1.30%	4.91%	1.91%

and 2,251 genuine and 643,565 impostor scores for the WVU nonideal iris database. Our comparative results in Fig. 4−9 consistently indicate outperforming results from such performance evaluation. It is important to note that the COTS (*VeriEye*) will discard the match score if it considers that the quality of the images does not satisfy the requirements even though the quality threshold is set to zero. As also detailed in IREX IX [110], blank templates from poor-quality iris images should produce high measures of dissimilarity. Therefore for a fair comparison, one needs to ensure the *same* number of genuine and imposter match scores, so a match score is considered to be zero when such (bad) matching happens.

4.3.6 Failure cases

We can analyze normalized iris images which failed from this approach and Fig. 4−10 presents some such image samples. These failed cases, that is, genuine class iris samples that failure to match, can be largely attributed to degradation in the iris image quality, segmentation error, and large off-angle iris images. Fig. 4−10 first provides image samples from the same-class (genuine) which failed to match and then also illustrates different-class (impostor) image samples which falsely matched from DRFNet-based framework. This figure also provides corresponding heat maps, which are generated from the real value output from DRFNet before the binarization step. The cold area toward blue color in these images represents the pixels values close to −1 while the warm area towards red color represents the respective pixel values that are closer to 1. The decision threshold was fixed as 0.3770 for these matching. The match scores from the genuine pairs are 0.3946 and 0.4063, while the match scores from the imposter pairs are 0.3569 and 0.3723 respectively.

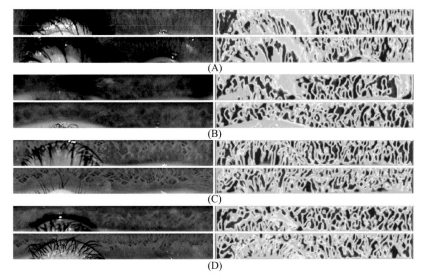

FIGURE 4−10 Sample images from ND-0405-Iris-Dataset that failed to correctly match: (A and B) genuine image sample pairs that failed to match and (C and D) imposter image pairs that incorrectly matched.

4.4 Discussion

This section provides details to understand on the choice of parameters for the DRFNet-based iris recognition framework. It will answer some common questions relating to the design, choice of training parameters, and configurations and present some new experimental results to validate such claims.

4.4.1 Choice of activation function for the network

Computer vision research has acknowledged that the application of traditional nonlinear units, such as sigmoid or hyperbolic tangent (*tanh*), can impede the training of deep neural networks [111]. As a result, rectified linear units (*ReLU*) has been widely utilized in popular convolutional neural networks (CNNs) such as ResNet [108], Inception [90], and DenseNet [112]. However, despite the prevalence of ReLU, our justification for tanh as the preferred nonlinear activation function merits some discussion.

The rectified linear unit *ReLU* has been widely used for the DCNN training for its sparsity and reduced likelihood for the vanishing gradient [111]. There are a few reasons for our preference to use *tanh* instead of *ReLU*. First, we expect our final output as a pseudo-binary feature since we perform Hamming distance computations during the test phase. The *tanh* whose output ranges from -1 to 1, is therefore more preferable than *ReLU*. Second, our network is not very deep and therefore we do not expect serious implications from the problem of vanishing gradients. We can also perform experiments using *ReLU*, instead of *tanh* in our model, and these comparative experimental results are illustrated in Fig. $4-11$. The EER results from our model with *tanh* and the new model with *ReLU* are 1.30% and 1.61%, respectively. These experiments were performed on ND-IRIS-0405 database and use the same train/test protocol as in Section 4.3.1. These results can also help to validate the choice of *tanh* over *ReLU* in the DRFNet.

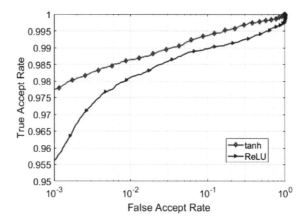

FIGURE 4–11 Comparative ROC results from different nonlinear activation units.

4.4.2 Choice of normalization for network training

In modern CNNs, normalization plays a crucial role in expediting network convergence and improving performance. While several normalization techniques are available, BN [111] has gained popularity and demonstrated success. Nevertheless, we have selected IN over BN. While IN performs BN-like normalization on each sample, it might result in less robust variance estimation compared to BN. Furthermore, the group normalization was introduced [113] for overcoming the limitations of current normalization methods.

We therefore present comparative experimental results with these competing normalization methods on the ND-0405-IRIS dataset. In the BN, we empirically selected batch size of 32 while for the group normalization, the group size of 8 was set for the best performance. These experimental results are shown in Fig. 4−12. The EER results from IN, BN, and group normalization are 1.30%, 1.35%, and 1.33%, respectively. The experimental results indicate superior performance using the IN and have therefore justified as prudent choice for the DRFNet.

4.4.3 Comparison with deep bottleneck architecture

Deep bottleneck architecture is another variation of ResNet [108] introduced to further simplify the networks with fewer parameters. However, the residual learning block shown in Fig. 4−3 and the bottleneck used in *ResNet* [108] are different. It is therefore crucial to compare the performance of these two architectures and elucidate why the conventional bottleneck was not utilized. When constructing a comparable network, it is essential to ensure that the parameters are equivalent to DRFNet. Additionally, to ensure fair comparison, it is necessary to replace the 3×3 convolutional layer in the bottleneck with a 3×3 dilated convolutional layer to maintain an identical receptive field.

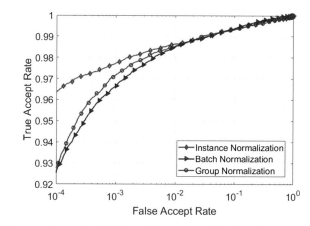

FIGURE 4–12 Comparative experimental results from different normalization schemes.

Such bottleneck design uses 1×1 convolutional kernels to reduce the number of channels and then perform the 3×3 convolutions on the smaller number of layers. After that, 1×1 convolution is performed again to increase the number of channels. We also perform experiments using the bottleneck architecture, with the configuration as shown in Table 4−9, using the ND-0405 IRIS dataset. The comparative experimental results from DRFNet without bottleneck architecture and DRFNet with bottleneck architecture are shown in Fig. 4−13.

It can be observed from these experimental results that the performance from this bottleneck design degrades seriously since we increase the depth and reduce the width. In the original *ResNet*, authors applied it to the wider layers, for example, 256 channels reduced to 64 channels by the 1×1 convolution and perform the 3×3 convolution and then perform 1×1 convolution to generate the 256 channels output. This strategy helped them to simplify the network. However, our training data and model size are relatively small compared with the *ResNet* trained for ImageNet [114], and this strategy further reduces the width of each layer and increases the depth of our model.

4.4.4 Comparison with dilated residual network

Over the past few decades, researchers have explored the use of dilated kernels to examine signals and features at various scales for multiple applications. In [115], the authors developed a dilated residual network for image classification, and their findings suggest that it can effectively perform semantic segmentation. This architecture, which is based on ResNet-18, categorizes all layers into five groups according to the feature map scale. The last two groups eliminate down-sampling by changing the convolution stride back to one and substitute the convolutional kernels with dilated convolutional kernels, which have a dilation factor of 2 and 4, respectively. Additionally, this study introduces degridding layers and boosts the total number of layers to 26. Before global average pooling, bilinear interpolation is used to up-sample the layer for semantic segmentation.

The differences between DRFNet and the dilated residual network (DRN) [115] can be summarized as follows. First, the model in [115] is a modified *ResNet* and it preserves the first three down-sampling layers while our model is a shallow network without any down-sampling and up-sampling. Second, we concatenate the layers from different scale, but the authors in [115] *only* up-sample the feature map before the global average pooling layer without concatenating feature maps from different scales. Third, we use the triplet architecture to compute the distance between different templates, while the authors in [115] use the sequential architecture with *softmax*, using the ground truth, to achieve the semantic segmentation. Fourth, the loss function is different since DRFNet uses specialized loss introduced for iris recognition in Chapter 2, that is, ETL function, while DRN uses the *softmax* cross-entropy loss. Finally, the authors in [115] use degridding layers and DRFNet does not incorporate these layers which can increase the complexity of model (from 18 to 26 layers).

Table 4–9   Details of *DRFNet* with bottleneck architecture.

Layer name	Layer type	Kernel size	Output channel	Dilated factor
Conv1	Convolution	3×3	16	1
Imnorm1	BatchNorm	–	16	–
Scale1	Scale	–	16	–
ReLU1	ReLU	–	16	–
Conv2a_1	Convolution	1×1	8	1
Imnorm2a_1	BatchNorm	–	8	–
Scale2a_1	Scale	–	8	–
ReLU2a_1	ReLU	–	8	–
Conv2a_2	Convolution	3×3	8	2
Imnorm2a_2	BatchNorm	–	8	–
Scale2a_2	Scale	–	8	–
ReLU2a_2	ReLU	–	8	–
Conv2a_3	Convolution	1×1	32	1
Imnorm2a_3	BatchNorm	–	32	–
Scale2a_3	Scale	–	32	–
Conv2b	Convolution	1×1	32	1
Imnorm2b	BatchNorm	–	32	–
Scale2b	Scale	–	32	–
Res2	Elementwise sum	–	32	–
ReLU2	ReLU	–	32	–
Conv3a_1	Convolution	1×1	16	1
Imnorm3a_1	BatchNorm	–	16	–
Scale3a_1	Scale	–	16	–
ReLU3a_1	ReLU	–	16	–
Conv3a_2	Convolution	3×3	16	4
Imnorm3a_2	BatchNorm	–	16	–
Scale3a_2	Scale	–	16	–
ReLU3a_2	ReLU	–	16	–
Conv3a_3	Convolution	1×1	64	1
Imnorm3a_3	BatchNorm	–	64	–
Scale3a_3	Scale	–	64	–
Conv3b	Convolution	1×1	64	1
Imnorm3b	BatchNorm	–	64	–
Scale3b	Scale	–	64	–
Res3	Elementwise sum	–	64	–
ReLU3	ReLU	–	64	–
Res	Concatenate	–	112	–
Conv4	Convolution	1×1	1	1
Imnorm4	BatchNorm	–	1	–
Scale4	Scale	–	1	–
Tanh	*tanh*	–	1	–

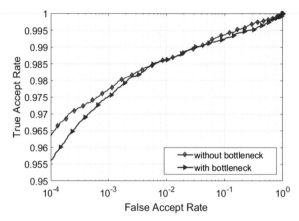

FIGURE 4–13 Comparative ROC results from different *ResNet* blocks.

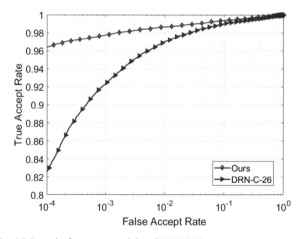

FIGURE 4–14 Comparative ROC results from our model and DRN-C-26.

The DRN-C-26 performs well for the semantic segmentation as detailed in [115]. Therefore to ensure a fair comparison, we use it as one branch of triplet networks and compute the ETL. We follow the same training protocols as detailed in [115], with the initial learning rate 0.1 and the parameter update scheme is SGD with momentum 0.9. The comparative performance using the ROC results from our model and DRN-C-26 is shown in Fig. 4–14 and the respective EERs are 1.30% and 2.19%. These experimental results can help to further validate the merit of DRFNet.

4.5 Chapter summary and further enhancements

In Chapter 2, we introduced *UniNet* model to generate a dense prediction from the normalized iris images using deep learning which can benefit from the spatial correspondences in the original iris images. This model matches the binarized dense predictions during the testing phase and has shown much improved accuracy as compared with other prior methods. This chapter attempts to further enhance such network with the dilated convolutional kernels and *ResNet* blocks.

Involuntary pupil dilation and scale changes during the iris imaging constitute the key source for the frequently observed iris deformations. The approach detailed in this chapter has attempted to address this problem by incorporating the dilated convolutional kernel and residual learning in the DRFNet-based framework. Such an approach can also simplify the architecture of the deep neural network.

It is worth noting that any direct usage of the feature vector from the deep neural network, like *ResNet* in [108], cannot preserve spatial-relationship among the randomly textured iris data as explained in Chapter 2 or provide superior performance than the *fully convolutional* network. DRFNet model is trained from scratch instead of transfer learning from the pretrained model. Our model only needs 1/170 (125,264 *vs.* 21.6 million) of the parameters as compared with the *ResNet-34* used in [115]. Table 4−5 provides a total number of parameters and the execution time in and is another advantage of this approach.

Iris images inherently illustrate ocular information and can be incorporated in the deep neural network model to further improve the iris image matching accuracy and it is part of further advancement that will be systematically discussed in coming chapters. Our current work uses a *MaskNet* which was separately trained. In Chapter 3, we introduced *UniNet.v2*, which provided complete deep learning-based pipeline for the iris recognition. Section 4.3.3, introduced network training using the binary-valued extended triples loss and the experimental results in Chapter 2 have indicated that this approach can offer superior performance over the real-valued ETL that was also used to train the DRFNet introduced in this chapter. Therefore further enhancement of this framework using the instance segmentation-based iris detection and segmentation, as discussed in Chapter 3, and using the binary-valued ETL as discussed in Chapter 2, is expected to offer significantly enhanced iris recognition accuracy. Such implementation has indeed appeared in a prototype design and is the right direction for the advancement of iris recognition.

5

Iris recognition with deep learning across spectrums

The deep neural network for matching normalized iris images introduced in the previous chapter was specially focused on matching images acquired from the standardized iris sensors. However, in many other real-world applications, iris images are acquired from sensors with considerable variability or under different illuminations and sensing environments. Significant degradations in the match accuracy are expected while matching such iris images that are acquired from different imaging domains or spectrums. To address such challenges, specialized deep-learning based methods can be employed to dramatically enhance the recognition of such iris images. This chapter focuses on creating a specialized pipeline to enhance the match accuracy of iris images obtained from different spectrums or sensors.

5.1 Introduction

The performance degradation issue in matching biometric images is widely acknowledged, particularly when attempting to match gallery images from one sensor with probe images from another or a degraded sensor. Such degradation for matching the cross-sensor iris images has been extensively studied, with significant declines in performance noted when matching conventionally near-infrared illuminated iris images with those captured under visible illumination. The acquisition of light pigmentated iris images, which are prevalent in diverse populations across various countries and regions, can be achieved with utmost convenience under visible illumination and is also known to offer high match accuracy. Conversely, a significant proportion of the global population, such as those hailing from the Indian or Chinese subcontinent, possess dark iris pigmentation, necessitating the use of near-infrared illumination to capture the distinctive iris texture to achieve remarkably high accuracy during the matching.

The advent of dual imaging sensors has brought forth a new era in iris recognition technology, enabling the simultaneous acquisition of near-infrared and visible illumination iris images with unprecedented accuracy. Building upon the first such research in [66] on the acquisition of iris images with pixel-to-pixel correspondences in bi-spectral domains, these cutting-edge capabilities hold tremendous potential for real-world applications, such as matching images stored in national ID databases that are widely acquired under near-infrared illumination. However, the inherently diverse appearance of iris texture under different spectral illumination poses a daunting challenge for such cross-spectral iris matching, necessitating the development of advanced algorithms to achieve accurate and reliable match results.

Iris and Periocular Recognition using Deep Learning. DOI: https://doi.org/10.1016/B978-0-443-27318-6.00012-7

The previous chapters have highlighted the remarkable success of specialized convolution neural networks (CNNs) in conventional iris recognition, demonstrating their outstanding ability to learn intricate anatomical features for precise user identification. This remarkable success has generated a strong motivation to delve deeper into the capabilities of deep learning architectures in tackling more arduous visible-to-near-infrared iris recognition challenges. As such, this chapter is dedicated to the development of cross-spectral iris-matching capabilities, leveraging the power of deep learning.

5.1.1 Motivation

Earlier work on cross-spectral iris recognition has made significant advances to improve matching accuracy. Such a summary of related work in Table 5−1 indicates that the earlier have predominantly focussed on extracting manually engineered features from the corresponding spectra during the learning phase. Despite yielding impressive results, the previous approaches warrant further enhancements to attain optimal matching accuracy for an array of pragmatic applications.

The crux of accurate cross-spectral iris image matching lies in the ability to automatically learn corresponding features rather than relying on limited performance gains from hand-crafted features. In this chapter, we explore the potential of deep learning capabilities to enhance cross-spectral iris recognition accuracy. We present experimental results using a range of deep learning architectures, for example, CNN, Siamese networks, Triplet networks, VGG, and deep residual networks (ResNet), to comparatively ascertain performance improvement against conventional methods in the literature. These findings showcase superior results on two publicly available cross-spectral iris image databases, affirming the efficacy of this approach for precise cross-spectral iris matching.

Smaller template sizes and higher template matching speeds are preferred in a variety of iris recognition applications. These experiments to enhance the cross-spectral iris matching accuracy indicate that the feature vectors recovered from the CNNs are generally sparse, and therefore there is significant potential to achieve compact iris template representations. By incorporating a supervised discrete hashing (SDH) scheme, we have demonstrated the potential to significantly reduce template size and improve match speed, utilizing the Hamming distance for features derived from our CNN-based models. The outcomes of our experiments, as detailed in Section 5.3.2, have shown a noticeable reduction in iris template size (a mere 1000 bits), while simultaneously improving cross-spectral matching accuracy. This 1000-bit template representation scheme yields a compact template size (merely 125 bytes) and represents a significant stride forward in cross-spectral iris recognition technology.

5.2 Cross-spectral iris recognition

The framework for cross-spectral iris recognition for challenging visible iris images is shown in Fig. 5−1. This framework, like earlier work [66,118], consists of an offline training phase

Table 5–1 Comparative summary of leading methods for matching cross-spectrum iris images.

Method	Database(s)	Public	Iris comparisons	Template size	Features	Match accuracy
A predictive NIR iris image is used from the color image [117]	WVU multispectral iris database	No	Genuine = 280 Impostor = 20,745 (estimated)	$128 \times 720 \times 8$ (estimated)	Hand-crafted	95.2% (FAR = 0.001)
IrisCode using 1D Log-Gabor filter [30]	(i) PolyU bi-spectral iris database (ii) Cross-eyed-cross-spectral iris recognition database	Yes	Genuine = 2800 Impostor = 195,3000 Genuine = 2160 Impostors = 516,240	$64 \times 512 \times 2$	Hand-crafted	(i) 52.6% (FAR = 0.1) (ii) 70.3% (FAR = 0.1)
NIR to VIS texture synthesis using MRF model [66]	(i) PolyU bi-spectral iris database (ii) Cross-eyed-cross-spectral iris recognition database	Yes	Genuine = 2800 Impostor = 195,3000 Genuine = 2160 Impostors = 51,6240	$64 \times 512 \times 2$	Hand-crafted	(i) 64.91% (FAR = 0.1) (ii) 78.13% (FAR = 0.1)
Deep Neural Network with an SDH for compression and classification	(i) PolyU bi-spectral iris database (ii) Cross-eyed-cross-spectral iris recognition database	Yes	Genuine = 2800 Impostor = 195,3000 Genuine = 2160 Impostors = 516,240	1000×1	Self-learned	(i) 90.71% (FAR = 0.01) (ii) 87.18% (FAR = 0.01)

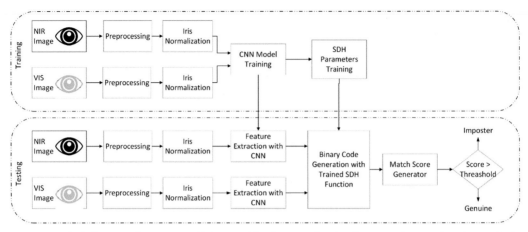

FIGURE 5–1 Block diagram of cross-spectral iris recognition framework using deep neural network and supervised discrete hashing.

where the parameters are automatically learned. Each of the iris images from both spectra is first subjected to the segmentation and image enhancement steps. The segmented images are used for CNN-based feature learning. The parameters for SDH are also learned during the training phase and employed to generate binarized features for the Hamming distance-based matching during the test phase. These match scores are used to establish the identity of the unknown input iris image pairs.

We investigate three CNN architectures to ascertain the learning for the cross-spectral iris features, that is, CNN with *softmax* cross-entropy loss, Siamese network, and Triplet network. Normalized image samples are used to extract fixed-length feature vectors, which are used for the classification. Two approaches for the classification of feature vectors can be considered; the first one is based on the joint-Bayesian inference [119], while the other one incorporates SDH [120], which generates match scores using Hamming distance. We now briefly introduce the CNN architectures that are considered to investigate such cross-spectral iris matching.

5.2.1 CNN with softmax cross-entropy loss

CNN with *softmax* cross-entropy loss can offer superior generalization capability and compact feature representations. The CNN employed in this framework adopts an architecture that is similar to AlexNet [127] architecture and is illustrated in Fig. 5−2. The network is composed of three convolutional layers, three pooling layers, and two fully connected (FC) layers. After each pooling layer and the first FC layer, there is a nonlinear activation function, and we use Rectified Linear Unit (ReLU) function in this work. The last FC layer is used for label prediction and calculation of softmax loss.

For every convolutional layer, we can compute i-th channel output y^i from Eq. (5−1). In this equation, x^j represents the j-th channel input from the previous layer, w^{ij} is the

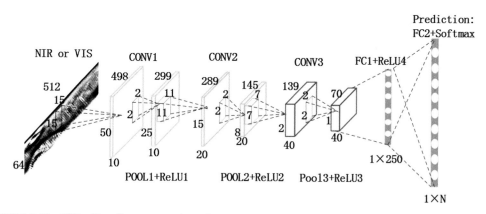

FIGURE 5–2 The CNN with *softmax* cross-entropy loss.

convolutional kernel between the x^j and y^i while b^{ij} is the neuron bias between input channel and the output channel.

$$y^i = \sum_j (b^{ij} + w^{ij} * x^j) \qquad (5-1)$$

The pooling layer shown in Fig. 5−2 extracts the maximum value from the kernel. It aims to downsample the input size for further processing so that features can be learned from a different scale. The ReLU activation function activates all the output with nonnegative values and can be defined as follows:

$$y^i = \max(y^i, 0) \qquad (5-2)$$

The FC layer will connect all the nodes in the current layer with one node to generate the output vector as in the following:

$$y^i = b_i + \sum_j w^{ij} * x^j \qquad (5-3)$$

The network is initialized randomly, and therefore there are variations in how accurately the neurons learn. The *softmax* cross entropy loss function is employed to compute the normalized error between the ground truth label and our prediction label as follows:

$$E = \frac{-1}{N} \log(p_n, l_n) \qquad (5-4)$$

where N is the number of classes in training samples, p_n is the predicted label, and l_n is the ground truth label. The final output is a $1 * N$ vector with positive elements. Each element value represents the probability prediction of the class label for the input image. Network training aims to minimize the loss by backpropagation so that the probability of predicting the ground-truth class can approach maximum.

5.2.2 Siamese network

The Siamese network [121] is essentially a twin-branch structure that learns the similarity between two comparable inputs. It contains two identical subnetworks whose parameters are simultaneously updated. The motivation for employing this architecture in our experiment is to ascertain inner correspondences between the NIR image pixels and VIS image pixels. One NIR image and one VIS image form an input pair for the Siamese network. Each input pair data has a binary label *l* indicating whether they are from the same iris/eye. The architecture of the Siamese network for matching cross-spectrum iris images is illustrated in Fig. 5−3, and each branch of this network has the *same* configuration as the CNN with *softmax* cross-entropy loss. In this network, the comparative loss from the last layer of twin branches is computed. This loss function can be written as follows:

$$E = \frac{1}{2N}\sum_{n=1}^{N}((l)d^2 + (1-l)\max(\alpha-d,0)^2) \qquad (5-5)$$

where N is the batch size set in forward propagation, l is the binary label indicating genuine pair and imposter pair, and d is the Euclidean distance between the two feature vectors generated from FC layers while α is the margin set during the training process. This loss function aims to minimize the distance between genuine pairs and enlarge the distance between the imposter pairs so that the overlap can be reduced and the matching performance can be improved.

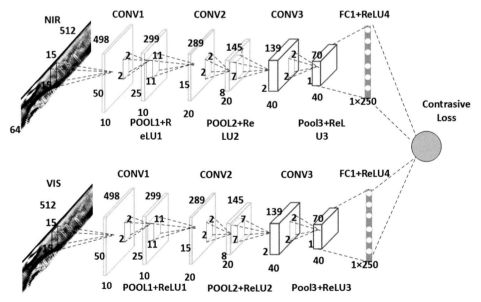

FIGURE 5–3 Siamese network for matching cross-spectrum iris images.

5.2.3 Triplet network

The triplet network [122] is comprised of three branches, as shown in Fig. 5–4, and has also been discussed earlier in Chapter 2. The three-channel inputs include one anchor image, one positive image, and one negative image. In this set of experiments, we select one NIR image as the anchor sample A, one VIS image from the same class as positive sample P, and one VIS image from a different class as negative sample N. The network architecture attempts to address a two-class classification problem, where the objective is to correctly classify the samples in P and N as belonging to the same class as A. The configuration of every branch is the same as for the CNN with *softmax* cross-entropy loss in Fig. 5–2. The triplet loss function in this network is the same as defined in Eq. (2.1) and can be rewritten for cross-spectrum network training as follows:

$$E = \sum_{i=1}^{N}\left(\left\|A_i - P_i\right\|^2 - \left\|A_i - N_i\right\|^2 + \alpha\right) \tag{5-6}$$

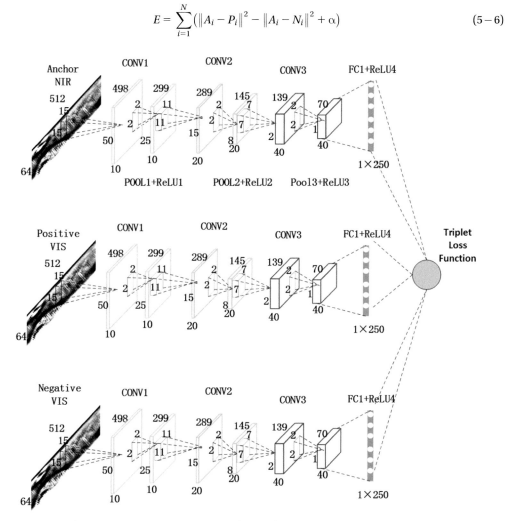

FIGURE 5–4 Network training using triplet architecture for matching cross-spectrum iris images.

where N is the batch size in the training, A_i is the anchor image whereas P_i is positive one and N_i is the negative one while α is the minimum margin fixed during the training stage. This approach attempts to simultaneously increase the distance between the imposter pairs and reduce the distance between the genuine pairs.

5.2.4 Joint-Bayesian formulation

The Joint-Bayesian formulation approach for the classification of deeply learned features, extracted from the trained CNN, has been shown to offer promising performance in the literature [119] and was therefore a judicious choice to explore cross-spectrum iris matching. The FC layer outputs *before* the prediction layer are utilized as the feature vector. Each of such templates from the CNN is therefore represented by this real-value vector.

In the theory of Joint-Bayesian, every feature vector x can be formulated as follows:

$$x = \mu + \varepsilon \tag{5-7}$$

where μ represents the class identity and ε represents intra-class variation. Under the assumption of Gaussian distributions, that is, $N(0, S_\mu)$, $N(0, S_\varepsilon)$, both variables are with zero mean. The covariance matrix of two observations $\{x_1, x_2\}$ can be written as follows:

$$\mathrm{cov}(x_1, x_2) = \mathrm{cov}(\mu_1, \mu_2) + \mathrm{cov}(\varepsilon_1, \varepsilon_2) \tag{5-8}$$

Let H_I denote the intra-class hypothesis indicating that two observations are from the same class, and H_E the extra-class hypothesis. Under H_I, μ_1, and μ_2 are the same due to the same class identity, and ε_1 and ε_2 are independent. Therefore the covariance matrix of the distribution $P(x_1, x_2 | H_I)$ can be written as:

$$\sum_{\mathrm{Intra}} = \begin{bmatrix} S_\mu + S_\varepsilon & S_\mu \\ S_\mu & S_\mu + S_\varepsilon \end{bmatrix} \tag{5-9}$$

On the other hand, under H_E, $\mu1$ and $\mu2$ are also independent; therefore the covariance matrix of $P(x_1, x_2 | H_E)$ becomes:

$$\sum_{\mathrm{Inter}} = \begin{bmatrix} S_\mu + S_\varepsilon & 0 \\ 0 & S_\mu + S_\varepsilon \end{bmatrix} \tag{5-10}$$

The log-likelihood ratio $s(x1, x2)$ can be obtained in a closed form after simple algebraic operations:

$$s(x1, x2) = \frac{P(x_1, x_2 | H_I)}{P(x_1, x_2 | H_E)} = x_1^T A x_1 + x_2^T A x_2 - 2 x_1^T G x_2 \tag{5-11}$$

where

$$A = \left(S_\mu + S_\varepsilon\right) - (F + G) \tag{5-12}$$

$$\begin{bmatrix} F+G & G \\ G & F+G \end{bmatrix} = \begin{bmatrix} S_\mu + S_\varepsilon & S_\mu \\ S_\mu & S_\mu + S_\varepsilon \end{bmatrix}^{-1} \tag{5-13}$$

The covariation matrix S_μ and S_ε can be estimated from expectation-maximization algorithm as described in [119]. In this work, the log-likelihood ratio $s(x1, x2)$ is considered as the match score between two respective features $\{x_1, x_2\}$.

5.2.5 Supervised discrete hashing

Hashing algorithms have shown to be quite effective in generating compact binary features for the representative high-dimensional data. One key advantage of such hashing is that it can reduce the storage requirements for the iris templates. The availability of such binarized templates can improve the matching speed as the Hamming distance operations required to compute the match score are significantly faster. Among several Hashing algorithms available in the literature, the supervised hashing framework introduced in [120] can generate optimal binary hash codes that can also be used for the linear classification of features and was therefore preferred in this work.

The match score generation with this hashing scheme incorporates the same feature vectors as incorporated for the formulation presented in Section 5.2.4. The training stage for the SDH aims to learn L bits binary code $B = \{b_i\}_{i=1}^n$ corresponding to every input image using n training feature vectors $X = \{x_i\}_{i=1}^n$ and the ground truth label matrix $Y = \{y_i\}_{i=1}^n$. The following Algorithm 5−1 summarizes the process for computing B.

Algorithm 5−1   Supervised discrete hashing.

Input: Training data $\{x_i, y_i\}_{i=1}^n$; code length L; number of anchor points m; maximum iteration number t; penalty parameters λ and v.

Output: Binary codes $\{b_i\}_{i=1}^n \in \{-1, 1\}^{L \times n}$; hash function $H(x) = \text{sgn}(F((x))$.

Step 1: Randomly select m samples $\{a_j\}_{j=1}^m$ from the training data and get the mapped training data $R(x)$ via the RBF kernel function.

Step 2: Initialize b_i as a $\{-1, 1\}^L$ vector randomly, $\forall i$.

Step 3: Loop until converging or reach maximum iterations;

− Projection step: compute P using Equ. (5−18) to form $F(x)$.
− Mapping step: compute W using Eq. (5−21).
− Bits calculation step: For the l_2 loss, iteratively learn $\{b_i\}_{i=1}^n$ bit by bit using the discrete cyclic coordinate descent (DCC) method with Eq. (5−26).

The expected binary code b should be ideal for classification, and the multiclass classification can be formulated as:

$$y = W^T b = [w_1^T b, \ldots, w_C^T b] \qquad (5-14)$$

where $w_k, k = 1, \ldots, C$ is the class vector for class k if we have C classes, and y is the label vector whose maximum value indicates the predicted class. To achieve high multiclass classification accuracy, the following optimization problem should be first considered:

$$\min_{B,W,F} \sum_{i=1}^{n} E(y_i, W^T b_i) + \lambda \|W\|^2$$

$$\text{s.t.} \quad b_i = \text{sgn}(F(x_i)), i = 1, \ldots, n \qquad (5-15)$$

where $E(.)$ is the loss function. $F(.)$ is the hash function which we wish to learn. Here, $\text{sgn}(.)$ is the sign function which produces $+1$ for the positive value and -1 for the negative value. λ is the regularization parameter. To achieve binary codes of better quality, we keep the binary constraints of b_i in the optimization. The problem outlined in (5.15) adds one more term modeling the fitting error of binary code b_i by the continuous embedding hashing function $F(x_i)$ and penalty term v as follows:

$$\min_{B,W,F} \sum_{i=1}^{n} E(y_i, W^T b_i) + \lambda \|W\|^2 + v \sum_{i=1}^{n} \|b_i - F(x)_i\|^2$$

$$\text{s.t.} \quad b_i \in \{-1, 1\}^L \qquad (5-16)$$

However, the optimization problem formulated in the above equation is highly nonconvex and difficult to solve. But it is tractable when we iteratively solve each variable one by one. Firstly, we can adopt the following nonlinear form for the hash function $F(x)$:

$$F(x) = P^T R(x) \qquad (5-17)$$

$R(.)$ outputs an m-dimensional column vector obtained by the RBF kernel mapping as described in [123,124]. The matrix P projects the mapped data $R(x)$ into the low dimensional space.

Projection-step: If the binary code b_i in (5.16) is fixed, the projection matrix P can be computed by regression:

$$P = (R(X)R(X)^T)^{-1}R(X)B^T \qquad (5-18)$$

This step is independent of the loss function $E(.)$.

In our experiments, we select l_2 loss as $E(.)$ in our classification model. The optimization task in Eq. (5−16) can be rewritten as follows:

$$min_{B,W,F} \sum_{i=1}^{n} \left\| y_i - W^T b_i \right\|^2 + \lambda \left\| W \right\|^2 + \upsilon \sum_{i=1}^{n} \left\| b_i - F(x_i) \right\|^2$$

$$\text{s.t.} \quad b_i \in \{-1, 1\}^L \tag{5-19}$$

The above equation can be further simplified as follows:

$$min_{B,W,F} \left\| Y - W^T B \right\|^2 + \lambda \left\| W \right\|^2 + \upsilon \left\| B - F(X) \right\|^2$$

$$\text{s.t.} \quad B \in \{-1, 1\}^{L*n} \tag{5-20}$$

Mapping-step: If B is fixed for the optimization of Eq. (5−20), we can solve W using the regularized least squares solution as follows:

$$W = (BB^T + \alpha I)^{-1} BY^T \tag{5-21}$$

Bits-calculation-step: When all variables but B fixed, we can rewrite Eq. (5−20) into form:

$$min_B \left\| L - W^T B \right\|^2 + \nu \left\| B - F(X) \right\|^2$$

$$\text{s.t.} \quad B \in \{-1, 1\}^{L \times n} \tag{5-22}$$

The solution for the above equation is still NP-hard. However, a closed-form solution can be achieved when we try to recover one-row B by fixing all the other rows. The optimization task in the above equation can be rewritten as:

$$min_B \left\| Y \right\|^2 - 2Tr(Y^T W^T B) + \left\| W^T B \right\|^2 + \nu(\left\| B \right\|^2 - 2Tr(B^T F(X)) + \left\| F(X) \right\|^2)$$

$$\text{s.t.} \quad B \in \{-1, 1\}^{L \times n}, \tag{5-23}$$

which is equivalent to:

$$min_B \left\| W^T B \right\|^2 - 2Tr(B^T Q)$$

$$\text{s.t.} \quad B \in \{-1, 1\}^{L \times n}, \tag{5-24}$$

where Q represents $WY + \nu F(X)$ and $Tr(.)$ is the conventional trace norm.

To minimize the l_2 loss, we need to iteratively learn every single bits in B using the discrete cyclic coordinate descent method. Let z^T be the lth row of B, $l = 1, 2, 3, \ldots, L$, and B' is the matrix of B excluding z. Then z is one bit for all n samples. Similarly, assume q^T be lth row of Q and v^T is lth row of W, Q' is the matrix Q excluding q and W' is the matrix W excluding v. As analyzed in [120], we finally rewrite Eq. (5−24) into the following form:

$$\min_z \left(v^T W'^T B' - q^T \right) z$$

$$\text{s.t.} \quad z \in \{-1, 1\}^n \tag{5−25}$$

It has the optimal solution:

$$z = \text{sgn}(q - B'^T W' v) \tag{5−26}$$

Each bit's b in B is computed from the pretrained $(L-1)$ bits vector B'. In our experiments, the whole L bits for X are iteratively learned from $5L$ times.

The feature vector extracted from CNN is largely sparse as observed during the experimentation. Therefore there is huge bits compression capacity for image representation with SDH. The SDH code learning includes the training process which is expected to further enlarge the margin between different classes, to improve the overall match accuracy.

5.3 Experiments and results

We performed a range of experiments to ascertain the comparative performance for matching cross-spectrum images. Two publicly available cross-spectral iris database, PolyU bi-spectral iris database [118,125] and cross-eyed-cross-spectral iris recognition database [255] are employed to ascertain performance improvement. To ascertain the usefulness of the cross-spectrum iris recognition framework for the cross-sensor iris recognition problem, we also performed additional experiments using publicly available (cross-sensor) UND dataset, and these are also detailed in Section 5.4.1. We briefly introduce the publicly available databases employed in our experiments in the following Section and discuss our experimental results in Section 5.3.2.

5.3.1 Cross-spectrum iris databases

Two publicly available cross-spectral iris image datasets provide iris images acquired from 209 subjects and 120 different subjects.

5.3.1.1 PolyU bi-spectral iris images database

The Hong Kong Polytechnic University (PolyU) bi-spectral iris images database includes 418 classes bi-spectral images acquired from 209 different subjects. There are 15 instances for every spectrum in each of the class. Images from two spectra were acquired simultaneously in this database. In total, there are 12,540 iris images ($209 \times 2 \times 2 \times 15$). The origin images dimension is 640×480 pixels. We used publicly available implementation for iris segmentation algorithm in [75] to accurately segment iris images for the experiments. The dimension of each of the automatically segmented and normalized iris image is 512×64 pixels. Sample images of this database are shown in Fig. 5−5A.

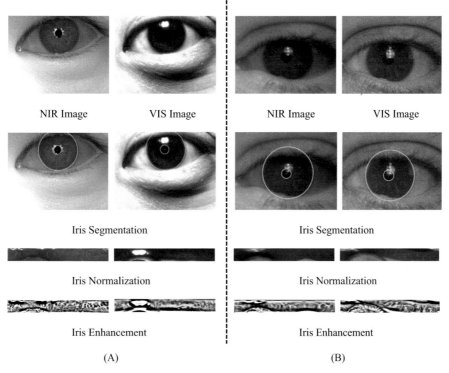

FIGURE 5–5 Sample iris image preprocessing for (A) PolyU bi-spectral iris database and (B) cross-eyed-cross-spectral iris recognition database.

5.3.1.2 Cross-eyed cross-spectral iris recognition databases

Cross-eyed-cross-spectral iris recognition database provides 3840 iris images from 240 classes acquired from 120 subjects. Each of the eye's images from every subject for both spectra has eight image samples of 400×300 pixels. We use the same iris segmentation algorithm [75] to automatically segment all the iris images. The dimension of all the segmented and normalized iris images from this dataset is 512×64 pixels. The sample images from the cross-eyed-cross-spectral database are shown in Fig. 5–5B.

Both the databases also have several low-quality iris image samples and such representative samples from these databases are shown in Fig. 5–6. The key image degradation factors in PolyU database are iris occlusion and poor lighting conditions. In the cross-eyed database, the degradation in image quality mainly results from the reflection and pose variations.

5.3.2 Matching results for cross-spectrum iris images

5.3.2.1 PolyU Bi-spectral iris images database

Our first set of experiments to ascertain the performance of cross-spectral iris recognition incorporated this publicly available dataset. To ensure fairness in the comparison using the conventional state-of-the-art approach in [66], we used iris images from 140 subjects for the

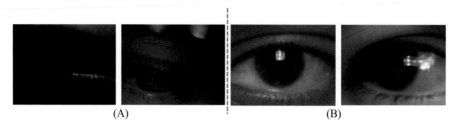

FIGURE 5–6 Low-quality image samples from (A) PolyU bi-spectral iris database and (B) cross-eyed-cross-spectral iris recognition database.

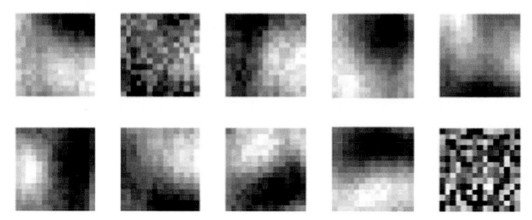

FIGURE 5–7 Visualization of CNN kernels from the first convolutional layer.

experiment. The first ten instances were selected for the CNN training and the rest five instances were employed for the matching. The matching protocol was all-to-all which generated 2800 ($10 \times 140 \times 2$) genuine scores and 1,953,000 ($6975 \times 140 \times 2$) imposter scores.

Fig. 5−7 depicts the visualization of kernels trained for the first convolutional layer of CNN with *softmax* cross entropy loss using PolyU bi-spectral iris dataset. It is generally observed [127] that the well-trained kernels present higher visual saliency reflecting its sensitivity to the edges with a different orientation. There are many kernels in this deep neural network architecture and samples in Fig. 5−7 are randomly chosen to visualize the effectiveness of the training and represents the self-learned features that are extracted from the edge, corners and other textures in the iris data.

The CNN with *softmax* cross-entropy loss is used as the feature extractor in this work. The feature vectors generated from this network are further classified by the joint-Bayesian inference and the SDH as discussed in Section 5.2. In SDH, all the feature vectors are hashed into a 1000 bits binary vector. The comparative matching results using the baseline MRF approach in [66] and using the popular *IrisCode* approach (similar to as in [30]) are used to ascertain the performance. The receiver operating characteristic (ROC) from this set of experiments is shown in Fig. 5−8 while the equal error rate (EER) results are summarized in Table 5−2.

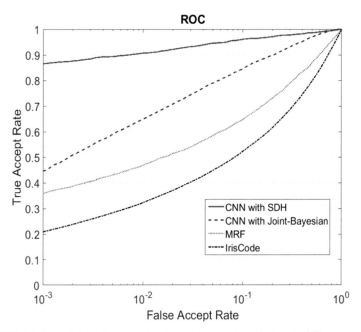

FIGURE 5–8 The ROC plots from PolyU bi-spectral iris dataset (same 140 subjects as in [3]).

Table 5–2   Comparative results using PolyU bi-spectral iris database.

Approach	EER
CNN-SDH	5.39%
CNN-Joint Bayesian	8.00%
MRF (*Baseline Method 1*) [66]	24.50%
IrisCode (*Baseline Method 2*) [30]	30.81%

The experimental results illustrated from the plots in Fig. 5−8 indicate that this deep learning-based approach for cross-spectral iris matching significantly improves the matching accuracy as compared with the algorithms with hand-crafted features in earlier or baseline methods in [66]. It can be observed from these results that the usage of SDH generates outperforming results as compared with those from the joint-Bayesian inference. It can be observed from Fig. 5−9 and Table 5−3 that the binary features generated from the SDH scheme increase the average separation between the genuine and imposter scores, as compared with those from the joint-Bayesian approach. The templates generated from SDH scheme are also significantly compact which can significantly reduce the storage requirements as Table 5−4 shows and also improves the matching speed between such compact templates (Fig. 5−10).

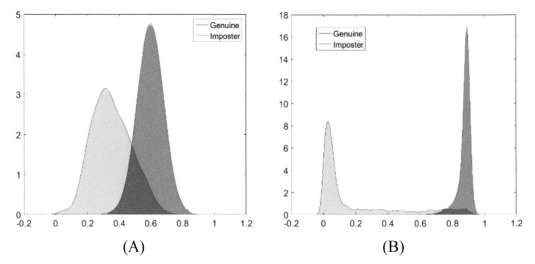

FIGURE 5–9 Match score distributions from PolyU bi-spectral Iris database for (A) CNN with Joint Bayesian and (B) CNN with SDH 1000 bits.

Table 5–3   Comparative DI from best-performing methods on PolyU bi-spectral iris dataset.

Approach	(DI)
CNN-SDH (1000 bits)	2.1275
CNN-Joint Bayesian	1.1943

Table 5–4   Compression ratio with SDH on PolyU bi-spectral iris dataset.

Origin templates (bits)	262,144
Binary vector (bits)	1000
Compression ratio	262.144

It is worth noting that the PolyU bi-spectral iris database provides images from 209 different subjects, but only the images from first 140 different subjects were employed in [66]. Therefore we also investigated comparative cross-spectral iris matching accuracy using the images from *all* the 209 subjects in this database. These experiments generated 4180 $(209 \times 2 \times 10)$ genuine and 4,367,650 $(209 \times 2 \times 10,425)$ imposter scores. The ROC from this set of experiments is shown in Fig. 5–11. It should be noted that as compared to the results in Fig. 5–8, the performance of CNN and SHD has comparatively degraded from EER of 5.39% to EER of 12.41% and this can be attributed to degraded image quality images from about 69 subjects. Such low-quality image samples have been illustrated in Fig. 5–6 and these were also used in this set of experiments.

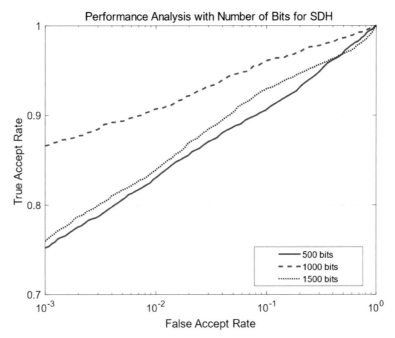

FIGURE 5–10 Performance analysis with number of bits for SDH on PolyU bi-spectral iris database.

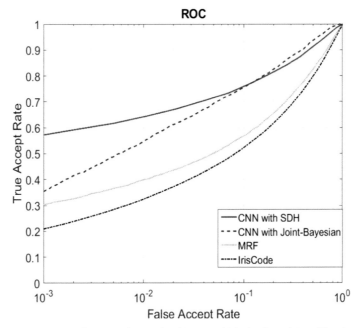

FIGURE 5–11 Comparative ROC performance from PolyU bi-spectral iris database (209 subjects).

5.3.2.2 Cross-eyed cross-spectral iris recognition database

Another set of experiments is performed using the cross-eyed database to ascertain the performance. In this set of experiments, first five instances from every subject are used for the CNN training while the left three instances from all the subjects are employed to test cross-spectral iris matching performance. Such all-to-all matching protocol generates 2160 ($120 \times 2 \times 9$) genuine and 516,240 ($120 \times 2 \times 2151$) impostor match scores for the performance evaluation.

This set of experiments also incorporated CNN with *softmax* cross-entropy loss and the two classification algorithms. The length of feature vector generated from the hashing process is still the same as 1000 bits. Comparative performance using two baseline methods, that is, MRF and the *IrisCode*, is evaluated. The resulting ROCs are shown in Fig. 5−12 and the EER are summarized in Table 5−5. These experimental results indicate that the combination of CNN with *softmax* cross-entropy loss and SDH consistently achieves outperforming results for the cross-spectral iris matching. Fig. 5−13 illustrates the distribution of genuine and impostor match scores to ascertain the influence of SDH scheme. The plots in this figure and the Decidability Index (DI) in Table 5−6 indicate that the usage of SDH improves the average distance between genuine and impostor scores.

The influence of the number of bits for SDH on the matching accuracy for this dataset is also investigated. The test results presented in Fig. 5−14 suggest that the choice of 1000 bits can still offer superior performance and reduction in template size. However, the difference in the performances from the template bit length changes is less significant compared with those for the PolyU bi-spectral iris database. Therefore when the template size is of key importance, 500-bits template size can be the judicious choice for faster template matching.

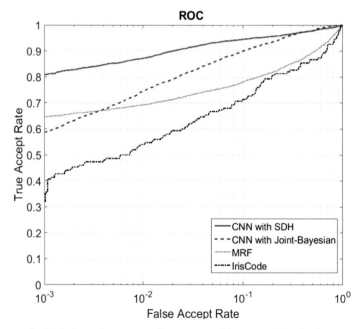

FIGURE 5–12 Comparative ROC plots using cross-eyed cross-spectral iris recognition database.

Table 5–5   Comparative results using cross-eyed-cross-spectral iris recognition database.

Approach	EER
CNN-SDH	6.34%
CNN-Joint Bayesian	10.07%
MRF (*Baseline Method 1*) [66]	18.40%
IrisCode (*Baseline Method 2*)	19.48%

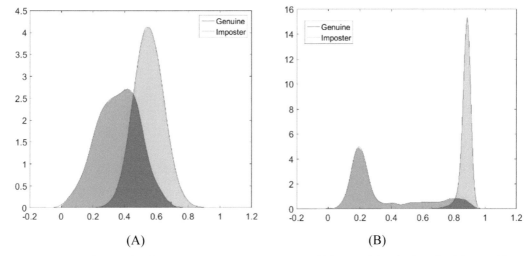

(A)   (B)

FIGURE 5–13 Match score distributions using cross-eyed cross-spectral iris recognition database for (A) CNN with Joint Bayesian and (B) CNN with SDH 1000 bits.

Table 5–6   Comparative DI from best-performing methods on cross-eyed-cross-spectral iris recognition dataset.

Approach	(DI)
CNN-SDH (1000 bits)	2.5346
CNN-Bayesian	1.6257

5.4 Comparisons with other CNN models and hashing methods

The experimental results presented in Section 5.3.2 indicate superior results as compared with the earlier methods presented in the literature* [118] for the cross-spectrum iris recognition. We also perform experiments using other popular networks to comparatively ascertain the performance of the scheme discussed in Section 5.2. The Siamese network and Triplet network are used to ascertain the performance using the *same* training and testing

---

* Reference [66] has provided comparisons with other cross-sensor iris recognition methods, for example, [81], to establish the merit of this approach and therefore these methods are not used as baseline method in this chapter.

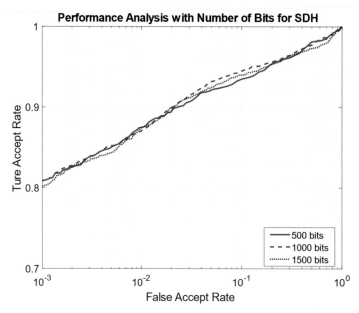

FIGURE 5–14 Performance analysis with number of bits for SDH using cross-eyed cross-spectral iris recognition database.

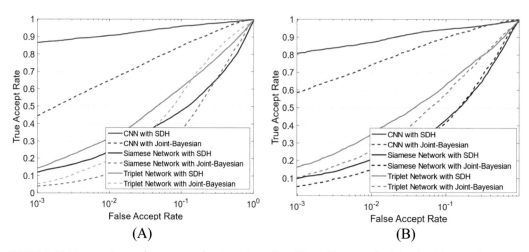

FIGURE 5–15 Comparative performance evaluation using other CNN architectures for (A) PolyU bi-spectral iris database and (B) cross-eye-cross-spectral iris recognition database.

data/protocols as detailed in Section 5.3.2. The results from these experiments using the ROCs are illustrated in Fig. 5–15. Both of these CNNs compute the loss based on the binary labels that indicate genuine or imposter pair rather than the class label used in a typical *soft-max* cross-entropy loss for the network in Fig. 5–2. It may be noted that the dataset used for the training generates a large number of imposter pairs than the number of genuine pairs.

Therefore the triplet loss function in used in these experiments can make it very difficult to span through all the possible cases during the training process. This is a plausible reason for inferior performance from these two architectures, as compared to CNN with *softmax* cross-entropy loss employed during the experiments detailed in Section 5.3.2.

More recent networks have shown impressive learning capability in large-scale image classification as compared to the AlexNet. Therefore we performed new experiments to evaluate the 1000-bits code generated from the SDH using VGG-16 [126] and also using ResNet-50 [108]. To ensure fairness in the comparison, we employed same protocols as detailed in Section 5.3.2. These experimental results are shown in Fig. 5−16 and Table 5−7. The training data available to us for our problem is too small to converge the VGG-16 net and ResNet-50. Therefore we performed the transfer learning by fine-tuning the *caffe* models trained from the *ImageNet* classification, despite the fact that the CNN model in our framework has been trained from scratch. The experimental results in Fig. 5−16 and Table 5−7 indicate that the VGG16 can further improve the performance of the CNN in our framework. However, there are two limitations that should be carefully considered with such alternative. First, VGG16 needs much more parameters as compared with the CNN in our framework (98,596,544 vs 635,650) which can be a burden for many thin-client operations. Secondly, the VGG16 is

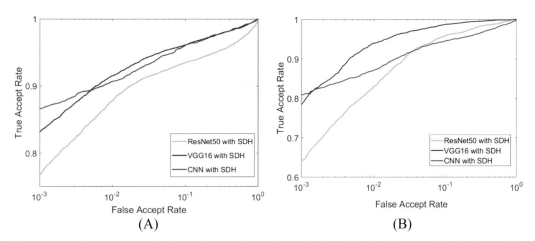

FIGURE 5−16 Different convolutional neural networks testing results from (A) PolyU bi-spectral iris database and (B) cross-eye-cross-spectral iris recognition database.

Table 5−7   Comparative results using the EER from two public databases.

	PolyU bi-spectral iris database	Cross-eye-cross-spectral iris recognition database
CNN with SDH	5.39%	6.34%
VGG16 with SDH	4.85%	3.13%
ResNet50 with SDH	7.17%	6.11%

fine-tuned from the pretrained model and it has already learned diverse features from *ImageNet*, which means the training data is not exactly same and it cannot be considered a fair comparison. We can also note that the *ResNet* performs poorly and this can be attributed due to the overfitting as our experiments indicated that the training loss gets minimized while the classification accuracy approaches to one after about one thousand iterations. The *DenseNet* [112] does not aim to address the overfitting problem, for which some regularization may bring a positive effect, and *ResNet* has already shown to saturated the training accuracy. Therefore *DenseNet* is not expected to further enhance the match accuracy for and was not investigated.

Although our framework focuses on cross-spectrum matching which is a more challenging problem, we also performed the following ablation tests with same spectral data from both databases. Each of the cross-spectral datasets was partitioned into two same-spectral ones and performs the same-spectral matching. The baseline results from the *IrisCode* employed in [66] using Log Gabor filter are also shown in Fig. 5—17. It can be observed these results that our approach outperforms the baseline algorithm in most cases even for the same-spectrum matching. During the NIR matching for the cross-eye-cross-spectral matching, our approach indicates slightly better performance except at the lower end of the high false acceptance. Since this framework is designed to address the cross-spectrum iris matching problem, these additional results also support the generalization capability of this framework for matching the same spectrum iris images.

There are many promising hashing algorithms in the literature, for example, Locality Sensitivity Hashing (LSH) [128], Spectral Hashing (SPH) [129], Kernel LSH (KLSH) [130], Locality-sensitive binary codes from shift-invariant kernels (SKLSH) [131], Kernel-based Supervised Hashing (KSH) [124], Discriminative Binary Code (DBC) [132], and Iterative Quantization (ITQ) [133], and deep supervised hashing (DSH) [134]. It is worth investigating their effectiveness as compared with the SDH and therefore separate experiments were performed. The codes length in these experiments was set to 1000 bits for the fair comparison.

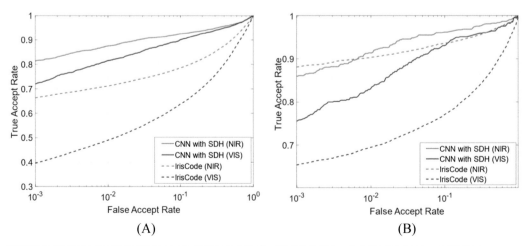

FIGURE 5–17 Same spectrum iris image matching results for (A) PolyU bi-spectral iris database and (B) cross-eye-cross-spectral iris recognition database.

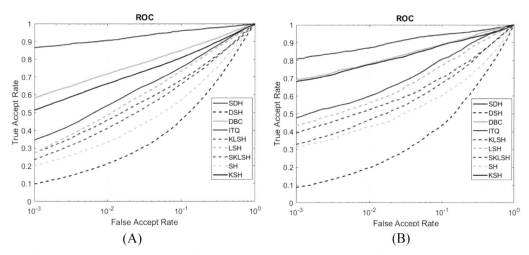

FIGURE 5–18 Comparative results using different hashing algorithms for (A) PolyU bi-spectral iris database and (B) cross-eye-cross-spectral iris recognition database.

Table 5–8   EER from two public datasets using different hashing algorithms.

Approach	PolyU bi-spectral iris database	Cross-eye-cross-spectral iris recognition database
SDH	5.39%	6.34%
LSH	19.13%	17.73%
SPH	26.75%	27.18%
KLSH	26.74%	22.68%
KSH	15.82%	10.77%
DBC	13.24%	10.69%
ITQ	18.15%	15.69%
DSH	31.32%	32.33%

DSH is an end-to-end hashing method that incorporates the deep convolutional neural network to generate the binary codes. The ROC results are shown in Fig. 5−18 and EER details are listed in Table 5−8. It can be observed from these results that the SDH significantly outperforms other methods for the hashing the feature vectors on both the datasets.

5.4.1 Performance evaluation for cross-sensor iris recognition performance

It will be interesting to ascertain the effectiveness SDH based cross-spectrum iris matching framework for more common cross-sensor iris recognition problem. It is also more frequent as the registration data, especially in the large-scale identification programs like Aadhaar [68], are generally acquired from different sensors than those used for the identification. Therefore a set of experiments using such cross-sensor iris image dataset were also performed. This set of experiments utilize *publicly* available UND 2012 cross-sensor database [135]. The train-test protocol is consistent with those for the experiments on the PolyU bi-spectral iris database in Section 5.3.2. We select iris images from the 214 different subjects in this database for the experiments. For every subject, ten instances are used for the training, and other five instances are used for the performance evaluation. Therefore a total of 5350 (214×25) genuine and 1,139,550 $(214 \times 25 \times 213)$ impostor scores are generated from the experiments and the resulting ROC curves are shown in Fig. 5–19. The plots with title "DANBNN after Adaptation" in this figure refers to the performance using the best of method introduced in reference [66]. Table 5–9 summarizes corresponding EER values from the experiments. These results are encouraging and indicate the effectiveness of the cross-spectral iris matching approach considered in Section 5.2.5 over other competing methods.

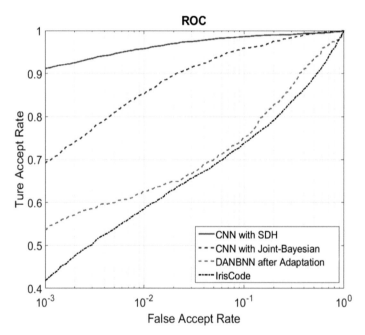

FIGURE 5–19 Comparative ROC plots using UND 2012 cross-sensor iris images database.

Table 5–9 Comparative results from UND 2012 cross-sensor iris images database.

Approach	EER
CNN-SDH	4.50%
CNN-Joint Bayesian	5.91%
DANBNN after adaptation (*Baseline Method 1*) [66]	18.20%
IrisCode (*Baseline Method 2*)	20.52%

5.5 Chapter summary and further enhancements

This Chapter introduces a deep learning-based framework for accurately matching cross-spectrum iris images. We present experimental results using two publicly available cross-spectral iris databases. These results indicate superior performance over the earlier state-of-the-art methods presented in the literature that incorporated hand-crafted features for matching cross-spectrum iris images. This chapter also systematically examined the effectiveness of SDH algorithm for enhancing the match accuracy of cross-spectrum iris images and reducing the template size. The experimental results presented in Section 5.3.2 indicate further improvement in the matching accuracy which is resulting from the improvement in the average distance between the genuine and imposter match scores generated from Hamming distance of the binary features.

The usage of noniris regions in [22] cannot be considered as the iris recognition but the ocular recognition [136] or as iris recognition with the usage of information in the vicinity. The key motivation in this work has been to evaluate cross-spectrum iris recognition capabilities, using the iris regions that are defined in [1] or widely incorporated in the deployed systems at border crossings or the national ID programs. Addition of periocular information, along with those from the iris regions in this work, is expected to further improve [136] cross-spectrum iris match capabilities. It is important to note that it is unreasonable to expect specialized deeply learned neural networks for matching cross-spectrum iris

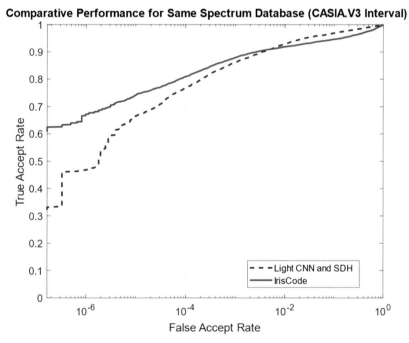

FIGURE 5–20 Comparative performance for matching same spectrum iris images.

images to also deliver outperforming results while matching same spectrum iris images. In this context, the comparative results for matching near-infrared-based images from CASIA-V3 interval database, accessible from weblink in [17], Fig. 5—20. This figure also presents the performance from *IrisCode* using the same set of genuine and impostor comparisons on the same dataset. There have been more recent advances in data-dependent hashing algorithms [137—139] and effectiveness of such algorithms to enhance cross-spectrum iris recognition capabilities can also be the part of further advancements in this area.

6

Semantics-assisted convolutional neural network for accurate periocular recognition

6.1 Introduction

The significance of periocular recognition has been emphasized earlier (in Section 1.5) for achieving accurate iris recognition across a spectrum of real-world applications. The potential of automated periocular recognition, utilizing eye images acquired under less constrained imaging setups, has been demonstrated in earlier studies. However, it is evident that further research and advancement in this area is imperative. Several databases, acquired under visible and near-infrared illuminations, have been introduced in the public domain[1] [17,141−143] and it can be observed that researchers require/use training samples from respective databases, primarily to select or learn the best set of parameters. The performance achieved on these less-constrained databases is encouraging but requires significant advancement to meet the expectations for the deployment. This chapter aims to address these limitations using the power of CNN for periocular recognition in less-constrained environments. This chapter introduces semantics-assisted CNN (SCNN) architecture, which leverages on recovering discriminative features from a limited number of training samples.

This approach for periocular recognition using SCNN does not require training samples from target datasets while achieving outperforming results, which is a crucial advantage over state-of-the-art conventional methods [16,63] that were briefly introduced in Section 6.5 of the first chapter. In our experiments, the SCNN is trained with one database and tested on totally *independent*/separate databases. The testing and training sets have mutually exclusive subjects and highly different image quality as well as imaging conditions and/or equipment. The SCNN architecture can also enable the recovery of more comprehensive periocular features from the limited training samples. Another key advantage of this method is its computational simplicity, that is, our trained model requires much less computational time for feature extraction and matching compared with other methods. The trained models and executable files of this method are made publicly available [144] to enhance reproducibility or evaluate them on new databases. Additionally, the SCNN architecture is not limited to periocular recognition and can be useful for general image classification tasks.

---

[1] Reference [140] provides a comprehensive summary of iris image databases in the public domain.

Iris and Periocular Recognition using Deep Learning. DOI: https://doi.org/10.1016/B978-0-443-27318-6.00008-5

By attaching branch CNN(s) that are trained with semantic supervision from the training data, the SCNN architecture can be easily used to extend and improve existing CNN-based approaches while limiting the general requirement of an increase in training data for such performance improvement. The SCNN enables the deep neural network to fully learn the training data in conjunction with the semantical correlation and therefore can benefit the final classification task, especially when the size of training data is limited to build a very deep network. Moreover, the SCNN architecture is easy to implement, and many public databases often include semantic annotations of their training samples.

6.2 Methodology

The key motivation for this methodology has been to incorporate CNN for the challenging periocular recognition problem due to its known ability to extract comprehensive features from images. In the context of CNN, this section will briefly introduce the theoretical background and then the practical architecture of the the SCNN model. This will then be followed by its application for the accurate periocular recognition problem iusing the sample images similar to those shown in Fig. 6−1.

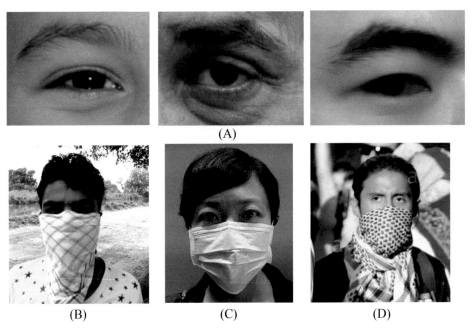

FIGURE 6−1 Sample images depicting the diverse applications of periocular recognition. Its more useful under certain circumstances such as (A) when the iris texture is compromised, or when faces are concealed for reasons such as (B) safeguarding against harsh environmental conditions, (C) during pandemic situations requiring face mask coverings, or (D) during the violent protests or riots.

6.2.1 Backbone network architecture for feature extraction

CNN is a biologically inspired variant of multilayer perceptron (MLP) and is well-known as one of the typical deep learning architectures. It is usually composed of convolution layers, pooling layers, and fully connected (FC) layers. At the output of each layer, there is often a nonlinear activation function, This work adopts the basic CNN architecture similar to AlexNet [127] and is shown in Fig. 6−2. The input image is passed through several convolutional units and then a few FC layers. The output of the last FC layer with N (number of classes) nodes would represent probabilistic prediction to the class labels.

Each of the convolution units is composed of three components—a convolution layer, a max-pooling layer, and a ReLU activation function, as can be observed from the backbone network architecture in Fig. 6−2. For the convolutional layer, each channel of its output is computed as:

$$y^{(i)} = \sum_j (\boldsymbol{b}^{(ij)} + \boldsymbol{k}^{(ij)} * \boldsymbol{x}^j) \tag{6-1}$$

where $\boldsymbol{y}^{(i)}$ is the ith channel of the output map, $\boldsymbol{x}^{(j)}$ is the jth channel of the input map, $\mathbf{b}^{(ij)}$ is called the bias term, $\boldsymbol{k}^{(ij)}$ is the convolution kernel between and $\boldsymbol{x}^{(j)}$, and the symbol * here denotes conventional 2D convolution operation. The parameters and $\boldsymbol{k}^{(ij)}$ will be learned by the back-propagation process during the network training. Therefore the convolution kernels are learned to automatically recover the most useful features that are discriminative among different subjects.

The pooling layer extracts one maximum or average value from each patch of the input channel. In this implementation, we use max-pooling with nonoverlapping patches. As a result, the input maps, after convolution, are down-sampled with a scale determined by the pooling kernel. The pooling operation aggregates low-level features from the input to high-level representation and thus could achieve spatial invariance among different samples.

At the output of each pooling layer and the first FC layer, for example, L7 in Fig. 6−2, we select the ReLU as the activation function:

$$y'_i = \max(y_i, 0) \tag{6-2}$$

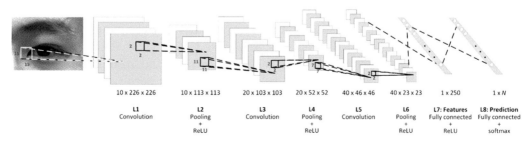

FIGURE 6–2 Architecture of the backbone deep convolutional neural network for SCNN.

The ReLU activation ensures the nonlinearity of the feature extraction process and is expected to be more efficient for training, as compared with the conventional activation functions like sigmoid or tanh employed in many other applications [145].

The FC layers process the input similarly to in any conventional neural network:

$$y_i = b_i + \sum_j x_j \cdot w_{ij} \qquad (6-3)$$

where x_j is the jth element of the vectorized input map to the current layer and y_i is the ith element of the output map, which is also a vector. b_i and w_{ij} are elements of the bias and weights to be learned through training. The last FC layer, as usually configured in classification problem, is not followed by ReLU but a *softmax* function:

$$y_i'' = \frac{e^{y_i}}{\sum_j e^{y_j}} \qquad (6-4)$$

The use of *softmax* function in the final output of the network results in a $1 \times N$ vector with positive elements which are summed up to one. Each element then is treated as the probabilistic prediction of the class label. The cross-entropy loss function is to be minimized, which is formulated as:

$$L(\mathbf{y}'') = -\log y_t'' \qquad (6-5)$$

where t is the ground truth label of the training sample. The loss function is minimized via back-propagation so that the predictions of the ground truth class of the training samples will approach unity.

6.2.2 Limitations of contemporary CNN-based methods

To enhance the performance of CNN-based methods, two common approaches are often employed. First, increasing the depth and comprehensiveness of the network by adding more layers is a popular method. In addition, incorporating a larger amount of labeled training data is crucial, considering CNN's typical supervised training nature. For instance, EfficientNet [146,147] boasts an impressive 342 layers, and Microsoft's deep network utilizes 152 layers [108]. However, training such deep networks poses challenges for researchers and small firms or startups due to the lack of enough computational power. Moreover, as networks grow deeper, the demand for training data also escalates. Unfortunately, in many research domains, obtaining a sufficient number of labeled training samples, such as in the case of ImageNet [148], can be a difficult task. Table 6−1 provides examples of several typical deep learning-based approaches and their employed training data. In reference [73] in Table 6−1, for instance, where the developed CNN is not very deep (nine layers), a total of ∼200,000 face images from more than 10,000 people were used for training to achieve superior performance. However, for other popular biometrics modalities like iris or periocular, there is currently no single public database with that many images. There are also privacy-related concerns associated with the acquisition and sharing of large-scale iris image

Table 6–1 Examples of deep learning-based models and their indicative number of training images.

References	Task	Size of training data	
		No. of classes	No. of samples
[146]	Image classification	18,000	300,000,000
[150]	Image classification	210,000	14,000,000
[90]	Image classification	1000	1,281,167
[73]	Face recognition	10,177	202,599
[151]	Face recognition	4030	4,400,000

databases, and new regulations, such as the GDPR [149], have restricted the development or sharing of such databases.

Therefore there is strong motivation to enhance the performance of existing CNN-based architecture in another way—to enhance CNN with supervision from explicit semantic information. When human recognizes objects, for example, while recognizing a face image, one would analyze not only the overall visual pattern but also the semantic information, such as gender, ethnicity, and age, to judge whether the face image belongs to a certain known person. Therefore it is reasonable to believe that semantic information is helpful for the visual identification task. For a CNN that is trained with the identity label only, it is possible that the network is already capable of acquiring semantic information. For instance, a popular deep learning model for face recognition, *DeepID2 +* [152], researchers discovered that although the network was trained using subject identities, certain neurons turn out to exhibit selectiveness to attributes like gender, ethnicity, age, etc. These semantic attributes contribute to discriminating identities [152]. However, such useful semantic information is expected to be *implicitly* learned by CNN. It is not easy to answer the following questions:

- How many types of semantic information can be acquired? Since the discriminative capacity of a certain CNN is limited, we cannot guarantee that all the semantic information we prefer to have has already been included.
- To what extent the semantic information can be analyzed by the trained CNN? Does it really help in the final identification task, or could it be further improved?

The above problems arise due to the nature of training popularly employed for the CNN, that is, the loss function is usually only related to the class labels. Therefore it is hard to reveal how semantic information can be *implicitly* acquired. To address these challenges, we can empower CNN with the ability to analyze semantic information *explicitly*. The idea is very simple and is illustrated in Fig. 6−3.

6.2.3 Semantics-assisted convolution neural network

As illustrated in Fig. 6−3, we simply add a branch, which is also a CNN, to the existing CNN. The attached CNN is not trained using the identity of the training data but the semantic groups.

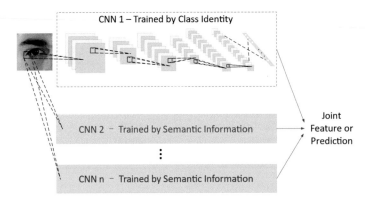

FIGURE 6–3 Semantics-assisted CNN (SCNN): the first branch CNN is trained by the label of the intended tasks, and other branch CNNs are trained using different semantic information. These ranches are jointly used to generate a comprehensive feature representation for the unknown periocular image and generate a more reliable match score.

For example, we could train CNN2 using the gender information of the training sample, that is, let CNN2 be able to estimate the gender instead of identity and train CNN3 using the ethnicity information. After the CNNs are trained, we can combine the output of each CNN in the way of feature fusion. We refer to such an extended architecture of the CNN as SCNN. Despite the simplicity of this idea, it can convincingly enhance the original CNN by adding more discriminative power to it, which has been shown from the experiments described in Section 6.3. Theoretically, the SCNN has the following benefits:

- Instead of letting the semantic information be learned from the identities by the CNN in an unpredictable and uncontrollable way, SCNN allows us to *explicitly* recover the preferred semantic information that can be helpful for the identification task. As a result, the feature representation from the SCNN is accompanied by more reliable semantic information that is closer to the mechanism in the human visual system.
- The training scheme for SCNN can reuse the same set of training data but just be labeled in another way than the simple identities. Since the labeling scheme is variable, the branches of SCNN learn the training data from different points of view, which is equivalent to increasing the data volume without really adding the number of training samples. This can relax the constraints on the requirements of enormous training data for deep neural networks to some extent, that is, instead of pursuing superior performance from a single CNN, we enhance the joint performance of branches of CNNs with fewer amounts of training data.
- The SCNN architecture and training scheme are naturally compatible with most of the existing CNN-based approaches. What we need is just to train some independent CNNs with semantic grouping labels and judiciously combine the features from multiple CNNs to benefit from such training, as the semantic annotations of training samples are also available for many public databases. In addition, the architecture of SCNN is highly friendly for parallel computing platforms.

6.3 Matching periocular images using SCNN

CNNs have proven to be highly successful in a range of face recognition applications, with numerous methods in the literature demonstrating exceptional performance [73,151,153]. Considering the fact that the periocular region encompasses vital facial components and harbors structural cues like eyebrows, eyelids, and eye ducts, it is a rational assumption that CNNs can be highly effective for periocular recognition. Unfortunately, such progress is impeded by the scarcity of large-scale periocular image databases, which are typically indispensable for adequately training deep neural networks. Consequently, we took it upon ourselves to develop and explore SCNN, a novel approach tailored specifically to address the challenges of accurately matching the periocular images.

6.3.1 Network architecture and supervision for accurate matching

The detailed SCNN structure used for accurately matching the periocular images is illustrated in Fig. 6−4. To ascertain the impact of adding a branch to an existing CNN, we simply designed one branch that is trained with semantic information, denoted as CNN2 in Fig. 6−4. While CNN1 is like the ones commonly trained with the subject identities from the training samples, CNN2 is designated to be trained with the side (left or right) and the gender information. More specifically, we labeled the training data as follows, also shown in Fig. 6−5:

    0—Left and male
    1—Right and male
    2—Left and female
    3—Right and female

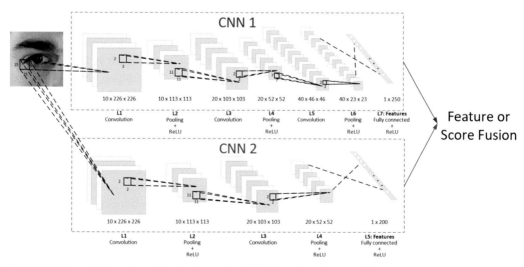

FIGURE 6–4 Consolidation of multiple features using SCNN for periocular recognition.

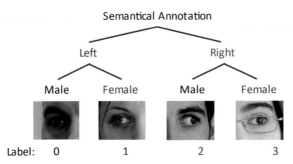

FIGURE 6–5 Semantical labeling employed to train the second CNN, that is, CNN2.

The reason for using left/right and gender information is that humans also tend to incorporate such judgment by visually inspecting the presented periocular images, although such accuracy may not reach a cent percent level. Therefore there is some scientific basis to believe that CNN can learn to distinguish the above semantic information from the periocular patterns and assist in the identification task. Another reason for using gender information is that the genders of subjects are often included in the metadata of many publicly available datasets, such as UBIPR [143]. Therefore we can directly use those labels to train CNN2. Other possible and useful semantic information includes iris color (light/dark), ethnicity, the shape of the eyebrow, etc.

Using such additional semantic information to supervise the network makes the overall architecture and learning process of SCNN similar to multilabel learning [154] to some extent. Nonetheless, there exists a fundamental distinction: our model introduces semantic labeling to aid and augment the prediction of subject identity labels, signifying their uneven importance, whereas traditional multilabel learning typically assumes equal significance among multiple labels. In addition, the learning processes of identities and other semantic information are separately undertaken to maximally ensure the explicitness of semantic learning and compatibility to other CNN-based models, while in general multilabel learning, features are usually jointly learned for predicting different labels. Nevertheless, in spite of the differentiation between the identity labels and other supportive labels, the semantic learning process (e.g., CNN2 itself) can also be conducted in the manner of multilabel learning alternatively.

6.3.2 Network training protocols and data augmentation

Among the original training samples, the last sample of each subject is selected to form the validation set, which is tested in every certain number of iterations to observe whether the training process is converging in the right direction or not. Furthermore, it is observed that the periocular images from the training set are well aligned and scaled to a similar level, while the samples from independent test datasets and real applications may have misalignments and scale variations. Such inconsistency can also be observed from the image samples in Fig. 6–6.

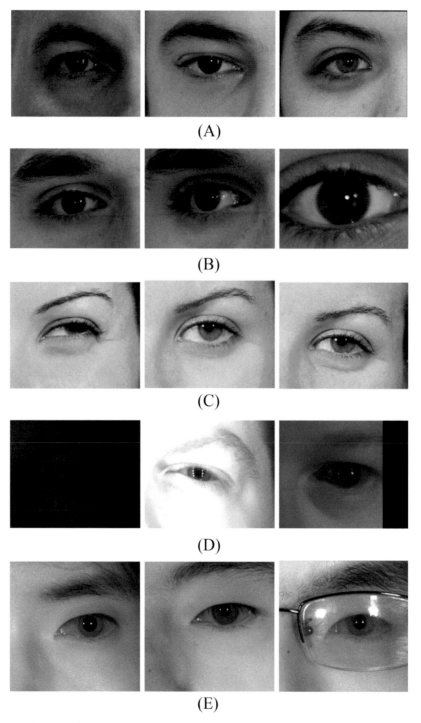

FIGURE 6–6 Sample images from the public databases that were employed during the experimentation: (A) UBIPR [143], (B) UBIRIS.v2 [199], (C) FRGC [141], (D) FOCS [142], (E) CASIA.v4-distance [17] Scale changes and misalignments are common for the images used during the performance evaluation.

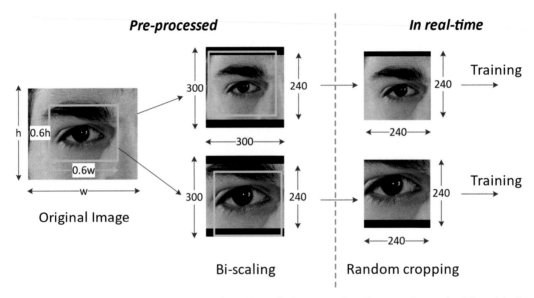

FIGURE 6–7 Illustration for the data augmentation using scale changes and random cropping. Each of the original images is augmented to two samples with different scales, and each augmented sample is cropped by a smaller window that is randomly placed before entering the network for each epoch of the training process.

If the deep network is trained with well-aligned and scaled images, it may not be effectively generalized to other datasets or data acquired by real applications. To address such problems, we first augmented the training data with a different scale to simulate scale inconsistency in the test environment. Then, we applied random cropping during the training process to ensure that the network could accommodate spatial variations among the periocular images. The scale augmentation and random cropping process is also illustrated in Fig. 6–7. As can be observed from this figure, each of the original input images in the training set is automatically cropped from its center with a size of $0.6w \times 0.6h$ where w and h represent its *original* width and height, respectively. The original images and their cropped patch are resized to 300×240 and then padded with symmetric edges filled with zeroes, to the size of 300×300. Therefore one original periocular image will generate two training samples. As a result, we have 6270 samples for training and 448 samples for validation while training for each side of the periocular images. Furthermore, during the training process, each training sample would be cropped by a 240×240 window which is randomly placed within the image region before entering the first layer of the network. Such a randomized cropping process from one training sample could produce abundant samples that have randomized misalignments with others. In this way, the network can be enforced to learn to extract features that are robust to misalignments.

6.3.3 Visualization of network kernels for trained SCNN

Once the networks have been trained, CNN1 is expected to lock into features that are directly relevant to the subject identities, while CNN2 is expected to analyze the features that are

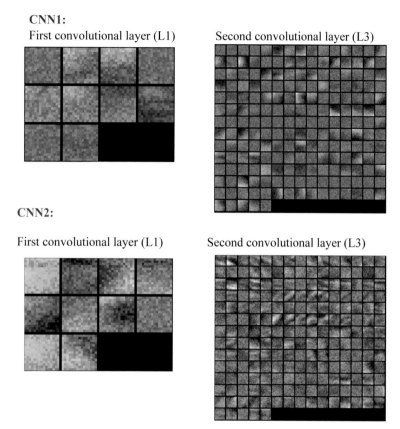

CNN1:

First convolutional layer (L1)   Second convolutional layer (L3)

CNN2:

First convolutional layer (L1)   Second convolutional layer (L3)

FIGURE 6–8 Visualization of the filter kernels from the first two convolutional layers of trained networks, that is, CNN1 and CNN2, respectively.

more related to the side and the gender difference. In order to observe the difference among features extracted by the two CNNs, we have visualized the filter kernels from the first two convolutional layers of trained CNN1 and CNN2 in Fig. 6–8.

6.3.4 Match score generation from feature vectors

The CNNs we use are trained in a classification protocol, that is, the category or identity of the input data is known and fixed. Therefore this network can be directly used in some classification or identification tasks. However, in biometrics, one-to-one matching for probably unseen subjects is the key problem and needs to be evaluated. Therefore we need to generalize the trained model to separate subjects that are not included in the training set and formulate a one-to-one matching scheme.

In this implementation, we use the output of the second last layer (L7 in CNN1 and L5 in CNN2) as the feature representation of the input data. While the last layer represents the class prediction during the training process, the second last layer should contain the most relevant and aggregated information that can contribute to distinguishing the classes or identities. Therefore it is reasonable to use the output of the second last layer as the feature representation and generalize the model to unseen subjects. Once we get the layer output vectors, we first normalize them by l^2 norm, then apply PCA to reduce the dimensionality of the vector. For the SCNN architecture, we simply concatenate the two independently normalized output vectors to form a longer vector before PCA. In our experiments, the dimension of output vectors after PCA is set to 80 for both the single CNN and SCNN cases. Then the joint Bayesian scheme [119] is utilized to predict the similarity between a pair of feature vectors. The joint Bayesian is primarily designed for face verification, in which a face (equivalent to the periocular feature vector here) is represented by:

$$f = \mu + \varepsilon \tag{6-6}$$

where f is the observation, in this paper the feature vector after PCA, μ is the identity of the subject, and ε is the intraclass variation. μ and ε are assumed to be two independent Gaussian variables following $N(0, S_\mu)$ and $N(0, S_\varepsilon)$, respectively, and then, the covariance of two observation is:

$$\text{cov}(f_1, f_2) = \text{cov}(\mu_1, \mu_2) + \text{cov}(\varepsilon_1, \varepsilon_2) \tag{6-7}$$

The joint distribution of a pair of observations $\{f_1, f_2\}$ is considered. Let H_I denote the intraperson hypothesis indicating that two observations are from the same person, and H_E the extra-person hypothesis. Under H_I, since μ_1 and μ_2 are the same, ε_1 and ε_2 are independent, the covariance matrix of the distribution $P(f_1, f_2|H_I)$ is:

$$\Sigma_I = \begin{bmatrix} S_\mu + S_\varepsilon & S_\mu \\ S_\mu & S_\mu + S_\varepsilon \end{bmatrix} \tag{6-8}$$

On the other hand, under H_E, μ_1 and μ_2 are also independent; therefore the covariance matrix has become:

$$\Sigma_I = \begin{bmatrix} S_\mu + S_\varepsilon & 0 \\ 0 & S_\mu + S_\varepsilon \end{bmatrix} \tag{6-9}$$

With above conditional joint probabilities, the log likelihood ratio which tells the difference between intra- and extraperson probabilities, can be obtained in a closed form:

$$r(f_1, f_2) = \frac{P(f_1, f_2|H_I)}{P(f_1, f_2|H_E)} = f_1^T A f_1 + f_2^T A f_2 - 2f_1^T G f_2 \tag{6-10}$$

where

$$A = (S_\mu + S_\varepsilon) - (F + G) \tag{6-11}$$

$$\begin{bmatrix} F + G & G \\ G & F + G \end{bmatrix} = \begin{bmatrix} S_\mu + S_\varepsilon & S_\mu \\ S_\mu & S_\mu + S_\varepsilon \end{bmatrix}^{-1} \tag{6-12}$$

The covariance matrix S_μ and S_ε can be estimated using an EM-based algorithm as detailed in [119], and the log-likelihood ratio $r(f_1, f_2)$ is used as the similarity score in our one-to-one matching scenario.

6.4 Experiments and results

In this section, we provide the details of the experiments and analyze the results. The experimental details on the periocular identification are first provided and this is followed by details on supporting experiments for the image classification.

6.4.1 Periocular recognition

6.4.1.1 Database organization and match protocols

We use the following publicly available databases for the experimental evaluation. Two different databases were employed for training the deep neural networks and three separate databases were employed for the performance evaluation (test).

6.4.1.1.1 UBIPR [143] (for network training)

We employed the UBIPR periocular database [155] for training the SCNN for the visible spectrum. This database originally contains 5126 images for each of left and right periocular regions from 344 subjects. However, we are also employing a subset of UBIRIS.v2 database [19] for separate test experiments, which has some overlapping subjects with the UBIPR database. In order to ensure that subjects of training set and testing set are mutually exclusive, we removed these overlapping subjects from UBIPR database before we perform training on the network. As a result, we only have 3359 periocular images from each of the two sides of 224 subjects. Such a scale is relatively small as compared with those in the training protocols in other typical deep learning work like ImageNet [114] or LFW [156]. Therefore the application scenario is good for validating the ability of SCNN for learning comprehensive information from a limited size of training data.

6.4.1.1.2 UBIRIS.v2 [19]

The UBIRIS.v2 database is primarily released for the evaluation of at-a-distance iris segmentation and recognition algorithms under visible illumination and challenging imaging environment. Since the eye images in this database contain surrounding regions of the eye, it is possible to perform periocular recognition on the UBIRIS.v2 database. Similar in [16], we use a subset of 1,000 images from this database that is released in NICE.I competition [157]. This subset contains left and right eye images together from 161 subjects that are captured from 3 to 8 m, bringing serious scale inconsistency.

Some images only contain the eye region without eyebrow and other surrounding texture which makes the task of periocular recognition highly challenging. Some sample images are shown in Fig. 6–6B.

6.4.1.1.3 FRGC [141]

The dataset of Face Recognition Grand Challenge (FRGC) is released by the National Institute of Standards and Technology (NIST) and has been primarily for the evaluation of new algorithms for the automated face recognition. Similar to [16], we automatically extracted the periocular region from the original face images of FRGC using publicly available face and eye detector [83,158]. A subset of 540 right eye images from 163 subjects, the same as also the ones used in [16], were employed in the experiments. Some sample images from [141] are reproduced in Fig. 6–6C.

6.4.1.1.4 FOCS [142] (for network training, performance evaluation)

The Face and Ocular Challenge Series (FOCS) dataset is also released by NIST and contains face, ocular images, and videos. We employed the "OcularStillChallenge1" section, which consists of 4792 left and 4789 right periocular images from 136 subjects that are cropped from face video clips acquired under near-infrared (NIR) spectrum. The periocular samples from this dataset, as shown in Fig. 6–6D, suffer from serious illumination inconsistency and misalignments, therefore this dataset is considered highly challenging. We used 3262 left and 3259 right periocular images of the first 80 subjects to train the CNNs and used the remaining images from 56 subjects for testing. Again, such a scale of training samples and subjects is small compared with other typical deep-learning tasks.

6.4.1.1.5 CASIA.v4-distance [17]

CASIA.v4 is the first publicly available long-range iris and face database acquired under NIR illumination, which was released by the Center for Biometrics and Security Research (CBSR) from the Chinese Academy of Sciences (CASIA). The full database contains 2,567 images from 142 subjects in a single session. The standoff distance of the subjects to the camera is from 3 m away. Similar to FRGC, we used a publicly available eye detector [83,158] to automatically segment left periocular images which are used in our experiments. The first eight samples of each subject, excluding a few badly segmented images, were used for the periocular matching experiment.

Above datasets were selected for evaluation because of the availability of periocular images acquired under less constrained environments that are close to real-world scenarios. The selected subsets from FRGC and UBIRIS.v2 contain multisession data and exhibit obvious scale/illumunation variation.

Samples in FOCS database suffer from significant illumination degradation and misalignment. Images from CASIA.v4-distance are more consistent than the other three databases, but were acquired at a distance and some contain artifacts like glasses and/or hair, therefore also represent less constrained scenarios. In addition, networks for visible and NIR spectrums were trained separately due to the significant difference between the image properties.

It is important to clarify that during these reproducible [144] experiments, the SCNN is tested in totally *cross-database* manner, that is, not only the subjects from the training and test set sets are totally separated, the databases themselves are independent from training for *three sets* of experiments. However, the methods we are going to compare with, [16] and [63], both require some samples of the target databases for the training. To compare with

Table 6–2 Organization of databases for network training and performance evaluation.

Spectrum	Visible			Near infrared (NIR)		
Division	Training set	Test set		Training set	Test set	
Dataset	UBIPR	UBIRIS.v2	FRGC	FOCS	FOCS	CASIA.v4-distance
Standoff distance	4–8 m	3–8 m	N/A	N/A	N/A	≥3 m
No. of subjects[a]	224	171(19/152)	163 (13/150)	80	56	141 (10/131)
No. of images[a]	Left: 3359 right: 3359	1000 (96/904)	540 (40/500)	Left: 3262 right: 3259	1530	1077 (79/998)

[a]The bracket (*a*/*b*) in the above last two rows indicates that *a* subjects or images were used for training for method in [16] and [63] (not for SCNN method), remaining *b* subjects or images were used for test or performance evaluation.

the best performance of [16] and [63] as well as to ensure the fairness in such comparison, we still divide the target datasets into training and testing sets, as summarized in Table 6–2. For example, 96 samples of the first 19 subjects in UBIRIS.v2 were used to train the models [16] and [63], the remaining were used for test as in [16,63] and also for our method. Such a configuration is highly disadvantageous to our methods because the interdatabase variance is always a key factor for the performance of all learning-based methods. However, our method has still been able to achieve outperforming results as detailed later.

We perform periocular matching using the all-to-all protocol, that is, every image is matched to all the other images in the testing set, and all the generated matching scores are taken into calculation of the ROC curve. Such a protocol is considered to be highly challenging because one bad sample may result in several poor genuine scores, which drops the overall matching performance.

6.4.2 Effectiveness of semantic cues in matching periocular images

We first examine the impact of the added branch that has been trained with the semantic information. We have compared the performance of a single CNN, that is, only CNN1 in Fig. 6–3, with the performance of the extended SCNN. The results from the verification experiments are illustrated in Fig. 6–9.

We can observe from Fig. 6–9 that the SCNN consistently achieves better performance than that of the original or single CNN. This observation suggests that the newly added CNN2 which is trained with semantic supervision has been successful in contributing to some useful information that is not reinforced in CNN1, and therefore improving the overall discriminative power of the network. In theory, we can add more branches that are trained with different semantic information (e.g., iris color) to further improve the final recognition accuracy. However, the need for computational power would also increase and the trade-off may need to be made according to the applications. In our example, since CNN2 shown in Fig. 6–4 has a relatively simplified structure, the additional training cost is minor.

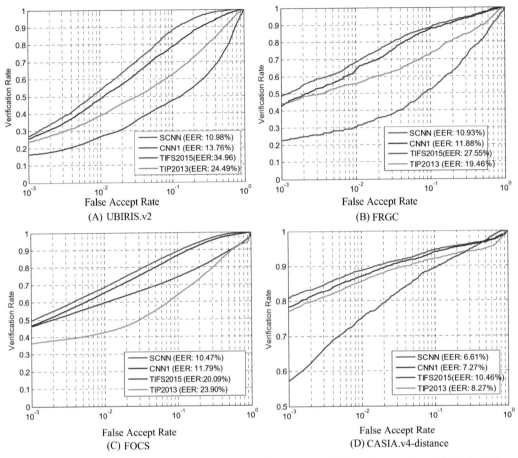

FIGURE 6–9 Comparative ROC curves of the periocular verification using SCNN and comparison with single CNN and other state-of-the-art methods for different databases.

6.4.3 Comparisons with earlier work on periocular recognition

We also compared the performance of our approach with state-of-the-art approaches [16,63] on the periocular recognition problem. While [16] is our previous work, we have carefully implemented the methods in [63] with the help of the original authors. The test protocols were kept exactly the same for different approaches during the experimental process, and therefore the comparisons of ROC/CMC curves are fair. However, several factors can be firstly clarified here to ensure clarity in understanding the experimental comparisons.

A. For UBIRIS.v2, we use the 1000 images set that was employed for the NICE.I competition. This subset is the same as was used in [16] but different from the one in [63]. In [63], test images were gathered from the full dataset, but only those acquired from 6 to 8 m were used, while the 1000-image set in [16] included samples acquired from 3 to 8 m. Due to the relatively consistent imaging distance, the subset used in [63] involves much less scale variance than those in [16] and also in this paper. As a result, the performance from our experiment using the exact method in [63] is not reproduced as well as what appears to be in [63], and this is reasonable due to the difference in the selection of images as explained above.

B. For FRGC, we also used the same subset as in [16] but different from the one used in [63]. As described before, the subset we used contains 540 periocular images, which were *automatically* segmented from the original face images and therefore may suffer from some misalignment. Moreover, images in this subset were acquired from *various sessions* with certain time-lapse and different imaging environments, which increases the difficulty for accurate recognition. However, the subset used in [63] only consists of images captured in consistent illumination and background in a *single session*, and the periocular regions were *manually* segmented. Therefore it is also a reasonable explanation for the degradation in performance in our reproduced results over the ones shown in [63] using the manual segmentation.

C. For FOCS, we used fixed division of training and testing sets, as shown in Table 6−2, while the original setup in [63] used fivefold cross-validation for the entire dataset. Although the subsets used in our experiment and their original experiment are not exactly the same, the quality of images is observed to be quite similar. Therefore these reproduced results are very close to those appearing in reference [63].

The verification results (ROC) for the above comparisons are also shown in Fig. 6−9, while the identification results (CMC) are shown in Fig. 6−10. In these figures, the Reference TIP 2013 and TIFS 2015 refer to the baseline methods in [16] and [63] respectively. It can be observed from the experimental results in these two figures that the proposed approach using SCNN consistently outperforms the two state-of-the-art non-deep learning based approaches.

To ascertain the statistical significance of the enhancements, the significance test for the ROC curves using the method described in [159], which judges from the area under the curve (AUC), was also performed. Table 6−3 shows the significance level (p-value) of the difference of the SCNN-based method over the comparative methods [16] and [63]. The results indicate that, by the commonly used confidence level of 95%, our approach significantly outperforms these two methods (p-value <0.05) on all the employed datasets. It may be noted that [63] performed poorly on the UBIRIS.v2 set because it adopts the patch-based matching scheme while, as explained above, the 1000-image set of UBIRIS.v2 used in our experiment suffers from serious scale variations among the samples, which results in significant loss of patch correspondence. The approach from [16], which uses DSIFT features, is more robust to scale variance, however, the extraction of DSIFT feature is especially time-consuming. In contrast, SCNN not only performs better than both of the baseline approaches on different databases but is also computationally simpler for deployment using the trained network. Table 6−4 presents the summary of the average time required for the feature extraction for the nondeep learning-based state-of-the-art approaches that were considered during our evaluation. These tests were performed using the Matlab wrapper and C + + implementation running on

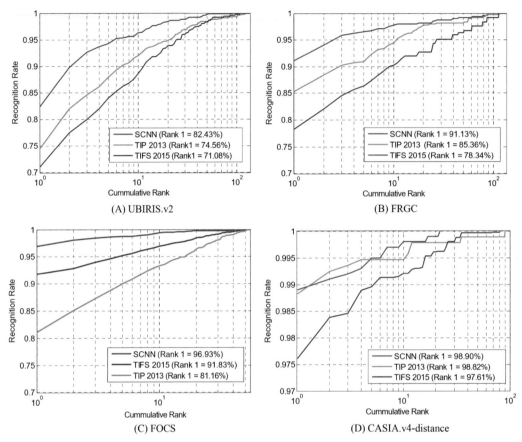

FIGURE 6.10 Comparative CMC curves of the periocular recognition using SCNN with state-of-the-art conventional (nondeep learning based) methods on different databases.

Table 6–3   Results of significance test for comparison of ROCs using method in [159].

	p-value			
Comparison	UBIRIS.v2	FRGC	CASIA.v4-distance	FOCS
SCNN and TIP2013 [16]	$<1e-4$	$<1e-4$	$<1e-4$	$<1e-4$
SCNN and TIFS2015 [63]	$<1e-4$	$<1e-4$	$<1e-4$	$<1e-4$

p-value indicates the probability of the null hypothesis that two methods have no difference statistically.
*The computed z-statistics are too large that the corresponding p-values exceed double precision, therefore expressed as $<1e-4$.

a computer with Linux OS, 16 GB RAM, 3.4 GHz Intel Core i7−4770 CPU (4 cores) and NVIDIA GeForce GTX 670 GPU. It can be observed that the SCNN based approach is much faster due to the straightforward architecture, and the use of more advanced GPU, for example, RTX 4090, can dramatically reduce the computational time.

Table 6–4 Comparison of time required to match two periocular images by different approaches, from Matlab implementation running on a computer with Linux OS, 16 GB RAM, 3.4 GHz Intel i7−4770 CPU (4 cores) and NVIDIA GeForce GTX 670 GPU.

Approach	Major time-consuming operations	Matching time (s)	
		GPU	CPU
SCNN	convolution, matrix multiplication	0.013	0.183
TIP'2013 [16]	DSIFT feature extraction, K-means clustering	/	15.478
TIFS'2015 [63]	Gabor feature extraction, correlation filter matching	/	1.441

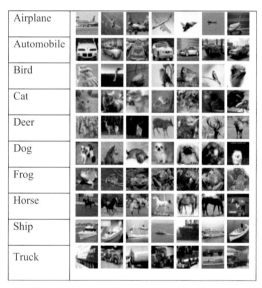

FIGURE 6–11 Sample images from each class of CIFAR-10 dataset [160].

6.4.4 Image classification

To examine that the proposed SCNN architecture is not only effective for the periocular recognition but can also be useful for more general problems, we performed experiment for image classification on the CIFAR-10 dataset [160].

The CIFAR-10 dataset contains 60,000, 32×32 color images from 10 classes. Among these images, 50,000 images are for training and 10,000 are for testing. Fig. 6−11 shows some randomly selected samples from each class. As we can see from Fig. 6−11, although the number of classes is not large, the intraclass variation is significant and the resolution is also smaller, which brings certain challenge for classifying those images. The CIFAR-10 has therefore emerged as a popular dataset for evaluating image classification algorithms along with others like ImageNet and CIFAR-100, etc.

Since the SCNN is developed to enhance existing CNN-based approaches, we select a baseline CNN to ascertain the improvement. We adopt the CNN originated from Krizhevsky's cuda-convnet [161], re-implemented and introduced in the Caffe tutorial [162]. Although the selected CNN is not the state-of-the for CIFAR-10 in terms of performance, we chose it because this model is publicly available under Caffe, the deep learning framework employed in the paper, and it is also quick to train. For simple annotation, we refer to this network as *cuda-convnet*. By following the tutorial, we can quickly get an accuracy of about 75% on the CIFAR-10 test set. Then, we trained a branch CNN to learn the semantic features of the images in CIFAR-10 to build the SCNN architecture. We define one possible groups of semantic information for the classes in the CIFAR-10 dataset as follows, also shown in Fig. 6−12.

$$
\begin{cases}
\text{Artificial} & \begin{cases} \text{rectangular, has wheel: (automobile, truck)} \\ \text{no/invisible wheel: (airplane, ship)} \end{cases} \\
\text{Natural} & \begin{cases} \text{round, short: (cat, dog, bird, frog)} \\ \text{slim, long: (deer, horse)} \end{cases}
\end{cases}
$$

With the above division, the entire dataset is grouped into four semantical classes. It may be noted that this is not the unique or the optimal division, but it is an easy-to-understand scheme to start with. To obtain a branch CNN that was trained to acquire the above semantic features, we simply duplicate the structure of the base cuda-convnet but replace the last FC layer having 10 neurons with a new FC layer with four neurons, since the task now is to recognize the four semantic groups. We then just repeat, as described in Caffe tutorial, but train the new network with newly labeled data. This new CNN is referred here as as cuda-convnet-s. Again, the above configuration is made because of the ease to execute and one has many choices for actual applications. We then built an SCNN with the architecture as in Fig. 6−13. As shown in this figure, we combine the branch CNN and the original one to obtain an extended structure. The components highlighted in red are retrained after the combination to aggregate the long concatenated features, and this process can be considered as a kind of finetuning. Since the number of layers to be retrained is small, the finetuning is very fast. Table 6−5 shows the classification results on the test set using the original cuda-convnet and the extended SCNN.

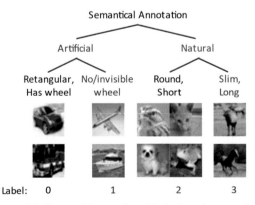

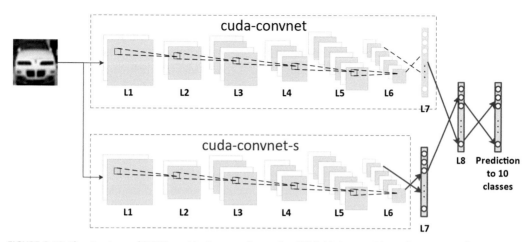

FIGURE 6–13 The structure of SCNN used in the experiment for CIFAR-10 dataset. The cuda-convnet is from the original Caffe tutorial, and the cuda-convnet-s is newly trained by the semantic information.

Table 6–5 Comparative results of classification for the CIFAR-10 testing set using original cuda-convnet and the SCNN enhancement on the cuda-convnet.

Approach	Accuracy
Cuda-convnet	74.95%
Cuda-convnet-SCNN	77.06%

We can observe from the results that the proposed SCNN can achieve an improvement of 2.11% over the original result. Although this may not be considered a very large improvement, the achieved results reinforce the motivation for SCNN to make solid and consistent enhancement on existing CNN-based approaches, especially for the scenario when the training data may not be enough to feed a complex network. In the CIFAR-10 dataset, the number of images per class is actually quite large and therefore the effect of SCNN is not significant, but it still offers a noticeable improvement with minor addition in the complexity. Moreover, as discussed above, the experimental setup can be easily recreated and made to execute in a straightforward manner. Therefore it is reasonable to expect certain space for further improvement.

6.5 Conclusions and further enhancements

This chapter has presented a deep learning-based periocular recognition framework SCNN which can deliver outperforming results and significantly smaller complexity. By training one or more branches of CNNs with semantical information embedded in the corresponding training data, the SCNN can recover more comprehensive features from the images and therefore achieve superior performance. The experimental results presented on four publicly available databases suggest that the SCNN approach can achieve outperforming results while requiring much smaller computational time for the matching process. The SCNN architecture can also be generalized for other image classification tasks, which can improve the performance over the single CNN-based approaches. The source and executable files of this approach are made publicly available [144] to encourage other researchers to easily reproduce our results and further advance research on accurate periocular recognition.

It may be noted that at the SCNN decouples the identity supervision and other semantic supervision, to ensure high level of explicitness of semantic learning and compatibility with the existing CNN-based approaches. However, it is believed that a well-designed network structure may explicitly incorporate semantic information itself and facilitate. efficient training in an end-to-end training manner. Such enhancement of this approach, along with the enhanced backbone network architecture, can explicitly enable the joint learning of semantic information and also preserve the integrity of the network.

7

Deep neural network with focused attention on critical periocular regions

Extensive research has confirmed the exceptional discriminative capabilities of the periocular region, making it a valuable alternative or supplement to iris and face recognition methods. This is particularly useful in scenarios where complete facial or clear iris images are unavailable. Moreover, the researchers and developers have observed that the periocular region is relatively less affected by expression variations and aging than the entire face. Despite these advantages, there remains significant room for improving the accuracy of periocular region matching. Meeting the demands of large-scale and real-world applications is a critical objective in this pursuit.

This chapter presents a robust and highly accurate deep learning-based architecture for periocular recognition. This approach incorporates an attention model that highlights crucial regions within periocular images. To achieve this, we employ a multiglance mechanism where specific components of the network focus on important semantical regions, namely the eyebrow and eye regions within the periocular image. By directing attention to these regions, the deep convolutional neural network learns additional discriminative features, thereby enhancing the overall recognition capability of the model. The remarkable performance of our method underscores the significance of the eyebrow and eye regions in periocular recognition, emphasizing the need for special attention during the deep feature learning process. Another contributing factor to our success is the utilization of a customized verification-oriented loss function, which can offer superior discriminating power compared to conventional contrastive or triplet loss functions.

7.1 Introduction

Numerous studies in human visual perception and advancements in deep neural networks have highlighted the advantages of incorporating visual attention to enhance performance in various image recognition and understanding tasks. Motivated by these findings, this chapter presents an attention-based deep learning architecture called *AttNet*, specifically designed for robust and highly accurate periocular recognition. The underlying assumption is that the eyebrow and eye regions play a critical role in periocular recognition and should receive additional attention during feature learning. As depicted in Fig. 7−1, when humans engage in recognition tasks, salient regions, such as the eye and eyebrow, within the periocular region tend to provide more discriminative information and naturally draw more

Iris and Periocular Recognition using Deep Learning. DOI: https://doi.org/10.1016/B978-0-443-27318-6.00002-4

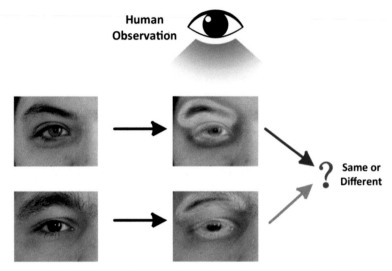

FIGURE 7–1 Illustration of implicit human visual attention while performing recognition tasks, such as periocular verification. Critical regions that can provide more discriminative information attract more attention, especially for fine-grained recognition.

attention compared to the surrounding areas. Leveraging this understanding, *AttNet* aims to capture and exploit these crucial regions for enhanced periocular recognition performance.

Based on the assumption that the eye and eyebrow regions are vital for accurate periocular recognition, the explicit attention-based deep neural network is introduced in this chapter. Our framework incorporates a region of interest detection network and an attention implication module, enabling the extraction of comprehensive periocular features with heightened discriminative capability. Our experimentation, detailed in Section 7.4, demonstrates the remarkable accuracy achieved by this approach for both visible and near-infrared (NIR) imaged periocular images. Notably, our attention-based model outperforms several state-of-the-art methods, as evidenced by the results obtained using four publicly available databases. These findings strongly support our assumption regarding the significance of critical regions, namely the eye and eyebrow, in achieving more precise periocular recognition. Additionally, our approach leverages a customized loss function called distance-driven sigmoid cross-entropy (DSC) loss, which offers superior supervision by demonstrating a marginal effect on both positive and negative training samples during verification-oriented learning. This distinguishes the DSC loss from other loss functions like contrastive loss and triplet loss, making it more effective in guiding the training process.

7.2 Methodology

This methodology introduces a significant innovation by integrating an attention model into the periocular recognition process, which directs the network's focus toward the specific

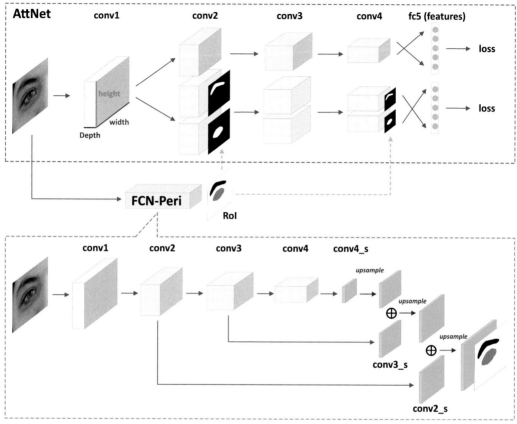

FIGURE 7–2 Architecture of the attention-based convolutional neuron network, referred to as *AttNet* (top), and the utilized fully convolutional network for specific region detection, called *FCN-Peri* (bottom).

regions of interest (RoI) during feature learning and matching. The overall framework is depicted in Fig. 7−2. Referred to as *AttNet* in this chapter, this network architecture first utilizes a convolutional unit (conv1) to extract low-level features from the input image. Subsequently, the network branches into two paths. The first branch processes the lower inputs in the customary CNN manner, while the second branch incorporates RoI information within its intermediate layers (conv2 and conv4), enabling a heightened emphasis on specific areas of the periocular input image. The first branch, without utilizing the attention mechanism, is designed to recover global features that a typical CNN can perform, which is able to maintain the− robustness of the network when RoI information is incorrect and improve overall performance by feature conjunction. The RoI information is provided by a fully convolutional network (FCN) [74], that is, *FCN-Peri* in Fig. 7−2. The detailed layer configuration of these two networks is provided in Table 7−1. Kindly note that both networks employed in this method are relatively simple compared with popular and very deep architectures, such as VGG [126] and ResNet [108], considering the availability of training data. Besides, we

Table 7–1 Detailed layer configurations for *AttNet* and *FCN-Peri*.

Unit	Layer	Type	# output channels	Kernel size	Stride
AttNet					
conv1	conv1_1	Convolution	32	5 × 5	1
	relu1_1	ReLU	/	/	/
	conv1_2	Convolution	32	5 × 5	1
	relu1_2	ReLU	/	/	/
	pool1	Max pooling	/	2 × 2	2
conv2	conv2_1	Convolution	32	3 × 3	1
	relu2_1	ReLU	/	/	/
	conv2_2	Convolution	32	3 × 3	1
	relu2_2	ReLU	/	/	/
	pool2	Max pooling	/	2 × 2	2
	att2[a]	Attention	/	/	/
conv3	conv3_1	Convolution	64	3 × 3	1
	relu3_1	ReLU	/	/	/
	conv3_2	Convolution	64	3 × 3	1
	relu3_2	ReLU	/	/	/
	pool3	Max pooling	/	2 × 2	2
conv4	conv4_1	Convolution	64	3 × 3	1
	relu4_1	ReLU	/	/	/
	conv4_2	Convolution	64	3 × 3	1
	relu4_2	ReLU	/	/	/
	pool4	Max pooling	/	2 × 2	2
	att4[a]	Attention	/	/	/
fc5	fc5	Fully connected	64	/	/
FCN-Peri					
conv1	conv1	Convolution	16	5 × 5	1
	relu1	ReLU	/	/	/
	pool1	Max pooling	/	2 × 2	2
conv2	conv2	Convolution	32	3 × 3	1
	relu2	ReLU	/	/	/
	conv2_s	Convolution	3	1 × 1	1
	pool2	Max pooling	/	2 × 2	2
conv3	conv3	Convolution	64	3 × 3	1
	relu3	ReLU	/	/	/
	conv3_s	Convolution	3	1 × 1	1
	pool3	Max pooling	/	4 × 4	2
conv4	conv4	Convolution	128	3 × 3	1
	relu4	ReLU	/	/	/
	conv4_s	Convolution	3	1 × 1	1

[a]Two branches of *AttNet* as shown in Fig. 7–2 have the same layer configuration, but attention layers are only placed in the second branch.

adopt the Siamese infrastructure for training the network in end-to-end verification protocol and develop a new compositional loss function which is referred to as DSC loss. This new DSC loss has been shown to offer superior performance than traditional verification-oriented loss functions like contrastive loss and triplet loss.

In this section, the detailed mechanisms for RoI detection and attention implication are explained in Sections 7.2.1 and 7.2.2, respectively; Section 7.2.3 presents the newly developed *DSC* loss function, followed by the details on the training and test configurations in Section 7.2.4.

7.2.1 Detection of semantical regions (FCN-Peri)

An essential consideration when incorporating a visual attention model is to identify regions of potential importance that warrant greater attention during the learning process. In general image classification and understanding tasks, the determination of these crucial regions is often learned jointly with the specific tasks, as the input data typically contains diverse background information, making predefined regions unfeasible. However, such strategies necessitate a substantial amount of training data with ample variation to constrain the learning process. In the case of fine-grained tasks like periocular recognition, a preference is given to predefined region detection, as prior knowledge about the input images is typically available. This allows for a better regularization of the learning process even with limited training data. In this approach, based on the human perception model, we assume that the regions containing the eyebrow and eye are relatively important for periocular recognition. Under such an assumption, we first exploit an FCN to detect the eyebrow and eye regions.

The FCN used in this work was initially introduced for semantic segmentation purposes [74]. In contrast to conventional CNNs, the FCN does not incorporate fully connected layers. Instead, it employs upsampling layers to merge intermediate convolutional feature maps of different scales. This approach ensures the preservation of spatial correspondence between the input image and output features, enabling pixel-to-pixel prediction. To train the FCN, a pixel-wise softmax loss function is employed, utilizing ground truth labels. In this method, we utilized a simplified version of the FCN introduced in [74] specifically designed for segmenting the eyebrow and eye regions from the background in the periocular input image. We refer to this as FCN-Peri. The detailed architecture of FCN-Peri is depicted in Fig. 7−2 (bottom row), and it consists of about 0.1 million parameters.

The initial FCN architecture outlined in [74] was primarily formulated to classify individual pixels into 21 predefined classes. However, for our problem, we redefine the task of distinguishing between the eyebrow and eye as two distinct classes. Consequently, our objective now involves segmenting the pixels within the original input image into three distinct categories: eye, eyebrow, and background. To train the *FCN-Peri* from scratch, we manually labeled the eyebrow and eye regions for about 100 images from the visible and NIR training datasets (further details about the datasets can be found in Section 7.5). It is important to clarify that when we mention the "eye region," we are referring to the region encompassing the iris, sclera, eyelid, and eyelash rather than solely the iris. Fig. 7−3 displays several region segmentation

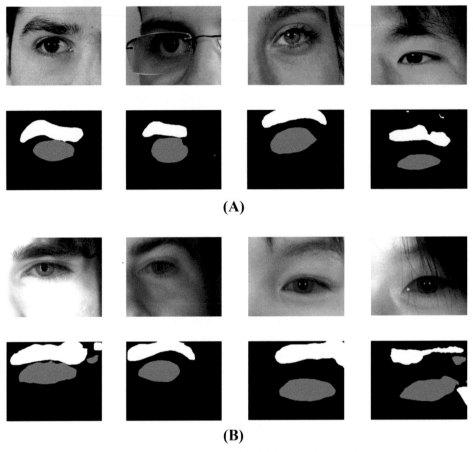

FIGURE 7–3 Samples outputs of *FCN-Peri* for test images with visible (A) and near-infrared (B) imaging. The black pixels represent the predicted background, and the white and gray pixels identify the predicted eyebrow and eye, respectively.

results obtained by applying the trained *FCN-Peri* to the test datasets. The predictions demonstrate remarkable robustness, although some errors are present in challenging samples. Nevertheless, we anticipate that the proposed attention-based deep neural network, *AttNet*, will exhibit tolerance toward such errors in a few samples. Additionally, it is worth noting that separate networks are trained for the visible and NIR spectrums.

7.2.2 Incorporating visual attention for periocular feature learning (*AttNet*)

Once the regions containing the eyebrow and eye are detected in an input image using *FCN-Peri*, we then incorporate the resulting RoI in *AttNet* for attention model implementation. As shown in Fig. 7–2, it can be observed that the output map from FCN-Peri, which indicates the positions of the eyebrow and eye, is employed to adjust the convolutional features after the conv2 and conv4 convolutional units. It is important to note that there is no standardized procedure for incorporating attention in deep neural networks. Different methods have been proposed, including using the RoI for affine transformation and alignment [163], applying blurring/masking techniques to the background of input images or intermediate features [164], or feeding cropped areas into multiple deep networks [165]. In this approach, we apply a straightforward yet effective mechanism for emphasizing important areas inferred by *FCN-Peri*, that is, increasing the magnitudes of the convolutional features within the RoI and decreasing those outside the RoI. More specifically, an *attention layer* is placed after a convolutional unit and performs the following operation:

$$f'_{x,y} = \begin{cases} \alpha f_{x,y} & , \text{if}\,(x,y) \in R \\ \dfrac{1}{\alpha} f_{x,y} & , \text{otherwise} \end{cases} \qquad (7-1)$$

where R is the set of x-y coordinates where the current position is considered as RoI, $\boldsymbol{f}$ is the convolutional feature map from the previous layer, $\boldsymbol{f}'$ is the processed feature map before entering the next layer, and α is a positive parameter controlling the intensity of adjustment. It was empirically fixed to 5 for all the experimental results presented in this chapter. Such an operation attempts to simulate human visual attention by weighting the features within the RoI more than those in the background for the subsequent layers of the network. The feature adjustments for eyebrow and eye are separately performed, each on half of the channels of the feature maps, respectively, as these two regions present quite different characteristics. We selectively incorporate such attention mechanisms for conv2 and conv4 to account for both low-level and high-level convolutional features. Since conv1 is shared by the RoI-aware and common branches, conv2 is therefore more appropriate to incorporate for low-level attention. On the other hand, conv4 is right before the fully connected layer fc5 (i.e., the layer generating feature vectors) and is also judicious to be selected to impart high-level attention. Fig. 7−4 visualizes the effect of the employed attention model on the features of the two convolutional units. It can be observed that the background features which do not belong to the RoI "fade" after the operation by attention layers. In this way, the foreground features make more impacts on the feature extraction process by subsequent layers. Although simply increasing the feature magnitudes inside the RoI may not be an optimal approach to incorporate visual attention, it is quite a scientific and easy-to-implement scheme to achieve the key objective of this research, that is, to investigate and evaluate the importance of eye and eyebrow regions to advance periocular recognition through the deep periocular feature extraction.

7.2.3 Distance-driven sigmoid cross-entropy loss for verification-oriented supervision

We adopt Siamese-like pair-wise network infrastructure for training our *AttNet*, that is, instead of classifying a single image into a standalone class, a pair of images are jointly

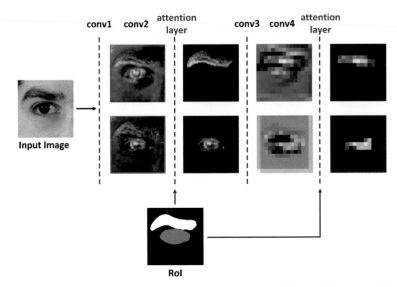

FIGURE 7–4 Visualization of convolutional features from intermediate layers before and after attention layers. The attention layers serve to enhance the feature values within the RoI while reducing those in the background. To facilitate a clearer understanding, feature maps of various scales are upsampled to a uniform size for better visualization.

evaluated to predict whether they belong to the same class or not. Such configuration is illustrated by Fig. 7–5. Contrastive loss [121] or triplet loss [77] are often used for pair-wise training. Compared with the classification training protocol, which usually uses a *softmax* loss function for supervision, the pair-wise protocol is closer to the verification problem (one-to-one matching), which is a fundamental application scenario for most biometric systems. A classification-based model, in contrast, may require additional transfer learning to make itself more effective and scalable, such as in [77]. Besides, the pair combination from training samples introduces more data variation, which is likely to reduce the overfitting of the trained model. In the following, we present a brief introduction to conventionally used loss functions for pair-wise training, followed by our newly designed *DSC* loss function.

7.2.3.1 Conventional verification-oriented loss functions

The conventional contrastive loss function for training Siamese network is formulated as follows:

$$L_{con} = td^2 + (1-t)\max(0, m-d)^2 \qquad (7-2)$$

where t is the label of the current pair, that is, $t = 1$ if the two samples come from the same class and $t = 0$ otherwise, and d is simply the Euclidean distance between the two input feature vectors $\boldsymbol{f}_X$ and $\boldsymbol{f}_Y$:

$$d = \left\| \boldsymbol{f}_X - \boldsymbol{f}_Y \right\|_2 \qquad (7-3)$$

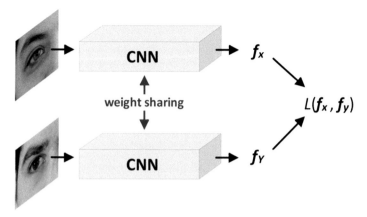

FIGURE 7–5 Illustration of Siamese architecture for training CNN in verification protocol. Two identical CNNs are placed in parallel to process a pair of samples. A specific pair-wise loss function (e.g., contrastive loss) is employed to supervise the training, and the weights (parameters) of the two networks are kept the same (weight sharing) during the entire training process.

m is a preset margin for regularizing the distance from a negative pair (i.e., a pair for samples from different classes). The contrastive loss is designed to reduce the distance between a positive pair as a quadratic energy term, while for negative pairs, the distance between a negative pair would be increased until it exceeds the hard margin m. The effect of m is to force the network to concentrate on relatively challenging negative pairs only. However, there is no regularization on the positive pair samples. As the training progresses, more and more negative pairs do not produce any losses due to the hard margin, while all the positive pairs still have a continuous impact on the backpropagation. This causes unbalanced training for positive and negative pair samples.

The above side effect is, to some extent, alleviated by triplet loss, which can be considered as a variant of contrastive loss. Instead of evaluating a simple pair, the triplet loss composes positive and negative pair into a triple structure and measures the loss by:

$$L_{tri} = \max \left(\left\| \boldsymbol{f}_{X_1} - \boldsymbol{f}_{X_2} \right\|_2^2 - \left\| \boldsymbol{f}_{X_1} - \boldsymbol{f}_{Y} \right\|_2^2 + m', 0 \right) \qquad (7-4)$$

where $\boldsymbol{f}_{X_1}$ and $\boldsymbol{f}_{X_2}$ are features from the same class while $\boldsymbol{f}_Y$ is extracted from another class. Different from contrastive loss, which uses an absolute margin to regularize negative pairs, the triple loss relies on a relative margin m' to enlarge the difference between the positive pair distance and negative pair distance. In this way, the balance of positive and negative pair samples is always retained during the training process. The verification-oriented applications, however, mostly use an absolute value as a threshold instead of a relative margin for decision making. Therefore slight inconsistency exists between the training process supervised by triplet loss and the actual test (matching) process.

7.2.3.2 Distance-driven sigmoid cross-entropy loss

In order to address the above limitations, we introduce a customized compositional loss function called *DSC* loss. Given the distance d between a pair of features to be evaluated, we first perform the following mapping on it:

$$s = b - ad^2 \tag{7-5}$$

$$p = \frac{1}{1 + e^{-s}} \tag{7-6}$$

where a and b are positive constants that are used for linear transformation on the square of the Euclidean distance, p is obtained by a sigmoid function on the transformed s and can be regarded as the probability that the two samples come from a same class. The motivation of using sigmoid function is that it maps any real value into (0, 1), and varies significantly near zero but much slower at two ends. Such property essentially enables a kind of soft margins for the low and high values of s. In this way, the learning process for both positive and negative pairs can be regularized so that it mainly focuses on challenging samples with s values near zero. The loss for the obtained probability p is then measured by the cross-entropy function:

$$L_{DSC} = -[t \log p + (1 - t) \log (1 - p)] \tag{7-7}$$

The sigmoid cross-entropy loss is widely used when the task is to predict probabilities of certain events. In this case, we regard our task as predicting the probability of a binary event — same class or different classes. Different from common approaches, which feeds a single neuron output spanning over $(-\infty, +\infty)$ into the sigmoid function, we originally map the Euclidean distance d to a term s that spans over $(-\infty, b]$, then transfer to approximated probability p. The constant b should be selected such that its sigmoid value $1/(1 + e^b)$ is very close to one. Such transfer is the key to the new *DSC* loss function, which utilizes the soft margins of the sigmoid function in a straightforward way.

Fig. 7−6 demonstrates the comparison of the newly developed *DSC* loss function and conventional contrastive loss function w.r.t d, for both positive $(t=1)$ and negative $(t=0)$ cases. It can be clearly observed that for negative cases, the two losses have a similar distribution that, when d is greater than certain values, the losses approach zero. Such marginal effects make sure that the learning process does not waste energy on unchallenging negative pairs that already have a large distance. However, for positive cases, the two losses exhibit notably different characteristics. The contrastive loss calculates the distance using a quadratic term, which means that even for easy positive samples, they continuously impact the learning process. Conversely, due to the hard margin m, several negative samples are overlooked by the contrastive loss. This imbalance can lead to a training process that overly emphasizes positive samples, even those that are not challenging. On the other hand, our *DSC* loss introduces a (soft) margin effect for positive cases. When the distance d falls within a small range, the loss approaches zero. The relatively small loss values indicate that the

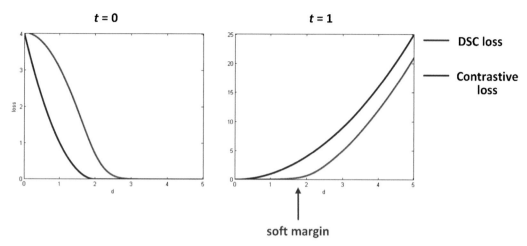

FIGURE 7–6 Comparison of *DSC* loss ($a = 1$, $b = 4$) and conventional contrastive loss ($m = 2$) with respect to d. The *DSC* loss provides a (soft) margin for positive cases ($t = 1$) which achieves better regularization for genuine pairs, such that the learning process mainly focuses on challenging samples.

current samples are generally easy for the network to handle, and they do not contribute significant gradients for the backpropagation during training. As a result, the training process remains focused on challenging samples, both positive and negative, in order to maximize the network's discriminative capacity.

The experiments analysis presented in Section 7.5.4.1 demonstrates that this DSC loss can offer superior discriminative power compared to the conventional contrastive loss and triplet loss, particularly at lower false acceptance rates.

7.2.4 Training and test configuration

To enhance the network's generalizability and the effectiveness of its features, we have adopted several commonly used data augmentation techniques for the training process, as well as feature composition during the matching phase. The details of these measures are elaborated upon in the subsequent sections.

7.2.4.1 Training data augmentation

All the training images are resized to 300×240 in advance. Besides, we have performed several *on-the-fly* image augmentation approaches. These approaches are randomly applied before each image is fed into the network, and are described in the following:

- Scaling—There is 80% probability for each image to be enlarged, with a factor randomly drawn from a uniform distribution over $(1, 1.3)$.
- Cropping—Each image is cropped with a window of 240×240 that is randomly placed across the entire image region.

- Color/intensity jittering—For an RGB image (visible imaging), a color augmentation method called Fancy PCA, as also described in [127], is applied. For a grayscale image (NIR imaging), a random value drawn from $\mathcal{N}$ (0, 0.02) is added to its pixel intensities to simulate illumination variation.

During the training process, the aforementioned random parameters are independently generated for each image in the mini-batch. When the same image appears again in a later iteration, the parameters will be randomly drawn again to create a different variant of that image. This approach allows a single source image to generate multiple diverse versions without requiring excessive storage space. By employing such augmentation techniques, the risk of overfitting in deep neural network training is effectively mitigated, especially when the number of training samples is not very large.

7.2.4.2 Test feature composition

As mentioned earlier, our network model accepts 240×240 square images as the input. On the other hand, the periocular source images used in our experiments have rectangular aspect ratios close to 5:4. During the test phase, we adopt feature composition similar to [73] and [126], to make our model adaptive (slightly) to different resolutions/aspect ratios, and also to obtain multi-scale feature representation. The composition process is described sequentially in the following:

1. The input image is resized to $w \times 240$, where w is larger than 240 and subject to the image's original aspect ratio.
2. The resized image is cropped with three 240×240 windows that are placed on the left end, center and right end of it respectively.
3. The resized image is enlarged with a factor of 1.2, then another 240×240 window is placed in the center of it to create the fourth cropped version.
4. Four cropped versions are fed into the network separately, each generating a 128-D feature vector. These four vectors are then concatenated into a 512-D vector for matching.

The Euclidean distance between two vectors is regarded as the dissimilarity score. The above feature composition process can cover the entire image region and account for the multiscale feature representation to a certain extent.

7.3 Visual attention analysis

In this section, we provide justification for the selection of predefined regions for visual attention enhancement. As outlined earlier, we selected eyebrow and eye as the RoI mainly due to the following two reasons:

- Inspired by human perception, eyebrow and eye regions will attract most of attention when humans observe periocular images. It is useful to note that many machine learning/deep learning algorithms are inspired by human perception/ behaviors, including neural networks, reinforcement learning, long-short term memory (LSTM), and also the referenced attention models in this chapter.

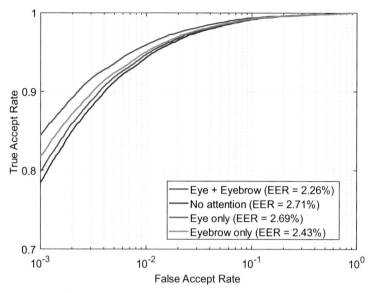

FIGURE 7-7 Comparison of different weights on the selected regions of interest for attention incorporation.

- The importance of eyebrow and eye characteristics for periocular recognition has been underlined in a number of earlier research work [51,63,166,167], where excluding or masking eyebrow or eye regions leads to performance degradation in most cases.

In order to statistically ascertain the effect of selecting these areas for attention enhancement, we also trained different versions of *AttNet* by adjusting the feature weights α in Eq. (7.1), detailed as follows:

- Eye + eyebrow: $\alpha_{eye} = \alpha_{eyebrow} = 5$
- Eye only: $\alpha_{eye} = 5, \alpha_{eyebrow} = 1$
- Eyebrow only: $\alpha_{eye} = 1, \alpha_{eyebrow} = 5$
- No attention: $\alpha_{eye} = \alpha_{eyebrow} = 1$

The aforementioned settings allow for an initial investigation into the impact of selected regions, with attention enhancement, on the recognition outcomes. The results from such comparative analysis using UBIPr database are shown in Fig. 7–7. It is evident that by explicitly enhancing attention on both the eye and eyebrow regions simultaneously, significant improvements in recognition accuracy can be achieved. Notably, emphasizing the eyebrow regions individually leads to greater improvements compared to solely focusing on the eye regions. This finding can be attributed to the fact that eyebrow characteristics are generally more stable and less affected by variations in illumination and eyeball movements, among other factors. These observations validate the positive effect of incorporating visual attention within the detected eyebrow and eye regions during the deep feature extraction process, thereby enhancing the accuracy of periocular recognition.

7.4 Network training analysis

The success of deep learning-based approaches relies heavily on the effectiveness of the training scheme, which is influenced by various factors, such as the nature of the classification task, network complexity, volume of training data, and learning algorithm. While deep learning has demonstrated significant achievements in tasks like ImageNet classification [90,108,112] and semantic segmentation [74], incorporating it into other biometrics problems poses specific challenges, primarily due to the *limited* availability of labeled training data. Insufficient training data can cause severe overfitting, that is, the model fits too well on the small scale of training data but is not able to properly classify test data that was unseen during the training phase. In this section, we present an analysis of the training processes employed for *AttNet* and *FCN-Peri* to ensure that the models analyzed in this chapter are sufficiently trained and that the level of overfitting remains within an acceptable range.

7.4.1 Training of *AttNet* network

There are no definite conclusions so far on the minimum required numbers to properly train a CNN for the classification problem. Generally, it is accepted that when there are more parameters to learn, and the problem is more complicated, the required amount of training data will be larger in order to avoid overfitting. A practical way is to refer to some typical architectures and the training configurations which have been widely adopted by researchers/developers in the literature. Table 7−2 presents the summary of the scale of our networks as well as some existing architectures for different classification tasks.

It can be inferred from Table 7−2 that (1) our network is much smaller than other typical network architectures in terms of parameter scale, and it is therefore reasonable to assume that the required number of training samples should be less than other examples in this table; (2) For the general image classification tasks, such as in [127] or [126], intra- and interclass variation are dramatically high, and therefore a large volume of training data should be devoted for sufficient learning. On the other hand, for typical biometric problems, such as

Table 7–2 Comparison of network configurations for our work and other typical architectures.

Architecture	Problem	# classes	# parameters	# train images
AlexNet [46]	Image classification	1000	60 M	∼1,000,000
VGG-16 [23]	Image classification	1000	138 M	∼1,000,000
ResNet-152 [12]	Image classification	1000	60 M	∼1,000,000
DeepIrisNet [50]	Iris recognition	356	138 M	∼30,000
PRWIS [48]	Periocular recognition	518	248 M	∼8000
AttNet	Periocular recognition	224	**7.7 M**	∼3000
FCN [25]	Semantic segmentation	21	134 M	∼8000
FCN-Peri	Semantic segmentation	3	**0.1 M**	100

Bold value emphasizes on the significance to indicate that from the method described in this chapter, both models need the "least" number of parameters and therefore the described method is the fastest among the others in this table.

for iris or periocular recognition, a relatively small amount of training has been employed to achieve promising results. This is probably because smaller interimage variation for biometric recognition may not require that many training samples to supply overcomplex information. The periocular recognition problem belongs to such category of problems. Considering the above two factors, our configuration for training the small *AttNet* with about 3000 (on the UBIPr dataset, which will be detailed in the next section) images is justifiable.

To statistically evaluate the convergence condition of our configuration, we vary the number of training samples to train *AttNet* on UBIPr database several times and observe the convergence status. These results are shown in Fig. 7−8. It can be observed that employing several hundreds of training images may easily cause overfitting as there is a large gap between the training loss and the test loss. However, when this number increases to 1000 or above, test loss converges to a similar level, and the gap becomes smaller. Note that it is difficult to totally eliminate the gap for most deep learning approaches. The above results indicate that the actual configuration in which approximately 3000 images were used for training *AttNet*, is practically appropriate to sufficiently train our network.

7.4.2 Training of *FCN-Peri* network

The problem of training an FCN for semantic segmentation is quite different from training a CNN for image classification. Semantic segmentation (e.g., detecting eyebrow and eye regions in this paper) is a pixel-wise classification task rather than an entire image classification task. In other words, with semantic segmentation, each pixel in the input image is classified into one of several predefined classes. Hence, when examining the number of training samples or data points, it is important to analyze at the pixel level rather than the image

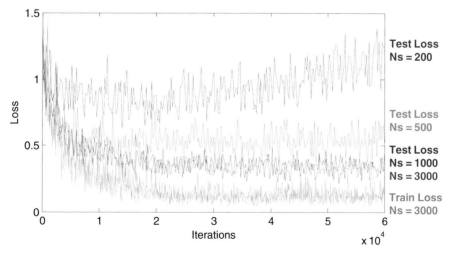

FIGURE 7–8 Learning status of *AttNet* with the different number of training samples (N_S). With N_S no less than 1000, test loss converges to a stable level. Train losses with different N_S are similar and therefore only one is plotted for clarity.

level. However, it is crucial to recognize that not all pixels can be treated as independent data points since adjacent pixels often contain highly redundant information. The concept of *receptive field* can help to more scientifically estimate meaningful data points in an image when training FCN.

In a single or multiple regular convolution/pooling operations, one output element or pixel is computed from a certain region in the input image/map, and this region is referred to as the *receptive field*. For example, with one convolutional layer in CNN/FCN having a 3×3 kernel, the receptive field is 3×3. With two such convolutional layers, the receptive field from input to output is 5×5. Fig. 7−9 can help to illustrate this concept. Since FCN mainly comprises convolutional layers and pooling layers, the output of each element/pixel is determined by a patch from the input rather than the entire image. We can therefore compute the receptive field of *FCN-Peri* first to estimate the approximate number of nonredundant data points available in the training process.

By employing a top-down approach, the receptive field can be calculated to determine the region at the bottom layer that influences a specific pixel at the topmost layer. Following the longest path from input to output in *FCN-Peri*, this process is illustrated in Table 7−3.

These observations indicate that each output pixel of *FCN-Peri* is determined by a patch of 80×80 from the input image, as also illustrated in the last row of Table 7−3. We can roughly assume that two patches can be considered as independent data points when the overlap between them is no less than 25% (otherwise, the information will be highly redundant). As a result, a 300×240 image we used as input can provide approximately 108 (9×12) nonredundant data points. As discussed earlier, we have labeled about 100 images for training *FCN-Peri*, generating approximately 10,000 data points for learning classification of three classes (i.e., eyebrow, eye, and background). On average, about 3000 training samples per class are available for training. Note that the network is more than 1000 times smaller than the original FCN, as revealed in Table 7−2, which suggests that the number of

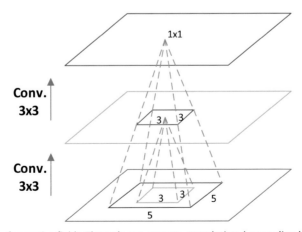

FIGURE 7–9 Illustration of receptive fields. Through one or more convolutional or pooling layers, each output neuron in the top layer is determined by a patch in the bottom/input layer.

Table 7–3   Computations for receptive field for *FCN-Peri*.

Layer	Kernel, Stride	Receptive Field
output	–	1×1
upsample $\times 3$	–	2×2
conv4	$3 \times 3, 1$	4×4
pool3	$4 \times 4, 4$	16×16
conv3	$3 \times 3, 1$	18×18
pool2	$2 \times 2, 2$	36×36
conv2	$3 \times 3, 1$	38×38
pool1	$2 \times 2, 2$	76×76
conv1	$5 \times 5, 1$	80×80

available training samples should be sufficient. In fact, the segmentation results on test data shown in Fig. 7–3, which were visually appropriate, can also validate that our *FCN-Peri* has been properly trained.

7.5 Experiments and results

Thorough experiments have been performed to evaluate the proposed approach from various perspectives, and comparisons are made with several state-of-the-art methods. These experimental results are reproducible via codes [168]. Two categories of experiments were performed which focuses on *Open-World* and *Closed-World* periocular images matching problems, respectively. In the following sections, we detail such problem definition and experimental configurations as well as observation and analysis of the obtained results.

7.5.1 Open-world versus closed-world verification

The open-world problem refers to the configuration that the subjects to be enrolled into the gallery in the deployment process may be *unseen* during the training phase. On the other hand, the closed-world problem has a constraint that all the subjects to be recognized in the deployment process are already *known* during the training phase.

The open-world problem is apparently more challenging but closer to the actual deployment environments for most applications, such as citizen authentication, general access control, and searching for missing people, as it is impractical for these systems to collect data from all possible subjects in advance during the training or development phase. The closed-world setting may result in higher recognition accuracy as more precise data adaptation can be achieved during training, but the system may be less scalable for deployment, which is also clarified by [169].

It should be clarified that the approach detailed in this chapter, especially the newly developed DSC loss function, is introduced for the open-world problem. However, it is woth noting that the several methods and contests [169,170] in the literature *only* focus on closed-world problems only, and therefore we investigate the performance under both settings.

7.5.2 Baseline methods for performance comparisons

Several state-of-the-art methods, that is, [16,63,136,169], are selected as baselines to evaluate the performance of the attention based model described in this chapter. These methods are used as baselines because they focus on the same problem as in this chapter, that is, less constrained periocular recognition, and report state-of-the-art performance on multiple datasets in recent years and with judicious theoretical significance. It should be noted that the methods in [16,63,136] are adaptive to the open-world setting, while [169] is only developed for closed-world settings, as also clarified in the respective reference.

7.5.3 Datasets and match protocols

Six publicly available databases are considered for the experimentation. Four of them are acquired under the visible spectrum, while the other two are with NIR imaging. The brief information on the employed datasets is described in the following.

- UBIPr [143]

  The organization of the UBIPr periocular database [155] is the same as introduced in the previous chapter (Section 4.1.1) for SCNN. We employed the same training set of 3359 images as used in the previous chapter for model learning. The remaining 1767 left images are used during the test phase for performance evaluation. This database is used for *open-world* experiments, and therefore no subjects are overlapping between the training and test sets.

- Face Recognition Grand Challenge (FRGC) [141]

  The details of this database were discussed in Section 4.1.1 of the previous chapter, and the same organization is also used here. Therefore the same 540 right eye images from 163 subjects are employed in our experiments, from which the first 40 images form the training set and the rest 500 form the test set. Experiments on this dataset also adopt the *open-world* configuration.

- Face and Ocular Challenge Series (FOCS) [142]

  The images from this dataset were the same as detailed in Section 4.1.1 of the previous chapter. Therefore we use the same 3262 left periocular images from the first 80 subjects for training and the remaining 1530 images from 56 subjects for testing. The *Open-world* configuration is incorporated for this dataset.

- CASIA.v4-distance [17]

  Images from this dataset are also the same as those used in the previous chapter and therefore 1077 images were used in the experimentation. The first 79 samples are used for training, while the remaining 998 samples are used during the test phase. Experiments on this dataset also follow the *open-world* protocol.

- UBIRIS.v2 [19]

  This dataset of noisy iris images acquired under the visible spectrum was also detailed in the previous chapter, and the same organization is also used here. Experiments on this dataset are mainly set for *closed-world* verification and comparison with method [169] but will also attach *open-world* results for comparative study. In the closed-world setting (as in [169]), 80% of images from all 518 subjects are used for training, and the remaining 20% are selected for testing. In the open-world setting, images from the first 400 subjects are used for training, while the remaining are used for the performance evaluation.

• VISOB [170]

   This competition dataset comprises ocular images captured with three different smartphones under three illumination conditions. The Visit-1 involves 550 subjects and was released for algorithm development. Visit-2 has images from 290 subjects and was used for performance evaluation in the competition. It is important to note that the competition organizers have *only* provided the Visit-1 part of this database in the public domain, which was also downloaded for this work. Therefore our experimental results were obtained on Visit-1 part only and should not be directly compared with the ranked methods in [170]. *Closed-world* setting was applied to the experiments on this dataset.

   The above datasets cover both visible and NIR spectrums and were acquired under varying and less constrained imaging environments that are close to real-world application scenarios. A few sample images from them were illustrated in Fig. 6−6 in the previous Chapter, except for the VISOB dataset, whose samples are illustrated in Fig. 7−10. More detailed information about the employed databases and training/test set division is presented in Table 7−4.

   For experiments carried out under open-world configuration, it is important to clarify the reasonable difference in training mechanisms for the four methods: (1) For our method and [13], the visible models are trained on UBIPr database and tested on UBIPr and FRGC databases; the NIR models are trained on FOCS and tested on FOCS and CASIA.v4-distance datasets. In other words, experiments on FRGC and CASIA.v4 are under *cross-database* scenarios. Such a training/test configuration is identical to the original one in the previous chapter (SCNN) which therefore provides a fair comparison. (2) For methods [16,63], the required training efforts are less, and it is observed that the *within-database* training and testing manner offers better results for these two methods. Therefore the training and test evaluations were performed on the same dataset for them. The aforementioned experimental configuration is also the same as used in SCNN, and justification has been provided to incorporate the best possible performance from these two baseline methods and ensure fairness in the performance comparisons.

FIGURE 7−10 Sample images from the VISOB database.

Table 7–4 Summary of the employed databases for training and testing.

Database	UBIPr		FRGC		FOCS		CASIA.v4-dist.		UBIRIS.v2		VISOB	
Spectrum	Visible		Visible		NIR		NIR		Visible		Visible	
Imaging distance	4−8 m		N/A		N/A		≥ 3 m		3−8 m		8−12 in.	
World scenario	Open		Open		Open		Open		Open/closed		Closed	
Division	Train	Test	Train	Test	Train	Test	Train	Test	Train	Test	Train	Test
#Subjects	224	120	13	150	80	56	10	131	518	518	484	475
#Images	3359	1767	40	500	3262	1530	79	998	8886	2215	5270	5103
#Genuine scores (Test)	12,351		826		39,614		3371		2215		4914	
#Imposter scores (Test)	1,547,910		123,425		1,130,071		494,132		1,145,155		2,464,938	

The training sets of FRGC and CASIA v4-distance databases are used for the training in [16] and [63]. This *AttNet* method and SCNN (Chapter 6) only adopt UBBIPr and FOCS database for the network training.

7.5.4 Open-world matching performance

7.5.4.1 Effectiveness of DSC loss function

The performance of the *DSC* loss function, which is designed for *open-world* verification, is firstly examined. We compare it with− conventional contrastive loss and triplet loss, which are also designed for 1:1 verification purposes. The experiment is performed on UBIPr, FRGC, FOCS, and CASIA.v4-distance. Three *AttNet* models with identical structures are trained with *DSC* loss, contrastive loss, and triplet loss, respectively. When training with contrastive loss and triplet loss, the margins are discretely tuned from {1, 2, 3, 4}, and the ones providing the best performance are used for comparison. The ROC curves are shown in Fig. 7−11.

It can be observed that *DSC* loss delivers noticeable and consistent improvements over the other two loss functions, especially for lower false acceptance rates (FAR). The performance at low FAR is regarded as more critical for biometric verification systems, and the key factor to this metric is the ability to verify challenging cases, that is, highly dissimilar genuine pairs and similar imposter pairs. The superiority of *DSC* loss is mainly attributed to the marginal effects for both positive and negative pair samples during the feature learning process, such that more training efforts can be put into challenging cases.

7.5.4.2 Comparisons with state-of-the-art methods

As discussed earlier, the performance of the proposed approach has been comparatively evaluated with state-of-the-art methods [16,63], and SCNN introduced in the previous chapter. The resulting ROC curves are provided in Fig. 7−12. We can observe from these results that our method consistently outperforms the other three baseline methods on all of the four employed databases. It is important to note that the advancements from our method are particularly significant at lower FAR, which indicates the outstanding capability of our method for verifying challenging periocular samples. Even under the challenging cross-database training and test protocol, the proposed method has exhibited high level of robustness. The promising results from the proposed attention-based model have further validated the importance of eyebrow and eye regions for periocular recognition.

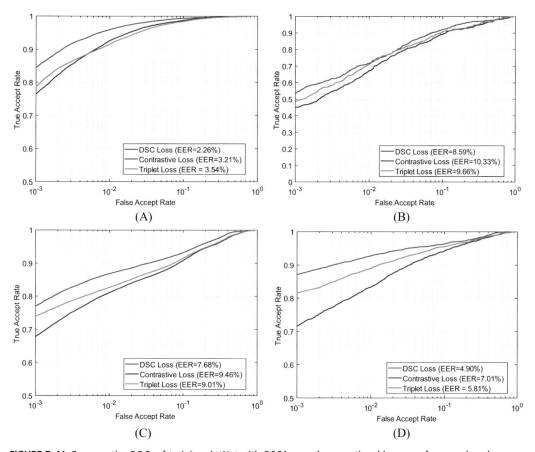

FIGURE 7–11 Comparative ROCs of training *AttNet* with *DSC* loss and conventional losses on four employed databases. The parameters of DSC loss are empirically set to $a = 10$ and $b = 5$; margins for contrastive loss and triplet loss are tuned among {1, 2, 3, 4}, and the best-performing ones are used here for comparisons, which are $m = 3$ and $m' = 4$.

We have also performed significance tests to ascertain the statistical significance of the improvements from our method. The method for the significance test is described in [159], which is based on the area under the curve of the ROC statistics. Comparison has been made with SCNN introduced in the previous chapter, as this method delivers the best performance among the three baselines. The results from the tests are provided in Table 7−5. It can be inferred that, with a widely used confidence level of 95%, the improvements from our method are statistically significant over its competitors.

7.5.5 Comparisons with other deep learning-based methods

As discussed earlier, the proposed approach is mainly designed for open-world verification problems. However, some other popular methods/competitions also adopt or focus on a

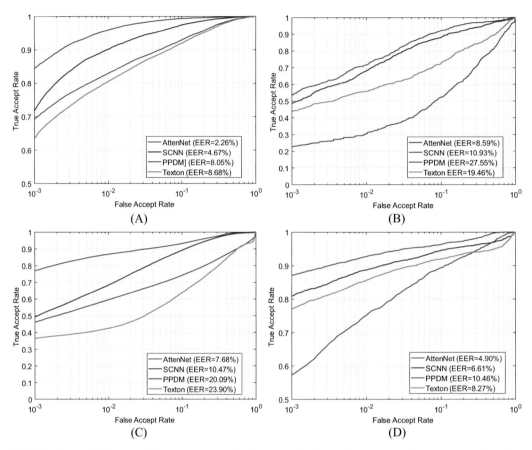

FIGURE 7–12 The ROC curves of the periocular verification using the AttenNet method and comparison with other state-of-the-art methods on different databases. (A) UBIPr, (B) FRGC, (C) FOCS, (D) CASIA.v4-distance.

Table 7–5   Results from the significance test for comparison of this method and SCNN.

Comparison with SCNN	UBIPr	FRGC	FOCS	CASIA.v4-distance
z-statistic	14.323	3.859	25.259	8.829
p-value*	$<10^{-4}$	1.14×10^{-4}	$<10^{-4}$	$<10^{-4}$

p-Value indicates the probability of the null hypothesis, that is, two sets of data do not differ significantly.
*p is here denoted as $<10^{-4}$ if the computed z is too large such that the corresponding p is too small for the computer to return the exact value.

closed-world setting, in which all the subjects to be recognized are known during the training or the development phase, and it is usually allowed to use the gallery set for the training process. Typical examples include [169–171]. Despite the fact that a closed-world setting is less challenging, it may be feasible for some applications to know all the interested subjects

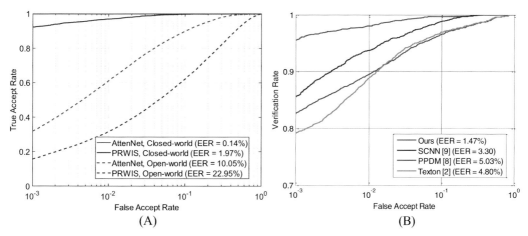

FIGURE 7–13 The ROC curves on UBIRIS.v2 database and VISOB database (iphone-day-light-short subset). The *AttNet* result under the closed-world setting on UBIRIS.v2 is close to line *y* = 1. (A) UBIRIS.v2 (Open-/Closed-world), (B) VISOB (Closed World).

in advance during the training phase, such as for the watchlist based surveillance system. Hence, we also supplement experiments under the closed-world configuration, which were conducted on UBIRIS.v2 and VISOB databases.

Under the closed-world setting, we maintained the architecture of *AttNet* but trained it in a different way. Similar to as in [169], we added a softmax layer after the feature layer (fc5 in Fig. 7−2) with N_C output neurons, where N_C is the number of classes (subjects) to be recognized. As a closed-world setting is applied, N_C is consistent during the training and test phases. Each output neuron at the softmax layer is regarded as the probability that the input sample belongs to a specific subject and therefore is used as the verification score. Fig. 7−13 provides ROCs for the verification results on UBIRIS.v2 with a comparison to [169], and on VISOB with a comparison to [16,63], and SCNN. Note that for experiments on UBIRIS.v2, we also attached open-world results for comparative study. To obtain the comparative open-world results from [39], we used the l2-norm distance between the feature vectors from fc7 layer as suggested in this reference.

From the results on UBIRIS.v2, we can observe that this approach consistently outperforms the state-of-the-art method, such as in [169]. Under the closed-world settings, our results have scored significantly high accuracy (0.14% EER), due to the reason that class-specific recognition has been learned with softmax loss function for given and fixed set of subjects (and the same for the baseline method). In contrast, when switched to an open-world setting, both [169] and this method suffer from obvious performance degradation, which reflects that an open-world problem inherently brings more challenges compared with a closed-world problem. However, our approach can still achieve superior results over that from the deep learning based method described in [169].

The results on the VISOB dataset reveal that our method still consistently outperforms other baseline methods considered in Chapter. It should be noted that the eye images in this

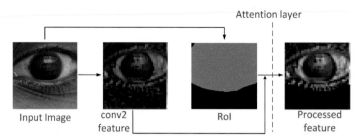

FIGURE 7–14 Visualization of convolutional features on a VISOB image which does not contain eyebrow. In this case, the attention mechanism does not much impact on the feature distribution, and *AttNet* will basically act like a common CNN to guarantee fundamental performance.

database do *not* include the eyebrow region, and the eye region occupies most of the image area (Fig. 7–10). This implies that the proposed visual attention mechanism may not benefit the recognition performance. Fig. 7–14 visualizes the intermediate features learned by *AttNet* on such data, from which we can observe that enhancing attention within the eye region does not affect much the feature contents. In this case, *AttNet* can serve as a common CNN for backing up the performance even if desired regions are absent or cannot be correctly segmented. Another aspect worth noticing is that, as discussed earlier, *only* the Visit-1 subset (550 subjects) is provided in the public domain but not the Visit-2 (290 subjects) part that was used for benchmarking in [170]. Therefore it will be unfair to directly compare the results provided in this chapter with those in [170].

7.6 Conclusions and further enhancements

This chapter has presented an attention-based CNN architecture for more accurate and robust periocular recognition. This framework includes *FCN-Peri*, which can accurately detect eyebrow and eye regions as key RoI, and *AttNet*, which makes use of the RoI information for more discriminative feature learning. A newly developed verification-oriented loss function, referred to as *DSC* loss, has also been introduced for this framework. The new loss function has shown to provide marginal effects for both positive and negative training samples during learning, which contributes to more robust feature representation for matching challenging periocular image pairs. Extensive experiments on four publicly available databases presented in Section 7.5 of this Chapter indicate that our attention-based framework achieves significantly better results than several state-of-the-art methods for periocular recognition. The effectiveness of the newly designed *DSC* loss function was also separately validated through comparison with conventional contrastive loss and triplet loss. The experimental results provide vital support to our assumption that information within eyebrow and eye regions is critical to periocular recognition and deserves more attention during feature learning and matching. The trained models and source for reproducing our experimental results are also made publicly available via [168].

Deep neural network architectures have witnessed notable progress with the integration of attention mechanisms in CNNs. These attention mechanisms effectively identify and emphasize relevant feature locations within the output of a convolutional block while reducing the impact of features from other regions [172]. The success of our method builds upon the foundation laid by these advancements in attention-based CNN architectures.

Various spatial and channel attention mechanisms exist that can compute attention weights automatically. For instance, reference [173] showcases an example of these mechanisms to achieve state of the art performance for the contactless palmprint matching, while reference [174] explores a more comprehensive approach for cross-spectral periocular matching. However, the attention model introduced in [174] presents a notable challenge: it requires feature reconstruction using multilinear principal component projection, which involves subspace learning. As a result, this approach incurs substantial computational overhead, making it less suitable for online matching scenarios where efficiency is crucial.

Most existing attention mechanisms, which include spatial and channel attention, are specifically designed to emphasize discriminative features. However, their performance is limited because they cannot effectively process both spatial and channel information together [175]. To overcome this limitation, extending the spatial and channel attention modules to generate a comprehensive global feature representation is a complex task that requires a substantial increase in network parameters. In Chapter 9, we delve into the challenges of designing a kernel-level attention module that addresses these limitations without introducing excessive parameter overhead. We further evaluate the success of this approach in matching periocular images.

8

Dynamic iris recognition through multifeature collaboration

The accuracy of matching segmented iris images decreases significantly when the images are acquired at a distance or under nonideal imaging conditions. With any increase in the stand-off distance, the quality and accuracy of the segmented iris images also degrade significantly. As underlined in the previous chapters, the periocular information is inherently embedded in such iris images and can be dynamically exploited to assist in iris recognition under such nonideal scenarios. Analysis of iris templates obtained from such images also shows a significant reduction in the region of interest. Instead of using the Hamming distance directly, as in the broad iris recognition literature, iris recognition in these scenarios can benefit from a similarity distance that considers the importance of different binary bits within the iris templates By accounting for the differences in the effective area of available iris regions, the periocular information can be dynamically reinforced to achieve higher accuracy for such iris recognition. This chapter introduces a deep learning-based dynamic iris recognition framework to accurately match such iris images acquired under cross-distance and nonideal imaging scenarios.

8.1 Introduction

The accuracy of iris recognition under less-constrained environments is known to degrade significantly, as compared to those from the conventional or stop-and-stare iris recognition systems. Such iris images are generally acquired with greater standoff distances for surveillance or from mobile devices with less cooperative individuals. This chapter examines such iris recognition challenges and evaluates iris recognition capabilities under more realistic scenarios.

Iris images acquired under less-constrained imaging environments often present varying regions of effective iris pixels. In this context, the conventional Hamming distance to match binarized iris templates may not be the best choice and is revisited in this chapter. Iris images under such less constrained imaging also present significant variations in occlusions, which should be carefully considered while simultaneously utilizing other available features within the same eye images. Since periocular information is inherently embedded in such iris images, the effectiveness of iris matching can benefit from the *relative* or adaptive attention on other areas in the same image, just like the adaptive attention that is imparted in the human visual systems.

This chapter introduces a new framework for periocular-assisted iris recognition. Iris images under a less-constrained imaging environment often present varying regions of

Iris and Periocular Recognition using Deep Learning. DOI: https://doi.org/10.1016/B978-0-443-27318-6.00001-2

effective iris pixels for iris matching. Such differences in the effective number of available iris pixels can be used to dynamically reinforce periocular information, which is simultaneously available from such iris images. Such dynamic reinforcement should also consider effective regions of discriminative features that receive varying attention during respective periocular matching. This framework therefore incorporates such discriminative information using a multilayer perceptron (MLP) network for less-constrained iris recognition. The experimental results presented in this chapter for within-database matching on three publicly available databases indicate outperforming results over state-of-the-art methods. Also, the ROC results show that such an algorithm outperforms others in cross-dataset matching. The results from within dataset matching and cross-dataset matching validate the effectiveness and generalization ability of this framework.

8.1.1 Challenges in accurately matching less-constrained iris images

The framework presented in the preceding chapters exhibits remarkable prowess in iris recognition, delivering unmatched reliability and accuracy for iris images acquired using conventional sensors and in indoor environments. Nevertheless, as the conventional iris imaging constraints loosen or the user's cooperation dwindles, encountering iris recognition challenges becomes inevitable.

The incorporation of iris segmentation is fundamental for extracting more discriminant information from the acquired images. However, the segmentation accuracy of the trained network can noticeably deteriorate for the less-constrained iris images, consequently impacting the overall match accuracy. This degradation can also be observed while utilizing the *MaskNet*, described in Chapter 2, for generating iris masks. Some examples of such segmentation samples using CASIA.v4 Distance iris dataset [17], with images of best/worst/average cases, are shown in Fig. 8−1. In the best case, the eyelid information and noise from the eyelash can be accurately segmented. Most of the iris pattern is considered as noniris part in the worst-case sample. In the average case, the mask will include part of the valuable iris region. Dynamic consideration of the effective number of iris pixels, after the iris segmentation, can lead to enhanced match accuracy and is one motivation for the unified framework introduced in the following section.

During the conventional iris recognition, or while matching two binarized iris templates, the black pixels (representing "0") and white pixels (representing "1") are given equal importance. However, with the templates generated from the iris images that are acquired under less constrained environments, such practice of imparting equal importance may not be the best choice and needs to be revisited. Therefore this chapter presents a new approach to match such templates using a specialized similarity measure instead of the conventional

(A)   (B)   (C)

FIGURE 8–1 Iris segmentation results from sample images in CASIA.v4 Distance dataset.

Hamming distance in the literature [69], which can accommodate the importance of different bits in iris templates. The experimental results presented in Sections 8.3.2 and 8.3.3, just for matching such iris templates from three publicly available iris databases, consistently indicate outperforming results and validate the effectiveness of such an approach, especially for the less constrained iris recognition.

8.2 Dynamic iris recognition framework

The framework for dynamic iris recognition is designed to benefit from multifeature collaboration schemes that can adaptively consider the importance and availability of ocular features to achieve significantly accurate iris recognition. The block diagram of this framework is illustrated in Fig. 8−1. A detailed explanation of the different blocks in this diagram is systematically introduced in the following three sections.

This framework adopts the *UniNet* architecture introduced in Chapter 2 to generate iris templates. It also attempts to recover reliable periocular features from the same eye or the iris images using the network architecture (consisting of *AttenNet* and *FCN-Peri*) for matching periocular images that was introduced in Chapter 7. This framework is trained during two different training or offline phases. Each of the acquired images is essentially an eye image that represents a range of ocular features, in addition to the embedded iris features in the sclera region surrounding the pupil. Therefore such input images are firstly preprocessed to independently recover the normalized iris images that are typically used in conventional iris recognition. The corresponding region of interest images are fed to the respective subnets and trained independently during the *first* network training phase. During the *second* training phase, all the parameters in two subnets are frozen and used to recover several cues that indicate the similarity among the iris and periocular templates, including the effective region of iris images among matched templates and the corresponding periocular region components among the matched templates.

Finally, these cues from the two subnets are employed to train an MLP network that can enable a binary prediction using the softmax cross-entropy loss. In the performance evaluation or test phase, the trained models take a pair of eye images as input and generate prediction results from the last softmax layer. These softmax layer results are considered as the consolidated match scores between the input or the unknown eye pair images. By utilizing these consolidated match scores, binary classification decisions are made for various applications involving at-a-distance or less-constrained iris images.

The subsequent sections in the following provide in-depth information and elaboration on the distinct components of the dynamic iris recognition framework.

8.2.1 Generation of iris templates

Initially, every acquired eye image undergoes a two-step process: localization of the region of interest through iris segmentation and subsequent image normalization. The image normalization preprocessing step follows the same approach as previously discussed in Section 1.2.1

or Section 2.1. The dimension of all the segmented and normalized iris images generated from the preprocessing steps from all the databases employed for the experimentation reported in this chapter is empirically fixed to 512×64 pixels. After the normalization, these images are also subjected to contrast enhancement, which saturates 5% of iris region pixels at high and low intensities.

The normalized rectangular iris images are used to extract feature templates and masks representing valid iris pixels or regions. For this purpose, the *UniNet* architecture, which has demonstrated state-of-the-art iris-matching capabilities, was employed, as introduced in Section 2.2. The *UniNet* includes two fully convolutional sub-networks called *FeatNet* and *MaskNet*, as detailed in Table 8−1. The *MaskNet* is responsible for generating binary masks that differentiate valid and unreliable regions within the iris templates, which can significantly impact iris match accuracy. To train the network, a triplet architecture is utilized, and triplets with a ratio of 1:3 between genuine match pairs and imposter match pairs are incorporated as the respective training sets. The *MaskNet* is pretrained using ND-IRIS-0405 Iris Image Dataset [76], and all its parameters are then frozen during the subsequent training of the *FeatNet*. The *FeatNet*, pretrained with ND-IRIS-0405 Iris Image Dataset, is finetuned using the triplet pairs generated from the respective training sets. The *FeatNet* is essentially a fully convolutional neural network, as detailed in Chapter 2. The loss function introduced for the *FeatNet* training is the extended triplet loss, which aims to enlarge the margin of the pseudo-Hamming distance between the intra-class and interclass matching. The extended triplet loss is defined in Eq. (2−2) and was also used for training the *FeatNet* network in Chapter 2. The margin between anchor-positive and anchor-negative distances was empirically set to be 0.1 for all the experimental results detailed in Section 8.3.

8.2.2 Iris template matching using similarity score

Hamming distance is widely employed to compute the dissimilarities between two binary feature templates in a range of biometric identification problems, such as for the iris as discussed in earlier chapters, or palmprint recognition [176]. Such Hamming distance-based matching implicitly assumes that all template values in the coding space have equal importance for distinguishing the user identity. However, the methods used for feature extraction, binarization, and the nature of input images can influence the significance of the white (ones) and black (zeros) areas in the encoded images. As a result, a more adaptable distance measure is introduced to account for this asymmetric importance while matching less-constrained iris images. Such measure is also referred to as the weighted similarity score (*WS*) with azzoo similarity measure [91] and is also incorporated for matching iris templates.

The effectiveness of white pixel matching and the black pixel matching in feature templates can also be experimentally evaluated. Let us assume that the number of white pixels and black pixels from one feature template A can be respectively represented as $P_w(A)$ and $P_B(A)$. While comparing two template A and template B, we can perform only white pixels matching $M_W(A, B)$ and only black pixels matching $M_B(A, B)$, and can compute the white

Table 8–1 Specification of *UniNet* incorporated in the Unified Framework (Fig. 8–2).

Layer name	Layer type	Kernel size	Output channel
FeatNet			
Conv1	Convolution	3×7	16
Tanh1	TanH activation	–	16
Pool1	Average pooling	2×2	16
Conv2	Convolution	3×5	32
Tanh2	TanH activation	–	32
Pool2	Average pooling	2×2	32
Res1	Deconvolution	4×4	32
Conv3	Convolution	3×3	64
Tanh3	TanH activation	–	64
Pool3	Average pooling	2×2	64
Res2	Deconvolution	8×8	64
Concat	Concatenation	–	112
Conv4	Convolution	3×3	1
MaskNet			
m_Conv1	Convolution	3×3	16
m_ReLU1	ReLU activation	–	16
m_Pool1	Max pooling	2×2	16
m_Conv2	Convolution	3×3	32
m_ReLU2	ReLU activation	–	32
m_Pool2	Max pooling	2×2	32
m_Score2	Convolution	1×1	2
m_Conv3	Convolution	3×3	64
m_ReLU3	ReLU activation	–	64
m_Pool3	Max pooling	2×2	64
m_Score3	Convolution	1×1	2
m_Conv4	Convolution	3×3	128
m_ReLU4	ReLU activation	–	128
m_Pool4	Max pooling	4×4	128
m_Score4	Convolution	1×1	2
m_Upscore4	Deconvolution	8×8	2
m_Score34	Elementwise sum	–	2
m_Upscore34	Deconvolution	4×4	2
m_Score234	Elementwise sum	–	2
m_Fuse	Deconvolution	4×4	2

pixel matching rates $R_w(A, B)$ and black pixel matching rate $R_B(A, B)$ as shown in the following two equations:

$$R_W(A, B) = \frac{2 \times M_W(A, B)}{P_w(A) + P_w(B)} \qquad (8-1)$$

$$R_B(A, B) = \frac{2 \times M_B(A, B)}{P_B(A) + P_B(B)} \qquad (8-2)$$

The difference in the contributions from different pixels matching, that is, average R_w and R_B from the genuine and imposter pairs, can also be empirically observed from the experiments using templates generated from the databases. We select 1000 genuine matching and 2000 imposter match from the test on CASIA-Mobile-V1-S3 dataset for empirical evaluation. It was observed that the average R_w is 0.5733 and the average R_B is 0.6138 for the genuine matches, while R_w is 0.4159 and the average R_B is 0.4563 for the imposter matches.

To accommodate differences in the discriminative information from the white pixel pairs and from the black pixel pairs, we use different weight and generate weighted similarity measure as follows:

$$WS\left(I_{i,j}^1, I_{i,j}^2\right) = \begin{cases} 2 - \alpha, & if \quad I_{i,j}^1 = I_{i,j}^2 = 1 \\ \alpha, & if \quad I_{i,j}^1 = I_{i,j}^2 = 0 \\ 0, & if \quad I_{i,j}^1 \neq I_{i,j}^2 \end{cases} \tag{8-3}$$

where $I_{i,j}^1, I_{i,j}^2$ are pixels in row i and column j in the two matched iris templates, and α is hyperparameter controlling the significance of coding pairs. In all our experiments, α is empirically set as 0.3. Assuming the image size of iris images are $H \times W$, we generate the match score using the weighted similarity as follows:

$$S_{ws} = \frac{1}{H \times W} \sum_{i=1}^{H} \sum_{j=1}^{W} WS\left(I_{i,j}^1, I_{i,j}^2\right) \tag{8-4}$$

It can be observed that when the α is unity, the value of S_{ws} is one minus the normalized Hamming distance. Therefore weighted similarity can be considered as a more flexible alternative for the template matching.

8.2.3 Periocular features generation and matching

The periocular preprocessing is more simplified and involves image normalization using a bilinear filter. The dimensions of all normalized periocular images are empirically fixed as 300×240. Detailed studies presented in Chapters 6 and 7 have demonstrated that periocular recognition with an attention model yields exceptional performance. Hence, for generating periocular templates, or features, the periocular recognition model employed here also encompasses two components: *FCN-Peri* and *AttenNet*. The architectures for these networks are provided in Table 8−2 for easy reference.

The *FCN-Peri* is a fully convolutional network designed to detect the eye region and eyebrow region in the periocular images presented. The *FCN-Peri* for the near-infrared images used here is the same as trained or generated in Chapter 7 and no additional fine tuning is performed. By automatically detecting the eye and eyebrow regions, *AttenNet* can provide pixel locations for these specific areas, enabling focused attention on these regions to generate more distinctive periocular features. The output of *AttenNet* is a feature vector comprising 512 elements. During the training phase, we compute the distance-driven sigmoid

Table 8–2   Details on architecture for the *AttenNet* and *FCN-Peri*.

Layer name	Layer type	Kernel size	Output channels
AttenNet			
Conv1_1	Convolution	5 × 5	32
ReLU1_1	ReLU activation	–	32
Conv1_2	Convolution	5 × 5	32
ReLU1_2	ReLU activation	–	32
Pool1	Max pooling	2 × 2	32
Slice_roi	Slice	–	32
Conv2_1, A_Conv2_1	Convolution	3 × 3	32
ReLU2_1, A_ReLU2_1	ReLU Activation	–	32
Conv2_2, A_Conv2_2	Convolution	3 × 3	32
ReLU2_2, A_ReLU2_2	ReLU activation	–	32
Pool2, A_Pool2	Max pooling	2 × 2	32
Att2	Attention	–	–
Conv3_1, A_Conv3_1	Convolution	3 × 3	64
ReLU3_1, A_ReLU3_1	ReLU activation	–	64
Conv3_2, A_Conv3_2	Convolution	3 × 3	64
ReLU3_2, A_ReLU3_2	ReLU activation	–	64
Pool2, A_Pool2	Max pooling	2 × 2	64
Conv4_1, A_Conv4_1	Convolution	3 × 3	64
ReLU4_1, A_ReLU4_1	ReLU activation	–	64
Conv4_2, A_Conv4_2	Convolution	3 × 3	64
ReLU4_2, A_ReLU4_2	ReLU activation	–	64
Pool4, A_Pool4	Max pooling	2 × 2	64
Att4	Attention	–	–
Feat, A_Feat	Fully connected	–	64
FCN-Peri			
Conv1	Convolution	5 × 5	16
ReLU1	ReLU activation	–	16
Pool1	Max pooling	2 × 2	16
Conv2	Convolution	3 × 3	32
ReLU2	ReLU activation	–	32
Conv2_s	Convolution	1 × 1	3
Pool2	Max pooling	2 × 2	32
Conv3	Convolution	3 × 3	64
ReLU3	ReLU activation	–	64
Conv3_s	Convolution	1 × 1	3
Pool3	Max pooling	2 × 2	64
Conv4	Convolution	3 × 3	128
ReLU4	ReLU activation	–	128
Conv4_s	Convolution	1 × 1	3
Upscore4	Deconvolution	8 × 8	3
Score34	Elementwise sum	–	3
Upscore34	Deconvolution	4 × 4	3
Score234	Elementwise sum	–	3
Fuse	Deconvolution	4 × 4	3

cross-entropy (DSC) loss between the Siamese pairs, generated from the corresponding training set. This DSC loss is the same as in Eq. (7−7). The ratio of genuine pairs and imposter pairs is set empirically as 1 : 2 for the network training.

8.2.4 Dynamic match score generation using multifeature collaboration

To develop any dynamic and effective dynamic mechanism to simultaneously utilize both iris and periocular cues available in the acquired images, various factors must be carefully considered. These factors include not only the similarity of individual features but also their importance as derived from the segmentation process, which can dynamically influence individual similarity scores. In less-constrained imaging conditions, acquired iris images often contain a varying number of effective iris pixels, contributing to the generation of respective iris match scores. Differences in the number of available iris pixels between two matched iris images can be utilized to dynamically reinforce periocular information, consolidating such cues to generate more reliable match scores. In addition, this dynamic reinforcement should account for the effective *regions* of discriminative features that receive varying attention during periocular matching. To address these considerations, an MLP network is incorporated. This network can dynamically consolidate multiple pieces of discriminative information and generates a more reliable consolidated match score between two unknown or input iris images. By carefully weighing the various cues and factors, such an approach can enable simultaneous utilization of both iris and periocular information, enhancing the overall performance of the system.

The dynamic feature collaboration mechanism can be visualized from the right-hand part of the framework in Fig. 8−2. The *UniNet* in this figure is employed to generate pseudo-binary feature maps, along with the respective masks, while the *AttenNet* generates the feature vectors that are used to compute Euclidean distance among respective ROI maps. This framework can therefore simultaneously generate iris match scores and periocular match scores using the Euclidean distance. Additionally, an essential input for the MLP is the mask

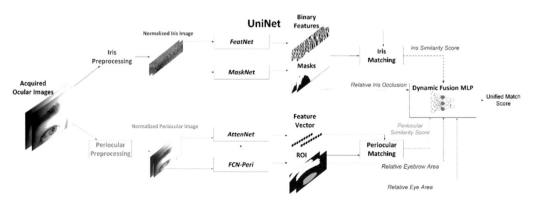

FIGURE 8–2 Unified framework for dynamic iris recognition using the collaboration of multiple features from deep neural networks.

Table 8–3   Architecture of MLP incorporated for the dynamic fusion.

Layer name	Layer type	Input channels	Output channels
FC1	Fully connected	8	32
Tanh1	TanH activation	32	32
FC2	Fully connected	32	16
Tanh2	TanH activation	16	16
FC3	Fully connected	16	8
Tanh3	TanH activation	8	8
FC4	Fully connected	8	2

rate, which effectively represents the importance or reliability of the respective iris match scores. This mask rate is quantified as the ratio between the valid pixels and all iris pixels among the two matches iris image templates. By considering the mask rate alongside the feature maps and vectors, we can make more informed decisions and obtain reliable consolidated match scores from both iris and periocular cues in the two matched images.

Similarly, the effectiveness of periocular feature template match scores is quantified using the eye and eyebrow ratio sum and the difference, that is, sum (also difference) of eye areas among matched periocular images and sum (also difference) of eyebrow areas among matched periocular images. These areas are automatically predicted or inherently available from *AttenNet*, as illustrated in Fig. 8−2. The MLP network therefore receives eight/seven element feature vector and is trained offline using respective genuine and impostor pairs from the training part of the dataset. This process allows the network to learn and comprehend the discriminative information necessary for matching any two iris images. Such a trained network can effectively generate consolidated match scores by extracting *softmax* values from the final layer output, which fall within the range of 0−1. The architecture of the MLP used in the experiments is summarized in Table 8−3.

8.3 Experiments and results

The framework introduced in Fig. 8−2 is validated using a series of experiments on three publicly available datasets, to ascertain its effectiveness for less-constrained iris recognition. This section first provides details on the three public datasets used in for the experimentation. The details of the experimental protocols are provided in the following section. This section also provides a comparative analysis of results from the dynamic iris recognition framework and with other state-of-the-art methods.

8.3.1 Less-constrained eye image databases and protocols

The experimental results presented in this section utilized the following three near-infrared eye image datasets in the public domain. Fig. 8−3 illustrates the sample eye images from these different datasets.

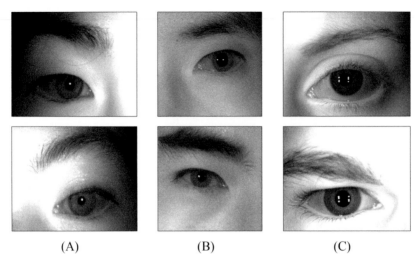

(A)   (B)   (C)

FIGURE 8–3 A Sample eye images from publicly available databases: (A) CASIA-Mobile-V1-S3 database, (B) CASIA iris image v.4 distance database, and (C) Q-FIRE-05-middle-illumination database.

8.3.1.1 Q-FIRE dataset

The Quality in Face and Iris Research Ensemble (Q-FIRE) dataset [18] is a publicly available dataset with at-a-distance iris images. The experiments in this section use Q-FIRE-05-middle-illumination subset which has been acquired from a distance of 5 ft. under middle-level near-infrared illumination. The periocular region images are automatically segmented using a trained Fast-RCNN detector. The processed dataset included both eye images from 159 different subjects. The first 15 right-eye images are used to train the network while the first 10 left-eye images are used for the test or the performance evaluation. This set of experiments therefore generated 7155 (45×159) genuine match scores and 1,256,100 ($159 \times 158 \times 50$) imposter match scores.

8.3.1.2 CASIA-Moblie-V1-S3 dataset

The CASIA-Mobile-V1-S3 dataset [177] is another publicly available dataset, which includes 3600 face images from 360 different subjects and these images have been acquired using a mobile device with near-infrared illumination. A Fast-RCNN detector [178] is trained with 100 manually labeled samples to detect the periocular region. We follow the same match protocols, both for the iris matching and periocular matching as described in [177]. Therefore the training set includes 3600 samples from 360 classes (eyes) in the first 180 subjects. The test set includes the other 3600 samples from 360 classes (eyes) in 180 subjects. The left eye is matched with all the left-eye images while the right-eye images are matched with all the right ones. Thereafter the left eye match scores and right eye match scores are combined using the sum rule and generate 8100 genuine and 1,611,000 imposter match scores.

8.3.1.3 CASIA iris image v.4 distance dataset

This subset of the CASIA.v4 database [17] contains the upper part of face images from 142 subjects. We detect the iris region images with an OpenCV-implemented iris detector [83], just as detailed and used in Chapter 2, and generate an eye images dataset with 2446 image instances. The training set comprises all the right eye samples, and the test set is composed of all the left eye samples just as for the experiments in Chapter 2. The test set therefore generated 20,702 genuine match scores and 2,969,533 imposter match scores.

8.3.2 Iris and periocular recognition

In this section, comparative experimental results are obtained by utilizing the framework introduced in Section 8.2, which allows for the simultaneous recovery of iris and periocular features. For these experiments, all models were trained using their respective training sets, and their verification performance was evaluated using the corresponding test set, as detailed in Sections 8.3.1.1−8.3.1.3. We use iris recognition results generated from the *UniNet* (Chapter 2), and periocular recognition results generated using the *AttenNet* (Chapter 7), as the baseline methods for the comparative performance evaluation. Also, we provide comparison using the static score level combination, using the iris match scores generated using similarity measure (8.4) by us with the periocular match scores, with weighted sum. These comparative results using the respective benchmarks are presented in Fig. 8−4 and summarized in Table 8−4.

The comparative ROC plots shown in 8.4, along with the GAR and EER values summarized in Table 8−5, indicate outperforming performance from this set of within-database experiments. It can be observed that the iris recognition itself, using the weighted similarity measure, achieves significantly superior performance over the prior state-of-the-art iris recognition methods, that is, both the conventional and deep learning-based methods. The combination of respective iris and periocular match scores using static fusion rules can also offer noticeable performance enhancement, while the dynamic fusion framework using DCNN provides consistently outperforming results on three different datasets This approach also outperforms the framework proposed in [16] or TIP13 as abbreviated here. This limited performance can be attributed to the lack of any specialized periocular matching algorithm in [16] and is plausibly the main constrain in limiting the overall performance. The Maxout CNN is based on our implementation [179] and the parameters provided in [177], since there is no publicly available code for the DCNN model and the employed segmentation algorithm. Also, the Bath dataset [41] used to pretrain the model in [177] is no longer publicly available.

8.3.3 Cross-database performance evaluation

This section presents the experimental results using the cross-database performance evaluation. Two sets of configurations were considered; first, incorporate the model which is trained using the CASIA.v4-distance database to match the iris images from the CASIA-Mobile-V1-S3

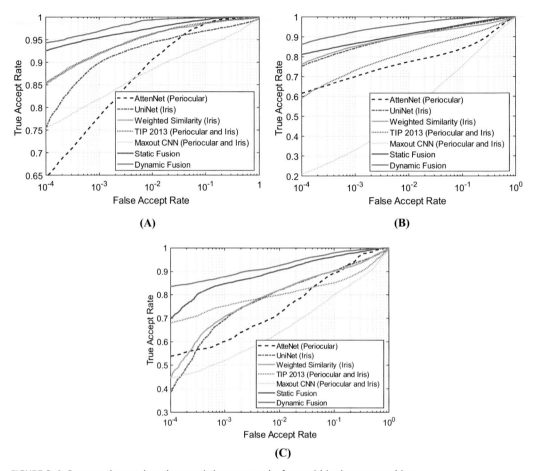

FIGURE 8–4 Comparative receiver characteristic curve results from within dataset matching.

and Q-FIRE databases directly without any fine-tuning. Second, we also present cross-database experimental results with the model, which is only trained using the CASIA-Mobile-V1-S3 database and used to match the iris images from the CASIA.v4-distance and Q-FIRE databases. This set of experiments is aimed to validate the generalization capability of the framework, especially when the image samples available for the training are quite limited. The EER values are summarized in Table 8−5 and the respective ROCs are illustrated in Fig. 8−5.

The results obtained from this set of cross-database experiments indicate consistent performance improvement which can indicate the generality of the dynamic iris recognition framework introduced to match less-constrained iris images. Additional cross-database experiments for the recognition problem were also performed and used the CMC plots to ascertain such performance in Fig. 8−6. In such a set of experiments, the leave-out-one protocol was followed, that is, we select one probe image from the test set and perform matching with other images. These results also present encouraging and superior performance, to a

Table 8–4 Comparative summary of match accuracy and equal error rates for within dataset comparison.

	CASIA-Mobile-V1-S3		CASIA.v4-distance		Q-FIRE	
	TAR@FAR $= 10^{-4}$	EER	TAR@FAR $= 10^{-4}$	EER	TAR@FAR $= 10^{-4}$	EER
TIP13 [16] (periocular and iris)	85.4%	2.43%	59.2%	9.93%	68.0%	13.86%
Maxout CNN [177] (periocular and iris)	75.4%	7.15%	21.0%	17.99%	44.5%	16.74%
AttenNet (Chapter 7) (periocular)	64.6%	3.93%	61.6%	14.27%	53.9%	10.55%
UniNet (*Iris*)	75.5%	3.94%	75.3%	5.54%	38.7%	9.72%
Weighted similarity (iris)	85.3%	2.57%	76.0%	6.12%	44.9%	9.85%
Static fusion	92.5%	1.85%	81.5%	5.23%	69.8%	4.95%
Dynamic fusion	94.3%	0.73%	86.3%	2.29%	83.6%	3.87%

Table 8–5 Summary of EER values during cross-database performance evaluation.

Training database	CASIA.v4-distance		CASIA-Mobile-V1-S3	
Test database	CASIA-Mobile-V1-S3	Q-FIRE	CASIA.v4-distance	Q-FIRE
AttenNet (periocular)	9.78%	10.15%	13.69%	12.79%
UniNet (iris)	4.11%	9.72%	7.06%	10.01%
Dynamic fusion	1.62%	6.49%	6.28%	6.43%

varying degree, and validate the generalization capability of the dynamic matching framework for the related iris recognition problem.

8.3.4 Open-set performance evaluation

A range of real-world applications of less-constrained iris recognition will require cross-database performance evaluation from such algorithms under open-set matching scenarios. Therefore open-set performance evaluation, using the cross-database settings as described in the previous section, was also performed to validate the effectiveness of the dynamic fusion framework. It is important to note that the closed-set identification, as detailed in Sections 8.3.2 and 8.3.3, involves comparisons between the gallery and the known probes.

In open-set identification, the gallery contains known subjects who have been enrolled, while the query subjects are unknown and only encountered during the query time. The goal of open-set identification is to correctly recognize the probe subjects that exist in the gallery while rejecting all other probe queries that as unknown. This approach is commonly used in surveillance and during person reidentification applications.

For the experimental analysis detailed in this section, we designate the last 30 test subjects as the unknown subjects in all or the respective datasets. These unknown subjects are *not* part

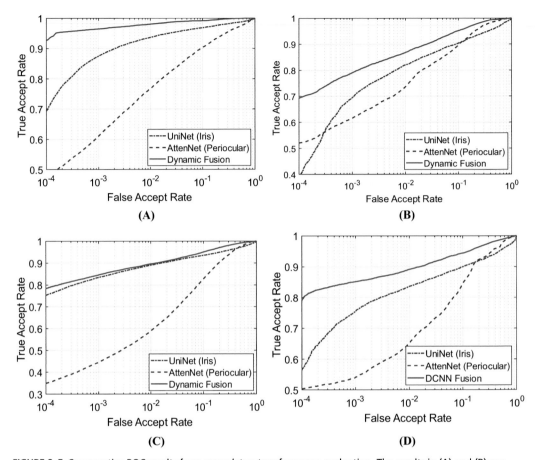

FIGURE 8–5 Comparative ROC results from *cross-dataset* performance evaluation. The results in (A) and (B) use the model trained with CASIA.v4 Distance database while the results in (C) and (D) use the model trained with CASIA-Mobile-V1-S3 database.

of the gallery or the enrollment. This configuration allows us to evaluate the performance of the open-set identification framework more comprehensively. We then ascertain the open-set performance using the false positive identification rate (FPIR) against false negative identification rate (FNIR), like in other references for the large-scale performance evaluation, for example, [14]. These plots are shown in Fig. 8–7, while their identification rates and equal error rates are summarized in Table 8–4. These results indicate consistent performance improvement, to varying degrees, and underline the merit of the dynamic iris recognition framework for cross-database open-set recognition applications.

8.3.5 Cross-distance performance evaluation

Cross-distance performance evaluation enables us to assess the effectiveness of the iris recognition framework in accurately matching iris images acquired from different distances,

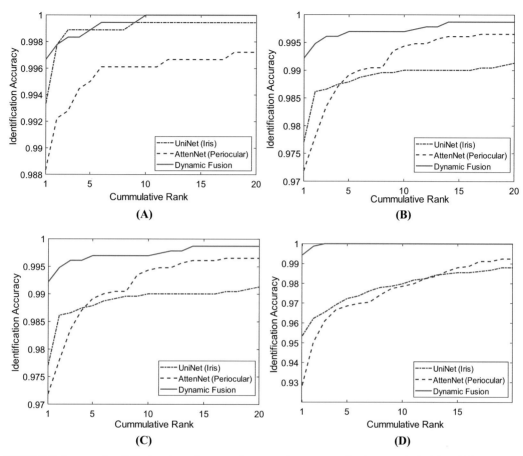

FIGURE 8–6 Comparative CMC plots from the *cross-dataset* performance evaluation. Results in (A) and (B) use the model trained with CASIA.v4 Distance database while those in (C) and (D) use the model which is trained using CASIA-Mobile-V1-S3 database.

even when the model is trained using databases that are only available from some other* distances. This evaluation provides valuable insights into the actual performance of iris-matching algorithms for surveillance-related operations, where enrolled subjects from one distance are matched with subjects imaged at some other (greater) distances.

In order to perform such performance evaluation, we use the model which is trained from the iris images that were acquired at a distance of 5 ft, that is, specifically using the Q-FIRE-05-middle-illumination database. This approach allows us to examine the framework's ability to generalize and relative performance when dealing with iris images captured at varying distances, resembling real-world scenarios with diverse imaging conditions. This model is used to match the same subjects' iris images acquired from 7-ft distance

---

* Generally, the iris image databases acquired from nearer (stop and stare) distances are widely available.

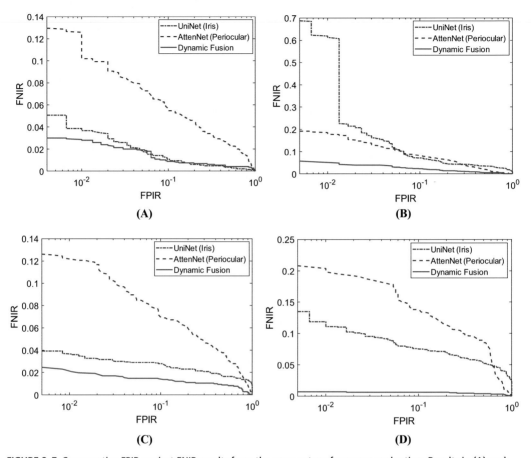

FIGURE 8–7 Comparative FPIR against FNIR results from the open set performance evaluation. Results in (A) and (B) use the model trained with CASIA.v4 Distance database while those in (C) and (D) use the model which is trained using CASIA-Mobile-V1-S3 database.

(available in the Q-FIRE-07-middle-illumination dataset) and from 11-ft distance (available in the Q-FIRE-11-middle-illumination dataset). These images have been acquired from 7- and 11-ft distances, respectively, under the same illumination condition and therefore represent more realistic scenarios for less-constrained iris recognition.

The 4703 samples from 159 right eyes in the Q-FIRE-05-middle-illumination dataset compose the gallery and attempt to use 10 samples from the same eye as the test probe to match with the respective gallery. There are 1576 test samples from the Q-FIRE-07-middle-illumination dataset and 1543 test samples from the QFRIE Q-FIRE-11-middle-illumination dataset. These matchings ensure that every genuine and impostor match pairs use two images that are acquired from different distances. After performing such matching, we get 46,110 genuine match scores and 7,365,318, imposter match scores for the Q-FIRE-07-middle-illumination dataset, and 45,665 genuine match scores and 7,215,767 imposter match scores for the

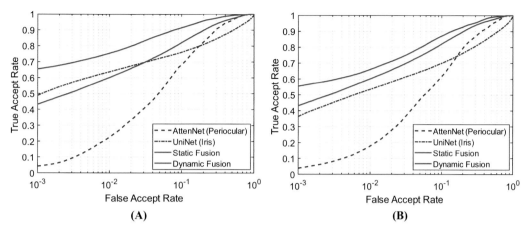

FIGURE 8–8 Comparative matching performance for *cross-distance* iris image matching.

Table 8–6   Summary of EER values from cross-database performance evaluation.

Approach	5 ft with 7 ft (%)	5 ft with 11 ft (%)
UniNet (iris)	19.29	22.44
AttenNet (periocular)	18.76	20.20
Static fusion	11.84	14.04
Dynamic fusion	9.11	11.57

Q-FIRE-11-middle-illumination dataset. The comparative ROC plots are shown in Fig. 8−8, while respective EER values are summarized in Table 8−6. It can be observed from these results that the average matching performance degrades under cross-distance matching and is quite expected. However significant improvement was observed in the matching accuracy, using the unified framework. These results can help to validate the effectiveness of the dynamic iris recognition framework for cross-distance iris matching.

8.4 Comparative analysis of static and dynamic fusion

The complementary nature of match scores generated from the deep features in our experiments is vividly demonstrated by the two-dimensional plots representing iris and periocular scores. Fig. 8−9 unveils these plots, portraying the distribution of (normalized) genuine and imposter scores derived from iris and periocular matching with their respective databases. In each axis, the subplots display kernel density estimation of each score distribution. Remarkably, these plots from less-constrained iris images reveal the immense potential of the joint use of individual match scores. This concerted approach allows for more effective separation between genuine and impostor identities, exemplifying the success of the dynamic framework for iris recognition.

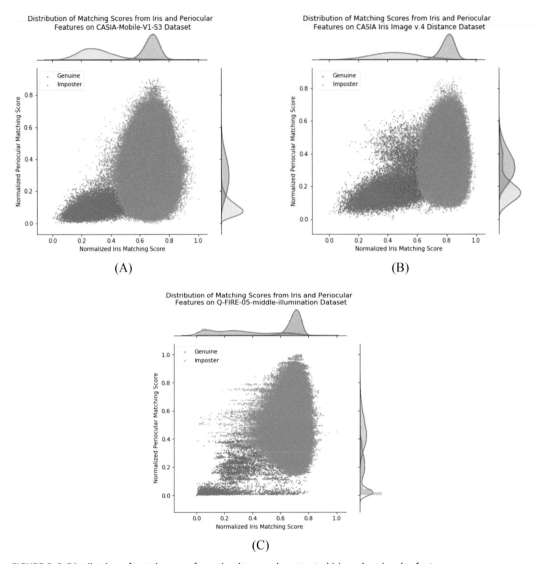

FIGURE 8–9 Distribution of match scores from simultaneously extracted iris and periocular features.

While discussing dynamic fusion, it is important to consider some well-established methods for static match score fusion that have shown merit in the biometrics literature. The weighted combination of individual match scores is computationally simpler, easy to implement, and is also used in many applications as it can enable superior performance. In addition, there are some other computationally simpler methods, for example, maximum or best of match scores, product of match scores, and nonlinear combination of match scores, which are also worth evaluating their fusion performance. The consolidated match scores from such static fusion rules can be obtained as follows:

$$s_a = \sum_{j=1}^{2} s_j w_j \tag{8-5}$$

$$s_b = \prod_{j=1}^{2} s_j^{w_j} \tag{8-6}$$

$$s_c = \max_{j=1,2} \left(s_j \right) \tag{8-7}$$

$$s_d = \sum_{j=1}^{2} \tanh(s_j) w_j \tag{8-8}$$

where $s_a, s_b, s_c,$ and s_d, respectively, represent the combined match score using weighed sum, product rule, max rule, and nonlinear combination. The weights for these fusion rules, for example, w_1 and w_2, are empirically computed with respective constraints ($w_1 + w_2 = 1$) and by sum. product rule, max rule, and nonlinear combination. The weights for these fusion rules, for example, w_1 and w_2, are empirically computed with respective constraints ($w_1 + w_2 = 1$) and by using the training part of the databases. The comparative experimental results from different fusion rules, on three different databases, are presented in Fig. 8−10. The respective EER values are summarized in Table 8−7. These results indicate the effectiveness of the dynamic fusion approach in significantly enhancing the match accuracy for the less-constrained iris images.

8.5 Ablation Study and Discussion

The experimental results presented in Section 8.3 indicate wide improvement in the performance using the dynamic iris recognition framework using deeply learned features. In the cross-dataset CMC plots in Fig. 8−6, we can observe that all the rank-one accuracy achieved is higher than 95%. Therefore there is still some room for further performance improvement for such closed-world performance from the respective databases. It should be noted that the images in these datasets were acquired from a distance and under a less-constrained environment. Therefore there are also several poor-quality or noisy test image samples in these databases, and these are resulting from varying degrees of occlusion, poor illumination, and blur from defocus. Fig. 8−11 illustrates such samples with poor-quality images and is to underline extreme challenges in discriminating the identities from such images.

There are several network-related parameters that are empirically determined for the framework in Fig. 8−2. Such parameter tuning process was performed using the CASIA-Mobile-V1-S3 dataset. Fig. 8−12A illustrates the performance plots for the different triplet

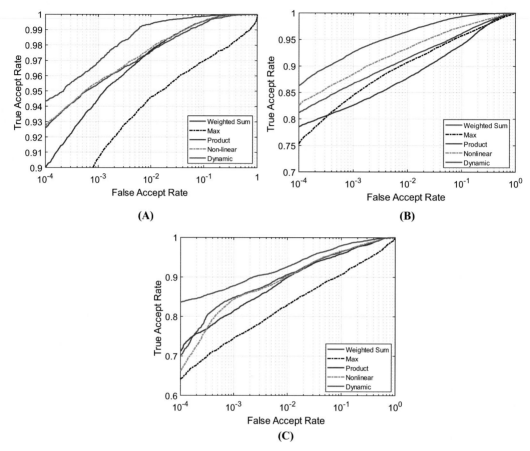

FIGURE 8–10 Comparative performance from different fusion algorithms using within-database performance evaluations.

Table 8–7   Summary of EER values from competing fusion methods.

	CASIA-Mobile-V1-S3	CASIA.v4 Distance	Q-FIRE
Weighted sum	5.23%	1.85%	4.95%
Max	5.54%	3.90%	9.50%
Product	6.94%	1.78%	5.34%
Nonlinear (Tanh)	4.00%	1.69%	4.84%
Dynamic	2.29%	0.73%	3.87%

margins m. The ratio of the genuine match scores and imposter match scores during the training of the network for iris ROI matching, using triplet architecture, was fixed to 1:3, and Fig. 8−12B illustrates the performance plots of different values of such ratio. These ablation studies' results are included to justify the choice of parameters for the framework. The ratio

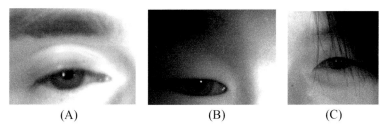

(A)   (B)   (C)

FIGURE 8–11 Image samples from less constrained iris image databases with significant image quality degradations: (A) defocus blur sample in Q-FIRE database, (B) poor illumination sample in CAISA-Mobile-V1-S3 database, and (C) severely occluded sample in CASIA v.4 Distance database.

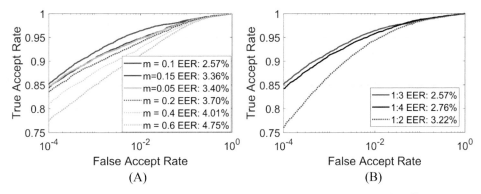

FIGURE 8–12 Comparative performance from ablation study with (A) different margins and (B) different triplet ratios.

Table 8–8   Average segmentation errors from *FCN-Peri*.

	Average segmentation error	
Approach	Eye area	Eyebrow area
MaskNet	3.54%	4.11%

of the genuine match scores and imposter match scores during the training of the Siamese network *AttenNet* for the periocular image matching was fixed to 1:2. This ratio is the same as used for the *AttenNet* introduced in Chapter 7.

The iris segmentation results performance using the *MaskNet* has already been evaluated in Table 2−5, and all the parameters for *MaskNet* were frozen for all the experiments on different databases. Therefore database-specific, or tuned parameters, were not employed for this network. The segmentation accuracy for the *FCN-Peri* employed in the framework (Fig. 8−2) using average segmentation error, defined earlier in Eq. (2−22), was evaluated. Therefore we also manually labeled 100 test images, as ground truth, from CASIA.v4 Distance database and computed the average segmentation error from *FCN-Peri*. These results are summarized in Table 8−8.

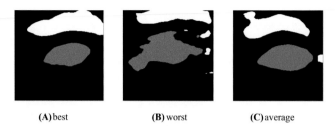

(A) best   **(B)** worst   **(C)** average

FIGURE 8–13 Periocular segmentation results from CASIA.v4 Distance database.

The *FCN-Peri* network is used to automatically locate the eye area and eyebrow area in the periocular image. In Fig. 8−13, sample periocular segmentation results from the same dataset are presented. This figure illustrates representative segmentation results from the best, worst, and average cases. In the best case, we can accurately detect the eye and eyebrow region. In the worst case, it cannot make precise pixel predictions, largely due to poor illumination. In the average case, some noisy points or regions are expected during the dense prediction.

8.6 Conclusions and further enhancements

This chapter systematically explained the design of a specialized framework for dynamic iris recognition. This design has been focussed to simultaneously recover periocular information to achieve enhanced match accuracy for the iris images acquired under less-constrained imaging environments. This framework incorporated weighted Hamming distances to achieve best of match scores from the iris features and also incorporated weighted (attention) measures to generate best matches for the periocular matching. Additionally, the fusion mechanism dynamically considers the significance of each modality, their relative importance, and the pertinent region of interest, leading to the generation of more dependable consolidated match scores. The experimental results, showcased using three publicly available datasets in this chapter, underscore the effectiveness of the proposed approach. The method demonstrates superior performance, evident through exemplary results in CMC and ROC plots, both within the dataset and in cross-dataset scenarios. Furthermore, this chapter extends its evaluation to *open-set* identification and *cross-distance* performance analysis, confirming the generalizability of the proposed approach. The results achieved in these assessments are significantly promising, reinforcing the potential and practicality of the presented methodology.

The dynamic framework discussed in this chapter incorporates an attention model with precomputed weights from the training database. This approach was chosen due to limited training data and to simplify visual interpretation. However, it's worth noting that this presents a limitation, which could be addressed by integrating a self-attention mechanism similar to as detailed in [180,181]. Self-attention mechanisms can highlight or compute the importance of relevant periocular features. In the context of less-constrained iris images, with the varying degrees of iris and periocular features, the capability to automatically guide the attention on more relevant iris features can remarkably enhance the performance for matching such real-world images. Such ability on top-down attention, as also introduced in [182] can enable periocular-adaptive representation for less-constrained iris recognition and can also be a promising extension for the framework discussed in this chapter.

Bispectral imaging of iris images, as demonstrated in [66], offers comprehensive details from ocular features and has demonstrated impressive matching results. Leveraging a dynamic combination of simultaneously acquired visible and near-infrared iris features within the same iris recognition framework (Fig. 8−2) could significantly enhance match accuracy, albeit with some added complexity.

Building an end-to-end framework for periocular and iris recognition framework is another possible direction to further enhance this framework. Iris recognition itself can be considered as an attention in the periocular recognition. Considering iris recognition itself as a form of attention within periocular recognition, an end-to-end framework that can perform segmentation, and simultaneously recover dynamically weighted discriminant features is expected to be a more attractive and elegant extension of the dynamic iris recognition framework using deep learning.

9

Position-specific convolutional neural network to accurately match iris and periocular images

In preceding chapters, we have systematically observed unparalleled success in accurately matching iris and periocular images using convolutional neural networks (CNNs). However, it's important to note that CNNs, by design, share the same parameters across the entire image. This presents a challenge, as the unique, distinguishing features within the iris and periocular images are typically spatially localized. Consequently, this parameter sharing can potentially limit the full realization of the CNN's capabilities. Thus in an attempt to address this challenge, we develop a specialized solution – a positional convolutional network, which is abbreviated to as *PosCNN* or *PosNet* in this chapter, that incorporates positional-specific convolutional kernels that are trained for each pixel. This chapter systematically describes this approach to extract more discriminant features, yielding superior match accuracy with considerably low complexity. Such feature representation is further refined to generate deeply learned 3D iris feature templates, which transcend the limited scope of 2D binary templates, for example, conventional *IrisCode* or FCN-based binary iris templates introduced in earlier chapters, to significantly enhance the model's performance. The similarity among these templates is computed using the *shifted* mean cosine distance, which can be executed at a remarkably faster speed using a conventional GPU card i.e. our implementation can compute over 30 million match scores within one second on a RTX 3080 GPU card. The experimental validation is presented using eight different publicly available databases: three public iris databases and five periocular image databases This specialized network architecture can offer consistently outperforming results, including many cross-database results, with relatively low computational complexity.

9.1 Introduction to new network design

CNNs are one of the most successful and widely used network architectures in deep learning, especially in computer vision. Its use of shared convolutional kernels throughout the input helps to reduce storage requirements [183] and leads to the "translation invariance" characteristics of CNN. Such use of shared weights in CNN significantly reduces the number of parameters, making the network easier to train. This is particularly beneficial in image detection or segmentation tasks, as the output should remain consistent regardless of the location of the target object or region of interest. However, this method of parameter sharing

Iris and Periocular Recognition using Deep Learning. DOI: https://doi.org/10.1016/B978-0-443-27318-6.00006-1

is less effective when matching ocular images, where iris images often have distinct features in different regions. Therefore it is more prudent to use positional-specific convolutional kernels.

One possible solution to address this challenge is to design a positional convolutional network that can incorporate position-specific convolutional kernels to compute the features. Selecting different kernels for various positions within images can extract more distinguishing features as compared to using shared kernels. However, this approach will significantly increase the number of parameters, making their optimization quite challenging. For example, if the original image size is 32*32 and we train a kernel for every pixel, the number of parameters would increase by over a thousand times. This increase is so substantial that implementing this idea is nearly unfeasible. To address this challenge, this chapter describes a new method for computing convolutional kernels based on position information. Through deduction, we can discover that this network structure can be divided into two regular convolutional layers, thereby increasing the feature representation ability while keeping the complexity only twice that of a conventional convolutional layer.

In addition to the design of *PosCNN*, we can enhance the representation of biometric feature templates. This model can generate a more accurate and reduced 3D feature template for each iris image rather than computing a 2D feature template or a 1D probability vector. Many state-of-the-art conventional or deep learning-based iris recognition algorithms generate binary feature templates that may be less precise in representing the feature. Therefore this approach extracts a reduced 3D feature template that requires less computation for matching as it reduces the need for calculating the shift distances, which is computationally demanding but a *must* operator for the binary feature templates like *IrisCode* or those generated from the trained deep network models in Chapters 2, 3 or 4. Since these feature templates are reduced, we only compute the mean of shifted cosine distance to generate the match score, instead of the Hamming distance as in Eq. 1-15 or Eq. 2-21, which can be computed more rapidly with amy conventional GPU card.

9.2 Position-specific convolutional neural network

9.2.1 Motivation

Deep learning-based iris recognition algorithms widely rely on the use of CNNs to extract the features. Compared to conventional hand-crafted texture features, convolutional networks can extract more discriminative features and offer improved accuracy, as also shown by the comparative results in Chapters 2 and 3. However, the architecture such CNNs may not be entirely suitable for the iris recognition tasks since these networks are designed for the generalized computer vision related tasks like image segmentation, object detection, and others.

CNNs rely on three crucial concepts: parameter sharing, sparse interactions, and equivariant representations [183]. Parameter sharing refers to the use of same parameter for multiple locations in a model, allowing for fewer parameters and easier training. The property of parameter sharing leads to translation invariance in convolutional layers. This property is useful in many computer vision tasks, like image segmentation and object detection, as the output should remain constant regardless of the object's location. However, this property is not as helpful for the iris or periocular recognition, as the features in such images can differ significantly in different spatial regions.

For such ocular recognition tasks, specific features are located in particular regions of the ROI images. For instance, in periocular images, there are typically eye browse and iris, and the eye browse is *always* located above the iris. Unless we rotate or flip the original image, we cannot find the eyebrows at the bottom of the periocular image while the iris is at the top of such an image. Therefore sharing the same parameter for every location does not make much sense. Sharing the same parameters for every location is also not efficient or complex, as it wastes computational resources by incorporating iris-specific kernels to the upper region and eye-browse-specific kernels to the lower region. Moreover, using inappropriate kernels in a specific region can negatively impact the final match performance. To address this challenge, we can train specific convolutional kernels in the upper region to extract the eyes-browse features and use different kernels in the bottom region to capture the iris' features. Such a design may lead to better performance for a range of ocular recognition tasks.

Therefore we are motivated to introduce a new network architecture that uses position-specific kernels rather than sharing the parameters.

9.2.2 Position-specific convolutional kernels

To build a position-specific convolutional network, the straightforward way is to train a set of convolutional kernels for every location, but it can result in a significant increase in number of parameters. For instance, when performing convolutional operations on a 128×128 image using 3×3 kernels (with a stride of 1 and padding of 1), the number of parameters is 16,384 times higher than that of a generic convolutional layer. Training such a network can be incredibly challenging. To address this challenge, we introduce a novel solution to tackle such problem from the *parameter explosion*. Instead of directly training position-specific kernels, we predict the kernels based on the position using a multilayer perceptron (MLP). Fig. $9-1A$ illustrates how we can build respective X matrix and Y matrix that holds the horizontal and vertical information of every pixel. We then train specific convolutional kernels using these two values for each pixel. Compared to a general convolutional layer, this method introduces only a few more MLP parameters, making it more feasible to train.

The use of position-specific kernels comes with high computational complexity. For instance, if the input and output channels are m and n, respectively, the input size is $w \times h$, and the convolutional kernel size is $k \times k$, then the output layer of MLP has $(m \times k \times k \times n)$ k^2mn neurons for the every picel.

Assuming that the hidden layers have p neurons, the resulting computational complexity will be at least $pwhk^2mn$ $(p \times k^2mn \times w \times h)$, which is a very large number especially when some parameters are not small. To mitigate this challenge and enhance the computational speed, several techniques can be employed: reducing the number of input/output channels,

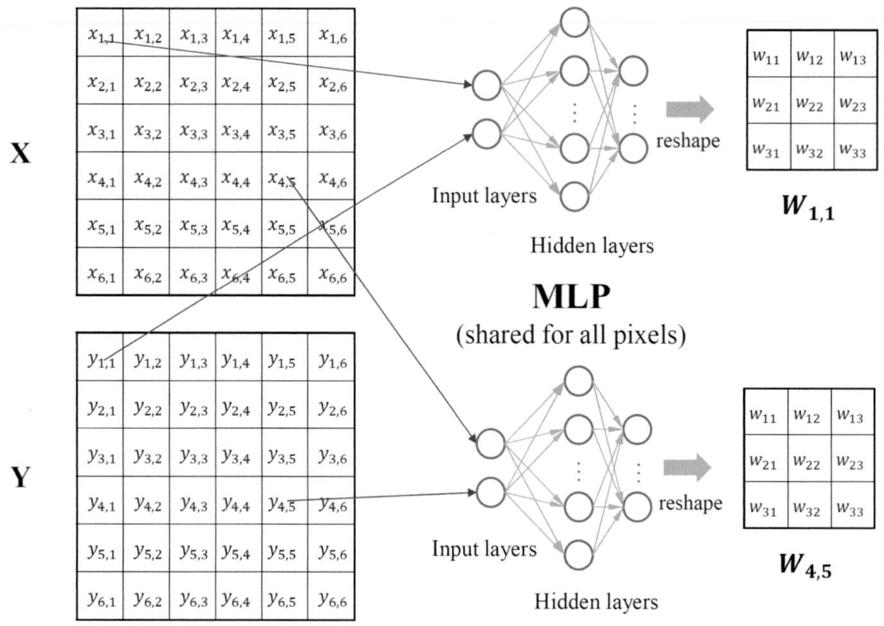

(A) MLP

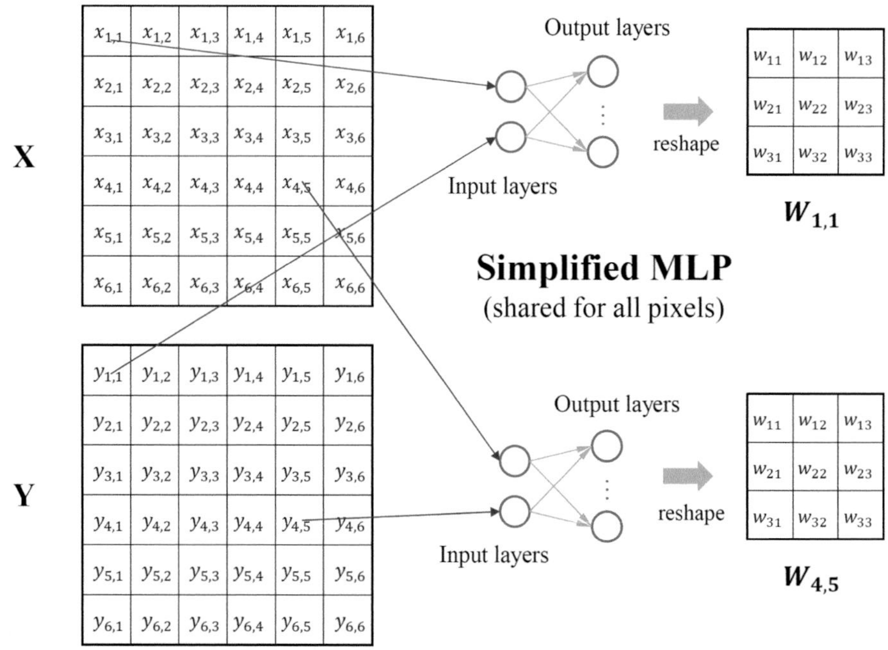

(B) Simplified MLP

FIGURE 9–1 Examples of position-specific convolutional kernels computation using MLP.

downsampling the feature size, decreasing the number of neurons in hidden layers, and adopting 1×1 kernels. Although these methods significantly reduce computational complexity, they can also degrade the match performance.

To address the difficulties resulting from the higher computational complexity due to position-specific kernels, we introduce an alternative method for efficiently computing them. Instead of MLP, we use a simplified network to *predict* the convolutional kernels. As illustrated in Fig. 9–1B, the hidden and activation layers are removed, turning it into a linear combination of the two input values. Computing the convolutional kernels directly would require a significant amount of computations ($pwhk^2mn$). However, we can simplify this architecture to significantly reduce such computations.

To simplify the derivation process, we can make certain assumptions. Let us assume that the input and output channels are denoted by m and n, respectively. X and Y are two position matrices with a size of $w \times h$ (w and h are the width and height of the input), where $X_{x,y}$ and $Y_{x,y}$ represent the position information of pixel (x, y), that is, the pixel in the xth row and yth column. For pixel at (x, y), $W_{x,y}^{i,j}$ is the trained convolutional kernel from input channel i to output channel j. Let matrix A and B represent the parameters of the simplified MLP, where $A^{i,j}$ and $B^{i,j}$ are the respective MLP parameters used for computing kernels $W_{x,y}^{i,j}$. Furthermore, let $I_{x,y}$ represent the input region responding to this kernel with m channels, and the region size is the same as the kernel size while centered at pixel (x, y). Lastly, let O denote the output matrix for the entire layer.

The convolutional kernels can be computed as follows:

$$W_{x,y}^{i,j} = X_{x,y} \cdot A^{i,j} + Y_{x,y} \cdot B^{i,j} \tag{9-1}$$

Therefore the output of the jth channel for pixel (x, y) can be computed as

$$O_{x,y}^j = \sum_{i=1}^{m} W_{x,y}^{i,j} \cdot I_{x,y}^i \tag{9-2}$$

$$= \sum_{i=1}^{m} \left(X_{x,y} \cdot A^{i,j} \cdot I_{x,y}^i + Y_{x,y} \cdot B^{i,j} \cdot I_{x,y}^i \right) \tag{9-3}$$

$$= X_{x,y} \sum_{i=1}^{m} A^{i,j} \cdot I_{x,y}^i + Y_{x,y} \sum_{i=1}^{m} AB^{i,j} \cdot I_{x,y}^i \tag{9-4}$$

We can now partition the output into two parts. We can observe that if we build a convolutional layer with m input channels and n output channels, and let the matrix $A^{i,j}$ be the convolutional kernels from i^{th} input channel to the jth output channel. Let P represent such output matrix of this convolution layer as follows:

$$P_{x,y}^j = \sum_{i=1}^{m} A^{i,j} \cdot I_{x,y}^i \tag{9-5}$$

Similarly, we can build another convolutional layer and let Q be its output matrix:

$$Q_{x,y}^j = \sum_{i=1}^{m} B^{i,j} \cdot I_{x,y}^i \qquad (9-6)$$

We can rewrite the above equation as

$$O_{x,y}^j = X_{x,y} \cdot P_{x,y}^j + Y_{x,y} \cdot Q_{x,y}^j \qquad (9-7)$$

This output from jth channel can be further simplified as follows:

$$O^l = X \cdot P^j + Y \cdot Q^j \qquad (9-8)$$

Since X and Y are the same for different output channels, we can unify the dot product for various output channel and generalize above Eq. (9−8) as follows:

$$O = X \cdot P + Y \cdot Q \qquad (9-9)$$

Eq. (9−9) reveals that the output matrix of the proposed positional-specific convolutional layer can be separated into two segments and processed by two regular convolutional layers. To this end, we design the positional-specific convolutional layers as depicted in Fig. 9−2. Two convolutional layers of equal size are utilized to extract two distinct features. These features are then multiplied by the X matrix and Y matrix, respectively, followed by the pixel-wise summation.

This approach significantly reduces the computational complexity. Specifically, compared to traditional CNNs, the positional convolutional layer only has twice the complexity, while greatly enhancing the feature extraction capabilities.

It is worth noting that we have omitted bias from the above derivation for the sake of simplicity. However this does not impact the conclusions or the illustrations presented in this section.

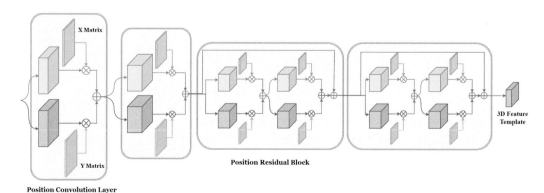

FIGURE 9–2 Overview of the network architecture using position-specific convolutional kernels. The input to this network can be normalized iris image or the normalized periocular image.

9.2.3 Generating matrix *X* and *Y*

There are various approaches to generate the *X* and *Y* matrix, but it is essential to ensure that they satisfy two criteria. First, these two matrices should be continuous. Second, the values must not be excessively small or large, as it can result in increased training difficulty.

Our experiments incorporate distinct methods to compute the position matrix for iris and periocular image databases. Such choice is quite reasonable as the nature of these two databases are quite different. For the normalized periocular images with width *w* and height *h*, wo compute this matrix as follows:

$$X[i,j] = 0.9 + 0.2 \times \frac{i}{\text{width}} \qquad (9-10)$$

$$Y[i,j] = 0.9 + 0.2 \times \frac{j}{\text{height}} \qquad (9-11)$$

The positional matrix for the normalized iris images is computed differently and as follows:

$$X[i,j] = 1 - 0.3 \times \frac{i}{\text{width}} \qquad (9-12)$$

$$Y[i,j] = 1 - 0.3 \times \frac{j}{\text{height}} \qquad (9-13)$$

Fig. 9−3 illustrates the heatmap of the position matrix for the periocular images while Fig. 9−4 illustrates the respective heatmap for the iris images.

9.2.4 Network architecture

We employed different network architectures for the iris and periocular image databases used in our experiments, as they exhibit distinct characteristics. Tables 9−1 and 9−2 detail

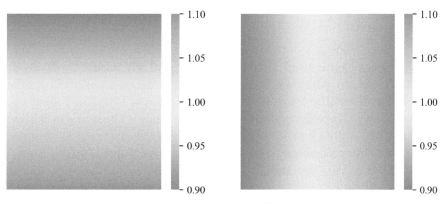

FIGURE 9–3 Heatmap of the weight matrix used in all experiments for the periocular images.

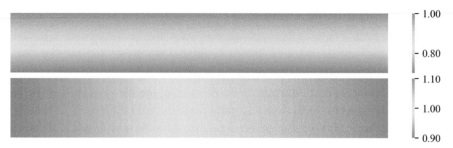

FIGURE 9–4 Heatmap of the weight matrix used in all experiments for the iris images.

Table 9–1   Network architecture for periocular recognition.

Type	Stride	# output channels
PosConv	2	32
PosConv	2	64
PosRes	2	128
PosRes	1	128
PosRes	1	128
Conv 1 × 1	1	16

Table 9–2   Network architecture for iris recognition.

Type	Stride	# output channels
PosConv	2	32
PosConv	2	64
PosRes	1	64
PosRes	1	64
PosRes	1	64
Conv 1 × 1	1	16

the specifics of architectures used for the periocular and iris images respectively. In this table, "PosConv" denotes positional CNN and "PosRes" denotes positional residual block (as depicted in Fig. 9–1). The iris *PosCNN* or *PosNet* outputs 16-channel templates for the improved performance. Since the periocular images database is larger in size as compared to those for the iris, we reduced it to 1/8 of the original size instead of 1/4. All "PosConv" layers are followed by a ReLU activation function and a batch normalization layer.

The experiments for the evaluation of iris recognition performance presented in this chapter utilize the *same* iris masks generated by *MaskNet* as detailed and used in Chapter 2 experiments. These masks are downsampled to 1/4 of the original size and combined them with feature templates when computing match scores. This is necessary because noniris regions in the normalized ROI images, such as the eyebrow and eyelid regions, significantly decreased performance.

9.3 3D feature representation

Many iris recognition algorithms generate a binary template for each image and match them using the Hamming distance [15,24,32,36,176]. More advanced deep learning-based algorithm, presented in Chapter 2-4, also generates compact binary templates. Some other deep learning-based methods, such as in Chapter 6, generate a softmax probability vector using the fully connected network. However, these representations have several limitations. First, binary features may not accurately represent the underlying features. Second, there can be translations between different ROI images of the same subject, which require these methods to shift the feature templates multiple times and retrieve or use the best result. As these algorithms generate binary feature template with the same size as the normalized RoI, they need a lot of computational time to generate the best match score or the result. For example, if shifting one template only by 5 pixels (up, down, left, and right) to match another template from the unknown identity, it will need to perform template matching. To address these limitations, we propose to compute a reduced 3D feature template for every image and match them using pixel-wise cosine distances. By computing the mean distance for every pixel, we can easily translate the matching process to a matrix multiplication operation and accelerate it using the GPU cards.

Let us assume that S and T represent two such 3D templates to be matched, each with a size of $m \times n \times c$, where c is the number of channels in the features. We first normalize all feature vectors into the unit sphere and generate two new normalized templates $|S|$ and $|T|$, then the mean cosine distance between templates S and T can be computed as follows:

$$d = \frac{\sum_{i=1}^{m} \sum_{j=1}^{n} |S| \cdot |T|}{mn} \qquad (9-14)$$

Therefore when matching one or several templates with many other templates, we can easily translate the matching process to matrix multiplication, which can be further accelerated using the conventional GPU card.

9.4 Experiments and results

The network detailed in Section 9.2 was trained using the Adam optimizer [184] with a fixed learning rate of 0.001 for the all databases in our experiments. However, we make slight adjustments for other parameters, such as the batch size and triplet margin, to achieve optimal performance for different databases. With a through experimentation during the training phase, it was determined that a triplet margin between 0.4 and 0.6 and a batch size of either 16 or 32 works quite well. Such hyperparameters can be selected for any sample database, largely representing the nature of images and imaging conditions

Table 9–3　Hyper-parameters for different databases during the network training.

Database	Margin	Batch size
ND-0405	0.3	16
WVU Nonideal	0.4	16
CASIA,v4-distance	0.4	16
UBIPR	0.5	32
FOCS	0.5	16
FRGC	0.5	16

Table 9–4　Summary of databases and protocols for periocular recognition experiments.

Database Division	UBIPR		FRGC[a]		FOCS		CASIA.v4[a]	
	Train	Test	Train	Test	Train	Test	Train	Test
No. of subjects	224	120	0	150	80	56	0	131
No. of images	3359	1767	0	500	3262	1530	0	998
No. of genuine scores	12,351		826		39,614		3371	
No. of impostor scores	1,547,910		123,425		1,130,071		494,132	

[a]Cross-database matching performance.

Table 9–5　Summary of databases and protocols for iris recognition experiments.

Database Division	ND-IRIS-0405		CASIA.v4		WVU Nonideal	
	Train	Test	Train	Test	Train	Test
No. of subjects	356	356	142	142	231	231
No. of images	9346	3394	2446	2446	1513	1528
No. of genuine scores	14,791		20,702		2251	
No. of impostor scores	5,743,130		2,969,533		643,565	

(distance, illumination, size, etc.) under deployment scenario, during the training phase to achieve higher accuracy. The network is trained using triplet architecture and the hyper-meters for different databases are summarized in Table 9–3. This table provides the parameters for iris (first three rows) and also for the periocular image databases (last three rows). The shifted triplet loss function, originally introduced in Chapter 2, was also used to train the network under triplet architecture.

9.4.1 Databases and protocols

To ascertain comparative performance with other state-of-the-art methods, several experiments were performed using publicly available iris and periocular databases. The training and match protocols, that is, number of training images, subjects, and the test images, are the same as those detailed in earlier chapters. However, these are also summarized in Tables 9-4 and 9−5 for convenience.

These experiments use four public periocular image databases for the respective experimental evaluation: UBIPR [143], FRGC [141], FOCS [142], and CASIA.v4-distance periocular databases [17]. This set of experiments uses the same match protocols as used in Chapter 7. We firstly train the network using the training set from UBIPR database and then test its performance using UBIPR test part of the database and also on FRGC test database. We then train another model using FOCS training images and test in FOCS test images and CASIA.v4-distance database. However, unlike for the experiments in Chapter 7, where we finetuned the model using FRGC and CASIA.v4 database (using only training set), results from the method introduced in this chapter do not use any such fine tuning. In other words, the results on UBIPR and FOCS database are within-database (*WithinDB*) results, while the results on FRGC and CASIA.v4-distance database are essentially the cross-database (*CrossDB*) experimental results.

The experimental results for matching normalized iris images utilize three public iris databases: ND-0405 database [76], CASIA.v4-distance iris databases [17] and WVU [85] database. The training and test protocols for iris images are the *same* as for the experiments detailed or employed for experiments in Chapter 4 (DRFNet).

9.4.2 Comparative experimental results for periocular recognition

This section presents comparative experimental results for the periocular image matching using the database and protocols discussed earlier (Table 9-4). The four baseline methods are the same as those used in the comparative experimental results presented in Chapter 7. The FCN-Peri here refers to the fully connected attention-based periocular recognition architecture that was presented in Chapter 7 and the respective baseline results are presented here for the ease in comparisons. The baseline methods PPDM [63] and Texton [16] are nondeep learning-based methods that have shown superior performance against several other nondeep learning-based methods.

The ROC plots for the respective comparative experiments are presented in Fig. 9−5. Comparative experimental results of the respective protocols (Table 9−4) are summarized in Tables 9−6−9−9. To conveniently visualize the comparative error rates at different false accept (FAR), these tables present respective genuine accept rate (GAR), in addition to the EER values. The GAR3 in this table refers to false accept rate (FAR) at genuine accept rate equals to 10^{-3} (GAR value when FAR = 0.1%). Similarly, the GAR4 refers to respective GAR value when FAR is 0.01%, and GAR5 refers to the respective GAR value when FAR = 0.001%.

It is worth noting that the CASIA.v4 distance database is used for iris recognition experiments in Section 9.4.3 and *also* used for periocular recognition here. It can be observed from these results that the use of proposed or position-specific convolutional neural network (*PosCNN* or *PosNet*) can consistently offer superior performance for matching periocular images.

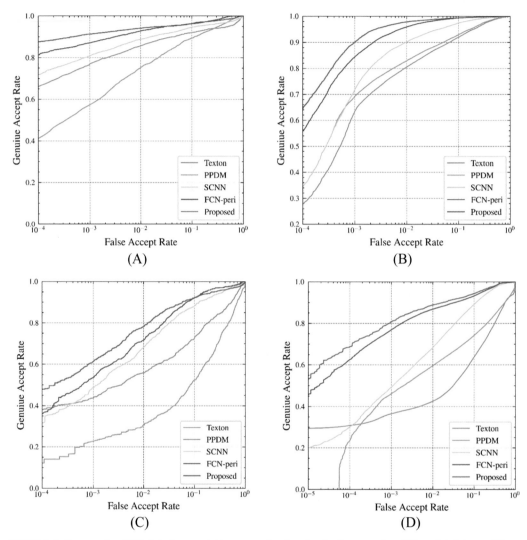

FIGURE 9–5 Comparative ROC plots from matching normalized periocular images using different databases: (A) CASIA.v4-distance database, (B) UBI periocular images database, (C) FRGC, and (D) FOCS database.

Table 9–6   Comparative experimental results (in %) for UBIPR (periocular) dataset.

	EER	GAR3	GAR4	GAR5
PPDM	8.05	69.27	34.77	13.68
Texton	8.68	63.59	27.54	11.53
SCNN	4.67	71.90	34.77	13.68
FCN-Peri	2.26	84.54	55.74	26.90
PosCNN	1.67	90.14	64.44	39.37

Table 9–7   Comparative experimental results (in %) for FRGC (periocular) dataset.

	EER	GAR3	GAR4	GAR5
PPDM	29.46	22.99	12.19	12.19
Texton	19.47	43.70	38.14	32.32
SCNN	11.93	48.79	31.72	19.98
FCN-Peri	8.75	53.75	36.32	30.51
PosCNN	7.32	69.35	54.03	39.34

Table 9–8   Comparative experimental results (in %) for FOCS (periocular) dataset.

	EER	GAR3	GAR4	GAR5
PPDM	23.95	36.61	30.94	29.51
Texton	20.06	46.25	23.97	0.00
SCNN	10.47	49.40	30.45	20.13
FCN-Peri	7.68	77.05	62.83	46.19
PosCNN	6.84	80.09	67.23	53.97

Table 9–9   Comparative experimental results (in %) for CASIA.v4-distance (periocular) dataset.

	EER	GAR3	GAR4	GAR5
PPDM	10.46	58.20	41.27	25.99
Texton	8.27	77.23	66.12	56.17
SCNN	6.61	80.95	72.00	62.00
FCN-Peri	4.58	87.12	81.28	74.61
PosCNN	3.89	92.38	88.73	85.08

9.4.3 Comparative experimental results for iris recognition

This section presents experimental results using three public iris databases, using the protocols as detailed in Section 9.4.1 (Table 9–5). The comparative ROC plots on respective databases are also presented in Fig. 9−6 and the red-colored ROC with "Proposed" label refers to those from the *PosCNN*-based method detailed in Section 9.2. Comparative experimental results from the iris recognition experiments are also summarized in Tables 9−10−9−12. These tables present specific error rates at different FAR from all the methods considered in the experiments. The GAR3 in this table also corresponds to the FAR when the genuine accept rate is 10^{-3} (or 0.1%). Similarly, GAR4 here also represents the GAR at a FAR of 0.01%, and GAR5 represents the GAR at a FAR of 0.001%. These experimental results consistently indicate outstanding performance and validate the effectiveness of the positional CNN for the iris recognition.

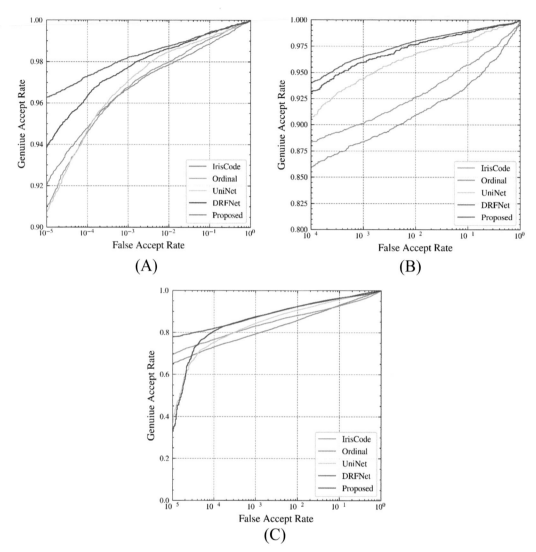

FIGURE 9–6 Comparative ROC plots for the matching normalized iris images using different databases: (A) ND-0405, (B) WVU-Nonideal, and (C) CASIA.v4-distance iris database.

Table 9–10   Comparative experimental results (in %) for ND-0405 (iris) dataset.

	EER	GAR3	GAR4	GAR5
IrisCode	1.88	96.69	94.81	92.08
Ordinal	1.74	96.78	94.60	91.05
UniNet	1.40	97.09	94.67	90.75
DRFNet	1.30	97.73	96.35	93.85
PosCNN	0.79	98.66	97.99	96.74

Table 9–11   Comparative experimental results (in %) for CASIA.v4-distance (iris) dataset.

	EER	GAR3	GAR4	GAR5
IrisCode	7.71	79.34	73.15	65.30
Ordinal	7.90	83.07	76.71	69.72
UniNet	5.54	84.31	75.31	37.24
DRFNet	4.91	87.49	80.66	32.93
PosCNN	3.87	89.47	85.63	74.32

Table 9–12   Comparative experimental results (in %) for WVU Nonideal (iris) dataset.

	EER	GAR3	GAR4	GAR5
IrisCode	6.82	88.37	85.95	83.05
Ordinal	5.19	90.11	88.37	85.76
UniNet	2.63	94.36	90.63	86.98
DRFNet	1.91	95.96	93.16	86.36
PosCNN	0.98	96.84	94.32	89.33

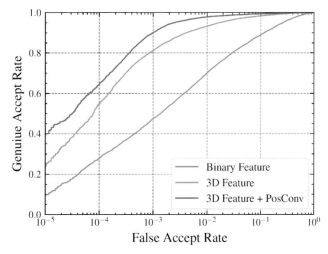

FIGURE 9–7 Comparative ROC curve of using binary features, 3D features, and *PosCNN* network on UBIPR database.

9.4.4 Ablation study

This section presents additional experimental results using UBIPR database. Three kinds of network architectures are used for the comparisons: regular CNN with binary features, regular CNN with 3D features, and positional CNN with 3D features. All these (three) networks have the same architecture and complexity. The comparative ROC plots are presented in Fig. 9−7. It can be observed from these results that after using 3D feature templates,

210 Iris and Periocular Recognition using Deep Learning

significant improvement in the performance is observed, and the match accuracy improves further when using the PosConv. This ablation study validates the effectiveness of the network architecture detailed in Sections 9.2 and 9.3.

9.5 Conclusions and further evaluation

This chapter has introduced the development of a new network architecture which can more effectively recover position-specific features from the iris and periocular images. The design to compute position-specific kernels based on the position matrix is quite simplified and effective. We also improve the feature representation and propose a more discriminative 3D feature template for accurate matching of iris and periocular images. Due to these design features, this method achieves outperforming results compared with all state-of-the-art baseline methods on multiple databases, which validates the effectiveness of this new network architecture.

The position-specific CNN offers enormous potential for other biometric modalities and is suggested for further evaluation. Further validation, especially for iris on very large databases is expected to generate more confidence for the real-world deployments and evaluate the trade-off between relatively enhanced complexity and the performance gain from *PosNet* architecture. Evaluating performance on very periocular datasets, for example, periocular images database provided in [185] from 1122 different subjects, will also generate more confidence on the *PosNet*, despite its evaluation of four challenging datasets in this chapter.

10

Biometrics security in the metaverse using egocentric iris recognition

Metaverse is an emerging platform for online business, government services and social interactions. With the advancement of electronic glasses, such as augmented-reality (AR), virtual-reality (VR), and mixed-reality (MR) devices, humans can now connect seamlessly with the Metaverse to unlock immense potential of emerging 5G networking technologies. Ocular images are inherently acquired during the immersion experiences from such devices, which offer tremendous potential for enabling high levels of security in various areas, including online education, e-business, healthcare, and entertainment or e-gaming. However, existing iris recognition techniques require good-quality images and are insufficient to realize the full potential of such very closely acquired and off-angled ocular images. This chapter presents a specialized approach for detecting, segmenting, and normalizing the iris region pixels from such off-angle ocular images, as well as a generalized framework that dynamically matches such iris images to achieve high security in various Metaverse applications.

10.1 Continuous biometric authentication in the metaverse

Real-world human users can conveniently access the metaverse, a multitude of interactive 3D virtual worlds, using wearable AR/VR/MR devices that have been significantly developed and offer tremendous potential to augment human capabilities. Metaverse is expected to offer tremendous benefits to users. However, there are also cybersecurity and privacy-related challenges as the users in such virtual worlds are represented by customized avatars. It will be challenging to establish the identity of persons who say what they are and with whom we interact in the virtual world. In addition to their choice of representation with preferred avatars, instead of real-face, we may never hear someone's real-world voice. The only real-world human interaction is facilitated by eyes, preferably via AR/VR/MR devices. Such wearable devices are a trend of electronic evolution, and they are potential substitutes for our smartphones if they are more portable [186]. However, significant algorithmic advances are required to achieve highly accurate user identification capabilities from such egocentric vision [187,188]. Foveated rendering [189] is one of the core technologies that enable a high-quality immersive experience with low computational cost and acquire egocentric iris images for gaze estimation. Eye interaction plays a crucial role in the metaverse, and iris recognition is therefore the most feasible biometric to establish the identity of real-world humans for

Iris and Periocular Recognition using Deep Learning. DOI: https://doi.org/10.1016/B978-0-443-27318-6.00004-8

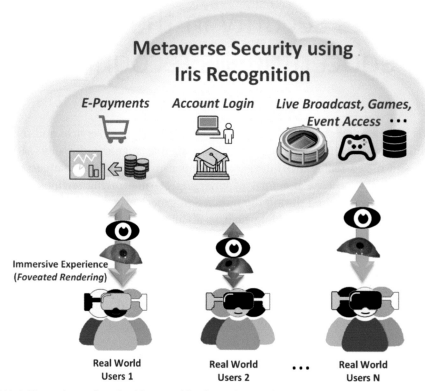

FIGURE 10–1 Biometric security using iris recognition for various applications in the metaverse.

access control. Images acquired for such gaze interaction provide tremendous potential for seamless iris recognition. Iris recognition has many potential applications in the Metaverse, as shown in Fig. 10−1, but significant algorithmic advances are needed to improve the currently available iris recognition capabilities to meet the expectations for stringent security.

10.1.1 Metaverse security and related work

The metaverse demands a fully immersive experience for a vast number of interconnected users, which poses many unprecedented challenges for a range of high-security applications [190]. Several studies have indicated that adopting zero-trust architecture (ZTA) can alleviate most security-related concerns [191]. The adoption of ZTA requires "continuous" verification of users along with identity and access management [192]. Knowing the entities who they say, especially during the immersive experience, is a key challenge. The entry into the metaverse is typically through an AR/MR/MR headset; compromising such a headset could result in a complete takeover of that user's avatar. The blockchain [193] is considered a key technology to address several other security and privacy-related challenges for large-scale metaverse applications. Detection of fake images and identities is another challenge for metaverse security. New methods besides GANs [194], such as Transformers [195], VQ-VAE [196,197], and the Diffusion model [198], are popular methods that are considered quite effective for such challenges.

The motivation of this work is to realize accurate iris recognition using ocular images that are commonly acquired for gaze estimation. The classical techniques to *segment* the iris from nonideal images [11] and off-angle images [199] cannot work for a range of images that are severely off-angled and acquired from closer distances. Another challenge with the use of classical methods for *matching* (summarized in Chapter 1) real-world iris images from popular AR/VR/MR sensors is related to the performance limitations. Specialized and deeply learned neural networks can help meet such expectations to accurately segment and match such iris images, which will be discussed in Section 10.2. Some other attempts in the literature have been utilized in deep neural networks to match the segmented and normalized iris images. Such attempts are relevant and bring promises to match AR/VR/MR-based iris images also. Therefore, these are briefly summarized in the following before introducing the specialized deep learning-based framework in the next Section.

The capabilities of deep neural networks in advancing the matching accuracy for normalized iris images have attracted wide attention from the researchers and the developers. Reference [22] details an approach called DeepIrisNet, which uses a deep convolutional neural network for general iris recognition. This work is a direct application of classic CNN on iris recognition problems without any iris-specific optimization and offers results that cannot match widely popular *IrisCode* when the right set of parameters is selected for the comparative experimentation reported in Chapter 2. Ref. [200] extracts features from different layers in VGGNet and uses convolutional features for iris recognition. Effective use of deep belief net (DBN) to match iris images is reported in [105]. Its core design is optimal Gabor filter selection for *IrisCode* generation, and then the generated *IrisCodes* are fed into DBN to extract self-learned features. Ref. [201] reports the off-the-shelf iris features extracted from pretrained open-source CNNs, and the final decision is made using a support vector machine (SVM). Ref. [202] attempted to use CNN to find patch similarity between poorly segmented iris samples and fed the generated quiver map of patch shift to distinguish the genuine and imposter pairs. Another dense iris feature learning framework using dilated residual kernel is investigated in [203]. Ref. [204] is an interesting attempt at iris recognition using an eye-gazing database [205] with several pretrained CNN models, including ResNet [108], DenseNet [112], and MobileNetV3 [206]. Periocular information is inherently available in the raw iris images, and therefore a range of methods have been incorporated for such periocular recognition. Attention-based deep networks can adaptively consider the importance of different ocular features and offer highly accurate results on multiple databases, as illustrated in Chapter 7. Therefore, such an approach can serve as a good baseline for developing more effective periocular image-matching techniques for the AR/VR/MR devices. Simultaneous use of iris and periocular features has enhanced iris recognition accuracy. Such a promising framework from the maxout CNNs to enhance mobile-based iris recognition performance is reported in [177]. Despite exciting results and from the less-constrained iris recognition, there has been a lack of any attention to close-range iris recognition using off-angle iris images often acquired in wearable AR or VR devices. Some eye gaze tracking databases developed in the past [205] are *not* in the public domain, do not provide user identity information for recognition tasks, are acquired from a small number of subjects, and therefore not much useful to advance such iris recognition capabilities for metaverse security.

10.2 Iris segmentation and normalization

Accurate recognition of human identities using head-mounted AR/VR sensors would require specialized preprocessing steps, and they are introduced in Fig. 10–2. These key steps in our iris recognition framework [116] to recover the normalized iris texture from such close distance and off-angle images are described in the following.

10.2.1 Pupil and iris boundary detection for off-angle images

Our first step is iris detection, which involves pixel-level identification of iris and noniris regions, that is, excluding sclera, eyelash, and source reflections to locate the region of interest (ROI) and predict the binary iris mask. We use. SOLOv2 [98] for such instance segmentation, which is finetuned using 150 images manually segmented egocentric iris images [207]. Earlier Refs. [199,208] have shown that the boundary of off-angle iris images cannot be fitted using circles that are widely used in conventional methods [21,36,177]. We therefore choose a nonconventional approach using an arc-support ellipse detector [209] to detect the pupil boundary and iris boundary on the ROI from the instance segmentation. To suppress the adverse effect of the eyelashes, we use the bilateral filter on the images for pupil ellipse detection. One can directly use the arc-support ellipse detector to locate the pupil boundaries without any parameter finetuning if the image quality is sufficient, that is, adequate contrast, occlusion, etc. However, the iris boundary may not appear as a sharp edge due to the limbus effect [210]; therefore detecting such boundaries in the ROI is difficult. To address such challenges, we use the mask segmentation results generated from the instance

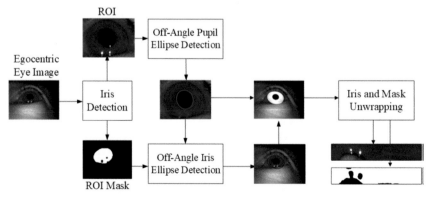

FIGURE 10–2 Key steps for deep-learning-based egocentric iris segmentation and normalization.

segmentation to assist in the accurate detection of iris boundaries. We use vertical Sobel operators with three different thresholds on the binary mask images to generate iris boundary candidates. Only the vertical one is employed in our experiments to eliminate the eyelid's effect. The final ellipse for the iris boundary is selected from the three candidates using the following heuristics: (h1) the pupil should be totally inside the predicted iris ellipse; (h2) the predicted iris ellipse should include 90% of predicted iris pixels; and (h3) if two or more candidates satisfy both (h1) and (h2) mentioned above, we select the ellipse more similar to the pupil ellipse as the iris or limbus boundaries. The similarity is computed by their respective semimajor axis length over the semiminor axis length.

The boundary information is represented with a ten elements vector $[x_p, y_p, l_p, s_p, \theta_p, x_i, y_i, l_i, s_i, \theta_i]$, where (x_p, y_p) and (x_i, y_i) are pupil ellipse center and iris ellipse center; l_p and l_i are the length of the corresponding semimajor axis; s_p and s_i are the length of the corresponding semiminor axis: θ_p and θ_i are orientation of the corresponding semimajor axis. The pupil radius r_p and iris radius r_i change with the rotation angle $\phi(0 < \phi \leq 2\pi)$. Such detected pupil ellipse and iris ellipse can be formulated as follows:

$$r_p^2 = (l_p \times \cos(\theta_p) \times \cos(\phi) - s_p \times \sin(\theta_p) \times \sin(\phi))^2$$

$$+ (l_p \times \cos(\theta_p) \times \sin(\phi) + s_p \times \sin(\theta_p) \times \cos(\phi))^2 \qquad (10-1)$$

$$r_i^2 = (l_i \times \cos(\theta_i) \times \cos(\phi) - s_i \times \sin(\theta_i) \times \sin(\phi))^2$$

$$+ (l_i \times \cos(\theta_i) \times \sin(\phi) + s_i \times \sin(\theta_i) \times \cos(\phi))^2$$

The images in Fig. 10−3 are sample ocular images acquired from a general-purpose VR sensor and the results for the detection of both the ellipses can be seen on respective images.

The iris segmentation scheme detailed in this section has been specially designed to introduce the off-angle and image quality-related challenges of the VR image sensors. If we attempt to use other popular iris segmentation schemes in references, the performance can degrade significantly. This aspect can be observed from the sample images in Fig. 10−4 which presents such comparative segmentation performance from other segmentation schemes used in the cited references. Even the elliptical segmentation scheme in [199] fails to normalize many AR/VR iris images acquired from the head-mounted AR/VR/MR sensors in operation. This is the key reason for the need to design a new preprocessing scheme.

10.2.2 Iris normalization

Similar to the conventional normalization of iris images discussed in Chapter 1, such normalization during the iris segmentation can be achieved by replacing the circles with the respective ellipses that are detected from the pupil and iris boundaries illustrated in Fig. 10−4. Different from the circles, the radius of such ROI region changes with the angle in the ellipse. The center of the detected pupil ellipse is the reference point to sample the pixels along the radial axis with a specific angle. Each of the iris region pixels, from the

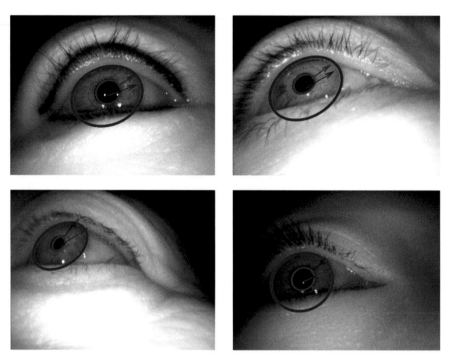

FIGURE 10–3 Sample images with the orientations of two detected ellipses.

intersection point $\left(x_p(\theta), y_p(\theta)\right)$ of the pupil boundary to the intersection point $(x_I(\theta), y_I(\theta))$ of the iris boundary, is scanned along the radial axis oriented at an angle θ and then in the anticlockwise direction for all other angles. This process is also illustrated in Fig. 10–5. The r here represents the radial distance between the pupil boundary and iris boundary, The locations of intersection points are computed using the respective slope from the pupil center. The mapping of every pixel in the off-angle iris image from the polar coordinate (r, θ) to the Cartesian coordinate (x, y) in the unwrapped iris image can be summarized as follows:

$$x(r, \theta) = (1 - r)x_p(\theta) + rx_i(\theta)$$

$$y(r, \theta) = (1 - r)y_p(\theta) + ry_i(\theta) \tag{10-2}$$

10.3 Egocentric iris recognition framework

Each segmented and normalized iris image is matched using a deep neural network that also uses the respective iris mask. We consider the network architecture introduced in Chapter 3 to preserve spatial feature correspondences in the generated templates. Such an FCN-based architecture (UniNet.v2) can aggregate features from three different scales and also be employed in this work. The genuine or within-class distances in close distance

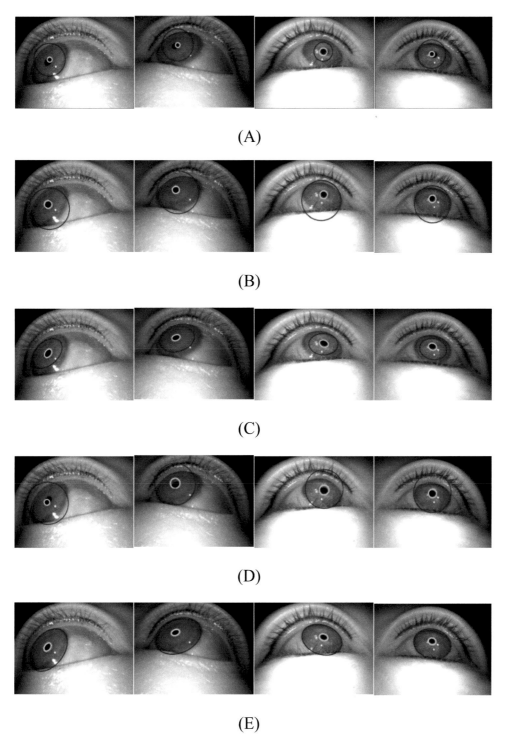

FIGURE 10–4 Illustrative comparisons with the baseline image normalization schemes on sample iris images in AR/VR database: (A) with normalization as in [87], (B) with normalization as in [21], (C) with normalization as in [199], (D) using normalization as in [11], and (E) using normalization as detailed in this section.

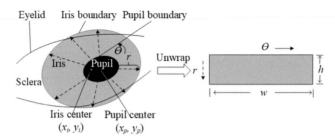

FIGURE 10–5 Elliptical unwrapping model for off-angle iris images.

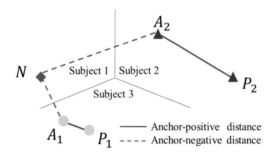

FIGURE 10–6 Limitations of conventional triplet architecture for egocentric iris recognition.

off-angle iris images are considerably higher than those for the conventional iris recognition [211–213] and can significantly degrade the matching accuracy. Therefore we use a quad-based network architecture and a newly introduced loss function in Section 10.3.1 to accurately match iris images. The motivation for using a quad architecture, instead of triplet architecture, is that the triplet architecture only considers the gap or distance between the genuine and impostor scores for same anchor images. This problem can be observed from the conventional triplet loss L_{trip} which is widely employed in such architecture that is

$$L_{\text{trip}} = \frac{1}{M} \sum_{i=1}^{M} \left[D_{A,P} - D_{A,N} + \alpha \right]_+ \qquad (10-3)$$

where M is the batch size, $D_{A,P}$ is the distance between the anchor image and genuine image, $D_{A,N}$ is the distance between the anchor and imposter images, α is a hyperparameter controlling the margin between the anchor-positive and anchor-negative distances, $[.]_+$ means truncating the value to zero if it is negative.

It should be noted that during the actual application, that is, verification or identification, a global threshold will be set for all the match scores instead of a unique threshold for each of the iris-class or the subject. This can be observed from an example case in Fig. 10−6 which shows five samples from three different subjects or classes where two triplets have already satisfied Eq. (10−3). However, we can note that the genuine distance between A_2 and P_2 is larger than the imposter distance between A_1 and N. If we deploy this system in our application, it will consider that A_1 and N are from the same class or subjects whereas

A_2 and P_2 are from different subjects. Therefore inspired by quadruplet [214], one more constrains is added to mitigate this effect and ensure the distance D_{A_2,P_2} is less than $D_{A_1,N}$. This can be achieved by adding one more branch for the negative sample from a different class regarding both the anchor and negative sample, as shown in Fig. 10−6. The new sample N' is from a third subject which is different from other samples, that is, A, P, N. Therefore we can compute one more imposter score $D_{N,N'}$ between the negative sample N and N'. The quadlet loss L_{quad} can be written as follows:

$$L_{quad} = \frac{1}{M} \sum_{i=1}^{M} \left(\left[D_{A,P} - D_{A,N} + \alpha \right]_+ + \left[D_{A,P} - D_{N,N'} + \alpha \right]_+ \right) \qquad (10-4)$$

10.3.1 Shifted and extended triplet loss function

The challenges in accurately matching the iris images from AR/VR sensors can be attributed to off-angle changes, rotation, segmentation errors, and deformations resulting from gazing changes. Conventional loss functions [214] are far from sufficient to accommodate such significant intraclass changes. Therefore we modify the loss function to accommodate the template shifts along the horizontal and vertical directions. The horizontal shift is circular since the unwrapped iris images are recovered from the elliptical ROI regions whose two ends are continuous. The pixels are horizontally shifted from $-u$ pixels to $+u$ pixels with the stepsize of t to accommodate iris pixel rotations in the range of $-\frac{2\pi u}{w}$ to $\frac{2\pi u}{w}$. We also include a vertical shift from $-v$ pixels to $+v$ pixels. However, such vertical shift is not circular shift as the out of range pixels in such vertical shifts will be occluded inside the iris masks, and therefore they will not influence the computation of gradients during the backpropagation. Therefore the shifted feature map satisfies following equations:

$$A_s(x_s, y_s) = A(x, y)$$

$$x_s = (x - u + w) \bmod w; \qquad (10-5)$$

$$y_s = (y - v + h) \bmod h$$

where x_s, y_s, x and y are the coordinates to represent a pixel in the feature maps A_s and A; w is the width of output feature maps; h is the height of the output feature map; u and v are the horizontal shift and vertical shift, respectively; and mod is the modulo operation. Accommodating such shifts for training the network using quad architecture in Fig. 10−7, we can write shifted and extended quadlet loss (SEQL) function as follows:

$$L_{\text{SEQL}} = \frac{1}{M} \sum_{i=1}^{M} \left(\left[D_p(A_s, P) - D_p(A_s, N) + \alpha \right]_+ + \left[D_p(A_s, P) - D_p(N_s, N') + \alpha \right]_+ \right) \qquad (10-6)$$

where $s \in (u, v)$ while A_s and N_s are the shifted feature maps that are generated for the computation of the minimum value of match distance $D_p(.)$ whose value ranges from 0 to 1. We cannot compute the Hamming distance in our training process because the XOR operation is not differentiable, so we compute the Euclidean distance between two real value

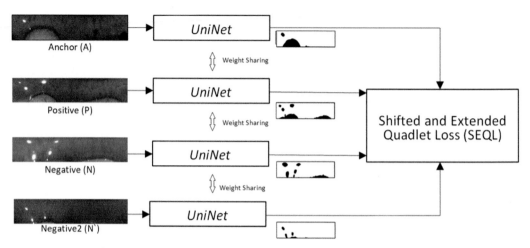

FIGURE 10–7 Network training architecture with *SEQL* loss function.

feature maps. The pixel value ranges from -1 to 1 since the second last layer is a *tanh* layer. Also, we only consider the pixels in the nonmask region, and the matching pairs have a common nonmask valid region V with $|V|$ valid pixels. The distance $D_p(.)$ between a shifted anchor image and positive image can be represented as:

$$D_p(A_s, P) = \frac{1}{|V|} \sum_{(x,y)\in V} (A_s(x,y) - P(x,y))^2 \qquad (10-7)$$

Above equation is differentiable when the feature map shift s is fixed. We denote the shift between the pairs $A - P, A - N$, and $N - N2$ respectively as s_{AP}, s_{AN} and s_{NN}

$$s_{AP} = argmin\big(D_p(A_s, P)\big)$$

$$s_{AN} = argmin\big(D_p(A_s, N)\big) \qquad (10-8)$$

$$s_{NN} = argmin\big(D_p(N_s, N')\big)$$

During backpropagation, we need to compute all the gradients from the four branches A, P, N, and N'. We can define the gradient from the positive sample P as:

$$\frac{\partial L_{\text{SEQL}}}{\partial P} = \begin{cases} 0 & \text{if}\quad L_{\text{SEQL}} = 0 \\[2ex] \dfrac{1}{M}\dfrac{\partial L_{\text{SEQL}}}{\partial D_p(A_s, P)}\dfrac{\partial D_p(A_s, P)}{\partial P} & \text{if}\quad D_p(A_s, P) - D_p(A_s, N) + \alpha \le 0 \\[1ex] & \text{or}\quad D_p(A_s, P) - D_p(N_s, N_2) + \alpha \le 0 \\[2ex] \dfrac{2}{M}\dfrac{\partial L_{\text{SEQL}}}{\partial D_p(A_s, P)}\dfrac{\partial D_p(A_s, P)}{\partial P} & \text{otherwise} \end{cases} \qquad (10-9)$$

The backpropagation for the negative sample N can be represented as:

$$\frac{\partial L_{\text{SEQL}}}{\partial N} = \begin{cases} 0 & \text{if} \quad L_{\text{SEQL}} = 0 \\ \dfrac{1}{M}\dfrac{\partial L_{\text{SEQL}}}{\partial D_p(N_s, N')}\dfrac{\partial D_p(N_s, N')}{\partial N_s} & \text{if} \quad D_p(A_s, P) - D_p(A_s, N) + \alpha \leq 0 \\ \dfrac{1}{M}\dfrac{\partial L_{\text{SEQL}}}{\partial D_p(A_s, N)}\dfrac{\partial D_p(A_s, N)}{\partial N} & \text{if} \quad D_p(A_s, P) - D_p(N_s, N') + \alpha \leq 0 \\ \dfrac{1}{M}\dfrac{\partial L_{\text{SEQL}}}{\partial D_p(A_s, N)}\dfrac{\partial D_p(A_s, N)}{\partial N} + \dfrac{1}{M}\dfrac{\partial L_{\text{SEQL}}}{\partial D_p(N_s, N')}\dfrac{\partial D_p(N_s, N')}{\partial N_s} & \text{otherwise} \end{cases} \tag{10-10}$$

Similarly, we can compute the backpropagation from the second negative sample N' as:

$$\frac{\partial L_{\text{SEQL}}}{\partial N'} = \begin{cases} 0 & \text{if} \quad D_p(A_s, P) - D_p(N_s, N') + \alpha \leq 0 \\ \dfrac{1}{M}\dfrac{\partial L_{\text{SEQL}}}{\partial D_p(N_s, N')}\dfrac{\partial D_p(N_s, N')}{\partial N'} & \text{otherwise} \end{cases} \tag{10-11}$$

We set the gradient as zero if the quadlet saturates, so we only need to derive the differential from a particular pixel when it is not zero. In our following steps, we only derive the equation when both triplets in the quadlet are not saturated for simplicity. Otherwise, the gradient for all the pixels will be set to zero. It is easy to find that the partial equation $\frac{\partial L_{\text{SEQL}}}{\partial D_p(.)}$ is equal to one or minus one in Eqs. (10−10)−(10−11) from Eq. (10−6). We can therefore derive the gradient for a particular pixel (x, y) for the second negative feature map N' first since it only appears once.

$$\frac{\partial L_{\text{SEQL}}}{\partial N'(x,y)} = \begin{cases} 0 & \text{if} \quad (x, y) \notin V_{N,N'} \\ \dfrac{2(N(x_{s_{NN}}, y) - N'(x, y))}{M|V_{N,N'}|} & \text{otherwise} \end{cases} \tag{10-12}$$

From the circular shift Eq. (10−6), we can find that shifting the N feature map to the left by s_{NN} bits is equivalent to shift N' feature map to the right by s_{NN} bits. That means $D_p(N_s, N') = D_p(N, N'_{-s})$. Therefore we can derive the gradient for the negative feature map N as follows.

$$\frac{\partial L_{\text{SEQL}}}{\partial N(x,y)} = \begin{cases} 0 & \text{if} \quad (x,y) \notin V_{N,N'} \text{ and } (x,y) \notin V_{A,N} \\ -\dfrac{2\left(N(x,y) - N'^{(x_{-s_{NN}},y)}\right)}{M|V_{N,N'}|} & \text{if} \quad (x,y) \notin V_{A,N} \\ \dfrac{2(A(x_{s_{AN}},y) - N(x,y))}{M|V_{A,N}|} & \text{if} \quad (x,y) \notin V_{N,N'} \\ \dfrac{2(A(x_{s_{AN}},y) - N(x,y))}{M|V_{A,N}|} - \dfrac{2\left(N(x,y) - N'^{(x_{-s_{NN}},y)}\right)}{M|V_{N,N'}|} & \text{otherwise} \end{cases} \tag{10-13}$$

Similarly, we can compute the partial derivatives for the positive feature map P:

$$\frac{\partial L_{\text{SEQL}}}{\partial P(x,y)} = \begin{cases} 0 & \text{if } (x,y) \notin V_{A,P} \\ -\frac{4\big(A\big(x_{S_{AP}},y\big) - P(x,y)\big)}{M\big|V_{A,P}\big|} & \text{otherwise} \end{cases} \qquad (10-14)$$

According to the shift rule discussed above, we can compute the gradient for the anchor feature map A as follows.

$$\frac{\partial L_{\text{SEQL}}}{\partial A(x,y)} = -\frac{\partial L_{\text{SEQL}}}{\partial P\big(x_{-S_{AP}},y\big)} + \frac{\partial L_{\text{SEQL}}}{\partial N\big(x_{-S_{AN}},y\big)} \qquad (10-15)$$

After computing the respective derivative maps for A, P, N, and N', the rest of the backpropagation-based network process is similar to the common DCNNs. The above equations show that the gradient is only computed when the loss value is greater than zero and the pixel is located in the valid mask region, else the information will be ignored during the training process.

10.4 Adaptive egocentric iris recognition

Raw images acquired from the AR/VR sensors are essentially periocular images with discriminative ocular features. Therefore such images can also be matched directly to generate periocular match scores that can be adaptively consolidated with iris match scores. Such an approach is illustrated in Fig. 10−8 and discussed in following. The implementation discussed in this chapter incorporated a powerful feature extractor ResNeSt [215] pretrained with ImageNet [114], and ArcLoss [216] function to learn periocular features from the input images. Any effective mechanism to simultaneously utilize the varying cues from the iris and periocular matching should carefully consider their image quality. A varying number of valid (ROI) iris pixels, incorporated to generate respective iris match scores, indicates the

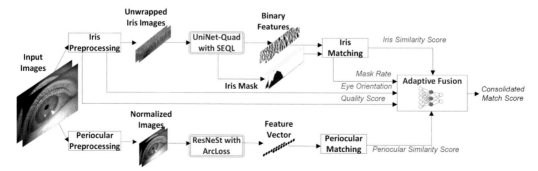

FIGURE 10–8 Adaptive iris recognition framework for egocentric images acquired using AR/VR devices.

reliability of such match scores and can serve as an important cue to adaptively consolidate the match score. We define the number of valid pixels as the *mask rate* and is computed as the fraction of occluded iris pixels, using the iris masks, in two matched iris templates.

The differences in mask rates can be utilized to adaptively reinforce the periocular information. Therefore we incorporate a multilayer perceptron network (MLP) to consolidate such multiple pieces of discriminative details and generate a more reliable match score. Our MLP is composed of three fully connected layers. It will receive a seven-element feature vector as an input, including the iris match score, periocular match score, mask rate, two eye image quality score from our quality checking network, and two eye orientation information from the segmentation steps. The eye orientation is the direction of the detected ellipse during iris segmentation. The network is trained offline using the genuine and impostor pairs from the respective training dataset. The trained network generates consolidated match scores, from the softmax value in the final output layer, in the 0−1 range.

10.5 Database development and organization

Lack of any *publicly* available database to date, for iris recognition using AR/VR devices is one of the critical limitations for much needed further research in this area. Therefore such two-session egocentric iris images database that includes images from 384 different subjects has been developed from this research [116] and made available in public domain [207]. This is the first *two-session* off-angle egocentric iris images database from a VR device in the public domain. Each of the subjects contributed to 360 samples acquired from nine different viewpoints and is a relatively large database for further research. A general-purpose sensor is employed to acquire the iris images for gaze estimation that also enable immersion experience in AR/VR environment. Therefore the acquired images reflect real-world and dual-use for the subject identification using close-range and off-angle iris patterns. The subjects who provided images in this database were volunteers from different ethnic communities, including Chinese, Indian and European. These volunteers consented to this research, were not paid any honorariums, and none of their personal details were acquired. They wore a head-mounted AR device and observed a 3D rectangular pattern with a green point displayed on the glasses. All the volunteers were requested to gaze sequentially at nine different locations as illustrated in Fig. 10−9, while the camera captured their iris images. Sample iris images acquired from different gaze points from a volunteer are shown in Fig. 10−10. Twenty different image samples from one eye at each of the gaze points were acquired. Therefore a total of 360 image samples have been acquired from one subject during a session.

The first session image samples from 384 different subjects are acquired while only 114 were available for the second session image acquisition. The minimum interval between two image sessions was four months. Therefore the entire database consists of 138,240 image samples from the first session and 41,040 image samples from the second session. This entire database is publicly available [207] to advance further research and deployments.

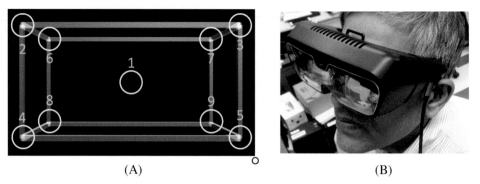

(A)   (B)

FIGURE 10–9 (A) Gaze points displayed on head-mounted display during the database acquisition using (B) a head mounted AR/VR device.

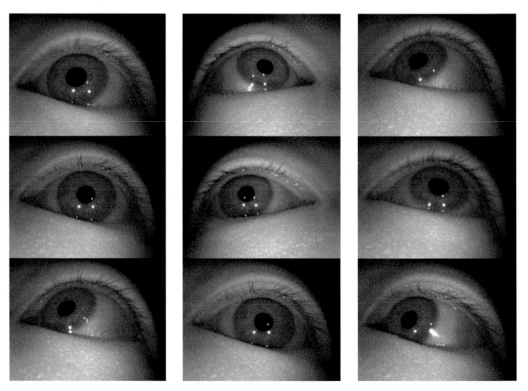

FIGURE 10–10 Sample ocular images from the developed dataset for the experimentation.

We can compute the average diameters D_i of the limbus ellipse, with major axis length L_i and minor axis length S_i, by assuming it to be circle with the diameter of D_i and with the same area as in the following:

$$\frac{\pi \times D_i^2}{4} = \frac{\pi \times L_i \times S_i}{4}, \text{or} \quad D_i = \sqrt{L_i \times S_i} \qquad (10-16)$$

Similarly, we can also estimate the size of pupil ellipse and compute effective iris diameter by computing the difference between the iris diameter and pupil diameter. In addition, we can compute the effective area of iris which is the total number of pixels in the valid iris region in the respective image. Table 10−1 presents the statistics of the AR/VR device based Iris Images dataset. Therefore considering the description in [24], this AR/VR dataset can be considered as quite challenging.

Fig. 10−11 illustrates the distribution of estimated iris image orientations from the egocentric views in the acquired database. The distributions in this figure illustrates two distinct peaks. The angle (x-axis) in this plot ranges from 0 to 180 degrees which is the angle between the horizontal right and major axis of the iris ellipse in an anti-clockwise direction, and most of our acquired samples are acquired from gazing at the four corners. When the subject stares at the top-left and down-right will look similar since the major axis angle ranges from 0 to 180 degrees instead of 0 to 360 degrees. Therefore, two peaks are observed along the angular distributions. Fig. 10−12A illustrates the distribution of effective iris pixels in the database images while Fig. 10−12B illustrates such distribution for the equivalent iris diameter. Each of the acquired images from the AR/VR sensor during the user engagement

Table 10–1 Statistics of the AR/VR device based Iris Images dataset.

	Min	Max	Mean
Iris diameter (pixels)	60	198	116.26
Iris area (pixels)	7166	34,258	18,434.39

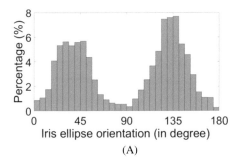 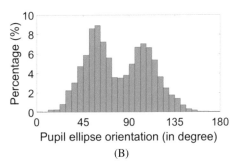

(A) (B)

FIGURE 10–11 Estimated distribution of (A) iris and (B) pupil ellipse orientations, from egocentric view, in the database images.

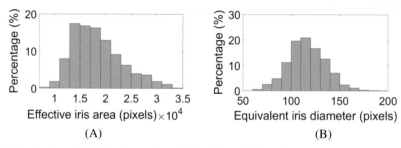

(A)   (B)

FIGURE 10–12 Distribution of (A) effective number of iris pixels and (B) equivalent iris diameter in the egocentric database images.

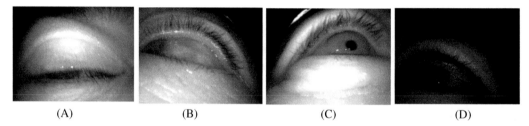

(A)   (B)   (C)   (D)

FIGURE 10–13 Sample images from egocentric iris image database with image quality degradation including (A) closed eye, (B) off-axis gaze, (C) motion blur, and (D) very low contrast.

may not be suitable for the continuous authentication as many of these images are of low quality. Fig. 10−13 shows such sample images with closed eye, serious off-axis gaze, motion blur, and very low contrast. Therefore an iris image quality checker is required to automatically discard such images and is discussed in the next section.

10.5.1 Iris image quality estimation and selection

Images that are acquired from the AR/VR sensor are often expected to include degraded quality samples, for example, closed eye, serious off-axis gaze, and motion blur. Therefore an iris image quality detector is required to automatically exclude such degraded images for their use in the recognition framework. The guidelines stated in IRIX V report [217] list common image quality degradation during the conventional iris image acquisitions. Among these potential iris image quality degradations listed in [217], Table 10−2 provides a list of these problems in the context of AR/VR iris images database acquired during this study.

A trained quality checker can discard such poor-quality iris samples and therefore a quality checker using MobileNetV3 [206] was trained to automatically discard very low-quality samples. We manually marked 4566 iris images that were separately acquired during the database development and classified them into one of the three categories, that is, 2054 good samples, 1404 bad samples, and 1108 ugly samples. Samples from such labeled images

Table 10–2 Common image quality degradations observed during egocentric iris acquisition using the head mounted devices.

Possible acquisition problem	AR/VR iris database
Occlusion by finger	No
Motion blur	Yes
Mislabeled eyes	No
Eye rotation	No
Closed or squinting eye	Yes
Specular highlights from glasses	No
Off-axis gaze	Yes
Highly dilated or constricted pupil	Yes
Focus blur	Yes
Iris absent from image	No
Poor illumination and low	Yes

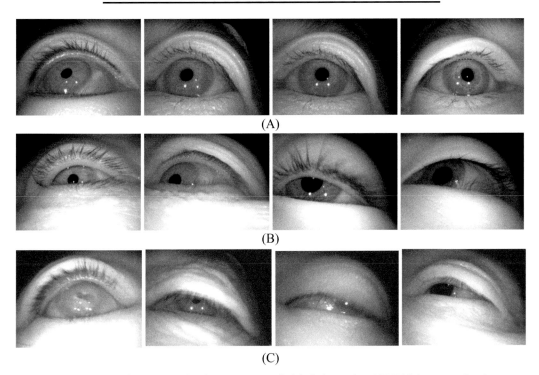

(A)

(B)

(C)

FIGURE 10–14 Example of image samples that were manually labeled to train a AR/VR iris image quality detector: (A) good samples, (B) bad samples, and (C) ugly samples.

are also shown in Fig. 10–14. Both bad and ugly samples are not expected to satisfy the expectations for conventional iris recognition [217] but we still believe that such bad-quality samples can help with the further extension of this research [116] as iris pattern imprints can

Table 10–3 Summary of statistics from images in the developed dataset.

	Session 1	Session 2
No. of subjects	384	114
No. of classes	768	228
No. of samples	138,240 (111,013)	40,140 (33,194)
Resolution	640 × 480	640 × 480

still be observed in many of such images. Our image quality checker using MobileNetV3 [206] was only trained using such labeled images. We train the model in 30 epochs using SGD with momentum with a learning rate of 0.001 and momentum of 0.9. This trained model was used as the quality checker, also made available from [207] and we only employed good quality image samples in our experiments.

The statistics of acquired egocentric iris images database is presented in Table 10−3 and the number in brackets (fourth row) represent images after the quality check that were used in our experiments. The image quality in the second session images is generally better than those from the session images. This can be observed from the number of samples retained (relative numbers in the fourth row of the table) i.e. the quality check discards many acquired image samples from the first session than those from the second session images. The reason is not difficult to understand. For almost all the volunteers in our data acquisition, this is the first time they have seen or used any AR/VR device. They are not familiar with wearing or use of such a device, and sometime they also fail to look at the expected gaze locations during the acquisition. Therefore, there are more low-quality samples, such as shown in Fig. 10−13, from our first session acquisition. In our second data acquisition session, all the volunteers were familiar with the AR/VR device, and they were more experienced in providing us with their data. Therefore, the overall quality of the second session images is relatively better.

10.6 Experiments and results

A range of experiments were performed to ascertain the performance of the approach described in previous sections for AR/VR sensor-based egocentric iris recognition. The details on the exact match protocols and the corresponding reproducible results are provided in the following section. The elliptical segmentation approach discussed in Section 10.2 is employed for the iris segmentation on all the other databases used for experiments in this chapter. The thresholds of the vertical Sobel operator were empirically fixed as 0.35, 0.4, and 0.45 for all our experiments. Our iris normalization generated unwrapped iris images of 512*64 pixels in Fig. 10−5 for all the experiments and databases used in this paper. For the network training using the quadlet architecture, we set the horizontal shift u as 32, step-size t as 2, vertical shift v as 5, and margin α as 0.15. The network is trained using SGD with learning rate of 0.001 and momentum of 0.9. The batch size is fixed as 8 for the 80,000 iterations.

10.6.1 Parameter selection for baseline methods

We have extensively tuned the parameters for benchmark methods to ensure that the best possible performances are employed for fair comparisons. We iteratively adapt possible combinations of the parameters for these approaches on each of the respective training set, within the empirically selected ranges, similar to as in Chapter 2. The best-performing parameters from such training sets are then employed, on the respective test sets, for the performance evaluation.

10.6.1.1 Parameter selection for IrisCode (2D)

A bank of six 2D Gabor filters are employed in the original OSIRIS implementation [87]. In addition to the default one, we generated five Gabor filter bands for tuning, using this tool, and obtain the best performance. A general purpose 2D Gabor filter for generating *IrisCode* [24] can be written as follows

$$g(x,y) = e^{-\left(\frac{x^2}{a^2}+\frac{y^2}{b^2}\right)} e^{-iwx} \qquad (10-17)$$

where a, b, w can determine two filters with the real and imaginary parts of the complex filter kernel. We incorporate three sets of parameters to form a band of six filters. The five additional Gabor filters can be listed as follows: (1)$\{(3, 1.5, 0.4\pi), (5, 1.5, 0.2\pi), (7, 1.5, 0.1\pi)\}$; (2) $\{(3, 1.5, 0.4\pi), (5, 1.5, 0.3\pi), (7, 1.5, 0.2\pi)\}$; (3) $\{(5, 2, 0.3\pi), (7, 2, 0.2\pi), (9, 2, 0.1\pi)\}$; (4) $\{(3, 2, 0.3\pi), (6, 2, 0.2\pi), (9, 2, 0.1\pi)\}$; and (5) $\{(5, 1.5, 0.3\pi), (7, 1.5, 0.2\pi), (9, 1.5, 0.1\pi)\}$

10.6.1.2 Parameter selection for IrisCode (1D)

The *IrisCode* implementation using 1D log-Gabor filters is provided in [30]. Its computationally efficient, also widely used in the literature to benchmark the performance and therefore justified as one of the baseline methods. There are two key parameters for this implementation. The first one is the wavelength λ, and its value ranges from 15 to 40, with the step size of one. The other parameter is the bandwidth over frequency σ/f and its value ranges from 0.2 to 0.5 with a step size of 0.05. There are a total of 182 different combinations.

10.6.1.3 Parameter selection ordinal filters

There are four parameters to be chosen for this method, as also detailed in reference [36]. The first one is the number of lobes n, and we can choose dilobe or trilobe ordinal filter. The second one is the lobe kernel size k which range from five to nine with step size two. The third one is the distance between lobes d, ranging from five to 17 with step size four. The last one is the standard deviation τ of each lobe, and we can choose from 1.5 to 1.9 with step size of 0.2. In total, there are 72 different combinations that are attempted for the best performance.

Table 10−4 lists the best set of parameters that were automatically selected from the above discussed steps. We can also note the need for different parameters for these benchmark methods for each dataset. In this context, our cross-database results in Section 10.6.3.3

Table 10–4   Best performing parameters for the baseline methods in the experiments.

Methods	Parameters	AR/VR dataset	QFIRE dataset	CASIA dataset
IrisCode (2D) [87]	$\{a, b, w\}$	(V)	(II)	(I)
IrisCode (1D) [30]	λ	26	18	20
	$\frac{\sigma}{f}$	0.25	0.35	0.35
Ordinal [36]	n	3	3	3
	k	7	5	9
	d	5	13	13
	τ	1.7	1.9	1.7

illustrate high generalization capability by achieving satisfactory performance without any need for any parameter tuning.

10.6.2 Databases and protocols

10.6.2.1 PolyU AR/VR iris images database

We perform experiments using the two-session and one session (all-to-all) match protocols. Two session experiments use 1967 images from 202 different classes in the second session to compose a probe set and 1879 samples in the first session to compose a gallery dataset. Such a two-session match protocol will generate 1967 genuine and 395,367 imposter match scores. One-session experiments selected samples from 242 subjects that are stated in a text file made available from [207]. We use image samples from the first 60 subjects for the training, whereas ten samples from the rest of 182 subjects are used for the performance evaluation. Test samples are evenly selected from the five different directions while considering the gaze points at the same corner as the same direction. Therefore there will be 3640 samples in the performance evaluation test dataset, and 16,380 genuine and 6,606,600 imposter match scores will be generated. The reason for such selection in one-session experiment is to ensure that there are at least two good-quality image samples at each gazing direction from both the eyes of each of the subjects. Similarly, we also attempt to select at least two good-quality images from each subject at each gaze direction for the two-session experiments. We can therefore only use images from 101 different subjects in two-session experiments.

10.6.2.2 Quality in Face and Iris Research Ensemble database

The Quality in Face and Iris Research Ensemble (Q-FIRE) database [18] is publicly available, providing off-angle iris images acquired using the OKI IRISPASS EQ5016A sensor. Although this database is not acquired from any AR/VR sensor that commonly generates close-range off-angle iris images, the iris images available in this database can help us ascertain the proposed approach's effectiveness for off-angle iris recognition. We select a subset of images acquired from a 5-ft distance under higher illumination. The original image samples illustrate the upper part of the face, and we automatically segment the periocular region with a

FIGURE 10–15 Sample off-angle iris images from QFIRE database.

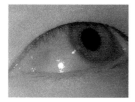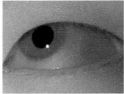

FIGURE 10–16 Sample off-angle iris images of the CASIA-Iris-Degradation-V1 dataset.

Fast-RCNN-based detector [178]. The samples in our experiments are chosen from the front, up, down, left, and right, as illustrated in Fig. 10−15. We selected iris samples from 44 subjects (88 classes) as our training set, 2640 iris samples from the last 132 subjects (264 classes) as our testing set. Therefore this database in our experiments generates 11,880 genuine and 3,471,600 imposter match scores.

10.6.2.3 CASIA-Iris-Degradation-V1 database
The CASIA-Iris-Degradation-V1 database [218] consists of 36,539 images from 255 subjects. The challenging samples are divided into 15 categories: illumination, off-angle, occlusion, etc. We use the off-angle subset composed of iris samples from frontal, top-left, down-right, down-left, and downright views, as shown in Fig. 10−16. We selected iris samples from 60 subjects (120 classes) as our training set, 2088 iris samples from the last 95 subjects (190 classes) as our testing set. Therefore this testing set in such experiments will generate 13,277 genuine scores and 2,165,551 imposter match scores.

10.6.3 Experimental results and performance comparisons

Rigorous experimentation was undertaken to validate the effectiveness of the framework introduced in Section 10.3. These experimental results are presented using the receiver operating characteristic (ROC) curves to evaluate the performance for the verification and cumulative matching characteristics (CMC) plots for the recognition problem. We can also ascertain the open set matching performance using the decision error trade-off (DET) plots generated by computing false positive match rates (FPIR) and false negative match rates (FNIR) curves. The generalization capability of this model using the cross-database performance is also presented.

10.6.3.1 Two-session matching performance

Matching AR/VR sensor-based iris images from the second session with those from the first session acquired during the registration can provide most realistic performance evaluation under the popular deployment scenario. Therefore this performance evaluation is firstly presented using the PolyU AR/VR Iris Images database. We also present comparative performance with many other classical and deep network-based competing benchmark methods. The original *IrisCode* (2D) introduced by Daugman [24] has been implemented in OSIRIS [87] and is an important baseline for the conventional iris recognition. *IrisCode* (1D) [30] is also a popular and widely used benchmark for iris recognition performance and uses 1D log-Gabor filter to generate *IrisCodes*. Another classical algorithm that can provide ordinal measurements using multilobe ordinal filters [36] was also considered during this evaluation. To ensure fairness, we use same test samples to evaluate all baseline methods under the same protocol as stated in Sections 10.6.1.1−10.6.1.3. We also compared with competing deep neural

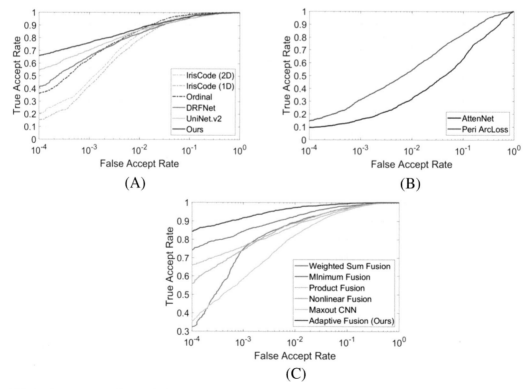

FIGURE 10–17 Comparative results for two-session verification performance on PolyU AR/VR Iris Images database. ROC plots from (A) iris, (B) periocular, and (C) the combined performance.

network-based methods that were proposed for the conventional iris recognition. The UniNet. v2 employs the fully convolutional network to generate binarized feature templates while DRFNet introduced in Chapter 4 generates consolidates features from the residual network using dilated kernels. It is important to note that only the iris encoding algorithms from these baseline methods are employed, and we use new segmentation approach introduced in Section 10.2 of this chapter to ensure fairness in such evaluation as the segmentation methods used in those baseline algorithms are *not* designed for the problem considered in this chapter, that is, close-range and off-angle iris recognition. Since the method proposed for matching off-angle periocular images in this work is new or not explored in the literatures, we also provide comparison of our periocular matching model with the AttenNet model detailed in Chapter 7. Our adaptive fusion results are also comparatively evaluated with the maxout CNNs [177] and some other classical fusion algorithms, including weighted sum, minimum, product, and non-linear fusion [219]. Comparative ROC plots for this evaluation are presented in Fig. 10−17 while Fig. 10−18 presents respective CMC plots for the recognition performance. Table 10−5 presents comparative summary of equal error rates (EER) and genuine or true accept rate (TAR) at low (10^{-4}) false accept rate (FAR).

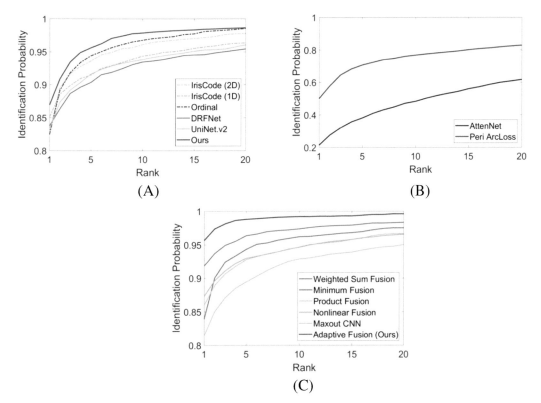

FIGURE 10–18 Comparative results for two-session *recognition* performance on PolyU AR/VR Iris Images database. CMC plots from (A) iris, (B) periocular, and (C) the combined performance.

Table 10–5 Comparative performance summary from two-session egocentric iris recognition.

Category	Methods	PolyU dataset two session	
		TAR@FAR $= 10^{-4}$	EER
Iris	IrisCode (2D) [87]	20.37%	5.65%
	IrisCode (1D) [30]	15.53%	5.50%
	Ordinal [36]	35.54%	5.56%
	DRFNet (Chapter 4)	41.38%	6.31%
	UniNet.v2 (Chapter 3)	54.75%	6.39%
	UniNet-Quad (ours)	**70.43%**	**3.26%**
Periocular	AttenNet (Chapter 7)	9.80%	22.04%
	Peri ArcLoss (ours)	14.38%	14.05%
Fusion	Weighted sum fusion	74.30%	3.61%
	Minimum fusion	32.28%	4.77%
	Product fusion	65.57%	4.28%
	Nonlinear fusion [219]	56.33%	5.43%
	Maxout CNN [177]	36.26%	6.07%
	Adaptive fusion (ours)	**88.15%**	**0.93%**

The bold emphasis indicates that the most accurate performance for the respective problem is achieved by this method. Its quite common to bold for easy attention and identifiication of best results among the others from the respective experimentation.

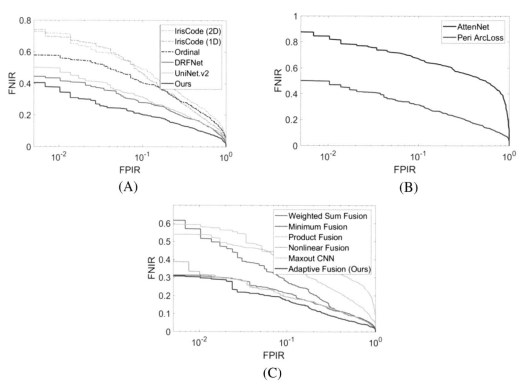

FIGURE 10–19 Comparative results for the *open set performance* evaluation on PolyU AR/VR Iris Images database. DET plots from (A) iris, (B) periocular, and (C) the combined performance.

We also evaluate the comparative performance for the open set matching problem as the unknown or not registered subjects can also appear during the actual application. The open set identification objective is to correctly identify probe subjects present in the gallery while rejecting all other probe queries as unknown, and it is widely applied in surveillance and person reidentification applications. These experiments use the first 30 test subjects as unknown subjects in all or respective databases, which are not enrolled in the gallery. We then ascertain the open set performance using the FPIR against the FNIR. Comparative plots from such evaluation are presented in Fig. 10−19. Additional performance comparisons using off-the-shelf CNN features and related complexity analysis are provided in Section 10.6.4.

10.6.3.2 One-session matching performance

Matching one-session iris images can generate large number of match scores [20], and such performance evaluation is also presented in this section. The comparative experimental results from our approach and the respective benchmark methods are presented in Fig. 10−20 for PolyU AR/VR Iris Images database. We also present respective ROC results in Fig. 10−21 using the QFIRE database protocol detailed in Section 10.6.2.2 and ROC results in Fig. 10−22 using the CASIA ID-V1 database protocol detailed in Section 10.6.2.3.

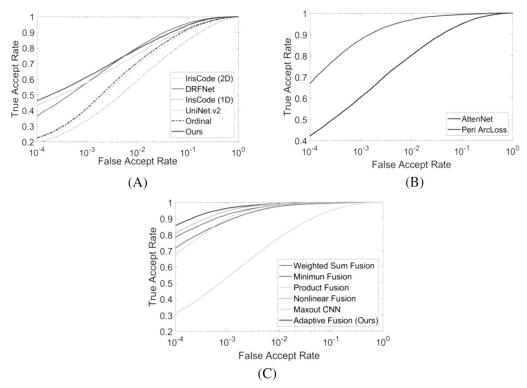

FIGURE 10–20 Comparative results for *one-session* verification performance on PolyU AR/VR Iris Images database. ROC plots from (A) iris, (B) periocular, and (C) the combined performance.

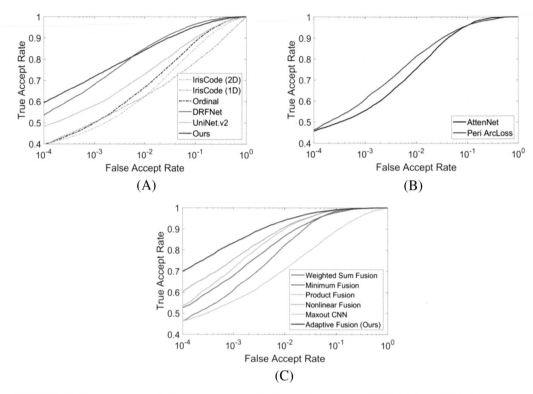

FIGURE 10–21 Comparative results for *one-session* verification performance on QFIRE database. ROC plots from (A) iris, (B) periocular, and (C) the combined performance.

Table 10–6 presents comparative summary of EER and TAR values at low (10^{-4}) FAR. As can be observed from this table, the performance improvement is quite consistent and can underline the merit of iris recognition framework for AR/VR sensor-based images.

10.6.3.3 Cross-database performance

Although there is no other publicly accessible close-range and off-angle egocentric iris database to the best of our knowledge, we still attempted to ascertain cross-database performance using the model trained on PolyU AR/VR Iris Images database and evaluated on the CASIA IDV1 database. Such cross-database evaluation can help to ascertain the generalization capability from the framework detailed in Section 10.3. Here we employ the directly trained model using PolyU AR/VR Iris Images database and use it to ascertain the matching performance for the CASIA ID-V1 database (Section 10.6.4) without any finetuning. We compare the performance with the other competing deep network-based algorithms. The number of test images is the same as respective database in the previous experiments. The comparative performance from the cross-databases experiment is shown in Fig. 10–23 while Table 10–7 summarizes respective EER and TAR values at low FAR (10^{-4}).

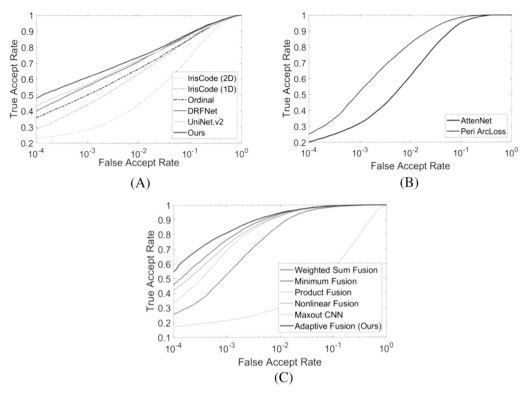

FIGURE 10–22 Comparative results for *one-session* verification performance on CASIA ID-V1 database. ROC plots from (A) iris, (B) periocular, and (C) the combined performance.

Table 10–6   Comparative performance summary from *one-session* matching.

		PolyU AR/VR		QFIRE		CASIA	
Modality	Method	TAR (%)	EER (%)	TAR (%)	EER (%)	TAR (%)	EER (%)
Iris	IrisCode (2D) [87]	22.16	9.45	40.10	12.66	22.86	17.12
	IrisCode (1D) [30]	18.19	12.57	39.52	17.04	28.92	12.58
	Ordinal [36]	22.21	8.80	39.80	10.98	35.90	12.65
	DRFNet (Chapter 4)	36.55	6.27	53.80	5.75	40.15	11.05
	UniNet.v2 (Chapter 3)	43.78	8.40	48.25	10.04	43.01	11.93
	Ours	**51.76**	**4.30**	**62.63**	**5.27**	**47.92**	**6.01**
Periocular	AttenNet (Chapter 7)	42.48	6.79	47.17	6.25	20.17	7.53
	Peri ArcLoss	66.89	1.87	46.22	6.18	25.31	4.75
Fusion	Weighted Sum	78.90	1.37	53.08	4.66	45.72	2.62
	Minimum	72.25	1.44	54.11	4.75	33.93	3.68
	Product	67.11	1.39	46.39	3.74	25.83	2.77
	Nonlinear [219]	81.33	0.95	60.40	3.70	42.22	2.80
	Maxout CNN [177]	31.87	7.50	46.31	10.56	17.19	25.05
	Adaptive fusion (ours)	91.87	0.17	78.57	0.62	57.98	0.70

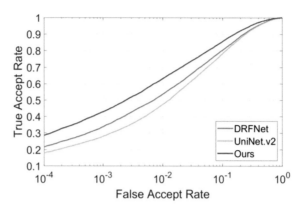

FIGURE 10–23 Comparative ROC from the cross-database performance evaluation.

Table 10–7   Performance summary from cross-database performance evaluation.

| | CASIA ID-V1 database | |
Method	TAR (%)	EER (%)
DRFNet (Chapter 4)	21.65	14.91
UniNet.v2 (Chapter 3)	17.90	15.31
Ours	30.16	11.03

10.6.4 Discussion

To ascertain the effectiveness of the proposed loss function for the iris recognition using AR/VR sensors, we also performed comparisons with popular CNN models using other loss functions. We performed comparisons with the quadlet loss using the same UniNetv2 architecture and provide additional comparison using the triplet loss. We also compare another baseline method, DeepIrisNet [22], which has shown promising results for conventional iris recognition. The hyperparameters for the effective training of respective network architectures were carefully investigated to achieve the best possible performance. All these comparisons were performed PolyU AR/VR Iris Images database in this work and the resulting performance is shown from the ROCs in Fig. 10−24. The poor performance from the quadlet loss function strongly suggests that it is necessary to account for the spatial bit translation to accurately learn the spatially corresponding features from the close-range and off-angle iris images.

Although our results from the proposed framework to adaptively match iris images have shown promising results, significant work is required to improve the performance for large-scale matching and deployment. Egocentric iris images from wearable AR/VR sensors can exhibit significantly high intraclass variations, and accurate localization of iris boundaries

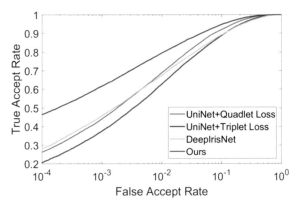

FIGURE 10–24 Comparative ROC from different loss functions.

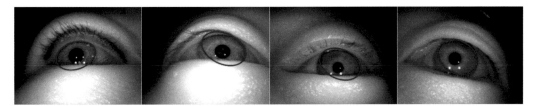

FIGURE 10–25 Falsely matched iris images with inaccurate localization of limbic boundaries.

in many such degraded quality images is quite challenging. Fig. 10−25 presents sample images from PolyU AR/VR Iris Images database that indicate erroneous localization of such iris boundaries in these images. Our analysis of the failed cases also indicates that the intraclass matching errors are largely introduced from the significant deformations of the off-angle iris images in the normalized images.

It can also be useful to perform two-session experiments using the same matching protocol to compare with the off-the-shelf features approaches [201]. There are five different feature extractors pretrained with ImageNet [114] employed to provide off-the-shelf features using normalized iris images, including AlexNet [114], VGGNet [126], InceptionNetV3 [220], ResNet152 [108] and DenseNet201 [112]. The feature vectors fed into the SVM are selected from the peak layers for performance, including layer 7 for AlexNet, layer 9 for VGGNet, layer 10 for InceptionNetV3, layer 12 for ResNet152 and layer 5 for DenseNet201 respectively. According to the description in the original paper, all the CNN models are not finetuned and only one-over-all multiclass SVMs are trained with corresponding training data. We use the predicted probability as the matching score, and plot the ROC in Fig. 10−26 while EER results are shown in Table 10−8. We can find that our approaches provide superior performance than the off-the-shelf approaches. The off-the-shelf features cannot effectively address the iris recognition problem under such challenging scenario without any iris-specific design, and one-over-all learning strategy is not

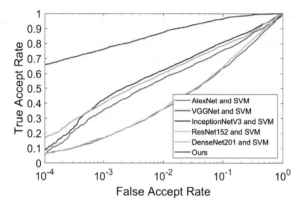

FIGURE 10–26 Comparative ROC results from off-the-shelf features using two-session matching protocol.

Table 10–8   Comparative EER values from off-the-shelf features using two-session matching.

Method	EER (%)
AlexNet and SVM	23.91
VGGNet and SVM	19.30
InceptionNetV3 and SVM	15.78
ResNet152 and SVM	22.45
DenseNet201 and SVM	17.27
Ours	5.43

Table 10–9   Comparative summary of complexity analysis for baseline models.

	Parameters	Extraction time (ms)
DRFNet (Chapter 4)	125 K	8.1
Maxout CNN [33]	4095 K	10.5
DeepIrisNet [44]	55,420 K	13.8
DenseNet201 [29]	20,242 K	24.6
Ours	129 K	8.9

expected to minimize the matching errors, especially those from the large intra-class differences.

We can also analyze the complexity of the iris recognition framework to ascertain its feasibility for the deployment. Table 10−9 presents comparative summary of the computational time for the feature extraction and storage requirements. One Ubuntu 18.04 machine with i9−7900X CPU, 32GB RAM, and 11GB 1080ti GPU was used for this analysis. These results indicate that the space and time complexity of our trained model is not large and quite suitable for the online iris recognition. The run time requirement for the iris image quality checker, iris and mask detection, ellipse detection with iris segmentation and normalization, are respectively 11.3, 62.4 and 223.7 milliseconds (Ms), which can be further reduced by the code optimization and choice of more simplified model.

10.7 Summary and further work

This chapter detailed a new framework to accurately match off-angle iris images especially those acquired from closer distances using head-mounted AR/VR devices. Systematic design of an SEQL function to provide effective supervision in learning discriminative features for the convolutional neural network was also discussed in this chapter. Extensive experimental results presented in Section 10.6 indicate outperforming results and validate the merit of this framework for iris recognition using popular AR/VR devices that inherently acquire ocular images under near-infrared illumination for gaze estimation.

There are also several ways for the practical use of the egocentric iris recognition framework introduced in this chapter. One way is to simultaneously use both the left and right eye images, which are essentially acquired or available in currently popular AR/VR sensors, to achieve significantly enhanced performance. When we combine *simultaneously* acquired left and right iris images' matching scores using the simple sum rule, we can drastically enhance the performance and the plots from such performance in Fig. 10−27. Such performance is obtained from the two-session images using the same protocols as in Section 10.6.3.1. It can be observed that the TAR@FAR $= 10^{-4}$ is 98.51% (and the EER is 0.01%). There are also some other ways that actual implementation can consider, for example, using best-of-the-match scores from several frames instead of every frame as estimated from the experiments in Section 10.6.

This chapter primarily focused on egocentric iris recognition, instead of iris segmentation as in [11] for example, which would require generation of a large number of manually

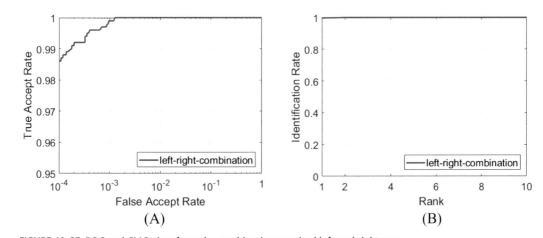

FIGURE 10–27 ROC and CMC plots from the combination acquired left and right eyes.

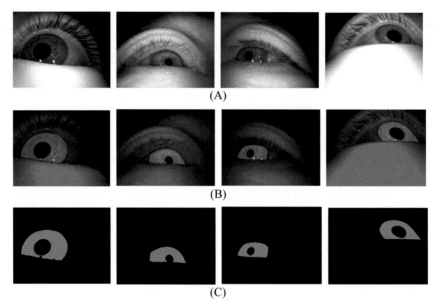

FIGURE 10–28 (A) Sample images from egocentric iris image database, (B) segmentation results (overlaid in green color) using segment anything model, and (C) segmented region of interest for iris recognition.

annotated iris and pupil regions in egocentric iris images. Therefore, further extensions of this work should aim for more precise localization of iris boundaries in the ocular images acquired from the head mounted AR/VR/MR devices. In this context, a range of more powerful and flexible segmentation models have emerged to address various types of image segmentation tasks. Despite their complexity, these models can be fine-tuned and integrated to achieve precise segmentation of iris regions from egocentric ocular images. Fig. 10–28 shows such results for the iris segmentation using *segment anything* [221] model which was fine-tuned using 500 sample images from the left eyes in our database. Despite the model's complexity, requiring 641,090,608 parameters and 7060 MB of GPU memory, the segmentation results are notably accurate and impressive. Further enhancement of this framework could involve analyzing feature consistency and fragility, evaluating performance on larger and cross-sensor AR/VR/MR sensing-based databases, and developing high-level feature representation from iris images with significant intra-class variations.

11

Inference and future pathways: reflections and exploration of new horizons

This book has introduced a range of deep learning-based models to match the iris images accurately and efficiently. The periocular region features are inherently acquired during a typical iris imaging setup, and therefore algorithms to accurately match such images with varying resolutions and under different illuminations were also introduced in earlier chapters. This chapter details the factors influencing the choice of iris recognition algorithms for real-world deployments, factors influencing the achievable performance, and application scenarios for different iris recognition algorithms. We also review the limitations of some of the deep learning-based iris recognition algorithms introduced in related literature. High-level feature representation for iris images, which is invariant to common preprocessing and/or imaging errors, is essential to realize the full potential for iris biometrics and is also introduced in this chapter. A range of other new ideas and frameworks, including iris recognition using adversarial learning and graph neural networks, are also discussed to advance iris recognition capabilities for challenging and large-scale applications.

11.1 Advancements and challenges

Robust iris recognition capabilities have traditionally been built from specialized iris segmentation and matching algorithms. Any direct use of conventional deep neural networks is only expected to offer limited performance. Comparative performance evaluations presented in Chapters 2, 3, or 10, using specialized models, have validated the merit of such specialized network architectures and loss functions introduced for the network training. It is worth noting that the most effective deep learning-based networks, introduced in Chapters 2, 3, or 10, were focused on enhancing the accuracy of the ROI segmentation networks and/or generating rich and robust feature templates. This section presents insights into various performance comparisons and further advancements to enhance the efficacy of these algorithms.

11.1.1 Iris detection and segmentation

The ISO Standard ISO/IEC 19794-6 [1] suggests minimum iris diameter in the detected iris images should be at least 200 pixels. Iris segmentation and detection for such images, meeting this criterion, have quite matured and are no longer considered a challenging

Iris and Periocular Recognition using Deep Learning. DOI: https://doi.org/10.1016/B978-0-443-27318-6.00011-5

problem for user authentication. However, efforts to impart enhanced flexibility and convenience using at-a-distance or iris-on-move imaging often result in many images with a variable background. Such images often pose challenges in the accurate localization (detection) or ROI segmentation to recover randomly textured iris patterns for identification. The accuracy of such detection and segmentation algorithms is also critical for matching the off-angle ocular images that are frequently acquired in a range of head-mounted virtual reality devices.

The pursuit of an iris detection and segmentation model in Chapters 3 or 10 has successfully fulfilled its primary objective of validating the deep learning-based alternative for accurately detecting and segmenting the ROI images from the acquired eye/ocular images. While the effectiveness of SOLOv2 [99] (as employed in Chapter 10) in segmenting the pupillary and limbic boundaries has been demonstrated in terms of both speed and accuracy, the utilization of more specialized instance segmentation models, such as SAM [221] or SEEM [102], holds the potential for further performance enhancement. By opting for complex segmentation models, such as in [103,104], it is also possible to achieve superior generalization capabilities through in-context training and seamlessly adapt them to the iris detection and segmentation tasks in UniNet.v2 framework.

11.1.2 Iris template generation and matching

Fully convolutional layer output from *UniNet* (Chapter 2) and *UniNet.v2* (Chapter 3) ensures that the iris template size remains fixed and is of the same size as the input ROI images. Consolidation of convolutional feature maps from three different scales in *FeatNet* has been incorporated to ensure balance the robustness of the features and spatial localization. However, the deep neural network for generating spatially corresponding features in Chapters 2 and 3 (*UniNet*) cannot be considered an end-to-end network, especially in terms of detecting noniris regions (*MaskNet*) and the generation of the final binary feature template. End-to-end training is highly desirable to achieve superior performance and adaptiveness from deep neural networks [222]. Therefore an end-to-end version of *UniNet* network is highly desirable. It can be achieved by jointly optimizing *FeatNet* and *MaskNet*, where a specific supervision mechanism for identifying effective iris region pixel is incorporated, and by designing learnable binary features on top of *FeatNet*, which may be similar to the supervised discrete Hashing mechanism incorporated in Chapter 5. Such measures are expected to enhance further the reliability of the extracted features and the robustness for more accurate iris recognition.

It should be noted that comparative experiments presented in Chapter 4 using dilated residual features and *UniNet* in Chapter 1 use different numbers of match scores, largely due to the exclusion of match scores due to failure to detect iris in a few images, and, therefore these should not be directly compared. It's also important to note that the use of multiple kernels for the approach in Chapter 4 significantly enhances the network complexity, as compared to those for *FeatNet* in *UniNet*, and therefore such complexity differences should be considered in any fair comparisons.

The *UniNet* framework performance can be further improved by incorporating more complex and backpropagation complaint iris contour fitting and normalization model to generate more robust spatially corresponding features.

11.1.3 Multitasking networks

Many successful deep learning-based architectures developed for iris recognition employ different networks that are even separately trained, and this is largely to address the challenge associated with a limited amount of iris images that can be used for network training. The UniNet.v2 framework introduced in Chapter 2 used a separate network (trained object detector) to detect the presence of the iris region, another network for the segmentation (*MaskNet*), and another network (*FeatNet*) for generating the feature templates. Similar attempts to segment iris and generate iris masks also appear in [223]. This was also the case for the AR/VR sensor-based iris recognition framework in Chapter 10, which employed a separate instance segmentation (SOLOv2) network for the iris segmentation and another trained network model for generating feature templates. A single deep network can instead be built to simultaneously and accurately perform these tasks using a multitasking network.

Popular multitasking networks are built on the assumption that different tasks are indeed related to each other. A key challenge in building such a successful network rests on the determination of the relationship among these tasks and the formulation of an effective learning model. One common approach is to learn a set of shared features for the different tasks and then train a generalized linear model that can represent different tasks with a weight vector [224]. It is not difficult to formulate similar relationships among tasks relating to iris detection, segmentation, masking, template generation, and matching. Such a model is, however, expected to be complex and will require a relatively large amount of training data to build such a model.

11.2 Factors influencing the performance of iris recognition algorithms

A range of algorithmic and demographic factors can influence achievable performance from iris recognition algorithms. These factors can be grouped under two categories, that is, factors impacting the achievable accuracy and the speed, and are elaborated in the following.

11.2.1 Accuracy

Match accuracy for iris recognition algorithms can depend on the nature of the application, that is, verification or identification, the mode of application, that is, bispectral, dual-eye comparisons, and demographical factors reflecting the users contributing the iris data. These are briefly discussed in the following.

11.2.1.1 Verification

The verification or user authentication applications require *one-to-one* comparisons among the matched templates. Its most widely deployed application for iris recognition systems and its performance is evaluated using the ROC plots. Some algorithms can perform better at *lower* FAR than others and are generally preferred for deployments, especially for high-security applications. Such importance is also reflected in the comparative evaluation of commercial iris recognition algorithms presented in [110] at the FAR of 10^{-5}.

11.2.1.2 Identification

The identification application requires *one-to-many* comparisons among the iris templates, and the user is not required to provide his/her claimed identity during such applications. There are *negative identification systems* that verify that a user is not enrolled in the system. De-duplication checks during the user enrollment of a new user in the Aadhaar program [68], or the (duplication) checks by NYPD [256] to prevent arrestees from pretending to be different arrestees during the arraignment is such an example of an iris-based *negative identification system*. On the other hand, *positive identification systems* are used to grant specific privileges to enrolled users, and the self-service iris kiosks at airports in the United Kingdom [24] are one such example of an iris recognition system. The performance from such *one-to-many* iris matching is evaluated using the CMC or DET plots. In addition to the number of enrolled users and the *number* of watchlist identities can significantly impact such performance from different iris recognition algorithms.

It is worth noting that the performance metrics for the verification and identification problem are quite different. The verification performance is measured using the ROC curve, which is based on the *aggregate statistics* of match scores corresponding to all identities. On the other hand, the identification performance is measured using the CMC curve, which is based on the *relative ordering* of match scores corresponding to each identity. The ROC is a "consistent" statistical estimator in that the two-dimensional values on the curve converge to a point as the number of genuine and impostor comparisons increase. The CMC curve is a metric that is applicable only to closed-set systems and not to identification systems in general. Here, the probability of the rank of the reference with the same source as the probe having a value less than or equal to M is plotted against M. The CMC curve is implicitly dependent upon the size of the closed-set, say N ($M \leq$ N), which is why the ISO/IEC 19795-1:2021 requires a statement of N for all CMC curves. Consequently, the CMC is an *inconsistent* statistical estimator of a probability that does not converge to any value other than 0 as N goes to infinity. Consequently, because CMC is dependent upon the number of comparisons, while the ROC is convergent with the number of comparisons, it immediately follows that *the same ROC curve can be accompanied by multiple CMC curves*. This is a scientific explanation of why a "poor" ROC curve can generate a "good" CMC curve for the *same* iris recognition system.

11.2.1.3 Bispectral and dual eye comparisons

A range of widely deployed iris recognition systems for access control and national ID programs use iris images from both eyes that are acquired *concurrently* from such dual-eye imaging devices. The performance of duel-eye iris matching offers significant improvement as compared to those for the single-eye matching from any given iris recognition algorithm. However, the NIST evaluation in [110] reports that that such improvement is not to a level that would be expected if the left eye iris and the right eye iris images were statistically independent.

Advances in iris sensing capabilities can generate pixel-to-pixel aligned visible and near-infrared iris images in a single imaging shot. Therefore such bispectral iris images can offer enhanced discrimination and superior match accuracy. Performance evaluation in [66] from the use of such bispectral iris images has shown significant performance improvement as compared to those from the conventional near-infrared imaged iris images.

11.2.1.4 Influence of pigmentation, gender, and ethnicity

The performance of iris recognition algorithms can be greatly influenced by the nature of iris image data acquired from the standardized iris sensors. Such demographic factors can relate to the gender, pigmentation, and ethnicity of subjects whose iris images are to be acquired or matched.

Iris pigmentation can be broadly categorized into two categories: light and dark. The iris with blue, green, and gray pigmentation can be considered light while those with brown or black pigmentation can be considered dark. Comparative performance evaluated on several commercial iris recognition algorithms in [110] has indicated that the majority of evaluated algorithms perform better on dark pigmentation iris data as compared to those for the light pigmentation. Such performance *bias* could be due to the differences in the performance of iris segmentation algorithms for the dark and light-pigmented iris images. It can also be due to the statistical richness in the iris texture and this can also depend on the nature of sensing techniques for the iris image acquisition. The nature of iris images employed for training the deep neural networks can significantly contribute to such *bias* between the light and dark pigmentation images.

Gender may also influence the accuracy of iris recognition algorithms. However, the comparative evaluation of commercial iris recognition algorithms from the male and female subjects' population has shown [110] inconsistent observations. A definitive explanation of such bias, if any, is yet to be discovered, but the differences in makeup for eyes of different genders can contribute to the varying accuracy in the localization of iris images.

The ethnicity of subjects can be considered in different aspects or ways, like Mongoloid Caucasoid, and Negroid; a related study in [225] has attempted to study the relative influence on the performance of conventional iris recognition (*IrisCode*) method using a database of the West African population. It reports a relatively small reduction in performance that can be compensated by a very small adjustment in the operational decision thresholds. Differences in the matching accuracy of subjects from different ethnic groups can be attributed to the differences in the proportion of training data from such groups. Deep learning-based algorithms are known to be susceptible to such bias in the training data.

11.2.2 Speed

Two key measurements can quantity the algorithmic speed: template *generation* time and template *matching* time. Template generation time is the amount of time the algorithm requires using a given iris image to generate the respective template for the enrollment or comparisons. A shorter template creation time is highly desirable to maintain high throughput in several access control applications like at the border crossings.

The template matching time refers to the amount of time required by any specific algorithm to generate a match score between two given templates. It's well known that for a given algorithm, template generation and matching time also depend on the implementation strategy and nature of the hardware adopted. For example, using multiple cores in CPU or advanced GPU hardware can significantly enhance achievable speed from a given algorithm.

It's also possible to achieve a trade-off between several algorithms' achievable speed and accuracy. Comparative performance evaluations of several commercial iris recognition algorithms during IREX III and IX [110] have reported such trade-offs for several evaluated algorithms. Adoption of more complex matching strategies can generally offer enhanced match accuracy.

11.3 Limitations with other published algorithms

Several interesting efforts to advance iris and periocular recognition algorithms using deep neural networks have appeared in the literature. Therefore it can be quite challenging for the readers to analyze competing claims on the performance, especially for the case when selecting algorithms for any typical real-world applications. This section outlines some of such instances and contradictions from the literature that pose genuine scientific questions on the stated claims.

Ref. [251] recently detailed an interesting attempt to advance iris recognition using complex networks [252] and shifted triplet loss introduced in Chapter 2. However, there are several technical flaws in the comparisons and fairness of performance evaluation with the employed baseline methods. For example, a careful look at ROCs "Fig. 13B" and "Fig. 13C" (p. 192) in [252] and EER values reported in "Table 3" of this reference reveals a large discrepancy. The EER values for *IrisCode*, DCT, DFT, and Ordinal algorithms on the UBIRIS.v2 dataset are all stated to be higher than 8%. However, in "Fig. 13C," we observe that the EER values are below 5% (estimated values from this ROC are 4.273%, 4.182%, 3.987%, and 3.857%, respectively for *IrisCode*, DCT, DFT, and Ordinal). We can also observe a similar inconsistency in the EER values on the CASIA-Iris-Thousand dataset as such stated EER values are higher than 3%. However, in "Fig. 13B," we observe that the EER values of *IrisCode* are about 2.23%, and for all other methods, it is smaller than 2%. The approach pursued in this paper "*employ a bank of M = 40 Gabor filters with 5 wavelengths and 8 orientations*" just for preprocessing. Therefore fair comparisons with baseline should also utilize multiple (40) *IrisCodes* to ascertain the merit of the performance from baseline method(s). Several other claims and comparisons presented in [251] lack fairness, for example, the achievement of an identical EER of 0.99% for Ref. [20] but on substantially different datasets or claims on complexity while using different hardware configurations and GPUs. A detailed analysis, also presented in [253], of the exact number of match scores employed in [251] indicates that this reference has selectively discarded certain match scores or used some nonstandard match protocols that have not been used in respective baseline methods. In either case, such experimentation cannot generate reliable results, and readers should exercise caution. For example, a remarkably elevated recognition accuracy can be achieved by selectively discarding low-value genuine and high-value imposter scores. Therefore even if an algorithm demonstrates very high performance under such unfair circumstances, as in this reference, we still cannot hastily conclude its superiority. In view of the significant errors and inconsistencies discussed in this section, Ref. [251] does not bring any advancement over the existing deep learning-based methods for iris recognition.

Ref. [15] tells us that 502 images are used for the test and 79 images for the training from the CASIA-at-a-distance database. On the other hand, Ref. [223] stated that only 100 images are used for the test and 300 images for the training from this database for the comparative performance evaluation. However, the numbers on the segmentation accuracy for the quantitative comparisons in Table 3, for example, 0.68, are directly lifted from [15], which uses different numbers of test and train images, as explained here. This cannot be considered a fair comparison and poses questions on the performance claims and methodology presented in [223]. There are some other instances of technical evaluation in this reference that underlines the need for more work in developing a multitasking framework for the iris recognition.

The *DeepIrisNet* [22] has been used as one of the baseline methods in many references, for example, [251]. However, the experimental comparisons presented in Chapter 2 on multiple databases indicate that with the right choice of parameters even the *IrisCode* can offer superior match accuracy over *DeepIrisNet*. Ref. [22] fails to utilize the best set of parameters for the conventional iris recognition method used as a baseline. Therefore comparisons presented in [253] lack fairness and those in Chapters 2 and 3 indicate need for significant work in developing a high-level deep feature representation (as underlined in Section 11.4.2).

There are also references to periocular recognition methods that have failed to use the same match protocols to establish the merit of deep network models for such tasks. For example, the comparisons presented in Ref. [174] for the *homogenous* periocular recognition use different match protocols while it lifts the error rates ("Table X" in Ref. [174]) from the baseline method that used *different* match protocols. Every research publication seeks to offer solutions for a specific problem, but it is not unusual for these attempts to have limitations or errors. It is, however, important to note such limitations and is key to developing the most effective solutions for real-world applications.

11.4 Further exploration and enhancements

Ocular images offer tremendous potential to identify a very large number of subjects accurately. Such potential can be realized by developing deep learning-based models and algorithms. The following section explores such enhancements and advancements that can enable the realization of the full potential of real-world ocular images.

11.4.1 Building generative models for iris recognition using adversarial learning

One of the important enhancements to achieve highly accurate capabilities, especially for the iris recognition from the *distantly acquired* images in a *less constrained environment,* can be realized by developing a generative and recognition model using adversarial learning. The generative model can help to address limitations resulting from the limited availability of iris images for the training. On the other hand, the recognition part of such a model can exploit diverse data from the generator network to achieve a significant improvement in the accuracy of the matching. Publicly available databases can be used for supervising adversarial learning and evaluating the performance of the recognition model. The segmented iris images after the normalization step, as incorporated in Chapter 3, are used as input for developing the generative recognition model, which is detailed in the following.

This model will utilize a generator network G and a discriminator network D, similar to in [226]. However, since the task of the discriminator is to recognize the identities of the iris samples instead of simply identifying real or synthetic, we here refer to it as recognizer network R. The motivation for adversarial training is to place G and R in *contest* with each other for simultaneous performance improvement, that is, G learns to generate realistic data that is similar to real samples while R learns to accurately recognize real data and synthetic data from G. More specifically, such a learning process attempts to optimize the following energy (loss) function:

$$\min_R \max_G V(G, R) = L(R(\boldsymbol{x})) + L(R(G(\boldsymbol{x}', \boldsymbol{z}))) \qquad (11-1)$$

where $\boldsymbol{x}$ and $\boldsymbol{x}'$ are sampled from real data, and $\boldsymbol{z}$ is the prior variable or random noise similar to as in [226] given to G for generating synthetic samples, optionally with reference to $\boldsymbol{x}'$. $G(\cdot)$ and $R(\cdot)$ are the function notations for network G and R respectively, and $L(\cdot)$ is the loss function for evaluating the output of recognizer (e.g., $L(p) = -t\log(p) - (1-t)\log(1-p)$, where p is the predicted probability of realness, $t=1$ for real and $t=0$ for synthetic in a binary detection case).

11.4.1.1 Preserving subject identities in the generative model

GANs are generally designed to ensure the realness of generated data for various applications. For example, Ref. [227] employed GAN for completing damaged/masked face images to generate highly realistic and natural results. However, as revealed from the experiments in [227], the identities of the generated images could not be guaranteed. Emphasis should not only be on realness but also on preserving subject identities from the generated data. Such efforts involve two perspectives, that is, (i) the design of generator G and (ii) the re-formulation of the loss function to incorporate subject identity imprints during training.

1. To provide adequate variation between the synthetic and real iris data to train the recognizer sufficiently, the *Encoder-Decoder* architecture [108,228] can be adopted for the generator network. As shown in Fig. 11−1, a reference sample, x', will be input to a CNN, which we refer to as encoder, to obtain a "code," that is, a high-level representation of input with reduced dimensionality. The code will then be associated with a prior variable z, and fed into another reversely symmetric CNN as a decoder to generate a new sample. The prior information mainly serves as variations, and by controlling the dimension of the intermediate code, the original image pixels can be compressed to alleviate the generation of the *same* image as reference input x'. Once it is well trained, the code will summarize the subject identity imprint while the prior provides an intra-person variation that is related to the iris imaging conditions (pose, resolution, illumination, etc.) for generating a synthetic sample with the given identity.

2. The second aspect of this approach is to re-formulate the loss function for training the generative model. Since the recognizer in such an approach aims to distinguish the *identities* of the samples, the loss needs to be redefined to embed the identity prediction other than the binary real/synthetic classification, similar to in [196]. Two possible recognition mechanisms for the problem formulation, as illustrated in Fig. 11−2, deserve consideration. The first one is to identify the subject ID for a single sample input (Fig. 11−2A). In this mode, the output of R is a $(n + 1)$-D vector $y \in \mathbf{R}^{n+1}$ which will be wrapped with a softmax function, that is, $p_i = e^{y^i}/(\sum_{j=1}^{n+1} e^{y^j})$. With such softmax wrapping, the first n elements of p represent the probabilities of the sample belonging to the corresponding n subjects and the $(n + 1)$ th element is the probability of synthetic sample, and the resulting loss function can be defined as follows:

$$L(p) = \begin{cases} -\log(p_k), & \text{if } t = 1 \\ -\log(p_{n+1}) + \log(p_{k'}), & \text{if } t = 0 \end{cases} \tag{11-2}$$

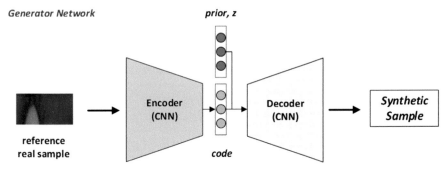

FIGURE 11−1 Illustration of generator network with encoder−decoder architecture.

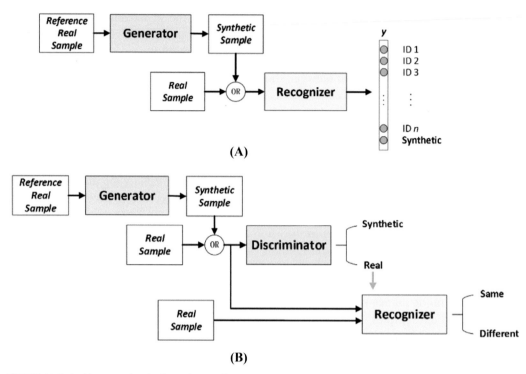

FIGURE 11–2 Architectures for the formulation of iris recognition problem during adversarial training: (A) a unified identification network for subject and real/synthetic classification and (B) hierarchical structure with preceding discriminator for real/synthetic classification and subsequent recognizer networks for identity verification. In both cases, the generator will receive feedback for both "real/synthetic" classification and subject identity recognition and therefore can learn to ensure high level of realness as well as preserving subject identities for the generated data.

where k is the ground-truth ID for the real sample, while k' is the reference ID for the synthetic sample. In the case of the synthetic sample $(t = 0)$, G attempts to synthesize a realistic image for subject k', and R will iteratively learn to classify it as a synthetic input. The second strategy is to adopt pair-wise input for the recognizer R, that is, the so-called Siamese architecture as in [229] (Fig. 11−2B). In this mode, the task of R is to verify whether two inputs originate from the same or different person. The recognizer network employs a hierarchical architecture, which comprises a preceding discriminator (judging sample realness) and subsequent pair verifier (judging identity). In this mode, the loss will consist of *two* parts, that is, the discrimination loss and the verification loss. This loss function is defined as follows:

$$L(\boldsymbol{p}) = \begin{cases} L_D - L_R, & \text{if } p_{real} \geq 0.5 \\ L_D, & \text{if } p_{real} < 0.5 \end{cases} \tag{11-3}$$

$$L_D = -t\log(p_{real}) - (1-t)\log(1-p_{real}) \tag{11-4}$$

$$L_R = -s\log(p_{sim}) - (1-s)\log(1-p_{sim}) \tag{11-5}$$

where p_{real} is the output of discriminator indicating the probability for the input being a real sample, p_{sim} is the verifier output as transformed probability for the pair of input belonging to the same subject. s is the identifier that whether two samples, no matter synthetic or real given by the generator side, are from the same person or not. In both recognition mechanisms, the generated subject identity will be evaluated and the feedback will be transferred to the generator G for learning to preserve identity information.

The effectiveness of identity preservation learning can be evaluated using the most effective deep learning models, iris recognition algorithms like those presented in Chapters 2 and 3, under scenarios of real-real, real-synthetic, and synthetic-synthetic matching. When the matching performance and the match scores distributions of the latter two settings are similar to the real-real setting, we can infer that the identity information from the referenced real samples is well retained during the synthetic data generation. It is worth noting that during the test or deployment phase, there will not be synthetic input, and the trained recognizer will only be used to differentiate identities from real or unknown data.

11.4.1.2 Recognizer based on state-of-the-art framework

The recognizer R is a standalone deep neural network that can recognize subject identities of input images, although in our case the input can be a synthetic image. A proper design of R can provide a robust starting point for the iris recognition task and facilitate convergence for the overall generative model. The *UniNet* architecture introduced in Chapter 2, has consistently shown outperforming results and therefore can provide judicious discriminating power for the adversarial training with the generator. Such architectural design can be further enhanced for fully leveraging real and synthetic data in a larger scale. First, instead of generating a single-channel feature map from multiscale intermediate convolutional features, we can exploit separate feature representations at each of the different scales to retain more scale-specific details. Secondly, during the test phase, one can consider to combine the features from recognizer R and the learned "code" from the generator that provides high level of identity information as illustrated in Fig. 11−2A, to obtain more discriminative iris representation. A comprehensive generative and recognition framework can be established for the iris recognition with such architectural designs and formulation. The adversarial training mechanism can boost the performance of the iris recognition network significantly by leveraging an unlimited number of synthesized images in addition to real images, thus providing superior accuracy over existing models that have incorporated a limited amount of training images.

11.4.2 Building high-level iris feature representation

Developing a high-level representation for real-world iris images, which can be invariant to common preprocessing and/or imaging errors in the acquired iris images, is essential to realize the full potential for iris biometrics. Almost all the iris recognition methods, available today incorporate low-level feature representation that can accurately recover local characteristics. However, achievable accuracy from such features heavily relies on the *accuracy* of iris segmentation, spatial alignment, and postprocessing operations, which are known to degrade iris images acquired under adverse environments. Therefore a high-level iris representation using the hierarchical fully convolutional network, by utilizing the local and global descriptors in iris pattern, can offer robust representation against the spatial deformations and degradations and is introduced in the following.

The segmented and normalized iris images, employed for training *UniNet* (Chapters 2 and 3), can be used to develop such a hierarchical network shown in Fig. 11–3. Two approaches can be considered for this hierarchical architecture and will be the key to its effectiveness. The first one is the *residual hierarchy* formed by convolutional features at different scales. The raw image is firstly passed through several convolutional units (convolution + activation + pooling layers) similar to as for the *UniNet*. The multichannel convolutional feature maps from bottom to top, f_1, f_2, and f_3 in our case, can be regarded as descriptors for the original image x at different scales: $f_i = F_i(x), i = 1, 2, 3$, where $F_i(\cdot)$ represents operation by one or multiple convolutional units. It can be inferred that the features at larger spatial scale (e.g., f_1) can better describe iris patterns but are least adaptive to deformation or blur, therefore have to incorporate spatial alignment (bit-shifting) for matching, while top features at smaller scale (e.g., f_3) may be less discriminative but relatively robust to spatial variations. We then stack the original input with each of the feature maps (optionally downsampled to the same resolution of the convolutional features), which is parsed by another convolutional layer: $f_{4,i} = F_{4,i}(x, f_i) = F_{4,i}(x, F_i(x))$. Such conjunction of convolutional features with original input is similar to the residual architecture introduced in [227]. The residual unit is expected to *refine* the previous features with the participation of past input instead of computing new representation as in [229]. The new convolution layers will output feature maps $f_{4,i}$ of uniform size from different scales by adjusting kernel sizes and strides for the bottom inputs.

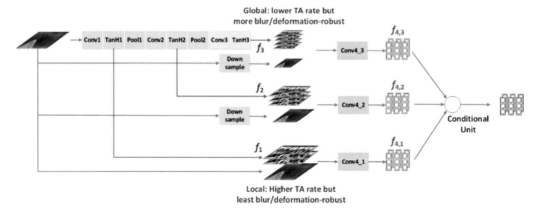

FIGURE 11–3 Hierarchical, conditional, and fully convolutional network for learning high-level iris feature representation. Different scales of features form a hierarchy, from local to global descriptors of iris pattern, which are then combined by a conditional unit for higher-level feature construction.

Such features form a hierarchical architecture from low-level to high-level convolutional representations and are subjected to the *conditional feature selection*, which is the second key component for this framework. Conditional components are often used in deep learning models [227,230] to address adaptive data routing/activation conditioned on potentially different global configurations for input pixels or intermediate features and have shown enhanced results over common deep neural networks. In our case, we use the conditional unit as the feature selector/fuser from the hierarchy of features introduced above. As discussed earlier, features computed from different scales exhibit varying distinctiveness to identity and robustness to deformation and blur, and therefore most discriminative features are expected to be adaptively selected to achieve as much accuracy as possible, conditioned on the feature distribution for this approach. Each of the candidate feature map is a 3-dimensional matrix, $\boldsymbol{f}_{4,i} \in \mathbf{R}^{W \times H \times C}$. We refer to each of the vectors along channel direction as *column vectors*, $\boldsymbol{c}_i \in \mathbf{R}^C$, and feature selection is performed column-wise. The conditional feature selector can be defined as a weight vector whose elements sum to one:

$$w_i = \frac{e^{z_i}}{e^{z_1} + e^{z_2} + e^{z_3}}, \boldsymbol{z} = \boldsymbol{a} \begin{bmatrix} \boldsymbol{c}_1 \\ \boldsymbol{c}_2 \\ \boldsymbol{c}_3 \end{bmatrix} + \boldsymbol{b} \qquad (11-6)$$

where $\boldsymbol{a} \in \mathbf{R}^{3 \times 3C}$ and $\boldsymbol{b} \in \mathbf{R}^3$ are the parameters of the conditional unit to be learned. The output weight vector $\boldsymbol{w}$ is then used to compute the weighted sum of the candidate column vectors to obtain an optimized column vector: $\boldsymbol{c} = w_1\boldsymbol{c}_1 + w_2\boldsymbol{c}_2 + w_3\boldsymbol{c}_3$, which is the final *high-level iris representation* to be used for matching. The matching process can adopt a distance (e.g., Euclidean) measure on all the column vectors for computing the dissimilarity metric and can therefore alleviate the need for complex bit-shifting operations as was employed in *UniNet*, since each fused column vector $\boldsymbol{c}$ contains high-level abstraction for a certain block in the original image and is expected to be robust to spatial translation. The network is then trained using the triplet loss function for the end-to-end optimization. The trained network can be employed to comparatively evaluate the performance, using cross-database evaluation, and metrics used in earlier chapters.

11.4.3 Synthesis of real-world iris image databases to advance iris recognition capabilities

More complex and deeply learned networks require a huge amount of training data and are critical for the success of such models. Therefore new capabilities to synthesize large-scale cross-view and cross-sensor ocular images can help to address a key privacy-related challenge associated with the acquisition and sharing of ocular biometric data, especially in view of new regulations, such as the GDPR [149].

The design and development of generative models to generate identity-specific and randomly textured iris images can address the limited availability of iris data with known identities. Fig. 11−4 presents samples of synthesized iris ROI images using generative adversarial

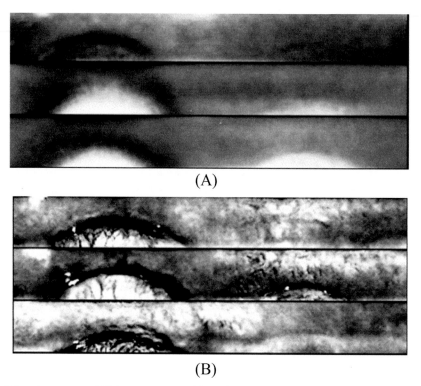

(A)

(B)

FIGURE 11–4 Sample *unwrapped* iris images generated from the generative models: (A) using BEGAN [233] and (B) using DCGAN [234]. These models are *not* designed to generate fine-grained random textures or iris images and are a key limitation of such methods.

networks (GANs). Synthesis of iris images using GANs has attracted some attention [231,232]. However, the GANs are notoriously difficult to train and face many unsolved difficulties in generating fine-grained iris texture and image samples in Fig. 11−4 indicate such limitations on the effectiveness of these models. Therefore algorithmic advancements are required to control the trade-off between iris texture randomness and visual quality, and to balance the convergence of discriminator against the generator.

Another approach to synthesize real-world ocular images is to model synthetic 3D ocular phantoms using Bezier surfaces. Modeling 3D ocular surfaces using Bezier surface [235] can be more effective, as compared to traditional parametric models that cannot accurately fit the shapes of different real-world ocular surfaces or generate fine-grained random texture deformations. Real-world ocular images from conventional devices also exhibit scale changes. Therefore besides random changes in the rotational angles, the distance between the camera and the ocular model can also be randomly changed by adjusting the extrinsic matrix of the camera. Such a synthesis approach for contactless fingerprints has shown impressive results in [236] and can also be adopted to synthesize multiview contactless 2D iris images.

11.4.4 Decision level enhancements

Iris recognition systems present multiple cues and contextual details for the targeted application. Consolidation of these simultaneous cues can significantly enhance the accuracy of such systems and such enhancements are discussed in the following sections.

11.4.4.1 Feature level consolidation using probabilistic modeling

Conventional iris images inherently reveal periocular features but to varying degrees which can depend on applications. The richest source of information is preserved in feature-level representations. Therefore feature-level combination of simultaneously acquired/available iris and periocular features can offer accuracy that may not be possible by any other methods for the combination. Iris and periocular modalities are however characterized by highly different statistical properties. Periocular features largely describe the global structural information of the sample in relatively abstracted and high level, often in the form of vector with closely correlated elements, and discriminative information lies in the global description of periocular images. On the other hand, iris features capture textural information in a certain spatial range instead of the whole image, as the least meaningful global structure is revealed in iris images. The significant difference in feature domains implies that *the numeric correlations within features of each modality are much stronger than that between different modalities* [237]. Therefore the correlation across iris and periocular is much harder to discover with simple models. As a result, linear or low-order modeling of these two types of features, such as *feature concatenation*, weighted sum of scores, or decision-level fusion, would easily learn to bias the dominant feature instead of capturing latent intermodality relationship. Another drawback of these approaches is that the learned or tuned parameters (e.g., weights of a weighted-sum scheme) frequently encounter overfitting for different databases.

As compared with previous multimodal learning methods [227,238], such an approach uses raw data (images) as input (visible units) to the multilayer RBMs, and we use features from pretrained deep CNNs as visible variables. This strategy can maximally take advantage of carefully designed and proven effective CNN architectures, rather than using RBM for feature extraction which can hardly incorporate modality-specific design and has too large parameter space (Fig. 11−5).

An ideal combination strategy for iris and periocular should model their relationship in a uniform space so that intermodality correlation can be more easily discovered, and allow more complex statistical inference other than simple low-dimensional operations. Such a combination using probabilistic modeling with a restricted Boltzmann machine (RBM) can, therefore, be more effective. Fig. 10−5 illustrates such an approach for the feature-level consolidation of the iris and periocular features, from the same ocular image. RBM is an undirected graphical model with stochastic visible units (input) $\boldsymbol{v} \in \{0, 1\}^D$ and stochastic hidden units $\boldsymbol{h} \in \{0, 1\}^F$. It defines an energy function as:

$$E(\boldsymbol{v}, \boldsymbol{h}; \theta) = -\boldsymbol{v}^{\mathrm{T}} \boldsymbol{W} \boldsymbol{h} - \boldsymbol{b}^{\mathrm{T}} \boldsymbol{v} - \boldsymbol{a}^{\mathrm{T}} \boldsymbol{h} \qquad (11-7)$$

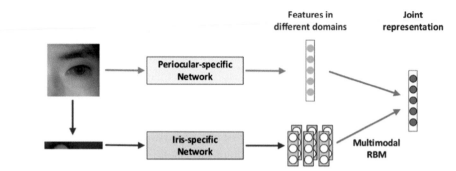

FIGURE 11–5 Learning joint feature representation for iris and periocular modalities. Probabilistic RBM can be reconstructed on modality-specific networks which can be separately pretrained. The RBM is optimized by learning joint probability distribution over multiple feature spaces.

where $\theta = \{\boldsymbol{a},\boldsymbol{b},\boldsymbol{W}\}$ are parameters to be learned. The joint probability distribution over the visible and hidden units can be defined as:

$$P(\boldsymbol{v},\boldsymbol{h};\theta) = \frac{1}{Z(\theta)}\exp(-E(\boldsymbol{v},\boldsymbol{h};\theta)) \qquad (11-8)$$

where $Z(\theta)$ is a partition function, that is, the sum of all $\exp(-E)$ over all possible configurations, for normalization purpose to ensure the probability distribution sums to one. Given visible units, the inference of hidden units is obtained by:

$$P(h_i = 1|\boldsymbol{v}) = \sigma(b_i + \sum_{j=1}^{D} w_{ij}v_j) \qquad (11-9)$$

where σ denotes the logistic sigmoid function. RBM is generally trained to maximize the product of probabilities (maximum likelihood) assigned to the training set using contrastive divergence (CD) algorithm or to minimize the variation of information according to [237,239]. In our case, the visible units can be formed by the separate periocular and iris features, and the hidden units, after learning, serve as a joint representation of the two modalities. Note that the input features may be real values while the visible units are binary. This can be achieved in several possible ways, for example, to convert the real-valued features into binary space (e.g., using hashing [78]) or by extending the original RBM to real value-compatible Gaussian RBM [239]. The learned RBM can be further fine-tuned using a recognition-oriented classifier in a supervised manner.

11.4.4.2 Incorporating user quality and cohort match scores in decisions

The *user quality* is a measure of the biometric distinctiveness of a particular user in the registered or enrollment database. Researchers have focused on the quantification of biometric image quality. However, in our approach instead of estimating the quality of the query images using conventional (nondeep learning-based) transforms, that is, Fourier transform, Wavelet transform, etc., individually, a single quality measure for each user is estimated based on their imposter match scores from the training data. Estimating the quality of the iris samples in such a way can be more effective in achieving performance improvement. Such a quality measure represents the quality of the biometric for an enrolled user rather than the quality of an image and therefore we designate this as *user quality*. The estimation of user quality is performed during the training phase and the minimum of all the imposter scores, for every user, is computed.

$$U_a = \min\{S_a^i\} \tag{11-10}$$

where, U_a represents the *user quality* of user "*a*" and S_a^i represents the imposter score vector for the user "a".

The estimated user quality score, generated during the enrollment or the training phase, is employed during the test image matching. For matching any two images, the minimum of the two *user quality* scores associated with the corresponding/claimed image class is used as the weight. For example, in case of Hamming distance-based match scores, from test and train/enrolled images using Eq. (2.21), the computed match score is normalized (divided in this case) by the weight obtained for that pair of matched images. This essentially means that if a user is more probable to be near any other class then its quality score would be low and dividing by that value will put that user away from the other classes.

$$S' = \frac{S}{\min(Ux, Uy)} \tag{11-11}$$

where S' is the new matching score, Ux is the *user quality* score of the claimed class, and Uy is the *use quality* score of the matched class. In this case, the larger the minimum imposter matching score, the better the *user quality* as this offers a large separation of user from the imposters.

The match scores from *other* enrolled users in the registered database can be directly incorporated into the decision-making to enhance the performance. Such use of cohort match scores is illustrated in Fig. 11−6. Acquired iris images are firstly preprocessed to generate RoI and extract feature templates from the trained model. Each of such templates is first matched with the user template corresponding to the claimed identity. If this match score m_u from an unknown user is less than the decision threshold (T), then the user is authenticated as a genuine user. However, we do not reject this user if his/her score m_u is more than threshold but employ cohort information to ascertain if he/she is genuine or imposter. This requires additional computations of match scores m_i ($\forall\, i = N - 1$) for the other users' (cohort) templates. If the score m_u is less than all the cohort matching scores m_i, then this unknown user identity is authenticated as a genuine user. However, even if any of the cohort scores, that is, m_i, is less than m_u then the user is authenticated as an imposter user. Effective use of cohort match scores is expected to enhance the performance of the iris recognition algorithms for many real-world applications. Fig. 11−7 presents sample

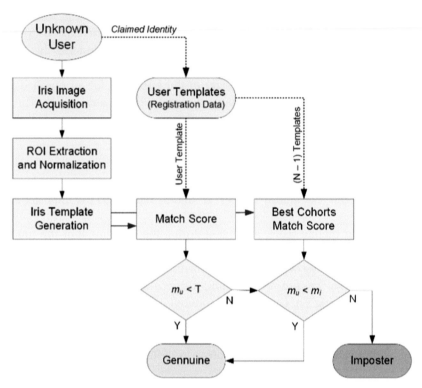

FIGURE 11–6 Enhancing iris identification decisions by incorporating cohort match scores.

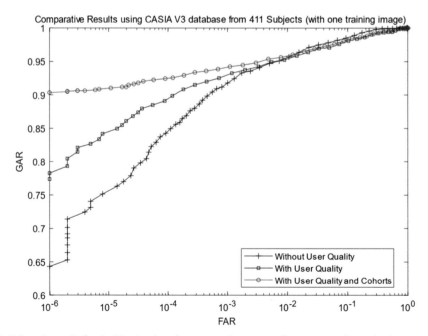

FIGURE 11–7 Sample results for decision-level performance enhancement from user quality and cohort match scores.

experimental results using CASIA.V3 iris images database. This set of experiments however uses only first seven images from each of the 411 subjects (only one eye) in this database. It can be observed from this figure that the performance improvement from the usage of user quality, and also the cohort scores, is quite significant.

11.4.5 Modeling complex feature relationships using transformers and diffusion models

Transformers offer a promising solution to the limitations of fully convolutional neural networks in capturing long-range spatial feature relationships in iris texture. With the introduction of self-attention mechanisms, transformers can effectively model these dependencies and achieve competitive accuracy in various domains. However, training transformers, such as the Vision Transformer [150], can be more challenging than traditional CNNs [240]. This challenge becomes even more pronounced when dealing with limited iris data, as transformers are complex architectures. Despite these difficulties, transformers offer great potential in accurately matching periocular images, making them valuable, especially for the large-very scale applications.

Despite the huge excitement generated by the capabilities of the transformers, these models are computationally intensive and formidably large for typical iris recognition applications. There are two key challenges with the use of such models: requirement of intensive computations during the training stage and exponentially growing requirement of training memory. Incorporating appropriate initialization and optimization paradigms [241] can help to accelerate the convergence rate and lower the computational costs. Similarly, the use of memory-efficient techniques can help to meet the prohibitive large training memory requirements.

The FCN used in Chapters 2, 3, or 10 considers the normalized iris images as a grid or sequence of random texture which lacks flexibility to accommodate frequent iris texture deformations due to variations in the pupil diameter. This challenge can be addressed by representing iris images as a graph structure. Iris images are also known to present several key point features, for example, iris crypts that are certain regions generally observed on the periphery of iris or near the collarette. Such key point features have been studied for the iris recognition [242,243] but with limited effectiveness. Such key point features can however be leveraged to *uncover* complex iris feature relationship using graph neural networks (GNN). Graph neural networks [244] are deep neural networks with graph embedding and are very effective in predicting or uncovering nodes, edges, and other graph-related complex tasks.

GNNs however operate on graph structure which is assumed to be fixed and homogenous. Therefore the normalized iris images should be firstly processed to recover reliable key points that can serve as the nodes for the graph. The GNNs can then recover the relationships, typically by accumulating the messages from the propagation of messages from one graph node to another, to model complex relationships among the nodes. The nodes can be recovered from a deep neural network-based preprocessing, for example, using Superpoint [245]. Another network can be utilized to recover matched correspondences [246] between key points between the pair of iris images during the training. The GNN can compute the similarity between such graphs, that is, matched correspondence pairs that compose such graphs.

A recent class of likelihood-based generative models with a specific Markov chain structure is referred to as diffusion probabilistic models or *diffusion models* in short. These network models learn the data distribution using an iterative noising and denoising process [247] and show its outperforming results for a range of computer vision-related problems [248,249]. These models have also achieved great success in converting them to hyperparameter-free classification models without the need for any additional training [250]. Iris recognition requires accurate classification of fine-grained iris texture under noising process which can be probabilistically modeled from the limited amount of available real-world data. Therefore the development of iris recognition models using diffusion models-based classification iris images is worth exploring to address challenges for the very large-scale iris recognition problems.

Bibliography

References

[1] ISO/IEC 19794-6:2011. Information Technology − Biometric Data Interchange Formats − Part 6: Iris Image Data. Standard, International Organization for Standardization, Geneva, 2011. <https://www.iso.org/standard/50868.html> (accessed 4.24).

[2] L. Flom, A. Safir, Iris recognition system, U. S. Patent No. 4, 641, 349, 1987.

[3] J. Daugman, Biometric personal identification based on iris analysis, U. S. Patent No. 5, 291, 560, March 1884.

[4] J. Daugman, High confidence visual recognition of persons by a test of statistical independence, *IEEE Trans. Pattern Anal. Mach. Intell.* 15 (1993) 1148−1161.

[5] A. Bertillon, La Couleur de l'iris, Rev. Sci. 36 (1885) 63−73.

[6] P. Grother, G.W. Quinn, M.L. Ngan, J.R. Matey, IREX IV: part 1, *evaluation of iris identification algorithms*, NIST Interag. Rep. 7949 (2013).

[7] Unique Identification Authority of India, *Iris Authentication Accuracy—PoC Report*, 2013. <http://uidai.gov.in/images/iris_poc_report_14092012.pdf>.

[8] ISO/IEC 19795-1:2021, Information technology—biometric performance testing and reporting—part 1: principles and framework. Technical report, 2023.

[9] UIDAI Iris, Authentication Device Specifications (STQC). <http://www.stqc.gov.in/sites/upload_files/stqc/files/Device_specification_BDCS_A-I-03-07-0.pdf>.

[10] NICE, I—noisy iris challenge evaluation, part I. <http://nice1.di.ubi.pt/index.html>.

[11] Z. Zhao, A. Kumar, An accurate iris segmentation framework under related imaging constraints, in: Proc, ICCV 2015, Santiago, Chile, 2015, pp. 3828−3836.

[12] A. Kumar, Dynamic security management in multibiometrics, in: B. Bhanu, V. Govindaraju (Eds.), Multibiometrics for human identification, Cambridge University Press; USA, 2011, pp. 302−320.

[13] P. Grother, M. Ngan, The IJB—a face identification challenge performance report, NIST Report, 2017. <https://zhaoj9014.github.io/pub/IJBA_1N_report.pdf>.

[14] Iris Exchange (IREX) 10. <https://pages.nist.gov/IREX10/> (accessed 2024).

[15] C.-W. Tan, A. Kumar, A unified framework for automated iris segmentation using distantly acquired face images, *IEEE Trans. Image Process.* 21 (9) (2012) 4068−4078.

[16] C.-W. Tan, A. Kumar, Towards online iris and periocular recognition under relaxed imaging constraints, *IEEE Trans. Image Process.* 22 (2013) 3751−3765.

[17] CASIA. v4 Iris Database. <http://biometrics.idealtest.org/dbDetailForUser.do?id = 4>.

[18] P.A. Johnson, P. Lopez-Meyer, N. Sazonova, F. Hua, S. Schuckers, Quality in Face and Iris Research Ensemble (Q-FIRE), in: Proc. 4th IEEE Int. Conf. Biometrics: Theory, Applications and Systems, BTAS, 2010, pp. 1−6.

[19] H. Proença, S. Filipe, R. Santos, J. Oliveira, L. Alexandre, The UBIRIS.v2: a database of visible wavelength images captured on the move and at-a-distance, IEEE Trans. Pattern Anal. Mach. Intell. 32 (8) (2010) 1529−1535.

[20] Z. Zhao, A. Kumar, Accurate and generalizable iris recognition using deep fully convolutional network and shifted triplet loss, in: Proc. IEEE Intl. Conf. Computer Vision, ICCV 2017, Venice, Italy, 2017, pp. 3829−3838.

[21] Z. Zhao, A. Kumar, A deep learning based unified framework to detect, segment and recognize irises using spatially corresponding features, Pattern Recogn. 93 (2019) 546−557.

[22] A. Gangwar, A. Joshi, DeepIrisNet: Deep iris representation with applications in iris recognition and cross-sensor iris recognition, in: Proc. Intl. Conf. Image Processing, ICIP, 2016, pp. 2301−2305.

[23] N. Liu, H. Li, M. Zhang, J. Liu, Z. Sun, T. Tan, Accurate iris segmentation in non-cooperative environments using fully convolutional networks, in: Proc. Int. Conf. Biometrics, ICB 2016, Halmstad, Sweden, June 2016.

[24] J. Daugman, How iris recognition works, IEEE Trans. Circ. Sys. Video Technol. 14 (2004) 21−30.

[25] Y. Zhou, A. Kumar, Personal identification from iris images using localized Radon transform, in: Proc. ICPR2010, Istanbul, Turkey, August 2010, pp. 2843−2840.

[26] M. Felsberg, G. Sommer, A new extension of linear signal processing for estimating local properties and detecting features, in: Proc. 2nd DAGM Symposium für Mustererkennung, Springer-Verlag, Berlin, 2000, pp. 195−202.

[27] T.-S. Chan, Ajay Kumar, Reliable ear identification using 2D quadrature filters, Pattern Recogn. Lett. 33 (14) (2012) 1870−1881.

[28] D. Boukerroui, J.A. Noble, M. Brady, On the choice of band-pass quadrature filters, J. Math. Imaging Vis. 21 (2004) 53−80.

[29] R. Corless, G. Gonnet, D. Hare, D. Jeffrey, D. Knuth, On the Lambert W function, Adv. Comput. Math. 5 (1996) 329−359.

[30] L. Masek, Recognition of Human Iris Patterns for Biometric Identification, The School of Computer Science and Software Engineering, The University of Western Australia, 2003. Matlab source codes. <https://www.peterkovesi.com/studentprojects/libor/index.html>.

[31] L. Zhang, L. Zhang, D. Zhang, MonogenicCode: a novel fast feature coding algorithm with applications to finger-knuckle-print recognition, in: Proc. Intl. Workshop on Emerging Techniques and Challenges for Hand-Based Biometrics, 2010, pp. 1−4.

[32] A. Kumar, T.-S. Chan, Iris recognition using quaternionic sparse orientation code (QSOC), in: Proc. CVPR 2012, Providence, USA, 2012, pp. 59−64.

[33] E. Stollnitz, T. DeRose, D. Salesin, Wavelet for Computer Graphics: Theory and Applications, Morgan Kaufmann, 1996.

[34] C.H. Daouk, L.A. Esber, F.O. Kanmoun, M.A. Alaoui, Iris recognition, in: Proc. ISSPIT, 2002, pp. 558−562.

[35] L. Shinyoung, K. Lee, O. Byeon., Efficient iris recognition through improvement of feature vector and classifier, ETRI J. 23 (2001) 61−70.

[36] Z. Sun, T. Tan, Ordinal measures for iris recognition, IEEE Trans. Pattern Anal. Mach. Intell. 31 (12) (2009) 2211−2226.

[37] R. Young, R. Lesperance, W. Meyer, The Gaussian derivative model for spatial-temporal vision: I. Cortical model, Spat. Vis. 14 (3−4) (2001) 261−319.

[38] S. Noh, K. Bae, J. Kim, A novel method to extract features for iris recognition system, in: Proc. 4th Intl. Conf. Audio- and Video-Based Biometric Person Authentication, AVBPA03, 2003, pp. 838−844.

[39] Q. Zheng, A. Kumar, G. Pan, A 3d feature descriptor recovered from a single 2d palmprint image, IEEE Trans. Pattern Anal. Mach. Intell. 38 (2016) 1272−1279.

[40] A. Kumar, A. Passi, Comparison and combination of iris matchers for reliable personal authentication, Pattern Recogn. 43 (3) (2010) 1016−1026.

[41] D.M. Monro, S. Rakshit, D. Zhang, DCT-based iris recognition, IEEE Trans. Patt. Anal. Mach. Intell. 29 (2007) 586−595.

[42] K. Miyazawa, K. Ito, T. Aoki, K. Kobayashi, H. Nakajima, An effective approach for iris recognition using phase-based image matching, IEEE Trans. Pattern Anal. Mach. Intell. 30 (2007).

[43] S. Rakshit, D.M. Monro, Iris image selection and localization based on analysis of specular reflection, in: Proc. IEEE Workshop on Signal Process. Applications for Public Security & Forensics, SAFE '07, April 2007.

[44] K.R. Park, H.-A. Park, B.J. Kang, E.C. Lee, D.S. Jeong, A study on iris localization and recognition on mobile phones, *EURASIP J. Adv. Signal Process.* (2008) 12. Available from: https://doi.org/10.1155/2008/281943.

[45] D. Kim, Y. Jung, K.-A. Toh, B. Son, J. Kim, An empirical study on iris recognition in a mobile phone, Expert. Syst. Appl. 54 (2016) 328−339.

[46] K. Hollingsworth, K. Bowyer, P.J. Flynn, The best bits in an iris code, IEEE Trans. Pattern Anal. Mach. Intell. 31 (6) (2009) 964−973.

[47] Y. Lee, R. Micheals, J. Filliben, J. Phillips, VASIR: An open-source research platform for advanced iris recognition technologies, J, Res. Natl Inst. Stand. Technol. 118 (2013) 218−259.

[48] D. Wenbo, S. Zhenan, T. Tieniu, Iris matching based on personalized weight map, IEEE Trans. Pattern Anal. Mach. Intell. 33 (9) (2011) 1744−1757.

[49] C.-W. Tan, A. Kumar, Accurate iris recognition at-a-distance using stabilized iris encoding and Zernike moments phase features, IEEE Trans. Image Process. 23 (2014) 3962−3974.

[50] G. Odinokikh, A. Fartukov, M. Korobkin, J. Yoo, Feature vector construction method for iris recognition, in: Proc. 2nd Intl. ISPRS Workshop on PSBB, Vol. XLII-2/W4, Moscow, Russia, 2017.

[51] D.L. Woodard, S. Pundlik, P. Miller, R. Jillela, A. Ross, On the fusion of periocular and iris biometrics in non-ideal imagery, in: Proc. 20th IEEE Intl. Conf. Pattern Recognition, 2010, pp. 201−204.

[52] R. Jillela, A. Ross. Mitigating effects of plastic surgery: fusing face and ocular biometrics, in: Proc. 5th Intl. Conf. Biometrics Theory, Appl. Systems, BTAS 2012, 2012, 402−411.

[53] K. Hollingsworth, K.W. Bowyer, P.J. Flynn, Useful features for human verification in near-infrared periocular images, Image Vis. Comput. 29 (2011) 707−715.

[54] F. Alonso-Fernandez, J. Bigun, A survey on periocular biometrics research, Pattern. Recog. Lett. 32 (2016) 92−105.

[55] B. Julesz, Textons, the elements of texture perception, and their interactions, Nature 290 (5802) (1981). 91−7.

[56] J. Malik, S. Belongie, J. Shi, T. Leung, Textons, contours and regions: cue integration in image segmentation, in: Proc. ICCV 1999.

[57] D.G. Lowe, Distinctive image features from scale-invariant keypoints, Int. J. Comput. Vis. 60 (2) (2004) 91−110.

[58] A. Oliva, A. Torralba, Modeling the shape of the scene: a holistic representation of the spatial envelope, Int. J. Comput. Vis. 42 (3) (2001) 145−175.

[59] T. Ojala, M. Pietikainen, T. Maenpaa, Multiresolution gray-scale and rotation invariant texture classification with local binary patterns, IEEE Trans. Pattern Anal. Mach. Intell. 24 (7) (2002) 971−987.

[60] N. Dalal, B. Triggs, Histograms of oriented gradients for human detection, in: Proc. CVPR 2005, 2005, pp.886−893.

[61] T. Leung, J. Malik, Representing and recognizing the visual appearance of materials using three dimensional textons, Int. J. Comput. Vis. 43 (1) (2001) 29−44.

[62] VLFeat: an open and portable library of computer vision algorithms. <http://www.vlfeat.org/>.

[63] J.M. Smereka, V.N. Boddeti, B.V.K. Vijaya Kumar, Probabilistic deformation models for challenging periocular image verification, IEEE Trans. Inf. Forensics Secur. 10 (2015) 1875−1890.

[64] Verieye SDK 12.0, 2023. <http://www.neurotechnology.com/verieye.html>.

[65] C. Boyce, Multispectral iris recognition analysis: techniques and evaluation. Graduate Thesis, Dissertations, and Problem Reports, 2476. <https://researchrepository.wvu.edu/etd/2476>.

[66] N.P. Ramiah, A. Kumar, Towards more accurate iris recognition using cross-spectral matching, IEEE Tran. Image Process. (2017) 208−221.

[67] G.W. Quinn, P. Grother, J. Matey, IREX IX part two multispectral iris recognition, NIST IR, 8252, June 2019, <https://nvlpubs.nist.gov/nistpubs/ir/2019/NIST.IR.8252.pdf>.

[68] UIDAI Technology Center, Aadhaar Technology & Architecture: Principles, Design, Best Practices, & Key Lessons, 2014. <https://ia600108.us.archive.org/17/items/Aadhaar-Technology-Architecture/AadhaarTechnologyArchitecture_March.pdf>.

[69] K.W. Bowyer, M.J. Burge (Eds.), Handbook of iris recognition, Springer, London, 2016.

[70] Z. He, Z. Sun, T. Tan, X. Qiu, C. Zhong, W. Dong, Boosting ordinal features for accurate and fast iris recognition, in: Proc. IEEE Intl. Conf. Computer Vis. Pattern Recognition, CVPR, 2008, pp. 1−8.

[71] J. Daugman, The importance of being random: statistical principles of iris recognition, Pattern Recogn. 36 (2) (2003) 279−291.

[72] K. Bowyer, K. Hollingsworth, P.J. Flynn, Image understanding for iris biometrics: a survey, Comp. Vis. Image Underst. 110 (2008) 281−307.

[73] Y. Sun, X. Wang, X. Tang, Deep learning face representation from predicting 10,000 classes, in: Proc. IEEE Intl. Conf. Computer Vis. Pattern Recognition, CVPR 2014, 2014, pp. 1891−1898.

[74] J. Long, E. Shelhamer, T. Darrell, Fully convolutional networks for semantic segmentation, in: Proc. IEEE Conf. Computer Vis. & Pattern Recognition. CVPR 2015, 2015, pp. 3431−3440.

[75] Source codes for an accurate iris segmentation framework under relaxed imaging constraints using total variation model, 2024. <https://web.comp.polyu.edu.hk/csajaykr/tvmiris.htm>.

[76] K. Bowyer, P. Flynn, The ND-IRIS-0405 iris image dataset, Notre Dame CVRL Technical Report, 2009.

[77] F. Schroff, K. Dmitry, P. James, Facenet: a unified embedding for face recognition and clustering, in: Proc. IEEE Intl. Conf. Computer Vis. Pattern Recognition, CVPR, 2015, pp. 815−823.

[78] X. Luo, H. Wang, D. Wu, C. Chen, M. Deng, A survey on deep hashing methods, ACM Trans. Knowl. Discovery Data 17 (15) (2023). Available from: https://doi.org/10.1145/3532624.

[79] H. Zhu, M. Long, J. Wang, Y. Cao, Deep hashing network for efficient similarity retrieval, in: Proc. Association for the Advancement of Artificial Intelligence Conference, AAAI 2016, 2016, pp. 2415−2421.

[80] Z. Cao, M. Long, J. Wang, P.S. Yu, Hashnet: deep learning to hash by continuation, in: Proc. ICCV 2017, Venice, 2017, pp. 5609−5618.

[81] J.K. Pillai, V.M. Patel, R. Chellappa, N.K. Ratha, Secure and robust iris recognition using random projections and sparse representations, IEEE Trans. Pattern Anal. Mach. Intell. 33 (9) (2011) 1877−1893.

[82] Web link to download the codes and executable files for accurate and generalizable iris recognition using deep fully convolutional network and shifted triplet loss. <http://www.comp.polyu.edu.hk/~csajaykr/deepiris.htm>.

[83] OpenCV based face and eye detector: <http://docs.opencv.org/trunk/d7/d8b/tutorial_py_face_detection.html>.

[84] IIT Delhi Iris Database. <http://www.comp.polyu.edu.hk/~csajaykr/IITD/Database_Iris.htm>.

[85] S. Crihalmeanu, A. Ross, S. Schuckers, L. Hornak, A protocol for multibiometric data acquisition, storage and dissemination, Technical report, WVU, Lane Department of Computer Science and Electrical Engineering, 2007.

[86] H. Proença, Iris recognition: on the segmentation of degraded images acquired in the visible wavelength, IEEE Trans. Pattern Anal. Mach. Intell. 32 (8) (2010) 1502−1516.

[87] N. Othman, B. Dorizzi, S. Garcia-Salicetti, OSIRIS: an open source iris recognition software, Pattern Recogn. Lett. 82 (2016) 124−131.

[88] A. Kumar, T.-S. Chan, C.-W. Tan, Human identification from at-a-distance face images using sparse representation of local iris features, in: Proc. ICB 2012, New Delhi, India, 2012.

[89] VeriEye SDK 9.0. <http://www.neurotechnology.com/verieye.html>.

[90] C. Szegedy, W. Liu, Y. Jia, P. Sermanet, S. Reed, D. Anguelov, et al., Going deeper with convolutions, in: Proc. IEEE Intl. Conf. Computer Vis. Pattern Recognition, CVPR, 2015, pp. 1−9.

[91] K.H. M. Cheng, A. Kumar, Advancing surface feature description and matching for more accurate biometric recognition, in: Proc. 24th Intl. Conf. Pattern Recognition, ICPR 2018, Beijing, China, Aug. 2018, pp. 1051−4651.

[92] H. Hofbauer, F. Alonso-Fernandez, P. Wild, J. Bigun, A. Uhl, A ground truth for iris segmentation, in: Proc. 22nd International Conference on Pattern Recognition, ICPR, 2014, Stockholm, Sweden, 2014, pp. 527−532. Available from: https://doi.org/10.1109/ICPR.2014.101.

[93] K. He, G. Gkioxari, P. Dollár, R. Girshick, Mask R-CNN, in: Proc. ICCV 2017, 2017, pp. 2961−2969.

[94] S. Ren, K. He, R. Girshick, J. Sun, Faster R-CNN: towards real-time object detection with region proposal networks, IEEE Trans. Pattern Anal. Mach. Intell. 39 (6) (2017) 1137−1149.

[95] COCO challenges. <https://places-coco2017.github.io/> (accessed 11.23).

[96] W. Luo, Y. Li, R. Urtasun, R. Zemel, Understanding the effective receptive field in deep convolutional neural networks, in: Advances in Neural Information Processing Systems, Proc. NeurIPS 2016, 2016, pp. 4898−4906.

[97] H. Proença, DeepGabor: a learning-based framework to augment IrisCodes permanence, IEEE Trans. Info. Forensics Secur. 17 (2022) 3748−3757.

[98] X. Wang, R. Zhang, C. Shen, T. Kong, L. Li, Solo: a simple framework for instance segmentation, IEEE Trans. Pattern Anal. Mach. Intell. (2021).

[99] X. Wang, R. Zhang, T. Kong, L. Li, C. Shen, SOlOv2: dynamic and fast instance segmentation, Adv. Neural Inform. Process. Syst. 33 (2020) 17721−17732.

[100] B. Cheng, I. Misra, A.G. Schwing, A. Kirillov, R. Girdhar, Masked-attention mask transformer for universal image segmentation, in: Proc. CVPR 2022, 2022, pp. 1290−1299.

[101] A. Kolesnikov, A.S. Pinto, L. Beyer, X. Zhai, J. Harmsen, N. Houlsby, UViM: a unified modeling approach for vision with learned guiding codes, Adv. Neural Inform. Process. Syst. (2022).

[102] X. Zou, J. Yang, H. Zhang, F. Li, L. Li, J. Gao, et al., Segment everything everywhere all at once, Adv. Neural Inform. Process. Syst. (2023).

[103] A. Kirillov, E. Mintun, N. Ravi, H. Mao, C. Rolland, L. Gustafson, et al., Segment anything, arXiv preprint arXiv:2304.02643, arxiv.org, https://segment-anything.com, November 2023.

[104] X. Wang, X. Zhang, Y. Cao, W. Wang, C. Shen, T. Huang, SegGPT: segmenting everything in context. April 2023, https://arxiv.org/pdf/2304.03284.pdf, https://github.com/baaivision/Painter/tree/main/SegGPT.

[105] F. He, Y. Han, H. Wang, J. Ji, Y. Liu, Z. Ma, Deep learning architecture for iris recognition based on optimal Gabor filters and deep belief network, J. Electron. Imaging 26 (2) (2017) 023005.

[106] H. Menon, A. Mukherjee, Iris biometrics using deep convolutional networks, in: Proc. IEEE International Instrumentation and Measurement Technology Conference (I2MTC), IEEE, 2018, pp. 1−5.

[107] F. Yu, V. Koltun, Multi-scale context aggregation by dilated convolutions, in: Proc. ICLR 2016.

[108] K. He, X. Zhang, S. Ren, J. Sun, Deep residual learning for image recognition, in: Proc. IEEE Intl. Conf. Computer Vis. & Pattern Recognition, CVPR 2016, 2016, pp. 770−778.

[109] S. Xie, R. Girshick, P. Dollár, Z. Tu, K. He, Aggregated residual transformations for deep neural networks, in: Proc. CVPR 2017, 2017, pp. 5987−5995.

[110] G.W. Quinn, J.R. Matey, P.J. Grother, IREX IX part one, performance of iris recognition algorithms, NIST Interagency/Internal Report (NISTIR), National Institute of Standards and Technology, Gaithersburg, MD. <https://doi.org/10.6028/NIST.IR.8207> (accessed 04.04.2024).

[111] S. Ioffe, C. Szegedy, Batch normalization: Accelerating deep network training by reducing internal covariate shift, arXiv Prepr. arXiv:1502.03167, 2015.

[112] G. Huang, Z. Liu, L. Van Der Maaten, K.Q. Weinberger, Densely connected convolutional networks, in: Proc. IEEE Conf. Computer Vis. & Pattern Recognition, CVPR 2017, 2017, pp. 4700−4708.

[113] Y. Wu, K. He, Group normalization, in: Proc. European Conference on Computer Vision, ECCV 2018, 2018.

[114] O. Russakovsky, J. Deng, H. Su, J. Krause, S. Satheesh, S. Ma, et al., Imagenet: large scale visual recognition challenge, Int. J. Comput. Vis. 115 (3) (2015) 211−252.

[115] F. Yu, V. Koltun, T. Funkhouser, Dilated residual networks, in: Proc. IEEE Conf. Computer Vis. Pattern Recognition, CVPR, 2017, pp. 472−480.

[116] K. Wang, A. Kumar, Human identification in metaverse using egocentric iris recognition, TechArXiv, 2022, pp 1−13. https://doi.org/10.36227/techrxiv.19750411.v1.

[117] J. Zuo, F. Nicolo, N.A. Schmid, Cross spectral iris matching based on predictive image mapping, in: Proc. Fourth IEEE International Conference on Biometrics: Theory, Applications and Systems, BTAS, 2010.

[118] N.P. Ramaiah, A. Kumar, Advancing cross-spectral iris recognition research using bi-spectral imaging, Mach. Intell. Signal. Process. Adv. Intell. Syst. Comput. (2016), vol. 390, pp. 1−10. Springer, New Delhi.

[119] D. Chen, X. Cao, L. Wang, F. Wen, J. Sun, Bayesian face revisited: a joint formulation, in: Proc. ECCV 2012, Lecture Notes Computer Sci., 2012, pp. 566−579.

[120] F. Shen, C. Shen, W. Liu, H.T. Shen, Supervised discrete hashing, in: Proc. CVPR 2015, 2015 IEEE Conference on Computer Vision and Pattern Recognition, 2015.

[121] S. Chopra, R. Hadsell, Y. Lecun, Learning a similarity metric discriminatively, with application to face verification, in: Proc. CVPR 2005, 2005.

[122] E. Hoffer, N. Ailon, Deep metric learning using triplet network, in: Similarity-Based Pattern Recognition, Lecture Notes Computer Sci., 2015, pp. 84−92.

[123] B. Kulis, T. Darrell, Learning to hash with binary reconstructive embeddings, Adv. Neural Inf. Process. Syst. (2009) 1042−1050.

[124] W. Liu, J. Wang, R. Ji, Y.-G. Jiang, S.-F. Chang, Supervised hashing with kernels, in: Proc. IEEE Conference on Computer Vision and Pattern Recognition, CVPR 2012, 2012.

[125] The Hong Kong Polytechnic University Cross-Spectral Iris Images Database, https://www4.comp.polyu.edu.hk/~csajaykr/polyuiris.htm, Accessed .06.24.

[126] K. Simonyan, A. Zisserman, Very deep convolutional networks for large-scale image recognition, in: Proc. Intl. Conf. Learning Representations, ICLR 2015.

[127] A. Krizhevsky, I. Sutskever, G.E. Hinton, Imagenet classification with deep convolutional neural networks, Adv. Neural Inf. Process. Syst. (2012) 1097−1105.

[128] A. Gionis, P. Indyk, R. Motwani, Similarity search in high dimensions via hashing, in: Proc. 25th Intl. Conf. Very Large Databases, VLDB 1999.

[129] Y. Weiss, A. Torralba, R. Fergus. Spectral hashing, in: Advances in Neural Information Processing Systems, NIPS, 2008.

[130] B. Kulis, K. Grauman, Kernelized locality-sensitive hashing for scalable image search, in: Proc. IEEE Intl. Conf. Computer Vision, ICCV 2009.

[131] M. Raginsky, S. Lazebnik, Locality-sensitive binary codes from shift-invariant kernels, in: Proc. Advances in Neural Information Processing Systems, NIPS 2009.

[132] M. Rastegari, A. Farhadi, D. Forsyth, Attribute discovery via predictable discriminative binary codes, in: Proc. ECCV 2012, Lecture Notes Computer Sci., 2012, pp. 876−889.

[133] Y. Gong, S. Lazebnik, A. Gordo, F. Perronnin, Iterative quantization: a procrustean approach to learning binary codes for large-scale image retrieval, IEEE Trans. Pattern Anal. Mach. Intell. 35 (12) (2013) 2916−2929.

[134] H. Liu, R. Wang, S. Shan, X. Chen, Deep supervised hashing for fast image retrieval, in: Proc. IEEE Conference on Computer Vision and Pattern Recognition, CVPR 2016.

[135] Y. Lee, R. Micheals, J. Filliben, P. Phillips, Robust iris recognition baseline for the grand challenge, NIST-IR Rep., 7777, 2011.

[136] Z. Zhao, A. Kumar, Accurate periocular recognition under less constrained environment using semantics-assisted convolutional neural network, IEEE Trans. Inf. Forensics Secur. 12 (5) (2017) 1017−1030.

[137] J. Gui, T. Liu, Z. Sun, D. Tao, T. Tan, Supervised discrete hashing with relaxation, IEEE Trans. Neural Networks Learn. Syst. (2016).

[138] J. Gui, T. Liu, Z. Sun, D. Tao, T. Tan, Fast supervised discrete hashing, IEEE Trans. Pattern Anal. Mach. Intell. 40 (2) (2018) 490−496.

[139] Y. Cao, H. Qi, W. Zhou, J. Kato, K. Li, X. Liu, et al., Binary hashing for approximate nearest neighbor search on big data: a survey, IEEE Access. 6 (2018) 2039−2054.

[140] L. Omelina, J. Goga, J. Pavlovicova, M. Oravec, B. Jansen, A survey of iris datasets, Image Vis. Comput. 108 (2021). Available from: https://doi.org/10.1016/j.imavis.2021.104109.

[141] FRGC dataset, 2023. <http://www.nist.gov/itl/iad/ig/frgc.cfm> (accessed 04.06.24).

[142] FOCS dataset, 2023. <http://www.nist.gov/itl/iad/ig/focs.cfm> (accessed 04.06.24).

[143] UBIPr dataset, 2023. <http://iris.di.ubi.pt/ubipr.html> (accessed 04.06.24).

[144] Weblink to download codes for SCNN. <http://www.comp.polyu.edu.hk/∼csajaykr/scnn.rar> (accessed 04.06.24).

[145] A. Kumar, Neural network based defection of local textile defects, Pattern Recogn. 36 (2003) 1645−1659.

[146] M. Tan, Q.V. Le, EfficientNet: rethinking model scaling for convolutional neural networks, in: Proc. Int. Conf. Mach. Learn., 2019, pp. 6105−6114.

[147] M. Tan, Q.V. Le, EfficientNetV2: Smaller models and faster training, in: Proc. Int. Conf. Mach. Learn., 2021, pp. 10096−10106.

[148] J. Deng, W. Dong, R. Socher, L.J. Li, K. Li, L. Fei-Fei, Imagenet: a large-scale hierarchical image database, in: Proc. IEEE Intl. Conf. Computer Vis. Pattern Recognition, CVPR, 2009, pp. 248−255.

[149] I. G. P. Team, EU General Data Protection Regulation (GDPR)—An Implementation and Compliance Guide, IT Governance Ltd, 2020.

[150] Dosovitskiy A., Beyer L., Kolesnikov A., Weissenborn D., Zhai X., Unterthiner T., et al. An image is worth 16x16 words: transformers for image recognition at scale, in: Proc. ICLR 2021.

[151] Y. Taigman, M. Yang, M.A. Ranzato, L. Wolf, Deepface: closing the gap to human-level performance in face verification, in: Proc. IEEE Intl. Conf. Computer Vis. Pattern Recognition, CVPR 2014, 2014, pp. 1701−1708.

[152] Y. Sun, X. Wang, X. Tang, Deeply learned face representations are sparse, selective, and robust, in: 2015 IEEE Conference on Computer Vision and Pattern Recognition, 2015, pp. 2892−2900.

[153] P. Li, BioNet: a biologically-inspired network for face recognition, in: Proc. IEEE Intl. Conf. Computer Vis. Pattern Recognition, CVPR, 2023, pp. 10344−10354.

[154] G. Tsoumakas, I. Katakis, Multi-label classification: an overview, Int. J. Data Warehous. Min. 3 (3) (2007) 1−13.

[155] C.N. Padole, H. Proenca, Periocular recognition: analysis of performance degradation factors, in: 2012 5th IAPR International Conference on Biometrics (ICB). IEEE, 2012, pp. 439−445.

[156] G.B. Huang, M. Ramesh, T. Berg, E. Learned-Miller, Labeled faces in the wild: a database for studying face recognition in unconstrained environments. vol. 1. no. 2, Technical Report 07-49, University of Massachusetts, Amherst, 2007.

[157] H. Proença, L.A. Alexandre, The NICE. I: noisy iris challenge evaluation-part I, in: 2007 First IEEE International Conference on Biometrics: Theory, Applications, and Systems (BTAS), 2007, pp. 1−4.

[158] P. Viola, M. Jones, Rapid object detection using a boosted cascade of simple features, in: Proceedings of the 2001 IEEE Computer Society Conference on Computer Vision and Pattern Recognition (CVPR), vol. 1, 2001, pp. I−511.

[159] E. DeLong, D. DeLong, D. Clarke-Pearson, Comparing the areas under two or more correlated receiver operating characteristic curves: a nonparametric approach, Biometrics 44 (3) (1988) 837.

[160] CIFAR-10 dataset, 2023. https://www.cs.toronto.edu/~kriz/cifar.html (accessed 30.05.23).

[161] cuda-convnet - High-performance C++/CUDA implementation of convolutional neural networks - Google Project Hosting. Code.google.com, 2023. <https://code.google.com/p/cuda-convnet/> (accessed 30.06.23).

[162] Caffe | CIFAR-10 tutorial, Caffe.berkeleyvision.org, 2023. <http://caffe.berkeleyvision.org/gathered/examples/cifar10.html> (accessed 30.05.23).

[163] V. Mnih, N. Heess, A. Graves, Recurrent models of visual attention, Adv. Neural Inf. Process. Syst. (2014) 2204−2212.

[164] F. Wang, M. Jiang, C. Qian, S. Yang, C. Li, H. Zhang, et al., Residual attention network for image classification, in: Proc. IEEE Conf. Computer Vis. Pattern Recognition, CVPR, 2017, pp. 6450−6458.

[165] T. Xiao, Y. Xu, K. Yang, J. Zhang, Y. Peng, Z. Zhang, The application of two-level attention models in deep convolutional neural network for fine-grained image classification, in: Proc. IEEE Conf. Computer Vis. Pattern Recognition, CVPR, 2015, pp. 842−850.

[166] U. Park, A. Ross, A.K. Jain, Periocular biometrics in the visible spectrum: a feasibility study, in: IEEE 3rd International Conference on Biometrics: Theory, Applications, and Systems (BTAS), 2009, pp. 1−6.

[167] J.M. Smereka, B.V. Kumar, What is a 'good' periocular region for recognition?, in: Proc. IEEE Conf. Computer Vis. Pattern Recognit. Workshops, CVPRW, 2013, pp. 117−124.

[168] Weblink to download codes for attention-based periocular recognition, <http://www.comp.polyu.edu.hk/~csajaykr/attnet.htm> (accessed 04.06.24).

[169] H. Proença, J.C. Neves, Deep-PRWIS: periocular recognition without the iris and sclera using deep learning frameworks, IEEE Trans. Inf. Forensics Secur. 13 (4) (2018) 888−896.

[170] A. Rattani, R. Derakhshani, S.K. Saripalle, V. Gottemukkula, ICIP 2016 competition on mobile ocular biometric recognition, in: Proc. IEEE Intl. Conf. Image Process., ICIP 2016, 2016, pp. 320−324.

[171] R. Raghavendra, C. Busch, Learning deeply coupled autoencoders for smartphone-based robust periocular verification, in: Proc. IEEE Intl. Conf. Image Processing, ICIP 2016, 2016, pp. 325−329.

[172] H. Fukui, T. Hirakawa, T. Yamashita, H. Fujiyoshi, Attention branch network: learning of attention mechanism for visual explanation, in: Proc. IEEE/CVF Conf. Comput. Vis. Pattern Recognit., CVPR, 2019, pp. 10705−10714.

[173] Y. Feng, A. Kumar, BEST: building evidences from scattered templates for accurate contactless palmprint recognition, Pattern Recogn. 138 (2023).

[174] N.B. Puhan, S.S. Behera, Holistic feature reconstruction-based 3-D attention mechanism for cross-spectral periocular recognition, IEEE Trans. Inf. Forensic Secur. 18 (2023) 435−448.

[175] L. Yang, R.-Y. Zhang, L. Li, X. Xie, SimAm: a simple, parameter free attention module for convolutional neural networks, in: Proc. Int. Conf. Mach. Learn., ICML, 2021, pp. 11863−11874.

[176] Q. Zheng, A. Kumar, G. Pan, Suspecting less and achieving more: new insights on palmprint identification for faster and more accurate palmprint matching, IEEE Trans. Inf. Forensics Secur. 11 (2016) 633−641.

[177] Q. Zhang, H. Li, Z. Sun, T. Tan, Deep feature fusion for iris and periocular biometrics on mobile devices, IEEE Trans. Inf. Forensics Secur. 13 (11) (2018) 2897−2912.

[178] R. Girshick, Fast R-CNN, in: Proc. IEEE Intl. Conf. Computer Vision, ICCV, 2015, pp. 1440−1448.

[179] Weblink to download codes for multi-feature collaboration-based iris recognition. https://www4.comp. polyu.edu.hk/~csajaykr/irisperifusion.htm (accessed 04.06.24).

[180] X. Zhu, D. Cheng, Z. Zhang, S. Lin, J. Dai, An empirical study of spatial attention mechanisms in deep networks, in: Proc. IEEE/CVF International Conference on Computer Vision, ICCV 2019, Seoul, 2019, pp. 6687−6696.

[181] H. Zhao, J. Jia, V. Koltun, Exploring self-attention for image recognition, in: Proc. IEEE/CVF Conf. Computer Vis. Pattern Recognition, CVPR 2020, 2020, pp. 10073−10082.

[182] B. Shi, T. Darrell, X. Wang, Top-down visual attention from analysis by synthesis, in: Proc. IEEE/CVF Conf. Computer Vis. Pattern Recognit., CVPR 2023, pp. 2102−2112.

[183] I. Goodfellow, Y. Bengio, A. Courville, Deep Learning, MIT Press, 2016.

[184] D.P. Kingma, J., Ba, Adam: a method for stochastic optimization, in: Proc. 3rd Intl. Conf. Learning Representations, ICLR 2015, May 2015.

[185] L.A. Zanlorensi, R. Laroca, D.R. Lucio, L.R. Santos, A.S. Britto Jr., D. Menotti, A new periocular dataset collected by mobile devices in unconstrained scenarios, Sci. Rep. 12 (2022) 17989.

[186] F.R.T. Azuma, A survey of augmented reality, Presence Teleop. Virt. Environ. 6 (4) (1997) 355−385.

[187] A. Fathi, A. Farhadi, J.M. Rehg, Understanding egocentric activities, *Proc. IEEE Intl. Conf. Computer Vision.*, ICCV 2011, 2011, pp. 407−414.

[188] A. Betancourt, P. Morerio, C.S. Regazzoni, M. Rauterberg, The evolution of first person vision methods: a survey, IEEE Trans. Circ. Syst. Video Technol. 25 (5) (2014) 744−760.

[189] A. Patney, M. Salvi, J. Kim, A. Kaplanyan, C. Wyman, N. Benty, et al., Towards foveated rendering for gaze tracked virtual reality, ACM Trans. Graph. 35 (6) (2016) 1−12.

[190] F. Tang, X. Chen, M. Zhao, N. Kato, The roadmap of communication and networking in 6G for the metaverse, IEEE Wirel. Commun. (2023) 72−81.

[191] S. Rose, O. Borchert, S. Mitchell, S. Connelly, Zero Trust Architecture, National Institute of Standards and Technology, Gaithersburg, MD, USA, 2020.

[192] E. Samir, H. Wu, M. Azab, C.S. Xin, Q. Zhang, DT-SSIM: A decentralized trustworthy self-sovereign identity management framework, IEEE Internet Things J. 9 (11) (2022) 7972−7988.

[193] Y. Wang, Z. Su, J. Ni, N. Zhang, X. Shen, Blockchain-empowered space-air-ground integrated networks: opportunities, challenges, and solutions, IEEE Commun. Surv. Tutor. 24 (1) (2022) 160−209.

[194] C. Dong, A. Kumar, E. Liu, Think twice before detecting GAN-generated fake images from their spectral domain imprintsJune *Proc.* CVPR 2022, Louisiana, USA, 2022, pp. 7865−7874.

[195] Y. Jiang, S. Chang, Z. Wang, TransGAN: two pure transformers can make one strong GAN and that can scale up, *NeurIPS*, 2021.

[196] A. Razavi, A.Vd Oord, O. Vinyals, Generating diverse high-fidelity images with VQ-VAE-2, *NeurIPS*, 2019.

[197] Y. Zhang, Y. Yan, P. Abbeel, A. Srinivas, VideoGPT: video generation using VQ-VAE and transformers, *ICLR*, 2021.

[198] J. Ho, C. Saharia, W. Chan, D.J. Fleet, M. Norouzi, T. Salimans, Cascaded diffusion models for high fidelity image generation, J. Mach. Learn. Res. 23 (2022) 1−33.

[199] J. Daugman, New methods in iris recognition, IEEE Trans. Syst. Man Cybern. B 37 (5) (2007) 1167−1175.

[200] S. Minaee, A. Abdolrashidiy, Y. Wang, An experimental study of deep convolutional features for iris recognition, in: Proc. IEEE Signal Processing in Medicine and Biology Symposium (SPMB), 2016, pp. 1−6.

[201] K. Nguyen, C. Fookes, A. Ross, S. Sridharan, Iris recognition with off-the-shelf CNN features: a deep learning perspective, IEEE Access 6 (2018) 18848−18855.

[202] H. Proença, J.C. Neves, IRINA: Iris recognition (even) in inaccurately segmented data, Proc. CVPR 2017, 2017, pp. 6747−6756.

[203] K. Wang, A. Kumar, Toward more accurate iris recognition using dilated residual features, IEEE Trans. Inf. Forensics Secur. 14 (2019) 3233−3245.

[204] F. Boutros, N. Damer, K. Raja, R. Ramachandra, F. Kirchbuchner, A. Kuijper, On benchmarking iris recognition within a head mounted display for ar/vr applications, in: Proc, IEEE Intl. Joint Conference on Biometrics, IJCB 2020, 2020, pp. 1−10.

[205] C. Palmero, A. Sharma, K. Behrendt, K. Krishnakumar, O.V. Komogortsev, S.S. Talathi, Openeds2020: open eyes dataset, arXiv preprint arXiv:2005.03876, 2020.

[206] A. Howard, M. Sandler, G. Chu, L.-C. Chen, B. Chen, M. Tan, et al., Searching for MobileNetV3, in: Proc. IEEE/CVF Intl. Conf. Computer Vision, CVPR 2019, 2019, pp. 1314−1324.

[207] Weblink to Access PolyU AR/VR Iris Images Dataset, 2024. <http://www.comp.polyu.edu.hk/csajaykr/metairis.htm>.

[208] W.J. Ryan, D.L. Woodard, A.T. Duchowski, S.T. Birchfield, Adapting starburst for elliptical iris segmentation, Proc. 2nd IEEE Intl. Conf. Biometrics: Theory, Appl. Systems. BTAS, 2008, pp. 1−7.

[209] C. Lu, S. Xia, M. Shao, Y. Fu, Arc-support line segments revisited: an efficient high-quality ellipse detection, IEEE Trans. Image Process. 29 (2020) 768−781.

[210] O. M. Kürtüncü, M. Karakaya, Limbus impact removal for off-angle iris recognition using eye models, in: Proc. 7th IEEE International Conference on Biometrics Theory, Applications and Systems, BTAS 2015.

[211] M. Karakaya, Deep learning frameworks for off-angle iris recognition, in: Proc. 9th IEEE Intl. Conf. on Biometrics Theory, Applications, and Systems, BTAS 2018, 2018.

[212] X. Li, L. Wang, Z. Sun, T. Tan, A feature-level solution to off angle iris recognition, Proc. IEEE Intl. Conf. Biometrics Theory Applications, BTAS, 2018.

[213] A. Abhyankar, S. Schuckers, A novel biorthogonal wavelet network system for off-angle iris recognition, Pattern Recogn. 43 (3) (2010) 987−1007.

[214] W. Chen, X. Chen, J. Zhang, K. Huang, Beyond triplet loss: a deep quadruplet network for person re-identification, Proc. IEEE Conf. Computer Vis. Pattern Recognition, CVPR, 2017, pp. 403−412.

[215] H. Zhang, C. Wu, Z. Zhang, Y. Zhu, H. Lin, Z. Zhang, et al., ResNeSt: split-attention networks, arXiv Preprint, arXiv:2004.08955, 2020.

[216] J. Deng, J. Guo, N. Xue, S. Zafeiriou, Arcface: additive angular margin loss for deep face recognition, in: Proc. IEEE Conf. Computer Vision and Pattern Recognition, CVPR 2019, 2019, pp. 4690−4699.

[217] G. Quinn, J. Matey, E. Tabassi, P. Grother, IREX V: Guidance for Iris Image Collection, 2014.

[218] J. Hu, L. Wang, Z. Luo, Y. Wang, Z. Sun, A large-scale database for less cooperative iris recognition, Proc. IEEE Intl. Jt. Conf. Biometrics, IJCB, 2021, pp. 1−6.

[219] A. Kumar, V. Kanhangad, D. Zhang, A new framework for adaptive multimodal biometrics management, IEEE Trans. Inf. Forensics Secur. 5 (1) (2010) 92−102.

[220] C. Szegedy, V. Vanhoucke, S. Ioffe, J. Shlens, Z. Wojna, Rethinking the inception architecture for computer vision, Proc. CVPR 2016, Las Vegas, USA, 2016, pp. 2818−2826.

[221] A. Kirillov, E. Mintun, N. Ravi, H. Mao, C. Rolland, L. Gustafson, et al., Segment anything, in: Proc. IEEE/CVF International Conference on Computer Vision, ICCV 2023, 2023, pp. 4015−4025.

[222] S. Sukhbaatar, J. Weston, R. Fergus, End-to-end memory networks, in: Proc. Advances in Neural Information Processing Systems, NIPS 2015, 2015, pp. 2440−2448.

[223] C. Wang, J. Muhammad, Y. Wang, Z. He, Z. Sun., Towards complete and accurate iris segmentation using deep multi-task attention network for non-cooperative iris recognition, IEEE Trans. Inf. Forensics Secur. 15 (2020) 2944−2959.

[224] X. Yin, X. Liu, Multi-task convolutional neural network for pose-invariant face recognition, IEEE Trans. Image Process. 27 (2) (2018) 964−975.

[225] J. Daugman, C. Downing, O.N. Akande, O.C. Abikoye, Ethnicity and biometric uniqueness: iris pattern individuality in a West African Database, arXiv, https://arxiv.org/pdf/2309.06521.pdf, September 2023

[226] J. Bao, D. Chen, F. Wen, H. Li, G. Hua, CVAE-GAN: fine-grained image generation through asymmetric training, in: Proc. IEEE Intl. Conf. Computer Vision, ICCV 2017, 2017, pp. 2764−2773.

[227] S. Zheng, S. Jayasumana, B. Romera-Paredes, et al., Conditional random fields as recurrent neural networks, in: Proc. CVPR 2015.

[228] D.P. Kingma, M. Welling, Auto-encoding variational bayes, arXiv Prepr. arXiv:1312.6114, 2013.

[229] K. Greff, R.K. Srivastava, J. Schmidhuber, Highway and residual networks learn unrolled iterative estimation, in: Proc. Int. Conf. Learning and Representation, ICLR 2017.

[230] Y. Ioannou, D. Robertson, D. Zikic, P. Kontschieder, J. Shotton, M. Brown et al., Decision forests, convolutional networks and the models in-between, arXiv preprint, arXiv:1603.01250, 2016.

[231] N. Kohli, D. Yadav, M. Vatsa, R. Singh, A. Noore, Synthetic iris presentation attack using iDCGAN, in: Proc. IEEE Intl. J. Conf. Biometrics, IJCB 2017, 2017, pp. 574−680.

[232] S. Yadav, C. Chen, A. Ross, Synthesizing iris images using RaSGAN with application in presentation attack detection, in: Proc. CVPR Workshop, CVPRW 2018.

[233] D. Berthelot, T. Schumm, L. Metz, BEGAN: boundary equilibrium generative adversarial networks, arXiv Apr. 2017.

[234] A. Radford, L. Metz, S. Chintala, Unsupervised representation learning with deep convolutional generative adversarial networks, in: Proc. 4th Intl. Conf. Learning Representations, ICLR 2016, San Juan, Puerto Rico, May 2−4, 2016.

[235] P. Shirley, M. Ashikhmin, S. Marschner, Fundamentals of Computer Graphics, AK Peters/CRC Press, 2009.

[236] C. Dong, A. Kumar, Synthesis of multi-view 3D fingerprints to advance contactless fingerprint identification, IEEE Trans. Pattern Anal. Mach. Intell. 45 (11) (2023) 13134−13151.

[237] K. Sohn, W. Shang, H. Lee, Improved multimodal deep learning with variation of information, Adv. Neural Inf. Process. Syst. 27 (2014).

[238] J. Nigam, A. Khosla, M. Kim, J. Nam, H. Lee, A.Y. Ng, Multimodal deep learning, in: Proc. ICML 2011, 2011.

[239] N. Srivastava, R.R. Salakhutdinov, Multimodal learning with deep Boltzmann machines, in: NIPS 2012.

[240] L. Yuan, Y. Chen, T. Wang, W. Yu, Y. Shi, Z. Jiang, et al., Tokens-to-token ViT: training vision transformers from scratch on ImageNet, in: Proc. IEEE/CVF Intl. Conf. Computer Vision, ICCV 2021, 2021, pp. 538−547.

[241] B. Zhuang, J. Liu, Z. Pan, Y. Weng, C. Shen, Survey on efficient training of transformers, in: Proc. Thirty-Second International Joint Conference on Artificial Intelligence, IJCAI-23, 2023, pp. 6823−6831.

[242] G.W. Quinn, J.R. Matey, P. Grother, E.C. Watters, Statistics of visual features in the human iris, NIST Technical Note TN 932452, August 2021.

[243] F. Shen, P.J. Flynn, Iris crypts: multi-scale detection and shape-based matching, in: Proc. IEEE Winter Conf. Applications of Computer Vision, WACV 2014, 2014, pp. 977−983.

[244] Z.-M. Chen, X.-S. Wei, P. Wang, Y. Guo, Learning graph convolutional networks for multi-label recognition and applications, IEEE Trans. Pattern Anal. Mach. Intell. 45 (6) (2023) 6969−6983.

[245] D. DeTone, T. Malisiewicz, A. Rabinovich, Superpoint: self-supervised interest point detection and description, in: Proc. CVPRW 2018, 2018, pp. 224−236.

[246] P.-E. Sarlin, D. DeTone, T. Malisiewicz, A. Rabinovich, Superglue: learning feature matching with graph neural networks, Proc. CVPR 2020, 2020, pp. 4938−4947.

[247] J. Ho, A. Jain, P. Abbeel, Denoising diffusion probabilistic models, Adv. Neural Inf. Process. Syst. 33 (2020) 6840−6851.

[248] S. Saxena, C. Herrmann, J. Hur, A. Kar, M. Norouzi, D. Sun, et al., The surprising effectiveness of diffusion models for optical flow and monocular depth estimation, in: Advances in Neural Information Processing Systems, NeurIPS, 2023.

[249] P. Dhariwal, A. Nichol, Diffusion models beat GANS on image synthesis, in: Advances in Neural Information Processing Systems, 2021.

[250] C. Li, M. Prabhudesai, S. Duggal, E. Brown, D. Pathak, Your diffusion model is secretly a zero-shot classifier, in: Proc. ICML Workshop on Structured Probabilistic Inference & Generative Modeling, PMLR 2023, Honolulu, Hawaii, USA.

[251] K. Niguen, C. Fookes, S. Sridharan, A. Ross, Complex-valued iris recognition network, IEEE Trans. Pattern Anal. Mah. Intell. 45 (1) (2023) 182−196.

[252] C. Trabelsi, O. Bilaniuk, Y. Zhang, D. Serdyuk, S. Subramanian, J.F. Santos, et al., Deep complex networks, in: Proc. Intl. Conf. Learning Representations, ICLR 2018.

[253] A. Kumar, Insights on Complex-Valued Iris Recognition Networks. IEEE Trans. Pattern. Anal. Mach. Intell, 2024. Available from: https://doi.org/10.36227/techrxiv.171744363.31782174/v1.

[254] X. Tang, J. Xie, P. Li, "Deep Convolutional Features for Iris Recognition," Proc. Chin. Conf. Biometric Recognit., pp. 391−400, 2017.

[255] A. Sequeira, L. Chen, P. Wild, J. Ferryman, F. Alonso-Fernandez, K. B. Raja, et al., "Cross-Eyed - Cross-Spectral Iris/Periocular Recognition Database and Competition," Proc. International Conference of the Biometrics Special Interest Group, BIOSIG 2016, 2016.

[256] Iris Recognition: Impact and use Policy, New York Police Department, USA. https://www1.nyc.gov/assets/nypd/downloads/pdf/public_information/post-final/iris-recognition-nypd-impact-and-use-policy_4.9.21_final.pdf (accessed June 2023).

Index

Note: Page numbers followed by "*f*" and "*t*" refer to figures and tables, respectively.